Mastering pfSense *Second Edition*

Manage, secure, and monitor your on-premise and cloud network with pfSense 2.4

David Zientara

BIRMINGHAM - MUMBAI

Mastering pfSense
Second Edition

Commissioning Editor: Vijin Boricha
Acquisition Editor: Shrilekha Inani
Content Development Editor: Priyanka Deshpande
Technical Editor: Mohit Hassija
Copy Editor: Safis Editing
Project Coordinator: Virginia Dias
Proofreader: Safis Editing
Indexer: Mariammal Chettiyar
Graphics: Tom Scaria
Production Coordinator: Shantanu Zagade

First published: August 2016
Second edition: May 2018

Production reference: 1040518

Published by Packt Publishing Ltd.
Livery Place
35 Livery Street
Birmingham
B3 2PB, UK.

ISBN 978-1-78899-317-3

`www.packtpub.com`

To my mother, Isabel Zientara, and to the memory of my father, Francis, for their constant encouragement and support, and for always keeping me focused on what is important. To my siblings, who have always been there when needed.

Contributors

About the author

David Zientara is a software engineer and IT professional living in northern New Jersey. He has 20 years of experience in IT, and he has been the lead software engineer for Oxberry since the mid-1990s. His interest in pfSense prompted him to create a pfSense website in June 2013, and eventually to author this book.

I wish to thank my editors for helping ensure that the final product is the best that it can be. I also wish to thank my parents for their constant support in my endeavors.

About the reviewer

Shiva V.N. Parasram is a professional cyber security trainer and the owner of the Computer Forensics and Security Institute (CFSI). He is also a Certified EC-Council Instructor (CEI), and his qualifications include an M.Sc. in network security (Distinction), CEH, CHFI, ECSA, CCNA, NSE, and more. He has successfully executed and delivered forensic investigations, penetration tests, and security training for large enterprises, and he is also the author of *Digital Forensics with Kali Linux, Packt Publishing*.

> *"If you have to be anything, be brave." – Indra J. Parasram.*
>
> *"Always be patient, son." – Harry G. Parasram.*
>
> *To my parents and best friends. The love that stayed, the love I know. Thank you.*

Packt is searching for authors like you

If you're interested in becoming an author for Packt, please visit `authors.packtpub.com` and apply today. We have worked with thousands of developers and tech professionals, just like you, to help them share their insight with the global tech community. You can make a general application, apply for a specific hot topic that we are recruiting an author for, or submit your own idea.

Table of Contents

Preface

pfSense is open source firewall/router software based on the FreeBSD packet filtering program PF that can be used as a perimeter firewall, router, wireless access point, DHCP server, DNS server, or VPN endpoint. *Mastering pfSense, Second Edition,* is a comprehensive guide to installing, configuring, and customizing pfSense.

Who this book is for

The target audience for this book should have at least an intermediate level of knowledge of computer networking. Some knowledge of pfSense is a plus, although it is not required.

The book should appeal to a wide range of technophiles; anyone interested in pfSense who has an aptitude for understanding networking and the resources to follow along with the examples will benefit from this book.

What this book covers

`Chapter 1`, *Revisiting pfSense Basics,* covers deployment scenarios for pfSense, hardware requirements, sizing and installation options, and it guides the user through the initial installation and configuration.

`Chapter 2`, *Advanced pfSense Configuration,* covers some of the commonly used pfSense services, such as DHCP, DNS, **Dynamic DNS** (**DDNS**), captive portal, **Network Time Protocol** (**NTP**), and **Simple Network Management Protocol** (**SNMP**).

`Chapter 3`, *VLANs,* covers how to set up a virtual LAN in pfSense, both from the command line and the web GUI, and provides examples showing how to configure some commercially available managed switches.

`Chapter 4`, *Using pfSense as a Firewall*, covers how to implement rules to block, pass, or divert network traffic, as well as virtual IPs, aliases, and scheduling.

`Chapter 5`, *Network Address Translation*, covers **Network Address Translation** (**NAT**) in depth, including outbound NAT, port forwarding, 1:1 NAT, and **Network Prefix Translation** (**NPt**).

`Chapter 6`, *Traffic Shaping*, covers how to use the pfSense's traffic shaping capabilities, using the traffic shaping wizard, by manually adjusting queues, and by creating custom floating rules.

`Chapter 7`, *Virtual Private Networks (VPNs)*, covers the advantages and disadvantages of VPNs and explains how to use pfSense to set up an IPsec, L2TP, or OpenVPN tunnel. Client-server and peer-to-peer options are covered.

`Chapter 8`, *Redundancy and High Availability*, covers load balancing, failover, and implementing redundancy via **Common Address Redundancy Protocol** (**CARP**), which allows the user to add one or more backup firewalls.

`Chapter 9`, *Multiple WANs*, covers ways to implement redundancy and high availability into internet connections by having multiple internet connections for failover, load balancing, and bandwidth aggregation. This chapter shows how to set up gateways and gateway groups.

`Chapter 10`, *Routing and Bridging*, covers bridging and static/dynamic routing, including when bridging network adapters is appropriate, as well when it is necessary to configure static routes and how to do it, and discusses the dynamic routing protocols available for pfSense.

`Chapter 11`, *Extending pfSense with Packages*, covers the most significant packages available for pfSense, such as Snort, Squid, HAProxy, and many others.

`Chapter 12`, *Diagnostics and Troubleshooting*, covers what to do when things go wrong. A problem-solving methodology is outlined, and common problems and available troubleshooting tools are discussed. A real-world example of troubleshooting is provided.

`Appendix A`, *Assessments*, answers to the questions mentioned in the chapters.

To get the most out of this book

I am assuming a basic understanding of networking. Enough knowledge to pass CompTIA's Networking+ exam should be more than enough knowledge. A basic knowledge of computers and how to use a CLI is also necessary. Since pfSense runs on FreeBSD, some experience with BSD and/or Unix-like operating systems such as Linux is helpful, though not strictly necessary. Experience with pfSense is also helpful; I am not assuming any prior knowledge of pfSense although the book does not discuss the initial installation and configuration in depth and instead progresses rapidly to more advanced topics. Readers with no prior knowledge of pfSense may be better served by starting out with a book targeted toward pfSense neophytes such as *pfSense 2 Cookbook* by *Matt Williamson*.

Since the focus in the second edition is more toward providing practical examples of pfSense in action, the reader will get more out of the book if they install pfSense and try some of the examples. Thus, having a system on which to install pfSense or being able to run pfSense in a virtual machine will be a plus. The book outlines the hardware requirements and sizing guidelines. If the reader intends to run pfSense in a virtual machine, they should run it on a system that supports 64-bit virtualization. For some of the examples such as VPNs and setting up a CARP failover group, it is helpful to set up a virtual network with multiple instances of pfSense running on the network.

Download the color images

We also provide a PDF file that has color images of the screenshots/diagrams used in this book. You can download it from `https://www.packtpub.com/sites/default/files/downloads/MasteringpfSenseSecondEdition_ColorImages.pdf`.

Conventions used

There are a number of text conventions used throughout this book.

`CodeInText`: Indicates code words in text, database table names, folder names, filenames, file extensions, pathnames, dummy URLs, user input, and Twitter handles. Here is an example: "The `nslookup` utility is available on Linux, Windows, and macOS."

Any command-line input or output is written as follows:

```
nslookup packtpub.com 8.8.4.4
```

Bold: Indicates a new term, an important word, or words that you see onscreen. For example, words in menus or dialog boxes appear in the text like this. Here is an example: "Navigate to **System** | **Advanced**. Make sure the **Admin Access** tab is selected and scroll down to the **Secure Shell** section of the page."

Warnings or important notes appear like this.

Tips and tricks appear like this.

Get in touch

Feedback from our readers is always welcome.

General feedback: Email `feedback@packtpub.com` and mention the book title in the subject of your message. If you have questions about any aspect of this book, please email us at `questions@packtpub.com`.

Errata: Although we have taken every care to ensure the accuracy of our content, mistakes do happen. If you have found a mistake in this book, we would be grateful if you would report this to us. Please visit `www.packtpub.com/submit-errata`, selecting your book, clicking on the Errata Submission Form link, and entering the details.

Piracy: If you come across any illegal copies of our works in any form on the internet, we would be grateful if you would provide us with the location address or website name. Please contact us at `copyright@packtpub.com` with a link to the material.

If you are interested in becoming an author: If there is a topic that you have expertise in and you are interested in either writing or contributing to a book, please visit `authors.packtpub.com`.

Reviews

Please leave a review. Once you have read and used this book, why not leave a review on the site that you purchased it from? Potential readers can then see and use your unbiased opinion to make purchase decisions, we at Packt can understand what you think about our products, and our authors can see your feedback on their book. Thank you!

For more information about Packt, please visit `packtpub.com`.

1
Revisiting pfSense Basics

While high-speed internet connectivity is becoming more and more common, many in the online world—especially those with residential connections or **small office/home office** (**SOHO**) setups—lack the hardware to fully take advantage of these speeds. Fiber-optic technology brings with it the promise of a gigabit speed or greater, and the technology surrounding traditional copper networks is also yielding improvements. Yet many people are using consumer-grade routers that offer, at best, mediocre performance.

pfSense, an open source router/firewall solution, is a far better alternative that is available to you. You have likely already downloaded, installed, and configured pfSense, possibly in a residential or SOHO environment. As an intermediate-level pfSense user, you do not need to be sold on the benefits of pfSense. Nevertheless, you may be looking to deploy pfSense in a different environment (for example, a corporate network), or you may just be looking to enhance your knowledge of pfSense. In either case, mastering the topics in this book will help you achieve these goals.

This chapter is designed to review the process of getting your pfSense system up and running. It will guide you through the process of choosing the right hardware for your deployment, but it will not provide a detailed treatment of installation and initial configuration. The emphasis will be on troubleshooting, as well as some of the newer configuration options.

This chapter will cover the following topics:

- A brief overview of the pfSense project
- pfSense deployment scenarios
- Minimum specifications and hardware sizing guidelines
- The best practices for installation and configuration
- Basic configuration from both the console and the pfSense web GUI

Technical requirements

The following equipment is required for installing and configuring pfSense 2.4:

- A 64-bit Intel, AMD, or ARM-based system with a 500 MHz processor or greater, at least 512 MB of RAM, and 1 GB of disk space onto which pfSense will be installed
- A USB thumb drive with at least 1 GB of disk space, or blank CD media if you prefer using optical media, which will serve as the installation media
- Internet access, for downloading pfSense binaries
- A second computer system, for accessing the pfSense web GUI
- An Ethernet switch and cabling, or a crossover cable, for connecting the second computer system to the pfSense system

If you want to try out pfSense without doing an actual installation, you can create a pfSense virtual machine. While this chapter does not provide a guide to installing pfSense into a virtual environment, I recommend the following for running pfSense in a virtual machine:

- A 64-bit Intel or AMD-based system with a 2 GHz processor or greater, at least 8 GB of RAM, and enough disk space to accommodate the virtual hard drive (likely 8 GB or greater)
- Either a Type 1 or Type 2 hypervisor:
    - Type 1 (bare-metal hypervisor; runs directly on the hardware):
        - VMware ESXi
        - Microsoft Hyper-V
    - Type 2 (requires an OS):
        - Proxmox (Linux)
        - Oracle VM VirtualBox (Linux, Windows, mac OS, Solaris)

Most likely you will have to create two virtual machines: one into which pfSense will be installed, and a second from which you will access the web GUI and test the functionality of the virtual pfSense system.

pfSense project overview

The origins of pfSense can be traced to the OpenBSD packet filter known as PF, which was incorporated into FreeBSD in 2001. As PF is limited to a command-line interface, several projects have been launched in order to provide a graphical interface for PF. m0n0wall, which was released in 2003, was the earliest attempt at such a project. pfSense began as a fork of the m0n0wall project.

Version 1.0 of pfSense was released on October 4, 2006. Version 2.0 was released on September 17, 2011. Version 2.1 was released on September 15, 2013, and Version 2.2 was released on January 23, 2015. Version 2.3, released on April 12, 2016, phased out support for legacy technologies such as the **Point-to-Point Tunneling Protocol** (**PPTP**), the **Wireless Encryption Privacy** (**WEP**) and **Single DES**, and also provided a facelift for the web GUI.

Version 2.4, released on October 12, 2017, continues this trend of phasing out support for legacy technologies while also adding features and improving the web GUI. Support for 32-bit x86 architectures has been deprecated (security updates will continue for 32-bit systems, however, for at least a year after the release of 2.4), while support for Netgate **Advanced RISC Machines** (**ARM**) devices has been added. A new pfSense installer (based on FreeBSD's bsdinstall) has been incorporated into pfSense, and there is support for the **ZFS** filesystem, as well as the **Unified Extensible Firmware Interface** (**UEFI**). pfSense now supports **OpenVPN 2.4.x**, and as a result, features such as **AES-GCM** ciphers can be utilized. In addition, pfSense now supports multiple languages; the web GUI has been translated into 13 different languages. At the time of writing, version 2.4.2, released on November 21, 2017, is the most recent version.

Possible deployment scenarios

Once you have decided to add a pfSense system to your network, you need to consider how it is going to be deployed on your network. pfSense is suitable for a variety of networks, from small to large ones, and can be employed in a variety of deployment scenarios. In this section, we will cover the following possible uses for pfSense:

- Perimeter firewall
- Router
- Switch
- Wireless router/wireless access point

The most common way to add pfSense to your network is to use it as a perimeter firewall, as shown in the diagram. In this scenario, your internet connection is connected to one port on the pfSense system, and your local network is connected to another port on the system. The port connected to the internet is known as the WAN interface, and the port connected to the local network is known as the LAN interface:

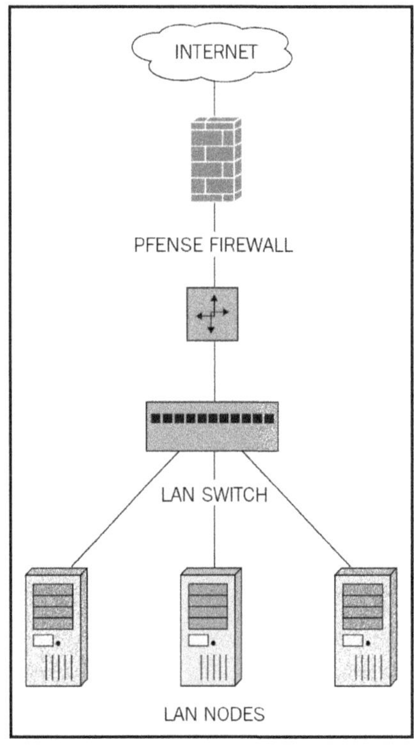

Diagram showing deployment scenario in which pfSense is the firewall

If pfSense is your perimeter firewall, you may choose to set it up as a dedicated firewall, or you might want to have it perform the double duty of a firewall and a router. You may also choose to have more than two interfaces in your pfSense system (known as optional interfaces). In order to act as a perimeter firewall, however, a pfSense system requires at least two interfaces: a WAN interface (to connect to outside networks), and a LAN interface (to connect to the local network).

The perimeter firewall performs two broad functions. The first, monitoring and controlling inbound traffic, should be fairly obvious. Allowing certain traffic on certain ports, while blocking all other traffic, is a core function of all firewalls. The second, monitoring and controlling outbound traffic, might seem less obvious but is also important. Outbound web traffic tends to pass through the firewall unchallenged. This, however, leaves our network vulnerable to malware that targets web browsers. To protect our networks against such threats, we need to monitor outbound traffic as well.

It is commonplace to set up the networks behind the firewall with a split architecture, with assets accessible from the internet being kept separate from the rest of the network. In such cases, the internet-accessible resources are placed on a separate network generally referred to as the **demilitarized zone** (**DMZ**). If your network requires such a setup, you can easily do this with pfSense as your perimeter firewall, as we will see later.

In more complex network setups, your pfSense system may have to exchange routing information with other routers on the network. There are two types of protocols for exchanging such information: distance vector protocols obtain their routing information by exchanging information with neighboring routers; routers use link-state protocols to build a map of the network in order to calculate the shortest path to another router, with each router calculating distances independently. pfSense is capable of running both types of protocols. Packages are available for distance vector protocols such as RIP and RIPv2, and link-state protocols such as **Border Gateway Protocol** (**BGP**). These protocols will be discussed in greater detail in `Chapter 10`, *Routing and Bridging*.

Another common deployment scenario is to set up pfSense as a router. In a home or SOHO environment, firewall and router functions are often performed by the same device. In mid-sized to large networks, however, the router is a device separate from that of the perimeter firewall.

In larger networks, which have several network segments, pfSense can be used to connect these segments. Traditionally, using a router to connect multiple networks requires multiple network interfaces on the router. However, with VLANs, we can use a single **network interface card** (**NIC**) to operate in multiple broadcast domains via 802.1q tagging. VLANs are often used with the ever-popular router on a stick configuration, in which the router has a single physical connection to a switch (this connection is known as a trunk), with the single Ethernet interface divided into multiple VLANs, and the router forwarding packets between the VLANs. One of the advantages of this setup is that it only requires a single port, and, as a result, it allows us to use pfSense with systems on when adding another NIC would be cumbersome or even impossible: for example, a laptop or certain thin clients. We will cover VLANs in greater depth in `Chapter 3`, *VLANS*.

In most cases, where pfSense is deployed as a router on mid-sized and large networks, it would be used to connect different LAN segments; however, it could also be used as a WAN router. In this case, pfSense's function would be to provide a private WAN connection to the end user.

Another possible deployment scenario is to use pfSense as a switch. If you have multiple interfaces on your pfSense system and bridge them together, pfSense can function as a switch. This is a far less common scenario, however, for several reasons:

- Using pfSense as a switch is generally not cost effective. You can purchase a five-port Ethernet switch for less than what it would cost to purchase the hardware for a pfSense system. Buying a commercially available switch will also save you money in the long run, as they likely would consume far less power than whatever computer you would be using to run pfSense.
- Commercially available switches will likely outperform pfSense, as pfSense will process all packets that pass between ports, while a typical Ethernet switch will handle them locally with dedicated hardware made specifically for passing data between ports quickly. While you can disable filtering entirely in pfSense if you know what you're doing, you will still be limited by the speed of the bus on which your network cards reside, whether it is PCI, PCI-X, or PCI Express (PCI-e).
- There is also the administrative overhead of using pfSense as a switch. Simple switches are designed to be Plug and Play, and setting up these switches is as easy as plugging in your Ethernet cables and the power cord. Managed switches typically enable you to configure settings at the console and/or through a web interface, but in many cases, configuration is only necessary if you want to modify the operation of the switch. If you use pfSense as a switch, however, some configuration will be required.

If none of this intimidates you, then feel free to use pfSense as a switch. While you're not likely to achieve the performance level or cost savings of using a commercially available switch, you will likely learn a great deal about pfSense and networking in the process. Moreover, advances in hardware could make using pfSense as a switch viable at some point in the future. Advances in low-power consumption computers are one factor that could make this possible.

Yet another possibility is using pfSense as a wireless router/access point. A sizable proportion of modern networks incorporate some type of wireless connectivity. Connecting to a network's wireless is not only easier, but in some cases, running an Ethernet cable is not a realistic option. With pfSense, you can add wireless networking capabilities to your system by adding a wireless network card, provided that the network card is supported by FreeBSD.

Generally, however, using pfSense as a wireless router or access point is not the best option. Support for wireless network cards in FreeBSD leaves something to be desired. Support for the IEEE's 802.11b and g standards is okay, but support for 802.11n and 802.11ac is not very good.

A more likely solution is to buy a wireless router (even if it is one of the aforementioned consumer-grade units), set it up to act solely as an access point, connect it to the LAN port of your pfSense system, and let pfSense act as a **Dynamic Host Configuration Protocol** (**DHCP**) server. A typical router will work fine as a dedicated wireless access point, and they are more likely to support the latest wireless networking standards than pfSense. Another possibility is to buy a dedicated wireless access point. These are generally inexpensive and some have such features as multiple SSIDs, which allow you to set up multiple wireless networks (for example, you could have a separate guest network which is completely isolated from other local networks). Using pfSense as a router, in combination with a commercial wireless access point, is likely the least-troublesome option.

Hardware requirements and sizing guidelines

Once you have decided where to deploy pfSense on your network, you should have a clearer idea of what your hardware requirements are. As a minimum, you will need a CPU, motherboard, memory (RAM), some form of disk storage, and at least two network interfaces (unless you are opting for a router on a stick setup, in which case you only need one network interface). You may also need one or more optional interfaces.

Minimum hardware requirements

The starting point for our discussion on hardware requirements is the pfSense minimum specifications. As of January 2018, the minimum hardware requirements are as follows (these specifications are from the official pfSense site, `https://www.pfsense.org`):

- CPU – 500 MHz (1 GHz recommended)
- RAM – 512 MB (1 GB recommended)

pfSense requires a 64-bit Intel (x86-64) or AMD (amd64) CPU. You should also use a CPU that supports the AES-NI instruction set extensions (or another hardware crypto offload), as such a CPU will be required, starting with version 2.5. There are three separate images provided for these architectures: CD, CD on a USB memstick, and an image for ARM-based Netgate systems. The active default console for the CD and CD on USB memstick images is VGA, while the active default console for the Netgate image is serial. The NanoBSD images (for embedded systems, which enabled the serial console by default) have been deprecated with the release of version 2.4. The serial console can be enabled on images which default to VGA via the web GUI under **System** | **Advanced**.

A pfSense installation requires at least 1 GB of disk space. If you are installing on an embedded device, you can access the console either by a serial or VGA port. A step-by-step installation guide for the pfSense Live CD can be found on the official pfSense website at: `https://doc.pfsense.org/index.php/Installing_pfSense`.

Version 2.3 eliminated the Live CD, which allowed you to try out pfSense without installing it onto other media. If you really want to use the Live CD, however, you could use a pre-2.3 image (version 2.2.6 or earlier). You can always upgrade to the latest version of pfSense after installation.

Installation onto either a hard disk drive (HDD) or a solid-state drive (SSD) is the most common option for a full install of pfSense, whereas embedded installs typically use CF, SD, or USB media. A full install of the current version of pfSense will fit onto a 1 GB drive, but will leave little room for installation of packages or for log files. Any activity that requires caching, such as running a proxy server, will also require additional disk space.

The last installation option in the table is installation onto an embedded system using the Netgate ADI image. Netgate currently sells several ARM-based systems such as the SG-3100, which is advertised as an appliance that can be used in many deployment scenarios, including as a firewall, LAN or WAN router, VPN appliance, and DHCP or DNS server. It is targeted towards small and medium-sized businesses and may appeal to home and business users seeking a reliable firewall appliance with a low total cost of ownership. Storage (without upgrading) is limited to 8 GB of eMMC Flash, which would limit which packages could be installed. Another Netgate option is the SG-1000, which is a bare bones router with only 2 Ethernet ports, 512 MB of RAM and 4 GB of eMMC Flash.

Hardware sizing guidelines

The minimum hardware requirements are general guidelines, and you may want to exceed these minimums based on different factors. It may be useful to consider these factors when determining what CPU, memory, and storage device to use:

- For the CPU, requirements increase for faster internet connections.

Guidelines for the CPU and network cards can be found at the official pfSense site at `http://pfsense.org/hardware/#requirements`.

The following general guidelines apply: the minimum hardware specifications (Intel/AMD CPU of 500 MHz or greater) are valid up to 20 Mbps. CPU requirements begin to increase at speeds greater than 20 Mbps.

- Connections of 100 Mbps or faster will require PCI-E network adapters to keep up with the increased network throughput.

If you intend to use pfSense to bridge interfaces—for example, if you want to bridge a wireless and wired network, or if you want to use pfSense as a switch—then the PCI bus speed should be considered. The PCI bus can easily become a bottleneck. Therefore, in such scenarios, using PCI-e hardware is the better option, as it offers up to 31.51 GBps (for PCI-e v. 4.0 on a 16-lane slot) versus 533 MBps for the fastest conventional PCI buses.

If you plan on using pfSense as a VPN server, then you should take into account the effect VPN usage will have on the CPU. Each VPN connection requires the CPU to encrypt traffic, and the more connections there are, the more the CPU will be taxed. Generally, the most cost-effective solution is to use a more powerful CPU. But there are ways to reduce the CPU load from VPN traffic. Soekris has the vpn14x1 product range; these cards offload the CPU of the computing intensive tasks of encryption and compression. AES-NI acceleration of IPSec also significantly reduces the CPU requirements.

If you have hundreds of simultaneous captive portal users, you will require slightly more CPU power than you would otherwise. Captive portal usage does not put as much of a load on the CPU as VPN usage, but if you anticipate having a lot of captive portal users, you will want to take this into consideration.

If you're not a power user, 512 MB of RAM might be enough for your pfSense system. This, however, would leave little room for the state table (where, as mentioned earlier, active connections are tracked). Each state requires about 1 KB of memory, which is less memory than some consumer-grade routers require, but you still want to be mindful of RAM if you anticipate having a lot of simultaneous connections. The other components of pfSense require 32 to 48 MB of RAM, and possibly more, depending on which features you are using, so you have to subtract that from the available memory in calculating the maximum state table size:

256 MB	~22,000 connections
512 MB	~46,000 connections
1 GB	~93,000 connections
2 GB	~190,000 connections

Installing packages can also increase your RAM requirements; **Snort** and **ntop** are two such examples. You should also probably not install packages if you have limited disk space. Proxy servers in particular use up a fair amount of disk space, which is something you should probably consider if you plan on installing a proxy server such as **Squid**.

The amount of disk space, as well as the form of storage you utilize, will likely be dictated by what packages you install, and what forms of logging you will have enabled. Some packages are more taxing on storage than others. Some packages require more disk space than others. Proxies such as Squid store web pages; anti-spam programs such as **pfBlocker** download lists of blocked IP addresses, and therefore require additional disk space. Proxies also tend to perform a great deal of read and write operations; therefore, if you are going to install a proxy, disk I/O performance is something you should likely take into consideration.

You may be tempted to opt for the cheapest NICs. However, inexpensive NICs often have complex drivers that offload most of the processing to the CPU. They can saturate your CPU with interrupt handling, thus causing missed packets. Cheaper network cards typically have smaller buffers (often no more than 300 KB), and when the buffers become full, packets are dropped. In addition, many of them do not support Ethernet frames that are larger than the **maximum transmission unit** (**MTU**) of 1,500 bytes. NICs that do not support larger frames cannot send or receive jumbo frames (frames with an MTU larger than 1,500 bytes), and therefore they cannot take advantage of the performance improvement that using jumbo frames would bring. In addition, such NICs will often have problems with VLAN traffic, since a VLAN tag increases the size of the Ethernet header beyond the traditional size limit.

The pfSense project recommends NICs based on Intel chipsets, and there are several reasons why such NICs are considered reliable. They tend to have adequately sized buffers, and do not have problems processing larger frames. Moreover, the drivers tend to be well-written and work well with Unix-based operating systems.

For a typical pfSense setup, you will need two network interfaces: one for the WAN and one for the LAN. Each additional subnet (for example, for a guest network) will require an additional interface, as will each additional WAN interface. It should be noted that you don't need an additional card for each interface added; you can buy a multiport network card (most of such cards have either two or four ports). You don't need to buy new NICs for your pfSense system; in fact, it is often economical to buy used NICs, and except in rare cases, the performance level will be the same.

If you want to incorporate wireless connectivity into your network, you may consider adding a wireless card to your pfSense system. As mentioned earlier, however, the likely better option is to use pfSense in conjunction with a separate wireless access point. If you do decide to add a wireless card to your system and configure it for use as an access point, you will want to check the FreeBSD hardware compatibility list before making a purchase.

The best practices for installation and configuration

Once you have chosen your hardware and which version you are going to install, you can download pfSense.

1. Browse to the **Downloads** section of **pfsense.org** and select the appropriate computer architecture (**32-bit**, **64-bit**, or **Netgate ADI**), the appropriate platform (**Live CD**, **memstick**, or **embedded**), and you should be presented with a list of mirrors. Choose the closest one for the best performance.

    You will also want to download the SHA256 checksum file in order to verify the integrity of the downloaded image. Verifying the integrity of downloads serves two purposes:

    - It ensures that the download completed
    - It safeguards against a party maliciously tampering with the images

In order to safeguard against the latter, however, be sure to download the checksum from a different mirror site than the site from which you downloaded the image. This provides an additional measure of security should an individual mirror site be compromised.

Windows has several utilities for displaying SHA256 hashes for a file. Under BSD and Linux, generating the SHA256 hash is as easy as typing the following command:

```
shasum -a 256 pfSense-LiveCD-2.4.2-RELEASE-amd64.iso.gz
```

This command generates the MD5 checksum for the 64-bit Live CD version for pfSense 2.4.2. You should compare the resulting hash with the contents of the `.sha256` file downloaded from one of the (other) mirrors.

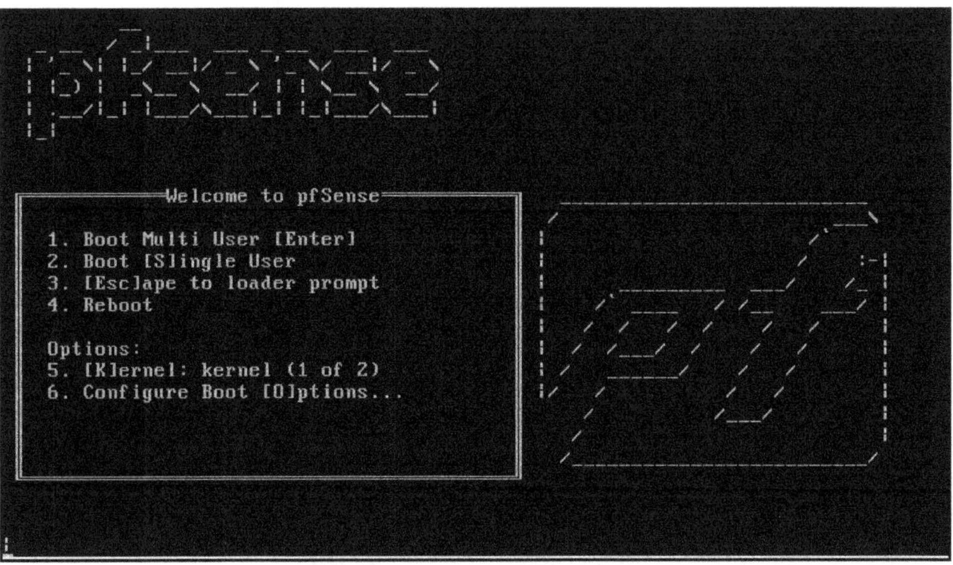

The initial pfSense boot menu when booting from a CD or USB drive

- If the system hangs during the boot process, there are several options you can try. The first menu that appears, as pfSense boots, has several options. The last two options are **Kernel** and **Configure Boot Options**. **Kernel** allows you to select which kernel to boot from among the available kernels.

If you have a reason to suspect that the FreeBSD kernel being used is not compatible with your hardware, you might want to switch to the older version. **Configure Boot Options** launches a menu (shown in the preceding screenshot) with several useful options. A description of these options can be found at: `https://www.freebsd.org/doc/en_US.ISO8859-1/books/handbook/`. Toggling **[A]CPI Support** to **off** can help in some cases, as ACPI's hardware discovery and configuration capabilities may cause the pfSense boot process to hang. If turning this off doesn't work, you could try booting in **Safe [M]ode**, and if all else fails, you can toggle **[V]erbose** mode to **On**, which will give you detailed messages while booting.

- While booting, pfSense provides information about your hardware, including expansion buses supported, network interfaces found, and USB support. When this is finished, the graphical installer will launch and you will see the copyright and distribution notice.

2. Select **Accept** and press *Enter* to accept these terms and conditions and continue with the installation.
3. The installer then provides you with three options: **Install pfSense**, **Rescue Shell**, and **Recover config.xml**. The **Rescue Shell** option launches a BSD shell prompt from which you can perform functions that might prove helpful in repairing a non-functional pfSense system.

For example, you can copy, delete and edit files from the shell prompt. If you suspect that a recent configuration change is what caused pfSense to break, however, and you saved the configuration file before making the change, the easiest way to fix your system may be to invoke **Recover config.xml** and restore pfSense from the previously-saved `config.xml` file.

- The next screen provides keymap options. Version 2.4.2 supports 99 different keyboard layouts, including both QWERTY and Dvorak layouts. Highlighting a keymap option and pressing *Enter* selects that option. There's also an option to test the default keymap, and an option to continue with the default keymap.

4. Select **Accept** and press *Enter* when you have selected a keymap.
5. Next, the installer provides the following disk partitioning options: **Auto (UFS)**, **Manual**, **Shell**, and **Auto (ZFS)**. The first and last options allow you to format the disk with the **Unix File System (UFS)** and Oracle's **ZFS** respectively.

- There are advantages and disadvantages to each filesystem, but the following table should help in your decision. Note that both filesystems support file ownership, and file creation/last access timestamps.

Filesystem	**UFS**	**ZFS**
Original release	August 1983 (with BSD 4.2)	November 2005 (with OpenSolaris)
Maximum volume size	2^{73} bytes (8 zebibytes)	2^{128} bytes (256 trillion yobibytes)

Maximum file size	2^{73} bytes (8 zebibytes)	2^{64} bytes (16 exbibytes)
Maximum filename length	255 bytes	255 bytes
Case sensitive	Yes	Yes
Support for filesystem-level encryption	No	Yes
Data deduplication	No	Yes
Data checksums	No	Yes

- In general, UFS is the tried-and-true filesystem, while ZFS was created with security in mind and incorporates many newer features such as filesystem-level encryption and data checksums.

pfSense does not support converting the filesystem to ZFS after installation; ZFS formatting must be done before installation.

- **Manual**, as the name implies, allows you to manually create, delete and modify partitions. There are several choices for partition types; you can even create an **Apple Partition Map (APM)** or a **DOS** partition, if that suits you. The **Shell** option drops you to a BSD shell prompt from which you can also manually create, delete and modify partitions, using shell commands.

6. If you chose ZFS, the next screen will present a series of options that allow you to further configure your ZFS volume.

    - **Pool Type/Disks** allows you to select the type of redundancy. The default option is **stripe**, which provides no redundancy at all. The **mirror** option provides for duplicate volumes, in which the array continues to operate as long as one drive is functioning. The **raid10** option combines mirroring and striping (it is an array of mirrored drives). It requires at least four drives; the array continues to operate if one drive fails; up to half the drives in the RAID can fail so long as they aren't all from the same subset.

- The next three options, **raidz1**, **raidz2**, and **raidz3**, are non-standard RAID options. Like RAID levels 5 though, they achieve redundancy through a parity stripe, although the parity stripe in Z1, Z2 and Z3 are dynamically sized. RAID-Z1 requires at least three disks/volumes and allows one of them to fail without data loss; RAID-Z2 requires four disks/volumes and allows two to fail; RAID-Z3 requires five disks/volumes and allows three to fail.

The installer will not let you proceed unless your RAID set has the minimum number of volumes for the configuration you selected.

7. If your ZFS RAID is configured correctly, the installer will next present you with a series of ZFS-specific options. You can change the **Pool Name** (the default is `zroot`), toggle Force 4K Sectors on or off depending on whether or not you want sectors to align on 4K boundaries, and toggle **Encrypt Disks** on or off. You can also select a partition scheme for the system.

    - The default is **GUID Partition Table (GPT)**, but the legacy **Master Boot Record (MBR)** is also supported. You can set it up to boot in **BIOS mode**, **Unified Extensible Firmware Interface (UEFI) mode**, or, if your system supports it, both modes. UEFI-based systems, by specification, can only boot from GPT partitions, while some BIOS-based systems can boot from GPT partitions (and all BIOS-based systems can boot from MBR partitions). There is also support for the FreeBSD patch that fixes a bug that prevents GPT partitions from booting on some Lenovo systems (**GPT + Lenovo Fix**). You can also set the **Swap Size**, toggle **Mirror Swap** on or off, and toggle **Encrypt Swap** on or off.
    - After you have made all desired modifications you can proceed; the installer will format all selected volumes, extract the archive files and install pfSense. You will also be given an option to open a shell prompt to make any final modifications. Otherwise, you can reboot the system and run the newly installed copy of pfSense.

- If you were unable to install pfSense on to the target media, you may have to troubleshoot your system and/or installation media. If you are attempting to install from the CD, your optical drive may be malfunctioning, or the CD may be faulty.

  You may want to start with a known good bootable disc and see if the system will boot off of it. If it can, then your pfSense disk may be at fault; burning the disc again may solve the problem. If, however, your system cannot boot off the known good disc, then the optical drive itself, or the cables connecting the optical drive to the motherboard, may be at fault.

- In some cases, however, none of the aforementioned possibilities hold true, and it is possible that the FreeBSD boot loader will not work on the target system. If so, then you could opt to install pfSense on a different system.
- Another possibility is to install pfSense onto a hard drive on a separate system, then transfer the hard drive into the target system. In order to do this, go through the installation process on another system as you would normally until you get to the **Assign Interfaces** prompt. When the installer asks if you want to assign VLANS, type `n`. Type `exit` at the **Assign Interfaces** prompt to skip the interface assignment. Proceed through the rest of the installation; then power down the system and transfer the hard drive to the target system. Assuming that the pfSense hard drive is in the boot sequence, the system should boot pfSense and detect the system's hardware correctly. Then you should be able to assign network interfaces. The rest of the configuration can then proceed as usual.

8. If you have not encountered any of these problems, the software should be installed on the target system, and you should get a dialog box telling you to remove the CD from the optical drive tray and press *Enter*. The system will now reboot, and you will be booting into your new pfSense install for the first time.

pfSense configuration

If installation was successful, you should see a screen similar to the one shown in the following screenshot:

```
FreeBSD/amd64 (thewookie.thewookie.duckdns.org) (ttyv0)

VirtualBox Virtual Machine - Netgate Device ID: b3bd7fcb975cb1b874f0

*** Welcome to pfSense 2.4.3-RELEASE (amd64) on thewookie ***

 WAN (wan)       -> em0        -> v4/DHCP4: 10.0.2.15/24
 LAN (lan)       -> em1        -> v4: 172.16.1.2/16
                                  v6: 1234:5678:9a::1/48
 OPT_WAN (opt1)  -> em2        ->
 PFSYNC (opt2)   -> em3        -> v4: 10.0.10.10/24

 0) Logout (SSH only)                  9) pfTop
 1) Assign Interfaces                 10) Filter Logs
 2) Set interface(s) IP address       11) Restart webConfigurator
 3) Reset webConfigurator password    12) PHP shell + pfSense tools
 4) Reset to factory defaults         13) Update from console
 5) Reboot system                     14) Disable Secure Shell (sshd)
 6) Halt system                       15) Restore recent configuration
 7) Ping host                         16) Restart PHP-FPM
 8) Shell

Enter an option:
```

The console menu in pfSense 2.4.3

Some of the initial configuration must be done at the console, while some aspects of the configuration, such as VLAN and DHCP setup, can be done from either the console or the web GUI.

Configuration takes place in two phases. Some configuration must be done at the console, including interface configuration and interface IP address assignment. Some configuration steps, such as VLAN and DHCP setup, can be done both at the console and within the web GUI. On initial bootup, pfSense will automatically configure the WAN and LAN interfaces, according to the following parameters:

- Network interfaces will be assigned to device IDs `em0`, `em1`, and so on
- The WAN interface will be assigned to `em0`, and the LAN interface will be assigned to `em1`

- The WAN interface will look to an upstream DHCP server for its IP address, while the LAN interface will initially be assigned an IP address of `192.168.1.1`

You can, of course, accept these default assignments and proceed to the web GUI, but chances are you will need to change at least some of these settings. If you need to change interface assignments, select **1** from the menu.

Configuration from the console

On boot, you should eventually see a menu identical to the one seen on the CD version, with the boot multi or single user options, and other options. After a timeout period, the boot process will continue and you will get an **Options** menu. If the default interface assignments are unsatisfactory, select **1** from the menu to begin interface assignment. This is where the network cards installed in the system are given their roles as WAN, LAN, and optional interfaces (OPT1, OPT2, and so on).

If you select this option, you will be presented with a list of network interfaces. This list provides four pieces of information:

- pfSense's device name for the interface (`fxp0`, `em1`, and so on)
- The MAC address of the interface
- The link state of the interface (*up* if a link is detected; *down* otherwise)
- The manufacturer and model of the interface (Intel PRO 1000, for example)

As you are probably aware, generally speaking, no two network cards have the same MAC address, so each of the interfaces in your system should have a unique MAC address.

1. To begin the configuration, select **1** and *Enter* for the **Assign Interfaces** option.
2. After that, a prompt will show up for VLAN configuration.

We will cover VLAN configuration in `Chapter 4`, Using *pfSense as a Firewall*, and we will cover both configuration from the command line and web GUI VLAN configuration.

3. If you wish to set up VLANs, see `Chapter 3`, *VLANs*. Otherwise, type `n` and press *Enter*. Keep in mind that you can always configure VLANs later on.
4. The interfaces must be configured, and you will be prompted for the WAN interface first.

5. If you only configure one interface, it will be assigned to the WAN, and you will subsequently be able to log in to pfSense through this port.

    This is not what you would normally want, as the WAN port is typically accessible from the other side of the firewall.

6. When at least one other interface is configured, you will no longer be able to log in to pfSense from the WAN port. Unless you are using VLANs, you will have to set up at least two network interfaces.

In pfSense, network interfaces are assigned rather cryptic device names (for example, `fxp0`, `em1`, and so on) and it is not always easy to know which ports correspond to particular device names. One way of solving this problem is to use the **automatic interface assignment** feature.

1. To do this, unplug all network cables from the system, and then type `a` and press *Enter* to begin auto-detection.
2. The WAN interface is the first interface to be detected, so plug a cable into the port you intend to be the WAN interface.

    The process is repeated with each successive interface.

3. The LAN interface is configured next, then each of the optional interfaces (OPT1, OPT2).

If auto-detection does not work, or you do not want to use it, you can always choose manual configuration. You can always reassign network interfaces later on, so even if you make a mistake on this step, the mistake can be easily fixed.

4. Once you have finished configuration, type `y` at the **Do you want to proceed?** prompt, or type `n` and press *Enter* to re-assign the interfaces.
5. Option two on the menu is **Set interface(s) IP address**, and you will likely want to complete this step as well. When you invoke this option, you will be prompted to specify which interface's IP address is to be set.

6. If you select **WAN interface**, you will be asked if you want to configure the IP address via DHCP. In most scenarios, this is probably the option you want to choose, especially if pfSense is acting as a firewall. In that case, the WAN interface will receive an IP address from your ISP's DHCP server. For all other interfaces (or if you choose not to use DHCP on the WAN interface), you will be prompted to enter the interface's IPv4 address.
7. The next prompt will ask you for the subnet bit count. In most cases, you'll want to enter `8` if you are using a Class A private address, `16` for Class B, and `24` for Class C, but if you are using classless subnetting (for example, to divide a Class C network into two separate networks), then you will want to set the bit count accordingly.
8. You will also be prompted for the IPv4 gateway address (any interface with a gateway set is a WAN, and pfSense supports multiple WANs); if you are not configuring the WAN interface(s), you can just hit *Enter* here.
9. Next, you will be prompted to provide the address, subnet bit count, and gateway address for IPv6; if you want your network to fully utilize IPv6 addresses, you should enter them here.

The advantages of IPv6 over IPv4 will be discussed more fully in `Chapter 2`, *Advanced pfSense Configuration*.

We have now configured as much as we need to from the console (actually, we have done more than we have to, since we really only have to configure the WAN interface from the console). The remainder of the configuration can be done from the pfSense web GUI.

Configuration from the web GUI

The pfSense web GUI can only be accessed from another PC. If the WAN was the only interface assigned during the initial setup, then you will be able to access pfSense through the WAN IP address. Once one of the local interfaces is configured (typically the LAN interface), pfSense can no longer be accessed through the WAN interface. You will, however, be able to access pfSense from the local side of the firewall (typically through the LAN interface). In either case, you can access the web GUI by connecting another computer to the pfSense system, either directly (with a crossover cable) or indirectly (through a switch), and then typing either the WAN or LAN IP address into the connected computer's web browser.

If you enabled the LAN interface but did not enable DHCP on LAN, or if you are accessing the web GUI on another computer on the LAN network, you must statically set the IP address on that computer to a valid IP address for the LAN network (for example, if the LAN interface IP address is `192.168.1.1` and the LAN network is `192.168.1.0/24`, set it to `192.168.1.2` or any number other than 1 for the last octet).

1. When you initially log in to pfSense, the default username/password combination will be **admin/pfsense**, respectively.
2. On your first login, the Setup Wizard will begin automatically.
3. Click on the **Next** button to begin configuration.

If you need to run the Setup Wizard after your initial login, select **System | Setup Wizard** from the top menu.

4. The first screen provides a link for information about a pfSense Gold Netgate Global Support subscription. You can click on the link to sign up to learn more, or click on the **Next** button.
5. On the next screen, you will be prompted to enter the hostname of the router as well as the domain. Hostnames can contain letters, numbers, and hyphens, but must begin with a letter. If you have a domain, you can enter it in the appropriate field.
6. In the **Primary DNS Server** and **Secondary DNS Server** fields, you can enter your DNS servers. If you are using DHCP for your WAN, you can probably leave these fields blank, as they will usually be assigned automatically by your ISP. However, your ISP's DNS servers may not be reliable. There are many third party DNS servers available, including OpenDNS (`208.67.220.220` and `208.67.222.222`) and Google Public DNS (`8.8.8.8` and `8.8.4.4`). Uncheck the **Override DNS** checkbox if you want to use third party DNS servers rather than the DNS servers used by your ISP. Click on **Next** when finished.
7. The next screen will prompt you for the **Network Time Protocol** (**NTP**) server as well as the local time zone. The NTP server configuration will be covered in greater detail in the next chapter; you can keep the default value for the server hostname for now. For the **Timezone** field, you should select the zone which matches your location and click on **Next**.
8. The next screen of the wizard is the **WAN configuration** page.

In most scenarios, you won't need to make any further changes to the WAN in comparison to what was done at the console (at least initially; a multi-WAN setup is more involved and will be discussed more fully in `Chapter 9`, *Multiple WANs*).

If you need to make changes, however, there are several options on this page.

1. For **Selected Type**, you have several options, but the most commonly used options are **DHCP** (the default type) or **Static**.

   If your pfSense system is behind another firewall and it is not going to receive an IP address from an upstream DHCP server, then you probably should choose **Static**. If pfSense is going to be a perimeter firewall, however, then **DHCP** is likely the correct setting, since your ISP will probably dynamically assign an IP address (this is not always the case, as you may have an IP address statically assigned to you by your ISP, but it is the more likely scenario).

2. The other choices are Point-to-Point Protocol over Ethernet (**PPPoE**) and Point-to-Point Tunneling Protocol (**PPTP**). Your ISP may require that you use one of these options for the WAN interface; if you are not sure, check with them.
3. If you selected either **PPPoE** or **PPTP**, you will have to scroll down to the appropriate part of the page to enter parameters for these connections.
4. At a minimum, you will likely have to enter the **Username** and **Password** for such connections. In addition, PPTP requires that you enter a local IP address and a remote IP address.
5. The **dial-on-demand** checkbox for PPPoE and PPTP connections allows you to connect to your ISP only when a user requests data that requires an internet connection. Both PPPoE and PPTP support an **Idle timeout** setting, which specifies how long the connection will be kept open after transmitting data when this option is invoked. Leaving this field blank disables this function.

PPP (Point-to-Point Protocol) and **L2TP** (**Layer 2 Tunneling Protocol**) are also valid choices for the WAN configuration type. However, the Setup Wizard does not allow the user to select either of these. In order to select **PPP** or **L2TP**, navigate to **Interfaces** | **WAN** from the top menu, and select **PPP** or **L2TP** in either the **IPv4 Configuration Type** or **IPv6 Configuration Type** drop-down box (or both). Setup is similar to the setup for **PPPoE** and **PPTP** – you will have to enter a **Username** and **Password** – and in the case of **PPP**, you will also have to enter your ISP's phone number in the **Phone number** field.

6. We can now turn our attention to the **General Configuration** section. The **MAC address** field allows you to enter a MAC address that is different from the actual MAC address of the WAN interface.

   This can be useful if your ISP will not recognize an interface with a different MAC address than the device that was previously connected, or if you want to acquire a different IP address (changing the MAC address will cause the upstream DHCP server to assign a different address).

7. If you use this option, make sure the portion of the address reserved for the **Organizationally Unique Identifier** (**OUI**) is a valid OUI – in other words, an OUI assigned to a network card manufacturer. (The OUI portion of the address is the first three bytes of a MAC-48 address and the first five bytes of an EUI-48 address).
8. The next few fields can usually be left blank. **Maximum Transmission Unit (MTU)** allows you to change the MTU size if necessary. **DHCP hostname** allows you to send a hostname to your ISP when making a DHCP request, which is useful if your ISP requires this.
9. The **Block RFC1918 Private Networks** checkbox, if checked, will block registered private networks (as defined by RFC 1918) from connecting to the WAN interface. The **Block Bogon Networks** option blocks traffic from reserved and/or unassigned IP addresses. For the WAN interface, you should check both options unless you have special reasons for not invoking these options. Click the **Next** button when you are done.
10. The next screen provides fields in which you can change the **LAN IP address** and **subnet mask**, but only if you configured the LAN interface previously.
11. You can keep the default, or change it to another value within the private address blocks. You may want to choose an address range other than the very common `192.168.1.x` in order to avoid a conflict.
12. Be aware that if you change the **LAN IP address** value, you will also need to adjust your PC's IP address, or release and renew its DHCP lease when finished with the network interface. You will also have to change the pfSense IP address in your browser to reflect the change.
13. The final screen of the pfSense Setup Wizard allows you to change the admin password, which you should do now.
14. Enter the password, enter it again for confirmation in the next edit box, and click on **Next**.

15. Later on, you can create another administrator account with a username other than admin and disable the admin account, for additional security, unless you plan on setting up multiple firewalls for high availability, in which case you will need to retain the admin account.
16. On the following screen, there will be a **Reload** button; click on **Reload**. This will reload pfSense with the new changes.
17. Once you have completed the wizard, you should have network connectivity. Although there are other means of making changes to pfSense's configuration, if you want to repeat the wizard, you can do so by navigating to **System | Setup Wizard**. Completion of the wizard will take you to the pfSense dashboard.

Configuring additional interfaces

By now, both the **WAN** and **LAN** interface configurations should be complete. Although additional interface configurations can be done at the console, it can also be done (and somewhat more conveniently so) in the web GUI.

1. To add optional interfaces, navigate to the **Interfaces | Assignments** tab, which will show a list of assigned interfaces, and at the bottom of the table, there will be an **Available network ports** option.
2. There will be a corresponding drop-down box with a list of unassigned network ports. These will have device names such as `fxp0`, `em1`, and so on.
3. To assign an unused port, select the port you want to assign from the drop-down box, and click on the + button to the right.
4. The page will reload, and the new interface will be the last entry in the table. The name of the interface will be **OPTx**, where **x** equals the number of optional interfaces.
5. By clicking on **interface name**, you can configure the interface.

   Nearly all the settings here are similar to the settings that were available on the **WAN** and **LAN** configuration pages in the **pfSense Setup Wizard**.

   Some of the options under the **General Configuration** section, that are not available in the Setup Wizard, are **MSS** (Maximum Segment Size), and **Speed and duplex.** Normally, MSS should remain unchanged, although you can change this setting if your internet connection requires it.

6. If you click on the **Advanced** button under **Speed and duplex**, a drop-down box will appear in which you can explicitly set the speed and duplex for the interface. Since virtually all modern network hardware has the capability of automatically selecting the correct speed and duplex, you will probably want to leave this unchanged.
7. The section at the bottom of the page, **Reserved Networks**, allows you to enable **Block private networks and loopback addresses** and **Block bogon networks** via their respective checkboxes. Although these options are checked by default when configuring the WAN interface, we normally want to allow private networks on internal interfaces, so these options are normally not enabled when configuring non-WAN interfaces.
8. If you chose an option other than **Static** for the **Configuration Type**, then other options will appear.

Since it is unlikely that internal interfaces will be configured as such, further discussion of these options will take place in the next section on WAN configuration.

Additional WAN configuration

Most likely, you won't have to do any additional configuration for the WAN interface; the configuration done in the Setup Wizard will be enough to get you started. If you need to make changes, however, follow these steps:

1. Navigate to **Interfaces** | **WAN** in the main menu.
2. The most likely scenario is that your ISP will provide an IP address via DHCP, but many providers will provide you with a static IP address if you require one. In such cases, you will need to set your **Configuration Type** to **Static** and then enter your WAN IP address and CIDR under either the **Static IPv4 Configuration** or **Static IPv6 Configuration** (or possibly both, if you plan to have both an IPv4 and IPv6 address).
3. You will also need to specify your ISP's gateway, which you can do by clicking on the **Add a new gateway** button. A dialog box will appear in which you can enter the IP address and a description.

4. If you have selected **DHCP** as the configuration type, then there are several options in addition to the ones available in the Setup Wizard. Clicking on the **Advanced** checkbox in the DHCP client configuration causes several additional options to appear in this section of the page.
    - The first is **Protocol Timing**, which allows you to control DHCP protocol timings when requesting a lease. You can also choose several presets (**FreeBSD**, **pfSense**, **Clear**, or **Saved Cfg**) using the radio buttons on the right.
    - There is also a **Configuration Override** checkbox which, if checked, allows you to specify the absolute path to a DHCP client configuration file in the **Configuration Override File** edit box. If your ISP supports pfSense, it should be able to provide you with a valid configuration override file.
    - If the **Configuration Override** checkbox is not checked, there will be three edit boxes in this section under the checkboxes. The first is **Hostname**; this field is sent as a DHCP hostname and client identifier when requesting a DHCP lease. **Alias IPv4 address** allows you to enter a fixed IP address for the DHCP client. The **Reject Leases from** field allows you to specify the IP address or subnet of an upstream DHCP server to be ignored.
    - The next section is **Lease Requirements and Requests**. Here you can specify **send**, **request**, and **require** options when requesting a DHCP lease. These options are useful if your ISP requires these options. The last section is **Option Modifiers**, where you can add **DHCP option modifiers,** which are applied to an obtained DHCP lease.
5. Starting with pfSense version 2.2.5, there is support for IPv6 with DHCP (DHCP6). If you are running 2.2.5 or above, there will be a section on the page called **DHCP6 client configuration**.
6. Similar to the configuration for IPv4 DHCP, there are checkboxes for **Advanced Configuration** and **Configuration Override**.
7. Checking the **Advanced** checkbox in the heading of this section displays the **Advanced DHCP 6** options:
    - If you check the **Information Only** checkbox on the left, pfSense will send requests for stateless DHCPv6 information.
    - You can specify **Send** and **Request** options, just as you can for IPv4.

- There is also a **Script** field where you can enter the absolute path to a script that will be invoked on certain conditions.
- The next options are for the **Identity Association Statement** checkboxes. The **NonTemporary Address Allocation** checkbox results in normal, that is, not temporary, IPv6 addresses to be allocated for the interface. The **Prefix Delegation** checkbox causes a set of IPv6 prefixes to be allocated from the DHCP server.
- The next set of options, **Authentication Statement**, allows you to specify authentication parameters to the DHCP server. The **Authname** parameter allows you to specify a string, which in turn specifies a set of parameters.
- The remaining parameters are of limited usefulness in configuring a DHCP6 client, because each has only one allowed value, and leaving them blank will result in only the allowed value being used. If you are curious as to what these values are here they are:

Parameter	Allowed value	Description
Protocol	Delayed	The DHCPv6 delayed authentication protocol
Algorithm	hmac-md5, HMAC-MD5, hmacmd5, or HMACMD5	The HMAC-MD5 authentication algorithm
rdm	Monocounter	The replay protection method; only monocounter is available

8. Finally, **Key info Statement** allows you to enter a secret key. The required fields are **key id**, which identifies the key, and **secret**, which provides the shared secret. **key name** and **realm** are arbitrary strings and may be omitted. **expire** may be used to specify an expiration time for the key, but if it is omitted, the key will never expire.
    1. If you do not check the configuration override checkbox (in which case you will specify a configuration override file, similar to how this option works with DHCP over IPv4), there will be several more options in this **DHCP Client Configuration** section . **Use IPv4 connectivity as parent interface** allows you to request an IPv6 prefix over an IPv4 link.
    2. **Request only an IPv6 prefix** allows you to request just the prefix, not an address. **DHCPv6 Prefix Delegation size** allows you to specify the prefix length.
    3. You can check the **Send IPv6 prefix hint** to indicate the desired prefix length, **Debug** for debugging, and select **Do not wait for an RA** (router advertisement) and/or **Do not allow PD/Address release,** if your ISP requires it.
9. The last section on the page is identical to the interface configuration page in the **Setup Wizard**, and contains the **Block Private Networks** and **Block Bogon Networks** checkboxes.

For information on how to configure other **Configuration Type** options such as **PPTP** and **PPPoE**, refer to the information about **Setup Wizard** configuration under the heading *Configuration from the web GUI*.

General setup options

You can find several configuration options under **System** | **General Setup**. Most of these are identical to settings that can be configured in the **Setup Wizard** (**Hostname**, **Domain**, **DNS servers**, **Timezone**, and **NTP server**). There are two additional settings available:

1. The **Language** drop-down box allows you to select the web configurator language.
2. Under the **Web Configurator** section, there is a **Theme** drop-down box that allows you to select the theme. The default theme of pfSense is perfectly adequate, but you can select another one here. There are several new theme options available for version 2.4, so if you have not tried these, you may want to do so.

pfSense 2.3 added new options to control the look and feel of the web interface and 2.4 has added some more; these settings are also found in the **Web Configurator** section of the **General Settings** page:

1. The top navigation drop-down box allows you to choose whether the top navigation scrolls with the page, or remains anchored at the top as you scroll.
2. The **Hostname** in the **Menu** option allows you to replace the **Help** menu title with the system name or **fully qualified domain name (FQDN)**.
3. The **Dashboard Columns** option allows you to select the number of columns on the dashboard page (the default is `2`).
4. The next set of options is **Associated Panels Show/Hide**. These options control the appearance of certain panels on the **Dashboard** and **System Logs** page. The options are:
    - **Available Widgets**: Checking this box causes the **Available Widgets** panel to appear on the **Dashboard**. Prior to version 2.3, the **Available Widgets** panel was always visible on the **Dashboard**.
    - **Log Filter**: Checking this box causes the **Advanced Log Filter** panel to appear on the **System Logs** page. **Advanced Log Filter** allows you to filter the system logs by time, process, PID, and message.
    - **Manage Log**: Checking this box causes the **Manage General Log** panel to appear on the **System Logs** page. The **Manage General Log** panel allows you to control the display of the logs, how big the log file may be, and the formatting of the log file, among other things.
    - **Monitoring Settings**: Checking this box causes the **Settings** section to appear on the **Status | Monitoring** page, which allows custom configuration of the interactive graph on that page.
5. The **Require State Filter** checkbox, if checked, causes the state table in **Diagnostics | States** to only appear if a filter is entered.
6. The last option on this page, **Left Column Labels**, allows you to select/toggle the first item in a group by clicking on the left column if checked.

7. The last three options on the page were added with version 2.4:
    - The **Alias Popups** checkbox, if checked, will disable showing the details of an alias in alias popups that appear when dragging the mouse over an alias on the **Firewall** page.
    - The **Login page color** drop-down box allows you to customize the login page color; the current default color is blue.
    - Finally, the **Login hostname** checkbox, when checked, will display the hostname on the login page. Having the hostname on the login page can be a helpful reminder if you are managing a large network with several firewalls, but it also potentially gives away what network is being secured.
8. Click on **Save** at the bottom of the page to save any changes.

Version 2.4.3 has added **Cross-site request forgery (CSRF)** protection to the dashboard widgets.

Summary

The goal of this chapter was to provide a brief overview of how to get pfSense up and running. Completion of this chapter should give you an idea of where to deploy pfSense on your network, as well as what hardware to utilize. You should also know how to troubleshoot common installation problems and how to do basic system configuration in the most common deployment scenarios.

We have barely scratched the surface here, however, and in the next chapter we will cover some of the more advanced configuration options. We will cover DHCP and DHCPv6, DNS and Dynamic DNS, as well as other capabilities you are likely to consider utilizing, such as captive portal, the Network Time Protocol (NTP), and the Simple Network Management Protocol.

The learning curve becomes somewhat steeper after this chapter, but fear not: if you have a solid understanding of computer networks and how they work, mastering pfSense can be both educational and fun.

Questions

Answer the following questions:

1. What term is used to refer to a network that is separate from the rest of the local network and provides services to users outside of the local network?
2. What are the minimum specifications for pfSense in terms of CPU, RAM and disk space?
3. How much memory does a state table entry require?
4. Why is it a good idea to use checksums?
5. What is the best filesystem choice for an organization that (a) requires support for filesystem-level encryption and data deduplication? (b) requires maximum backward compatibility?
6. Identify the two places from which interface assignment can be done in pfSense.
7. Identify at least four different valid configuration types for a pfSense interface.
8. What is the default setting for **Block Private Networks and loopback addresses** (a) on the WAN interface? (b) an the LAN interface? (c) why?
9. Identify two places within the web GUI where the time zone can be set.
10. Identify at least three parameters that can be set in the Setup Wizard.

Further reading

- The official pfSense documentation wiki is a good place to get started. There you will find a guide for downloading and installing pfSense, a features list, a packages list and documentation for packages, as well as an FAQ document. You can find the wiki at: `https://doc.pfsense.org/index.php/Main_Page`.
- During the WAN and LAN configuration, you may have noticed the description of block private addresses and loopback addresses makes reference to RFC 1918 and RFC 4193. **RFC** stands for **Request for Comments**; these are documents published by the **Internet Engineering Task Force** (**IETF**), and in spite of their deceptively informal title, RFCs are actually specifications and standards for internet-related technologies. RFC 1918 and 4193, for example, describe private addressing for IPv4 and IPv6 networks respectively. If you wish to read an RFC, navigate to: `https://tools.ietf.org/html/`, which allows you to retrieve RFCs by numbers or draft names.

2
Advanced pfSense Configuration

The information provided in the first chapter should be enough to get you started with your pfSense router/firewall and deploy it on your network. In this chapter, we will go beyond this basic functionality. Some of the features covered in this chapter overlap with features provided by consumer-grade routers, and as a result you may be somewhat familiar with configuring them. Others, however, go beyond what the typical consumer-grade router provides.

By the end of this chapter, you should know how to configure the following pfSense services:

- **Secure Shell** (SSH) login
- **Dynamic Host Configuration Protocol** (DHCP)
- **Domain Name System** (DNS)
- **Dynamic DNS** (DDNS)
- Captive portals
- **Network Time Protocol** (NTP)
- **Simple Network Management Protocol** (SNMP)

Technical requirements

You should be able to configure of all of the services listed previously with the computer hardware listed under the *Technical requirements* for `Chapter 1`, *Revisiting pfSense Basics*. Having internet access on the other side of your pfSense firewall is useful for testing Dynamic DNS; often the easiest way to do this is with a mobile connection that provides internet access via a network separate from your home/office broadband connection. A wireless access point or router can be useful if you want to set up DHCP or captive portal on a wireless network. Just remember to disable DHCP if you are using a wireless router (put the router in wireless access point mode and let pfSense act as the DHCP server).

SSH login

In the previous chapter, we referred several times to configurations that can be done at the pfSense console. The same functionality is available via remote SSH login, if you enable it.

1. To do so, navigate to **System** | **Advanced**. Make sure the **Admin Access** tab is selected and scroll down to the **Secure Shell** section of the page.
2. Check the **Secure Shell Server** checkbox to enable SSH login.
3. If all you want to do is enable traditional login via the standard SSH port (`22`), then you can click on the **Save** button at the bottom of the page.
4. If you want to change the login port, you can do so by entering a port number other than `22` in the **SSH port** edit box. Changing the SSH port is a good additional security measure, especially if you plan on making SSH login accessible from the WAN side of the firewall.
5. If you set a strong password, SSH login should be pretty secure, but you can add another layer of security by checking the **Disable password login for Secure Shell (RSA/DSA key only)**. If you invoke this option, you must create authorized SSH keys for each user that requires SSH access.
6. The process for generating SSH keys differs depending on what program and OS you use. One handy program for generating SSH keys is PuTTYgen, a companion to the PuTTY terminal program. This program can be downloaded here: `https://www.chiark.greenend.org.uk/~sgtatham/putty/latest.html`.
7. PuTTYgen's interface takes the form of a dialog box. In the **Parameters** section at the bottom you can select the type of key to generate (select either **RSA** or **DSA** to generate a valid SSH-2 key for pfSense) and the number of bits in the key.

8. When you are finished setting the parameters, click the **Generate** button in the **Actions** section to generate a public/private key pair. The program will request that you move the mouse over the top area of the dialog box to generate some entropy. When the key is generated, the dialog box should look similar to the following screenshot:

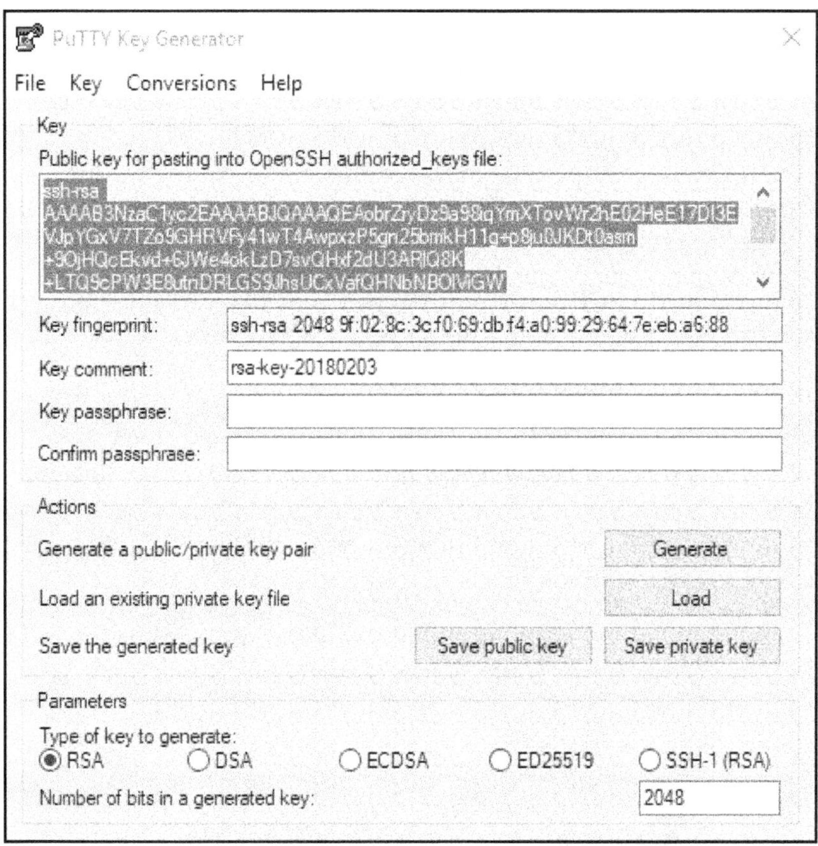

PuTTYgen after generating a public/private key pair

9. Click the **Save private key** button to save the private key; you will need this later to log in to pfSense. Once you have saved the private key, copy the public key in the textbox at the top of the dialog box to the clipboard.
10. The next step is to paste the public key into pfSense. From the web GUI, navigate to **System** | **User Manager**. Scroll down to the **Keys** section, and paste the public key into the **Authorized SSH Keys** edit box. Once you have done this, scroll to the bottom of the page and click on **Save**.

11. Now you can launch PuTTY and configure your session. Enter the IP address of the pfSense system in the **Host Name (or IP address)** edit box. Enter the port in the **Port** edit box. Keep the default **Connection Type** on **SSH**.
12. In the left pane, navigate to **Connection** | **SSH** | **Auth** (you may have to expand **Connection** and **SSH** to reveal the **Auth** settings page). In the **Private key for authentication:** edit box, enter the full path and filename of the private key. This is the private key you saved previously.
13. You can now save the current configuration by clicking on **Session** at the top of the left pane, typing a name into **Saved Sessions** and clicking on **Save**, or you can just click on **Open** to connect to the pfSense console.
14. At the **login as:** prompt, type in the administrator username; the next prompt will be for the key's passphrase. Enter the passphrase and press *Enter*, and you should be logged into the console.

If you were unable to log in to the console, then you need to make sure you went through the process correctly; namely, the following steps must have been completed:

1. Enabling SSH login in pfSense.
2. Generation of a valid SSH-2 public/private key pair.
3. Adding the public key to the list of authorized SSH keys for the administrator in pfSense.
4. Configuring PuTTY to log into pfSense, remembering to add the private key to the SSH authorization options.

If there was a public/private key mismatch, make sure the keys are correct and that there aren't any additional characters or white spaces in them.

DHCP

If you only have a few devices on your network, you could easily configure them with static IP addresses and not use a DHCP server at all. In such cases, internet connectivity will be established more quickly, since computers on the network won't have to go through the DHCP discovery-offer-request-acknowledge process. As the size of your network grows, however, a DHCP server becomes essential, as keeping track of statically assigned IP addresses will become far too cumbersome. Fortunately, configuring pfSense to act as a DHCP server is relatively easy, and can be done from either the console or the web GUI.

DHCP configuration at the console

DHCP configuration at the console can be done with the following steps:

1. At the console, select **Set interface(s) IP address** on the menu.
2. Select the interface on which you want to run the pfSense DHCP server (this is usually a LAN, but it could be any interface other than the WAN interface). You will be prompted for the interface's IPv4 IP address.
3. Type in the address (or leave the line blank for none) and press *Enter*.
4. The next prompt is for the subnet bit count. Type in the correct bit count and press *Enter*.
5. Next, you will be prompted for the upstream gateway address. You do not need to provide this information, so just press *Enter*. IPv4 address configuration is now complete.
6. The next prompt will be for the IPv6 address. If you have a small network, IPv6 configuration is not necessary, although there are some advantages to IPv6 configuration, such as the ability to assign addresses automatically, enhanced security, and even better mobility features. Enter an IPv6 address if you want to use IPv6 on the interface.
7. After you enter the IPv6 address, you will be prompted to enter the subnet bit count, so enter the bit count and press *Enter*. Since you don't need to specify an upstream gateway, you can press *Enter* there as well.
8. The next two prompts will ask you whether to start the DHCP server on IPv4 and IPv6, respectively. If you specify `y` for either one, you will be prompted to enter the address range for DHCP. Here you can specify any valid address range for your subnet. Keep in mind that you don't have to start the DHCP server for IPv6 unless you want clients to have their IPv6 addresses assigned to them. Instead, you can utilize client address configuration.

Now that you have enabled DHCP at the console and assigned addresses ranges, you should be able to connect to your network via DHCP. Configuring networking on the client for DHCP will be different for each platform, but virtually all modern OSes allow you to select either static IP assignment or DHCP (if it's not explicitly called DHCP, it will likely be called **automatic IP assignment** or something like that). You may have to reset your network connection, but once you do, the DHCP server should assign you an IP address.

DHCP configuration in the web GUI

You can also set up your DHCP server in the web GUI, which includes many more options than the console does.

1. Navigate to **Services** | **DHCP Server**. There will be a separate tab for each non-WAN interface.
2. Click on the tab for the interface you want to configure. The following screenshot shows the configuration page for the LAN interface:

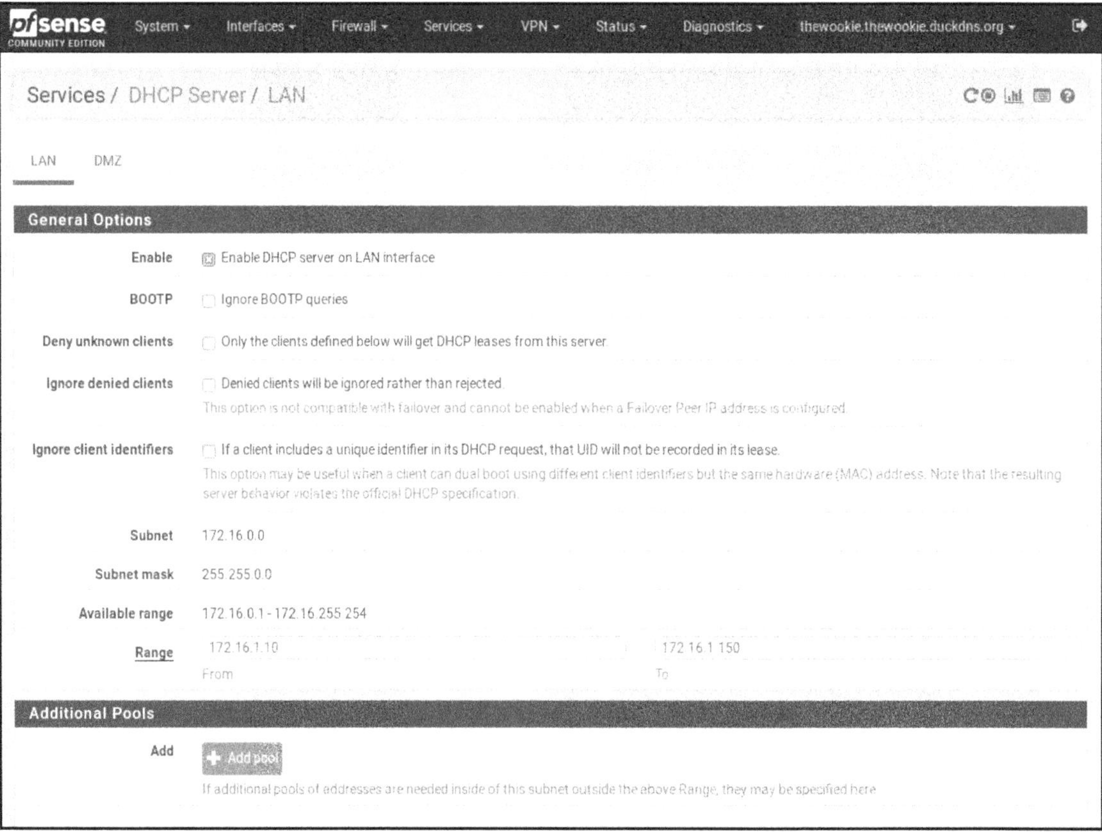

The DHCP configuration page (for IPv4) in pfSense

3. In the **General Options** section, there is an **Enable** checkbox, which, as you probably guessed, enables the DHCP server on the interface.
4. There are also **Range** edit boxes where you can define the range of assigned addresses. If this is all you wanted to do (which is no more than the level of DHCP configuration the console provides), you can click on the **Save** button at the bottom of the page and the DHCP server will now be up and running.

One of the options added in version 2.4, the **BOOTP** checkbox, if checked, will cause the DHCP server to ignore BOOTP queries. BOOTP is a protocol by which networks can assign IP addresses to users. Like DHCP, it uses port `67` and port `68` to communicate. It also predates DHCP (it was originally defined in RFC 951 in September 1985, while DHCP was not defined until March 1997). Both BOOTP and DHCP are methods of automatic IP assignment. However, BOOTP differs from DHCP in several significant ways:

- BOOTP uses the **User Datagram Protocol** (**UDP**), while DHCP uses the **Transport Control Protocol** (**TCP**)
- BOOTP only works with IPv4 networks, while DHCP has been revised to support IPv6 networks
- BOOTP does not support DHCP, but the reverse is true: parts of BOOTP provides services to DHCP, and DHCP servers provide legacy BOOTP functionality

Therefore, a DHCP server will normally also act as a BOOTP server. This can be problematic, however, because BOOTP leases do not have a maximum lease time by default (the original definition of BOOTP does not even include the lease concept). Therefore, BOOTP leases can easily exhaust the DHCP address pool. One possible solution is to just ignore BOOTP queries, which may seem like overkill, but it also eliminates the possibility of DHCP support for BOOTP ever being a problem. If you ever have problems with BOOTP queries, you can enable this option.

1. The **Ignore denied clients** checkbox, if checked, will cause pfSense to ignore denied clients rather than reject them. This, however, is not compatible with failover, because another pfSense system in the failover group will assume that the failure to respond to a DHCP request indicates a failure of the other system.
2. The **Additional Pools** section allows you to specify additional pools of addresses outside of the range specified in **General Options**.
3. You add address pools by clicking on the **Add pool** button and entering the new range.
4. Once a new pool has been added, it will appear under the **Additional Pools** section, and you will be able to edit or delete the pool from the **DHCP Server** page.

5. You may want to set up your system so that only devices with certain MAC addresses receive DHCP leases. If so, check the **Deny unknown clients** checkbox.
6. You will then have to scroll down to the **Other Options** section and click on the **Advanced** button next to the **MAC Address Control** section.
7. In the **MAC Allow** edit box, specify the MAC addresses of the devices (as comma-separated values with no spaces) to which you want to allow access. If you want to deny access to certain devices, you can specify their MAC addresses in the **MAC Deny** edit box.

Be aware that MAC address control only provides a minimal level of security. A user who relies on auto-configuration to connect to the internet will be locked out, but a determined hacker can easily resort to MAC address spoofing which, as you probably know, is one of pfSense's capabilities. Therefore, it's not a good idea to rely on MAC address control as a security measure.

There may be devices on your network (for example, file servers and printers) which need to have the same IP address at all times. For these devices, you can rely on static mappings.

8. If you scroll down to the bottom of the page, you will find a section labeled **DHCP Static Mappings for this Interface**. Following this heading and to the right, there will be an **Add** button which will launch a page on which you can add a mapping.
9. The first setting on this page is **MAC Address**. Here, you must enter the MAC address of the device which is to receive a static mapping.
10. To the right of the **MAC Address** edit box, there is a **Copy My MAC** button that will copy the MAC address of the device currently being used to connect to pfSense; this is provided for your convenience.
11. The MAC address is the only field you must enter. If this is all you enter, this MAC address will be added to the list of allowed MAC addresses for the DHCP server. To obtain a static mapping for this device, you need to enter an IP address in the **IP Address** field.

A bug in pfSense prevented multiple MAC addresses being mapped to a single IP address. Version 2.4.3 fixed this bug, and this is now possible.

12. There is also a **Hostname** field, in which you can specify the hostname, minus the domain. This field is optional, but, if specified, will be forwarded to the DNS server to help identify the client.
13. Another optional field is **Description**, which just allows you to enter a text description of the static mapping.
14. The **Client Identifier** field allows you to enter a client identifier string which will then be sent to the DHCP server. If the client identifier is specified, this identifier, along with the assigned network address, will be used by the DHCP server to identify the client, per RFC 2131. The **Client Identifier** field allows you to enter a client identifier string which, when specified, is used along with the assigned network address by the DHCP server to identify the client, per RFCs 2131 and 6842.
15. In the **Servers** section, you can specify both WINS servers and DNS servers. WINS servers provide Windows with a means of mapping NetBIOS names to network addresses. If you don't have a WINS server on your network, you can leave this blank.
    - The **DNS Servers** fields need not be filled in most cases. If these fields are left blank and the DNS forwarder is enabled, pfSense will automatically assign itself as the DNS server for client PCs.
    - If the DNS forwarder is disabled and these fields are left blank, the default DNS servers specified in **System | General Setup** will be used. There are, however, circumstances in which you may want to override either the default DNS servers or the DNS forwarder:
        - When you need to specify custom DNS servers (for example, an Active Directory configuration in which Active Directory has its own DNS servers)
        - If you are using the **Common Address Redundancy Protocol** (**CARP**) in conjunction with the DNS forwarder, you should specify the CARP IP here.
16. If you want to register the client with a DDNS server, you can enter this information by scrolling down to **Dynamic DNS** and clicking on the **Advanced** button.
17. The **Enable registration of DHCP client names in DNS** checkbox enables DNS registration. If you want to enable DDNS registration, you must fill in the **DDNS Domain** field. There are also fields for the primary domain name server IP address, as well as the DDNS key name and key secret.

With the release of version 2.4.3, several options have been added to the DHCP Dynamic DNS options. The DDNS **Hostnames** checkbox, if enabled, will force the dynamic DNS hostname to be the same as the configured hostname for static mappings, rather than the hostname supplied by the DHCP client. The **key algorithm** drop-down box provides several options for the server key encryption algorithm. **HMAC-SHA512** is the most secure of these options. The **DDNS Client Updates** drop-down box provides options controlling who is allowed to update DNS. If it is set to **Allow**, the client is allowed to update DNS; the DHCP server is prevented from updating forward entries. If it is set to **Deny**, the DHCP server will do the updates and the client will not. If it is set to **Ignore**, then the DHCP server will do the update, but the client can also attempt an update, usually using a different domain name.

DHCPv6 configuration in the web GUI

As with DHCP configuration on IPv4 networks, DHCP configuration on an IPv6 network (DHCPv6) has many options. The DHCPv6 configuration page combines DHCPv6 and router advertisement configuration. This section will focus on options that are only available with DHCPv6 rather than options that are present in both DHCP and DHCPv6.

To configure DHCPv6, navigate to **Services** | **DHCPv6/RA**. Under **DHCPv6 Options**, there are several useful settings. The purpose of the **Prefix Delegation Range** option, as the name implies, is to delegate to clients the ability to act as DHCPv6 servers. This is done by assigning portions of the subnet to them. To illustrate this, consider one of the common IPv6 prefix examples: `fd12:3456:78:9a::` with a subnet mask of `48`. The remaining bits are available for delegation, so we have an available range of `fd12:3456:789a::` to `1234:5678:9a: ffff:ffff:ffff:ffff:ffff`. We can delegate any subset of this range. The prefix delegation size indicates the CIDR of the client's subnets. It must be on the boundaries of the range indicated in the **DHCPv6 Prefix Delegation Size**.

In our previous example, we had a ULA with a prefix of `fd12:3456:789a::/48`. If we wanted our clients to receive portions of the subnet, then we could set a **Prefix Delegation Range** of `fd12:3456:789a:0000::` to `fd12:3456:789a:ff00::` with a **Prefix Delegation Size** of `56`. This would provide a maximum of 256 blocks of addresses to be delegated.

While it is possible to use a prefix longer than 64 bits, doing so is discouraged, since features such as **stateless address autoconfiguration** (**SLAAC**) depend on the DHCPv6 server advertising a prefix of 64 bits.

There is another tab on this page for **Router Advertisements** (**RA**). This enables an IPv6-capable router to advertise its presence to other routers, and keep other nodes informed of any changes in the network.

Understanding the RA configuration options requires an understanding of the RA flags. Two flags that are in every RA packet are the `M` flag and the `O` flag. The `M` flag stands for **managed address configuration** and it informs the host receiving the packet that there is a DHCPv6 server available and that the host should get its IPv6 address from this server. If the `M` flag is set to zero, then it means that the host should not look for a DHCPv6 server. The `O` flag stands for **other configuration** and it tells the host that it should get other configuration information (for example, DNS) from the DHCP server.

In addition, many packets have an `L` flag and an `A` flag. The `L` flag tells the host that other devices with the same prefix as the prefix contained in the RA packet are on the same subnet. Therefore, they should communicate at the switch level and not send every packet to the router. The `A` flag tells the host to use the prefix inside the RA packet and the host's own MAC address to generate its own IPv6 address. Thus the host should use SLAAC.

With this in mind, here is how these flag settings correspond to the router mode options:

	`M` **flag**	`O` **flag**	`L` **flag**	`A` **flag**
Router Only	0	0	0	0
Unmanaged	0	0	1	1
Managed	1	1	1	0
Assisted	1	1	1	1
Stateless DHCP	0	1	1	1

In addition to these options, there is also a **Disabled** option to completely disable router advertisements.

Most modern operating systems support both SLAAC and DHCPv6, so you should be able to choose either **Unmanaged** or **Managed** in most cases. If you are not sure which modes are supported on your systems, you can choose **Assisted** mode.

The **Default valid lifetime** field defines the length of time in seconds that the prefix is valid for the purpose of on-link determination. The **Default preferred lifetime** field defines the length of time in seconds that the addresses generated from the prefix via SLAAC remain preferred. The defaults are 86,400 seconds and 14,400 seconds, respectively.

The **RA Subnets** field allows you to specify subnets on which RA will take place. If no subnet is specified, the RA daemon will advertise on the subnet to which the router's interface is assigned. You must specify both the subnet and the CIDR mask. This option allows you to perform RA only on selected subnets.

The **DNS Servers** section allows you to specify different DNS servers than the default ones (the interface IP if **DNS Forwarder or Resolver** is enabled, or the servers configured on the **General** page if neither of these is enabled). In the **Domain search list**, you can specify an optional list, and there is also a **Use same settings as DHCPv6 server** checkbox if you just want the RA daemon to use the same DNS servers specified on the **DHCPv6** tab.

DHCP and DHCPv6 relay

Especially in larger networks, it is possible that you don't want to run the DHCP server on your system, but instead want to pass on DHCP requests to another server. In this case, you can use the pfSense DHCP relay, which can be found by navigating to **Services** | **DHCP Relay**. In order to use **DHCP Relay**, the DHCP server must be disabled on all interfaces. Note, however, that the DHCPv6 server may still be enabled. The converse is also true: in order to use **DHCPv6 Relay**, you must disable the DHCPv6 server on all interfaces, but you do not have to disable the DHCP server.

If you later enable the DHCP server, the DHCP relay will be automatically disabled, and if you enable the DHCPv6 server, the DHCPv6 relay will be disabled.

To enable to DHCP relay, refer to the following steps:

1. To enable the DHCP relay, check the **Enable** checkbox.
2. There is also an **Interface(s)** list box where you can select the interfaces on which the DHCP relay will be enabled. If you want the DHCP relay to append the circuit ID (the pfSense interface number) and the agent ID, you should check the **Append circuit ID and agent ID to requests** checkbox.

3. The **Destination server** edit box allows you to specify the IP address of the DHCP server. You can specify more than one IP address; you can use the **Add** and **Delete** buttons to add/delete entries.

The DHCPv6 relay can be enabled by navigating to **Services** | **DHCPv6 Relay**. The settings for the DHCPv6 relay are identical to the settings for the DHCP relay.

DHCP and DHCPv6 leases

If you want to see what DHCP leases have been issued, navigate to **Status** | **DHCP Leases**. This page offers several pieces of information about active and inactive leases:

- The IP address of the lease.
- The MAC address of the client that has received the lease.
- The hostname of the client.
- A description of the client, if one is available.
- The start and end time of the lease.
- Whether the client is online, and the type of lease: static, active, inactive. Static is for statically mapped DHCP leases; active and inactive is for dynamically allocated leases. Active denotes those clients that are using their leases, while inactive is for inactive clients whose DHCP leases have not yet expired.

To find out what DHCPv6 leases have been issued, navigate to **Status** | **DHCPv6 Leases**. All of the information about DHCP leases that the **DHCP Leases** page contains is contained on the **DHCPv6 Leases** page with respect to DHCPv6 leases. The leases table also has two additional fields. **IAID** is each lease's Identity Association ID. An **Identity Association** (**IA**) is a collection of addresses assigned to a client, and each IA has its own ID – the IAID. **DUID** is the DHCP Unique Identifier, which is a globally unique identifier each DHCPv6 client and server has for identification purposes.

There is a second table on this page called **delegated prefixes**. The purpose of this table is to list all prefixes that have been assigned to clients, so they can act as routers. Once again, the IAID and DUID are present in the table, as well as the start and end time of the delegation, and the state of the delegation. Note that a client must request a delegation from pfSense before it appears in this table.

DNS

It seems only appropriate that we should follow up a lengthy discussion on how to configure pfSense to handle the task of granting hosts IP addresses with a discussion on how to configure pfSense to handle the service that maps hostnames to IP addresses, thus making the internet much more user friendly. You may never have the occasion to set up your own DNS server, but there are compelling reasons to do so. Having your own DNS server can reduce administrative overhead and improve the speed of DNS queries, especially as your network grows. Moreover, the ease with which a DNS server can be set up with pfSense makes it that much more appealing.

It should be noted that pfSense has two separate services for DNS. Prior to version 2.2, DNS services were configurable via **Services** | **DNS Forwarder**, which invokes the dnsmasq daemon. For version 2.2 and later, unbound is the default DNS resolver, and it is configurable by navigating to **Services** | **DNS Resolver**. New installs of version 2.2 or greater, have DNS resolver enabled by default, while upgrades from earlier versions will have DNS forwarder enabled by default. You can still use DNS forwarder on newer versions, but if you do, you will have to disable DNS resolver or change the port settings for it. By default, both DNS forwarder and DNS resolver are configured to bind to port `53`, and both services cannot bind to the same port.

DNS resolver

Since DNS resolver is the default resolver in the current version of pfSense, we will begin by looking at the options available for it.

General Settings

The first tab is labeled **General Settings**, and the first section on the page is **General DNS Resolver Options**. The first option is **Enable**, which enables **Unbound**, and is checked by default. The next option is **Listen Port**, which allows you to set the port used for responding to DNS queries. The default port is port `53` (DNS traditionally uses port `53` and the UDP, although DNS also uses TCP for responses larger than a datagram, including DNSSEC and some IPv6 lookups, so take this into account when creating firewall rules for DNS).

The **Network Interfaces** list box allows you to select which interface IPs are used by **Unbound** to respond to queries from clients. Queries to interfaces not selected are discarded. If **Unbound** is enabled, however, you must select either **All** or **localhost** for this option. The **Outgoing Network Interfaces** list box allows you to choose which network interfaces the DNS resolver may use to send queries to authoritative servers and receive their replies.

When there is no domain match from local data, **System Domain Local Zone Type** determines how the DNS resolver handles the query. There are several options available in this drop-down box:

- **Deny**: The DNS resolver will only answer the query if there is a match in the local data. If there is no such match, then the query will be dropped silently.
- **Refuse**: This option is similar to **Deny**, except that when there is no match from the local data, the rcode `REFUSED` will be returned, so the client knows the query was refused.
- **Static**: The DNS resolver looks for a match in the local data. If there is no match, it returns `nodata` or `nxdomain`, but it will also return the **Start of Authority** (**SOA**) for the root domain, provided that such information exists in the local data.
- **Transparent**: The DNS resolver will answer the query from local data if there is match. If there is no match in local data, the query will be passed on to upstream DNS servers. If there is a match in the local data, but the type of data for which the query is being made does not exist in the local data, then the DNS resolver will return a `noerror/nodata` message.
- **Type Transparent**: This option is similar to **Transparent**, but in cases in which there is a match in the local data but the type of data being asked for does not exist, the DNS resolver will pass the query on to upstream DNS servers.
- **Redirect**: The DNS resolver will attempt to answer the query from local data. If there is no local data other than the zone name, the query will be redirected.
- **Inform**: Identical to **Transparent**, except that the client IP address and port number will also be logged.
- **Inform/Deny**: Identical to **Deny**, except that the query will be logged.
- **No Default**: Default contents for AS112 zones will not be returned by queries.

Enable DNSSEC support

The next option, enabled by default, is **Enable DNSSEC Support. DNSSEC** is a means of protecting DNS data from attacks which use forged or manipulated DNS data, such as DNS cache poisoning. If you enable it and the upstream DNS server to which you will be forwarding DNS requests does not support DNSSEC, however, DNS resolution may not work.

The **Enable Forwarding Mode** checkbox allows you to control whether **Unbound** will query root servers directly (if this option is unchecked) or if queries will be forwarded to the upstream DNS servers. You should only enable this option if the upstream DNS servers are trusted. If you have enabled DNSSEC support, and you consider this to be important, you should also make sure the upstream DNS servers provide DNSSEC support. Forwarding mode is necessary if you are using a multi-WAN configuration which does not have default gateway switching.

The **Register DHCP leases in the DNS Resolver** option allows you to register DHCP static mappings. This in turn enables the resolving of hostnames that have been assigned IP addresses by the DHCP server. The **Register DHCP static mappings in the DNS Resolver** option is similar to the **Register DHCP leases in the DNS Resolver** option, except the former allows you to register DHCP static mappings instead of DHCP leases. The **Display Custom Options** button reveals a textbox when you click on it. You can enter any additional parameters here.

Host Overrides and Domain Overrides

The next two sections are **Host Overrides** and **Domain Overrides**. **Host Overrides** allows you to configure a specific hostname to resolve differently than it otherwise would with the DNS servers being used by the DNS forwarder. This can be used for split DNS configurations; it also provides one possible way of blocking access to certain sites (although the user could always defeat this measure by simply entering the correct IP address of the target domain).

Domain Overrides is similar, except that it allows you to specify a different DNS server to use when resolving a specific domain. This can be useful in certain scenarios; for example, if you have a Windows Active Directory configuration and DNS queries for Active Directory, servers must be directed to Active Directory's DNS server.

The next tab is **Advanced Settings**. We will not cover all the settings that are configurable in this section, but here are some of the more interesting settings:

- **Prefetch DNS Key Support**: Enabling this option causes DNS keys to be fetched earlier in the validation process, thus lowering the latency of requests (but increasing CPU usage).
- **Message Cache Size**: This controls the size of the message cache, which stores DNS response codes and validation statuses. The default size is 4 MB.
- **Experimental Bit 0x20 Support**: The small bit size (16 bits) of a DNS transaction ID makes it a frequent target for forgery, which creates a security risk. One of the ways of improving the security of DNS transactions is to randomize the 0x20 bit in an ASCII letter of a question name. For example, the names `www.mydomain.com` and `WWW.MYDOMAIN.COM` will be treated the same by a requester, but could be treated as unequal by a responder. It can thus serve as a sort of covert encryption channel and make DNS transactions more secure.

Access Lists

The final tab is **Access Lists**, which enables you to allow or deny access to your network's DNS servers for specified blocks of network addresses (known as netblocks). This can be useful if you need to grant access to them for remote users (such as users connecting through a VPN), or to deny access to certain local netblocks. You can add an access list entry by clicking on the green **+Add** down button and to the right of the access list table.

The first option is the **Access List name**, in which you can specify a name for the access list. The next option is the **Action** drop-down box, in which you can specify what to do with DNS queries that originate on the netblock defined by this access list entry. The options are as follows:

- **Deny**: Stops queries from the defined netblock. Queries are dropped silently.
- **Refuse**: Stops queries from the defined netblock. Instead of dropping the query silently, it sends back a DNS rcode `REFUSED`.
- **Allow**: Allows queries from hosts within the defined netblock.
- **Allow Snoop**: Similar to **Allow**, but allows both recursive and non-recursive access from hosts within the defined netblock. This should only be configured for the administrator for such uses as troubleshooting.

The **Description** field allows you to enter a (non-parsed) description. Finally, the **Networks** field is where you enter the netblock (subnet) on which the access list takes effect. You must also select the CIDR of the subnet in the adjacent drop-down box. To the right, you can enter a description of this netblock. You can add the newly defined access list by pressing the green **Add Network** button at the bottom of the page.

DNS forwarder

Although the DNS resolver is the default DNS service in pfSense 2.2 and later, you can use DNS forwarder instead.

1. To do so, navigate to **Services** | **DNS Forwarder** and click on the **Enable DNS forwarder** checkbox (make sure to disable DNS resolver first). Many of the settings for DNS forwarder are identical to the DNS resolver settings. In this section, we will focus on the settings which are unique to DNS forwarder.
2. As with the DNS resolver, you can register DHCP leases and static mappings, but there is also an option called **resolve DHCP mappings first**.
3. Invoking this option causes the DHCP mappings to be resolved before the names provided in the **Host Overrides** and **Domain Overrides** tables.
4. The **DNS Query Forwarding** section has several unique options. The **Query DNS servers sequentially** checkbox, as the name implies, causes the DNS servers specified on the **General Setup** page to be queried sequentially instead of being queried at the same time.
5. The **Require domain** checkbox will drop DNS queries from upstream servers if they do not contain a domain (in other words, queries for plain names). The **Do not forward private reverse lookups** option, if enabled, results in the DNS forwarder not forwarding reverse lookups for RFC 1918 private addresses (`10.0.0.0` addresses, `172.16.0.0` to `172.31.0.0` addresses, and `192.168.0.0` addresses).
6. The **Strict interface binding** checkbox causes the DNS forwarder to only bind to the IP addresses of interfaces selected in the **Interfaces** list box. If this option is not enabled, DNS forwarder will bind to all interfaces. Some of the settings available in the DNS resolver are also available in the DNS forwarder, such as the ability to set the port for resolving DNS queries, and the ability to bind only to selected interfaces.

One significant limitation of the DNS forwarder is that strict interface binding does not work with IPv6 addresses. As with the DNS resolver, the DNS forwarder allows you to add **Host Overrides** and **Domain Overrides**, and there is a field for **Custom Options** as well.

DNS firewall rules

After you have been diligent enough to configure pfSense to act as a DNS server, it would be a shame if end users on your network could circumvent pfSense and specify whatever DNS server they want. Yet that's exactly what most modern OS allow the end user to do. Thus, even if we have set up pfSense to act as the DNS server for the local network, the user's computer will bypass pfSense and go directly to `8.8.4.4`. Other than the fact that the user is subverting the policy we were trying to enforce, this is bad for a number of reasons:

- Every time the user accesses a site that requires a new DNS lookup, his computer will only cache the results on his computer. If the user had used pfSense as his DNS server, the results of the lookup would be cached on the pfSense system, and therefore would be available to everyone else on the local network.
- The user could specify a DNS server whose security has been compromised, and his computer would now be vulnerable to DNS cache poisoning and other attacks.

Fortunately, there are ways of preventing this sort of end user behavior. Although we have not covered firewall rules yet, it might prove useful to demonstrate how such rules can be used to block users from manually specifying a DNS server.

We know that DNS uses port `53` to communicate, so rules blocking or allowing port `53` traffic is what we need. Specifically, we need the following:

- A rule allowing port `53` traffic on the LAN network whose destination is a LAN node
- A rule blocking all other port `53` traffic on the LAN network

We begin by creating the rule allowing port `53` traffic to a LAN node:

1. Using the top menu in the web GUI, navigate to **Firewall** | **Rules** and click on the **LAN** tab.
2. There should already be at least two rules there: default **Allow LAN to any rules** for IPv4 and IPv6 respectively. Since firewall rules are applied from top to bottom with the first rule encountered that applies to the traffic being applied, we want to create a rule above those rules. Otherwise, pfSense will apply one of the **Allow LAN to any rules** first to the DNS traffic, which will defeat the purpose of our rule. Therefore, we click on the green **Add** button with an up arrow next to create a rule at the top of the list.

3. We want this rule to allow traffic, so we leave the **Action** set to **Pass**.
4. We know that DNS traffic uses the UDP protocol, so we set **Protocol** to **UDP**.
5. Scrolling down, we leave the **Source** set to **Any**, but we want to change the **Destination** to **LAN address**. We want to change the **Destination port range** to port `53`, and we can do that either by selecting it in the **From** drop-down box, or by just typing `53` into the first **Custom** edit box. You can enter a brief description in the **Description** edit box (example, `Allow DNS to LAN nodes`) and then click on the **Save** button, which will return us to the main **Firewall** page and the rules table for LAN.

We still need a rule to block all other DNS traffic. Actually, what we will be doing is creating a rule that blocks all DNS traffic on the LAN network and placing it after the rule we just created so that all DNS traffic on the LAN network whose destination is not a LAN address will be blocked. It will be easiest to just modify the rule we just created.

1. So, navigate to the rule we just created in the table, and under the **Actions** column, click on the icon that looks like two sheets of paper to copy the rule. This will create a duplicate of the rule which we can now modify.
2. Change **Action** to either **Block** or **Reject**, and change **Destination** to **Any**. You probably also want to change the **Description** (for example, `Block all DNS`). That is all you need to do, so you can click on **Save**.
3. When you return to the main **Firewall** page, make sure that the rule for allowing DNS traffic to a LAN node comes before the block DNS rule. If the order is incorrect, you can drag and drop the rules until they are in the correct order.
4. When you are done, click on the green **Apply Changes** button at the top right of the page.

You probably want to confirm that the rules we added do what they are supposed to do, so go ahead and use `nslookup` to try to look up a domain name using a different server. The `nslookup` utility is available on Linux, Windows, and mac OS, and by specifying a domain name as the first parameter and a DNS server as the second parameter, you can bypass the default DNS server. For example:

```
nslookup packtpub.com 8.8.4.4
```

Will do a DNS lookup for `packtpub` using one of the Google DNS servers. If the rules we created work, this should fail, while invoking the same command while omitting the second parameter (so `nslookup` will use the default DNS server) should work.

These rules can be fairly effective in preventing the end user from bypassing the pfSense DNS server, but there are at least two major flaws:

- The rules only apply to the LAN network. On a larger network, there will be several network segments. We will want a means of applying these rules to more than one network.
- The end user can still defeat the rules we created by connecting to a VPN.

We will revisit these issues in `Chapter 4`, *Using pfSense as a Firewall.*

DDNS

Although DNS changes propagate through networks relatively quickly, the distributed nature of DNS and the fact that it is not fully automated means that it may take several hours to distribute a DNS change. While this is adequate for a service that only changes its IP address infrequently, it can be a problem if your IP address changes more often. For example, if you are running a server on an ISP that assigns IP addresses via DHCP, your public IP address will likely change more frequently. This is where DDNS, which provides a means of rapidly updating DNS information, comes in handy.

DDNS actually refers to two separate services. The first involves using a client to push the DNS change out to a remote DNS server. The second involves updating traditional DNS records without manually editing them (this mechanism is specified by the IETF's RFC 2136). pfSense provides the ability to configure clients for use with both services, and we will cover both of them.

DDNS updating

DDNS updating without RFC 2136 can be configured by navigating to **Services** | **Dynamic DNS** and clicking on the **Dynamic DNS** tab (the first tab). This tab will show you a table with all the DDNS clients that have been added.

To utilize DDNS, you must first find someone that provides DDNS services. Your ISP may provide DDNS services; if not, there are several organizations that provide DDNS services for a variety of costs (some provide them for free). Cost, ease of use, and the existence of additional security features (such as invisible domains) are all factors you might consider when choosing a service.

Once you have chosen a DDNS service, you can begin the configuration process from your DDNS service's website. First, you will need to create at least one (sub) domain. Here we can see one such domain configuration page; this one is from the DuckDNS website. Once you have created a domain, you need to find out the username and password (if any) that are required for the service, as well as the update URL. You should be able to find this information on the service's website.

Once you have this information, you can go back to the **Dynamic DNS** page in the pfSense web GUI, make sure you have selected the **Dynamic DNS** tab, and click on the green **+Add** button to add a DNS client. This will launch the client configuration page.

The first option on the page is the **Disable this client** checkbox. This allows you to enter the client information without activating DDNS. The **Service Type** drop-down box allows you to select your service from a number of options; many DDNS service providers are listed here (in some cases, there are multiple listings for the same provider). Select your provider here; if there is more than one listing for your provider, check your provider's website for guidance on which option to choose. If your provider is not listed, you can select **Custom**.

Note that if you select **Custom**, several options will appear below the **Service Type** drop-down box that would not appear otherwise. The **Enable verbose logging** checkbox, if checked, provides more detailed logging information. Normally, if both IPv4 and IPv6 addresses are enabled, IPv6 addresses will be preferred, but if you want IPv4 resolution instead, you can check the **Force IPv4 resolving** checkbox. Finally, **Verify SSL peer** will cause **libcurl** to verify peer certificates, thus providing the greatest possible level of security on SSL/TLS connections between pfSense and the DDNS provider.

If you do not select **Custom**, then the next option will be the **Interface to monitor** drop-down box. In virtually all cases, this should be set to **WAN**. In the **Hostname** edit box, you need to enter the fully qualified hostname of the hostname you added on your service provider's website. The **MX** edit box allows you to add an IP address of a mail server. Not all services allow you to set up a separate mail server, but if yours does, this is where you would specify it. The **Enable Wildcard** checkbox, if checked, causes anything typed before your domain name to resolve to your domain name: for example, if your domain name is `mydomain.duckdns.org`, `www. mydomain.duckdns.org` will resolve to `mydomain.duckdns.org`. The **Enable verbose logging** option provides for a more verbose level of logging, which can be helpful in troubleshooting.

Finally, the **Username** and **Password** fields are where you enter the username and password combination you got from your DDNS provider's website. You may be able to leave these fields empty; in other cases, you may have to enter an API user/ key combination or some other key or token. Finally, in the **Description** field you can enter a brief description. Press the **Save** button at the bottom of the page to save the client information. This should return you to the page with the DDNS client table, and the entry you just made should be in the table.

Once you have entered the DNS client information, you still need a means of sending out DNS changes to your DDNS provider. This often comes in the form of updater software that must be run on one of your computers. Once the software is installed, the parameters that you must enter may include such things as:

- The domain which you want to update
- A token or some other kind of identifier
- The refresh interval (5 minutes, 10 minutes, and so on)

The software may also provide a means of forcing an update, so that when your WAN address changes, you don't have to wait for the automatic update. Your DDNS provider will have more detailed information on how to install and configure your updater software.

RFC 2136 updating

The other form of DDNS supported by pfSense is RFC 2136 updating. This form of DDNS is more like traditional DNS, and is the standardized method of dynamically updating DNS records. It offers the following advantages over the DDNS method described in the previous section:

- **More secure**: RFC 2136 uses **Transaction Signature** (**TSIG**), which uses shared secret keys and one-way hashing in order to provide a cryptographically secure means of authenticating DNS updates.
- **Good for enterprises**: RFC 2136 is supported by many enterprise-level applications, including such directory services as LDAP and Windows' Active Directory. It is also supported by BIND servers and Windows Server DNS servers.
- **Standardized**: Whereas the DDNS services described in the last section often must be configured in different ways depending on which provider you use, all systems that utilize RFC 2136 are following the same standard; thus, configuration is somewhat easier.

There are also some disadvantages to using RFC 2136. Wildcarding is not supported by this standard. Also, there does not seem to be a means of forcing updates, so it may take somewhat longer for updates to take effect.

1. You can get started with RFC 2136 configuration by navigating to **Services** | **Dynamic DNS** and clicking on the **RFC 2136** tab. You will see an RFC 2136 client table which is similar to the table on the **Dynamic DNS** tab.
2. Click on the green **+Add** button down and to the right of the table to add a client.
3. While the DDNS client configuration page had a **Disable** checkbox, the RFC client configuration page starts off with an **Enable** checkbox that you must check for this client to be enabled.
4. The next option is the **Interface** drop-down box. The selected interface should almost always be **WAN**.
5. Next is **Hostname**, in which you must enter the fully qualified domain name of the host to be updated.
6. After that there is **TTL**, which controls how long the DNS record to be updated should be cached by caching name servers. You will likely want to make this a relatively small number (smaller than the traditional 86,400 seconds), as this parameter controls how long a DNS server could be showing the old value after an update.
7. The next value is **Key Name**, which is whatever name you gave the key when you created it on your DNS server. Usually it is identical to the fully qualified domain name. The **Key Type** value must match the type of the key specified in **Key Name**; usually you can specify **Host** as the option.

Version 2.4.3 has removed the **Key Type** option and has added a **Key algorithm** drop-down box in which you can select the key encryption algorithm (**HMAC-SHA512** is the most secure of the options). The **Key** field should be the secret key generated when you created the specified key.

8. In the **Server** field, you must specify the IP address of the DNS server the client will be updating.
9. The next option is the **Use TCP instead of UDP** checkbox. DNS uses TCP for zone transfers and for queries larger than 512 bytes and UDP for name queries, so in most cases, you should leave this unchecked. If you are updating a zone record, however, you will want to check this box. You should probably check this box, especially if you are using DNSSEC and/or IPv6.
10. The **Use public IP** checkbox will attempt to use the public IP address to fetch if the DNS server's IP address is private.

11. The **Record Type** option allows you to specify whether the client should update A records (for IPv4), AAAA records (for IPv6), or both.
12. Finally, in **Description** you can enter a brief (non-parsed) description of this entry. Click on the **Save** button to save the entry, and you should be returned to the client table with the new entry in the table.

Troubleshooting DDNS

If you tried to implement dynamic DNS but it is not working, there are several potential causes. If you are using DDNS via a DDNS provider, you should confirm that you set up the domain correctly and also confirm that your provider's service works with pfSense. Once you have done that, you should go through the client configuration step by step. Many DDNS providers have instructions for different routers, including pfSense routers, and if such instructions are available, you should follow them. Also, make sure you have installed and configured your provider's updater software correctly. If you have gone through all of these steps and DDNS is still not working, you may want to contact your provider's technical support, if such support is available.

Captive portal

Businesses providing internet access for customers (usually via a wireless connection) is something that has become ubiquitous. Consequently, network administrators need a form of access control that covers such scenarios. You may want to redirect users to a login page to control access. Even if you don't want to require authentication, you may still want to redirect users to a page containing your terms of service. In such cases, you can utilize pfSense's captive portal service. Captive portal can be used to redirect wireless users to a login page, and it can also be used for wired users. Earlier versions of pfSense were limited to use of one interface on your firewall, but the current version allows you to enable captive portal on multiple interfaces.

Implementing captive portal

To get started implementing a captive portal on your network, perform the following steps:

1. Navigate to **Services** | **Captive Portal**. This page displays a table with all of the defined captive portal zones. There is a green **+Add** button down and to the right of the table; pressing this button allows you to add a zone.

2. When you add a zone, you are initially directed to the **Add Zone** page. Here you are required to enter **Zone Name**, which can only contain letters, digits, and underscores. You can also enter a brief (non-parsed) description in the **Description** field. Enter this information and press the **Continue** button.
3. Now we will be directed to the **Configuration** page, where we are presented with a warning which contains the following information:
    - Make sure you enable the DHCP server on the captive portal interface
    - Make sure the maximum DHCP lease time is longer than the captive portal hard timeout
    - Make sure the DNS forwarder or DNS resolver is enabled, or DNS lookups will not work for unauthenticated clients
4. To begin configuration, check the **Enable Captive Portal** checkbox. Once this box is checked, the other options will appear on the page.
5. We will begin by considering the options that must be changed in order for captive portal to work. You must select at least one interface on which the captive portal will be enabled, and you can do this in the **Interfaces** list box. The first option is the **Interfaces** drop-down box, in which you select the interface on which captive portal will be enabled. In most scenarios where you are setting up a captive portal, you probably want to have a separate interface or interfaces for captive portal users.
6. Next, scroll down to the **Authentication** section. Here you must select an authentication method: **No Authentication**, **Local User Manager/Vouchers**, or **RADIUS Authentication**:
    - If **No Authentication** is selected, the captive portal user will not be prompted for a username and password or a voucher code—usually at most they will be required to accept the network's terms of service.
    - **Local User Manager/Vouchers** covers the cases in which pfSense will handle authentication. Either the user will be prompted for a username/password combination for a user who was previously entered into the pfSense user manager, or the user will be prompted for a voucher code that was generated by pfSense.
    - In the case of **RADIUS Authentication**, the authentication will be done by an external RADIUS server. This will be covered in detail in a subsection, but we will note that if you choose this option, at a minimum you will have to enter the RADIUS protocol and the IP address of the primary RADIUS server.

The next section is **HTML Page Contents**. At a minimum, you will probably find it necessary to replace the portal page, contents page, and to upload a portal page that is appropriate for the type of authentication you selected. If you are not requiring authentication, all you need is a form with a **Submit** button and a hidden field with the name `redirurl` and the value `$PORTAL_REDIRURL$`. If you require authentication, then you need to have either `auth_user` and `auth_pass` or `auth_voucher` (or both if you support both username/password login and vouchers).

The pages you uploaded may contain images, and as you probably guessed, you're going to need a means of uploading these images. This is what the **File Manager** tab is for. Any files you upload via this tab with the filename prefix of **captiveportal-** will be made available in the root directory of the captive portal server. This is useful if you have files which you want to reference in your portal page (for example, a company logo). In addition, you can upload PHP files for execution. The total size limit for all files uploaded via this tab is 1 MB.

1. To add a file, click on the **+Add** button, which is below the **Installed Files** table and to the right. This loads a separate page where you can upload the file.
2. Click on the **Browse** button to launch a file dialog box.
3. Select a file, click on the **Open** button in the file dialog box, and then click on the **Upload** button.

User manager authentication

If you chose **No Authentication**, then you have configured as much as is necessary to get captive portal up and running. If you chose one of the other options, however, you need to configure some form of authentication:

1. If you want to utilize the user manager, navigate to **Services** | **User Manager**. You will then need to add as many users as you need to for captive portal access.
2. It might also be a good idea to set up a separate group for captive portal users, and you can do that by clicking on the **Groups** tab.
3. Once there, you can click on the **+Add** button on the right side of the page below the table to add a group.

4. There is a single section on this page titled **Group Properties**, and in this section, you need to enter a **Group Name**. You can also enter a description in the **Description** field. In the **Group membership** list boxes, you can add other groups to which you want members of the new group to belong. Once you are done, press the **Save** button.
5. We still haven't assigned captive portal privileges to the newly created group, so once you are redirected to the table, find the group in the table and, under the **Actions** column, click on the **Edit group** icon (the pencil).
6. Once again, the **Group Properties** section is there, but underneath it is a section called **Assigned Privileges** where, as you probably guessed, you can assign privileges to the group.
7. Clicking on the **Add** button will enable you to add privileges. This will load a page with a list box with many options; for this group we want to select **User – Services: Captive Portal login**. Select this and click on the **Save** button at the bottom of the page. This will take you back to the previous page, so you need to click on the **Save** button on that page, which will return you to the main **Groups** page. We have created a group with captive portal login privileges.
8. Now you need to go back to the **Users** tab and add users to the group that you created in the previous step by pressing the **+Add** button, adding information for each user, pressing the **Save** button, and repeating the process for as many users as you need to add. At a minimum, you need to enter a username and password for each user, and make the user a member of the new group. There are also options to create a user certificate, add an SSH key (so the user can connect to pfSense via SSH without entering a username/password combination), and a field for an IPsec pre-shared key.
9. Now that we have created some captive portal user accounts, we can return to the **Captive Portal** configuration. Note that below the radio buttons where we select the authentication mention, if **Local User Manager/Vouchers** is selected, there is an **Allow only users with "Captive Portal login" privilege set** checkbox. Although this checkbox is selected by default, when we click on the **Local User Manager/Vouchers** radio button, we can uncheck it, thus eliminating the need to create a group with this privilege added to it.

Voucher authentication

You can also use vouchers for authentication. This is done by clicking on the **Vouchers** tab under **Captive Portal**. This page has two sections: **Voucher Rolls**, which shows any existing vouchers, and **Create, Generate and Activate Rolls with Vouchers**.

The **Enable** checkbox, when checked, begins the process of creating vouchers. The next two fields are for the **Voucher Public Key** and the **Voucher Private Key**. Here, you should paste an RSA public key and RSA private key (64 bits or smaller). The next field is **Character set**; this defines the characters contained in the generated tickets. You can probably keep the default value. The **# of Roll Bits** field reserves a range in each voucher to store the roll number to which it belongs. The **# of Ticket Bits** field reserves a range in each voucher to store the ticket number to which it belongs. Finally, the **# of Checksum Bits** field reserves a range in each voucher to store a checksum over the roll number and ticket number. The sum of roll, ticket, and checksum bits must be one less bit than the RSA public/private key.

The **Magic number** field defines a magic number to be stored in each voucher, that is only stored if there are bits left over in the roll, ticket, and checksum bits. The **Invalid voucher message** and **Expired voucher message** fields define messages to display when the voucher is invalid and expired, respectively.

The **Voucher Database Synchronization** section of the page allows you to enter the master voucher database ID, sync port, and username/password combination. If this node is the master voucher database node, or if it will be the only node using vouchers, you can leave these fields blank. Press the **Save** button at the bottom of the page when you are done.

When the **Voucher** page reloads, there will be a new section at the top of the page called **Voucher Rolls**. You can generate new voucher rolls by pressing the **+Add** button below the table on the right side. There are fields for the **Roll #** (the number found on top of the generated vouchers), the **Minutes per ticket** (the time in minutes a user is allowed access), and **Count** (the number of vouchers generated). There is also a **Comment** field where you can enter a non-parsed comment. When you have filled out these fields, press the **Save** button.

When you return to the main **Voucher** page, the newly created voucher roll will be listed in the table at the top. Under the **Action** column, you can click on the export vouchers icon (the sheet) to download the voucher roll as a `.csv` file. The file contains a series of vouchers that can be used for captive portal authentication. In order to accept captive portal login via vouchers, your portal login page must include the following field: `<input name="auth_voucher" type="text">`.

RADIUS authentication

The third authentication option is **RADIUS Authentication**. **Remote Authentication Dial-In User Service** (**RADIUS**) provides a means of centralized authentication, authorization, and accounting for network users. To use RADIUS to authenticate captive portal users, you must have a RADIUS server. It is beyond the scope of this book to explain how to configure a RADIUS server, but we will cover some of the more important RADIUS options on the **Captive Portal Configuration** page.

pfSense supports several protocols for sending and receiving data from the RADIUS server. **Password Authentication Protocol** (**PAP**), **Challenge Handshake Authentication Protocol** (**CHAP**), MS-CHAPv1, and MS-CHAPv2 are all supported. You can supply a primary authentication source and secondary authentication source, each of these having a primary RADIUS server and secondary RADIUS server. You can supply an IP address, port, and shared secret for each. Entering an IP address for each RADIUS server used is required. If the **RADIUS port** field is left blank, pfSense will use the default RADIUS port. Entering RADIUS shared secret is not required, but is recommended.

One of the authentication options under **RADIUS Options** is the **Reauthenticate connected users every minute** checkbox. If this option is enabled, pfSense will send access-requests to RADIUS for each user every minute. If an access-reject is received for any user on one of these requests, the user is disconnected from the captive portal immediately. There is also an option called **RADIUS MAC Authentication**. Checking this box will cause RADIUS to try to authenticate captive portal users by sending their MAC address as the username and the **MAC authentication secret**, specified in the next edit box, as the password.

Other settings

The preceding guide should be enough to get captive portal running on your network. There are, however, many other settings on the captive portal configuration. Most of them can be kept at their default settings most of the time, but in certain circumstances they can be altered to ensure the captive portal works smoothly.

On the main captive portal configuration page under the **Interfaces** list box is the **Maximum concurrent connections** edit box. This setting controls not how many users can be logged into the captive portal, but rather how many concurrent connections are allowed per IP address.

The next two settings are **Idle Timeout (Minutes)** which controls how long it is before an idle client is disconnected, while **Hard Timeout (Minutes)** controls how long it is before a client is disconnected even if they are active. Both settings are optional and leaving them blank disables them. Applying a timeout for idle clients is a good way to prevent exhaustion of the DHCP pool.

The next setting is the **Pass-through credits per MAC address** edit box. Entering a number here allows a client to pass through the captive portal this number of times without being directed to the captive portal page. Once this number is exceeded, the user is directed to the captive portal login page again. As the name implies, this is done on a per-MAC address basis.

The **Reset waiting period** checkbox, if checked, will result in the waiting period on login attempts being imposed on clients whose pass-through credits have been exhausted. If not checked, such users will be allowed to log in again immediately. The **Logout popup window** checkbox, if checked, will display a pop-up logout page when the users initially pass through the captive portal. This can be used to allow users to explicitly log out, but it also can be used if you want to display a page informing the user that they have successfully passed through the captive portal.

HTTPS Options initially has a single option: the **Enable HTTPS login** checkbox, which when checked, will cause the captive portal username and password, over an HTTPS connection, to take advantage of the SSL encryption such a connection provides. If this box is checked you must provide the HTTPS server name and the SSL certificate. The server name should match the **Common Name** (**CN**) in your certificate.

By default, when HTTPS login is enabled, clients can connect to the captive portal via HTTPS. You can prevent this by checking the **Disable HTTPS Forwards** checkbox, in which case attempts to connect to port `443` sites will not be forwarded to the captive portal. Users will then have to attempt a connection to port `80` to get forwarded to the captive portal.

There are several other options on other tabs worth mentioning. The **MACs** tab allows you to control access to the captive portal based on MAC addresses. Clicking the **+Add** button on this page allows you to add a MAC address. Once you do this, you will be at the **Edit MAC Address Rules** page. Here you can specify a **MAC address** (the button to the right of this option allows you to copy your MAC). The **Action** drop-down box allows you to choose what to do with traffic from this MAC address (the options are **Pass** and **Block**). You can also specify **Bandwidth up** and **Bandwidth down** limitations for the MAC address (in kbit/s), as well as a non-parsed description in the **Description** field.

The **Allowed IP Addresses** tab allows you to control captive portal access by IP address. Clicking on the **+Add** button on this page takes you to the **Edit Captive Portal IP Rule** page. At a minimum, you must enter the IP address and the CIDR of the address. You can also specify the direction of the access. **From** allows access from the client IP through the captive portal. **To** allows access from all the clients behind the portal to the IP. The **Both** option allows traffic in both directions. As with MAC addresses, you can specify **Bandwidth up** and **Bandwidth down** for the specified IP address.

The **Allowed Hostnames** tab allows you to control captive portal access based on hostname. Again, the **+Add** button on this tab allows you to add entries. You need to enter a hostname in the **Hostname** field, and, as with **Allowed IP Addresses**, you can control the direction of the access, as well as **Bandwidth up** and **Bandwidth down**. You may also enter a non-parsed description in the **Description** field.

Troubleshooting captive portal

pfSense's captive portal service has many options, which means that there are many more things that can go wrong with captive portal access. We can divide these issues into two general categories:

- Authentication issues (client cannot authenticate, even with seemingly valid credentials)
- Client can establish a captive portal connection, but some other aspect of the service is not working (for example, DNS is not functioning, websites are blocked, and so on)

We will first consider authentication issues. The authentication options are **Local User Manager/Vouchers** and **RADIUS Authentication**. If you are using the local user manager, you should confirm that you have created the user accounts correctly and, if **Allow only users/groups with "Captive portal login" privilege set** is checked, you should confirm that the users have this privilege. You can, of course, disable this option and see if the users can connect to troubleshoot the issue. If you are using vouchers to authenticate, you should confirm that your captive portal login page has `<input name="auth_voucher" type="text">` for entering the voucher.

One possible issue that might arise is that you are trying to use MAC addresses for authentication, but the captive portal service cannot confirm that the MAC address is correct. This could happen if there is a router between the captive portal client and pfSense, and this issue could occur both in cases where a RADIUS server is being used for authentication, and without a RADIUS server. For troubleshooting, you might try allowing users access by IP address and see if this works. If it does, there's a good chance pfSense is unable to confirm the MAC address.

One other possibility is that the user is trying to access the captive portal page through HTTPS, but your captive portal zone is only configured for HTTP access. In this case, the solution is for the user to try again with HTTP at the beginning of the URL.

One problem that has been reported is that sometimes, when using captive portal on a VLAN, the captive portal page will not load. This apparently happens when the parent interface of the VLAN is also being used as a separate interface on pfSense. To prevent this problem, when a parent interface is partitioned into VLANs (VLAN1, VLAN2, and so on), the parent interface (for example, OPT1) should not be used separately; only the VLANs should be used.

If a RADIUS server is being used for authentication, then the problem could be either a client or server issue. The RADIUS server may be misconfigured, or it may be down entirely. If you have confirmed that the RADIUS server is functioning properly, the problem may be an incorrect configuration of pfSense. The log files can be helpful in further pinpointing the exact problem. Navigate to **Status** | **System Logs** and click on the **Captive Portal Auth** tab. If pfSense cannot connect to the RADIUS server at all, you should check the IP address/port settings for the RADIUS servers, as well as the shared secret.

The second category of issues is when the user is able to pass through the captive portal, but there are other issues. For example, the user may be having DNS issues. Once again, a good indication that a problem is related to DNS is when you can ping the IP address of a site, but you cannot ping the hostname. DNS is likely not functioning if pinging a valid hostname (for example, `https://www.google.com`) returns the following result:

```
ping: unknown host google.com
```

If it looks like DNS resolution is the problem, you should check to make sure either DNS forwarder or DNS resolver is running, but not both. If you have confirmed that one of these is running and you are still having problems, the issue may be a DNS server that is down or is not configured properly.

If the user cannot access certain websites, the problem may be that the firewall or proxy server has blocked access to the site. You should navigate to **Firewall** | **Rules** and check to see if there are any rules for the captive portal interface that might block access. Proxy servers usually have the capability of blocking websites, so if you are running one, you will want to check the settings for the proxy server. We will cover both firewall rules and proxy servers in greater depth in future chapters.

NTP

NTP is an application layer protocol that controls the synchronization of various devices over the internet to within a few milliseconds of **Coordinated Universal Time** (CUT). NTP is hierarchical, with servers organized into different strata. At stratum 0 are high-precision time devices such as atomic clocks. At stratum 1 are computers that are synchronized within a few microseconds to their directly connected stratum 0 devices. At stratum 2 are computers that are directly connected to stratum 1 computers, and so on. Synchronization is achieved by adjusting the system time based on an offset. The offset is calculated by taking an average of the differences of the timestamps on request and response packets between the client and the server. The clock frequency is then adjusted to reduce the offset gradually, and the newly adjusted clock provides timestamps for the next request and response packets, creating a feedback loop known as clock discipline.

NTP is often overlooked, mainly because it does its job and in pfSense, it requires minimal configuration. You may recall that in the **Setup Wizard**, you were asked to specify a time server, but a default time server was provided. Many users will give no further thought to NTP configuration. You may, however, have reason to deviate from the default settings:

- Your pfSense system may be involved in validating certificates as part of a PKI infrastructure, in which case time synchronization is essential
- You may be running pfSense on an embedded system which does not have a battery to preserve the time and date settings
- Even if you don't fall into either of these categories, maintaining the proper time is still important, since it determines the timestamp on logs

pfSense's NTP service provides for synchronization via a conventional NTP server, as well as from **Global Positioning System** (**GPS**) devices and **Pulse Per Second** (**PPS**) devices. We will cover all of these methods in this section. The following are the steps:

1. Navigate to **Services** | **NTP**, as shown in the following screenshot:

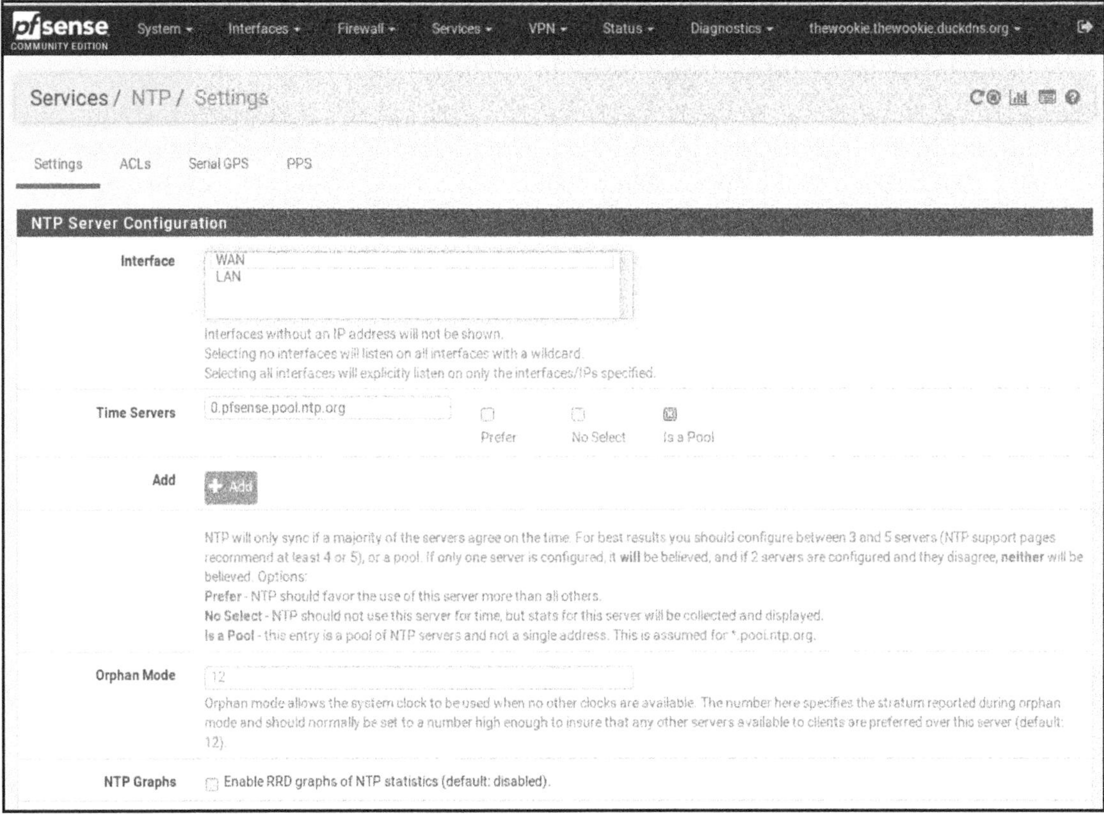

The NTP settings page.

2. The **NTP** page has three tabs and the first (and default) tab is **Settings**. The first option on this page is the **Interfaces** list box, in which you can select the interfaces on which the NTP service will listen. The default setting is to listen on all interfaces, but since the NTP server is probably upstream, you can select **WAN** as the only interface on which to listen (or multiple WAN interfaces if you have them).
3. The next option is **Time Servers**.

4. The time server you specified when you initially configured the system will be listed here, but you can also specify additional servers by clicking on the **Add** button.
5. You need to specify the hostname. You can optionally check either the **Prefer** or **No Select** option.
6. **Prefer** indicates that the NTP services should favor this server over all others.
7. **No Select** indicates that NTP should not use this server for time, but it will collect and display stats from the server.
8. You can check more than one **Prefer** checkbox, but when you save the settings, only the first **Prefer** checkbox on the list that you checked will remain checked.
9. The **Orphan Mode** option allows pfSense to use the system clock when no other clocks are available.
10. The number entered in this edit box specifies the stratum reported during orphan mode. You might recall that stratum indicates how close the computer is to a high-precision time device; higher numbers indicate that the device is further away from such a device and thus have a lower priority. Whatever number you set here should be high enough to ensure that all other servers are preferred over this server. The default is `12`.
11. The **NTP Graphs** checkbox, if enabled, generates **round-robin database** (**RRD**) graphs of NTP data.
12. You can view these graphs by navigating to **Status** | **RRD Graphs** and clicking on the **NTP** tab.
13. The next two subsections involve logging options. **Log peer messages**, if enabled, logs messages between the NTP client and server, while **Log system messages** logs other messages generated by the NTP service.
14. Log reference clock statistics logs statistics generated by reference clocks, which are generally radio time code receivers synchronized to standard time (for example, a GPS or PPS device).
15. Log clock discipline statistics logs statistics related to the clock synchronization process, while log NTP peer statistics logs statistics related to NTP client/server communication.
16. The next subsection is **Access Restrictions**, and it contains a number of important options. The first option is **Enable Kiss-o'death packets**. When checked, this enables the client to receive kiss-of-death packets, which are packets sent by the NTP server to tell the client to stop sending packets that violate server access controls. This in turn will cause the client to stop sending data to the server.

17. The next option is **Deny state modifications by ntpq and ntpdc**. The **ntpdc** daemon queries the **ntpd** daemon about its current state and then requests changes to that state. If this option is checked (the default), then ntpdc's change requests will be denied.
18. The next two options are inverses of each other: **Disable ntpq and ntpdc queries** and **Disable all except ntpq and ntpdc queries**. **Deny packets that attempt a peer association**, if checked, will block any peer associations that are not explicitly configured.
19. Finally, **Deny mode 6 control message/trap service**, if enabled, will decline to provide mode 6 control message trap service to hosts. This service is a subsystem of mode 6, which is intended for use for remote event logging.
20. The final option on this page is **Leap seconds** which have been implemented to keep UTC close to mean solar time, and are added to UTC on an average of one per 18 months. This option allows the NTP service to advertise an upcoming leap second addition or subtraction.
21. You must add a leap second configuration routine in order to do this; it can be pasted into an available edit box or uploaded in a file. Configuring this option is only important if your NTP server is a strata 1 server, in which case it likely has other NTP servers making queries to it.
22. When you have finished configuring these options, you can press the **Save** button at the bottom of the page.

If configuring all these options doesn't provide enough accuracy for you, you can always connect either a GPS or a PPS device to the serial port and use it as a reference clock. Also, if the GPS device supports PPS, it may be used as a PPS clock reference. Using a USB GPS is not recommended owing to USB bus timing issues; however, a USB GPS device may work. You can configure a GPS device by following points:

1. Clicking on the **GPS** tab. The first option is the **GPS Type** drop-down box, which lets you select a predefined configuration.
2. If your GPS type is listed in the box, you should select that type. If it is not listed, you should select **Generic**. Selecting **Default** is not recommended.
3. The next option is the **NMEA Sentences** list box. NMEA defines an electrical and data specification for communication between marine electronics; GPS is but one of the types of devices that utilize it. There are different NMEA sentence types, and they are listed in this list box.
4. If you know what sentence type your device uses, you can select it here; otherwise, you can leave it set to **All**.

5. The **Fudge Time 1** edit box allows you to specify a GPS PPS signal offset, while **Fudge Time 2** allows you to specify the GPS time offset.
6. The **Stratum** edit box allows you to set the GPS clock stratum. Normally you would probably want to set it to **0** (and that is the default value), but you can change it here if you want ntpd to prefer a different clock.
7. There are several flags you can set. Prefer this clock, as the name implies, causes the GPS clock to be preferred over all other clocks.
8. If you went through the trouble of setting up a GPS clock, you probably want to use it, but if you don't, you can check the **Do not use this clock, display for reference only** checkbox.
9. The **Enable PPS signal processing** checkbox, if enabled, treats the GPS as a PPS device.
10. By default, PPS processing occurs on the rising edge of the pulse, but checking **Enable falling edge PPS signal processing** will cause processing to occur on the falling edge.
11. The **Enable kernel PPS clock discipline** checkbox, if checked, will result in NTP using the **ppsu** driver, which reduces incidental jitter sometimes associated with PPS clocks. Normally, the GPS will send location data to ntpd, but if you check the **Obscure location in timestamp** checkbox, it won't.
12. Finally, if you need to fine-tune the GPS time offset (**Fudge Time 2**), you may want to check the **Log the sub-second fraction of the received timestamp** checkbox.
13. In the **Clock ID** edit box, you can enter a GPS clock ID.
14. If the **Advanced** button in the **GPS Initialization** subsection is clicked, you will see the GPS initialization commands, and you will also be able to edit them.
15. Finally, **NMEA Checksum** allows you to calculate an NMEA checksum by entering an NMEA command string and pressing the **Calculate** button. The result will appear in the box to the right of the **Calculate** button.
16. When you are done making changes, press the **Save** button at the bottom of the page.
17. If you have a serial PPS device such as a radio that receives WWV (time) signals, you can configure it as follows:
    1. Click on the **PPS** tab.
    2. The first option on this page is the **Fudge Time** edit box, which is used to specify the PPS signal offset.
    3. In the **Stratum** edit box, you can enter the PPS clock stratum. As with GPS devices, you probably want to leave it at **0** (the default), but you can change it here.

4. The first two flags, **Enable falling edge PPS signal processing** and **Enable kernel PPS clock discipline**, are identical to the flags available on the **GPS** tab. The only unique flag on this tab is the **Record a timestamp once for each second** option, which is useful in constructing frequency deviation plots.
5. The last option is the **Clock ID** edit box, which is identical to the **same** option on the **GPS** tab and simply allows you to change the PPS clock ID. When you are done making changes, click on the **Save** button at the bottom of the page.

SNMP

SNMP is another application layer protocol supported by pfSense. SNMP collects and organizes information about managed devices, and is often used for monitoring network devices. SNMP-managed networks consist of managed devices, software running on the managed devices (known as agents), and software running on the manager, known as a **network management station** (**NMS**). The management data is organized hierarchically in structures known as **management information bases** (**MIBs**).

Enabling SNMP in pfSense will allow it to act as a network management station, and this in turn will enable you to monitor network traffic and flows, pfSense queues, as well as system information (for example, CPU, memory, and disk usage). It is also capable of running traps on managed devices that are triggered by certain events. SNMP is implemented under pfSense with the bsnmpd service. It contains the most basic MIBs available, but it can be extended by loadable modules.

Version 2.4.3 has changed SNMP notification handling so that notifications are batched in order to avoid sending multiple emails in a short period of time.

1. To activate the SNMP daemon, navigate to **Services** | **SNMP** and check the **Enable** checkbox under the **SNMP Daemon** section. You can run SNMP without changing any of the defaults, but you should review the options before continuing.
2. The second section is **SNMP Daemon Settings**, and the first option under it is the **Polling Port** edit box. The default port is `161` (the standard port for SNMP), but you can change it if necessary.

3. You can enter an optional **System Location** and **System Contact** in the next two edit boxes.
4. In the **Read Community String** edit box, you can enter a passphrase that will be required by all hosts querying the SNMP daemon. You should enter a strong passphrase here.
5. The next section is **SNMP Traps Enable**, under which there is an **Enable** checkbox for enabling traps. Checking this box reveals the **SNMP Trap Settings** section with several trap options.
6. In the **Trap server** edit box, you should enter the hostname or IP address of the trap server. In the **Trap Server Port**, you can enter the port where the traps will be received. The default is `162`, but if your SNMP trap receiver is on a different port, you can change it here. The **SNMP Trap String** field is a string that will be sent along with any generated trap.

Under the **SNMP Modules** section, you can choose which modules to run. The choices are as follows:

- **MIBII**: This provides information provided in the management information base tree (defined by RFC 1213), which covers networking information and networking interfaces. This module will allow you to query network interface information.
- **Netgraph**: This module provides some netgraph-related information. Netgraph is a graph-based kernel networking subsystem that is a part of FreeBSD.
- **PF**: This provides information about pfSense, including the rules, states, interface information, tables, and so on.
- **Host Resources**: A module that provides additional information from the MIB tree (for example, system uptime, the amount of physical memory, and so on).
- **UCD**: A module which implements parts of the UCD-SNMP-MIB toolkit. It allows you to get memory, load average, and CPU usage, among other things.
- **Regex**: A module which produces counters from logs or other text files.

The last section of the page, **Interface Binding**, has only one option: the **Interface Binding** drop-down box, which determines which interfaces on which the SNMP daemon is listening. The default is **All**, but you can select a single interface on which to listen (or **localhost**). Selecting multiple interfaces without using the **All** option is not supported. When you have finished making changes, click on the **Save** button at the bottom of the page.

Summary

In this chapter, we covered several useful services that are available with pfSense. SSH login, DHCP, DDNS, and DNS are four services that you will probably want to implement at some point, even if you are using pfSense in a home or SOHO environment. The remaining services—captive portal, NTP, and SNMP—are services you might not be likely to implement unless you are using pfSense in a corporate environment. Nonetheless, it's a good idea to have a working knowledge of these services.

In the upcoming chapters, you will learn how to further unleash the power of pfSense, with an eye towards making our networks more robust and scalable. One of the ways we can make our networks more scalable is by implementing VLANs, and we will examine that in the next chapter.

Questions

Answer the following questions:

1. (a) What transport layer protocol does DHCP use? (b) What ports does DHCP use? (c) What transport layer protocol does BOOTP use? (d) What ports does BOOTP use?
2. What are the Router Advertisement (RA) flag settings that correspond to enabling Stateless DHCP (also known as SLAAC)?
3. What are the two services pfSense has for DNS?
4. (a) What transport layer protocol does DNS use? (b) What port does DNS use?
5. What advantage does DDNS have over traditional DNS services?
6. What are the three types of authentication that pfSense's captive portal service supports?
7. What field must exist in the captive portal login page if voucher authentication is supported?
8. Name a device that can be connected to the serial port to attain greater time accuracy than NTP normally would provide.
9. What are management information bases (MIBs)?
10. What is the default port for SNMP?

3 VLANs

The networks we have contemplated so far have been relatively simple networks with two interfaces (WAN and LAN). As our networks get larger, we have two primary concerns. The first is the increase in broadcast traffic (packets received by every node on the network). The second is the need to segregate network traffic based on management and/or security concerns.

One way of solving these issues is to divide our networks into different segments. For example, in a corporate network we may have different subnets for the engineering department, the sales department, and so on. The problem with this approach is that it does not scale well in the traditional networking paradigm. Each subnet requires a separate physical interface, and there is a limit to how many physical interfaces we can place in a single router.

A better solution is to decouple the physical organization of our network from the logical organization of it. Virtual LANs accomplish this objective. By attaching a special header to an Ethernet frame (known as an **802.1Q tag**, named after the IEEE standard that defines VLANs), we can accomplish two feats we could not otherwise do: single interfaces can now support multiple networks; also, networks can now span multiple interfaces (less common, but possible).

In addition, VLANs provide some advantages over traditional networks. With VLANs, if a user moves from one location to another, the user's computer's network settings do not have to be reconfigured—the user just needs to connect to a switch port that supports the VLAN of which the user is a member. Conversely, if the user changes their job function, they do not need to move; they only need to join a different VLAN which contains the resources they need to access. Moreover, since broadcast traffic is confined to a single VLAN, it is significantly reduced, cutting down on unnecessary network traffic and improving security, since it is less likely a user can eavesdrop on network traffic not intended for that user.

In this chapter, we will consider some concrete examples of how VLANs can be used to improve network design. We will then cover VLAN configuration within pfSense, and also discuss VLAN switch configuration as well as troubleshooting.

Completing this chapter will enable you to master the following topics:

- Basic VLAN concepts
- VLAN configuration at the console
- VLAN configuration in the web GUI
- VLAN configuration at the switch
- Troubleshooting VLANs

Technical requirements

To work through the examples in this chapter, you will need a working pfSense system with at least one optional interface. To actually implement a working VLAN, you will need a managed switch as well. The TP-Link TL-SG108E, which is used for the first example in this chapter, is an example of a relatively low-cost SOHO managed switch. Cisco managed switches are often found in corporate environments and are generally more expensive, although they can often be purchased used at a reasonable price.

Basic VLAN concepts

Before we consider the technical aspects of VLANs, it might be helpful to consider an example network, step back and consider how it might be implemented using a traditional networking model, then consider how the same network might be implemented with VLANs to provide a more concrete illustration of their advantages.

Example 1 – developers and engineering

To illustrate the usefulness of VLANs, let's consider the simple case of a mid-sized company that has a software department and an engineering department. The software department occupies floors one and three, while the engineering department occupies floors two and four, and each floor has its own wiring closet with a switch connected to the company router.

Let's also assume that we want to have separate networks for software developers and engineers, so that the developers can communicate with each other via the developers' network, and the engineers can communicate with each other via the engineering network, but the developers shouldn't be able to access the engineering network and engineers shouldn't be able to access the developers' network. The following diagram shows this setup:

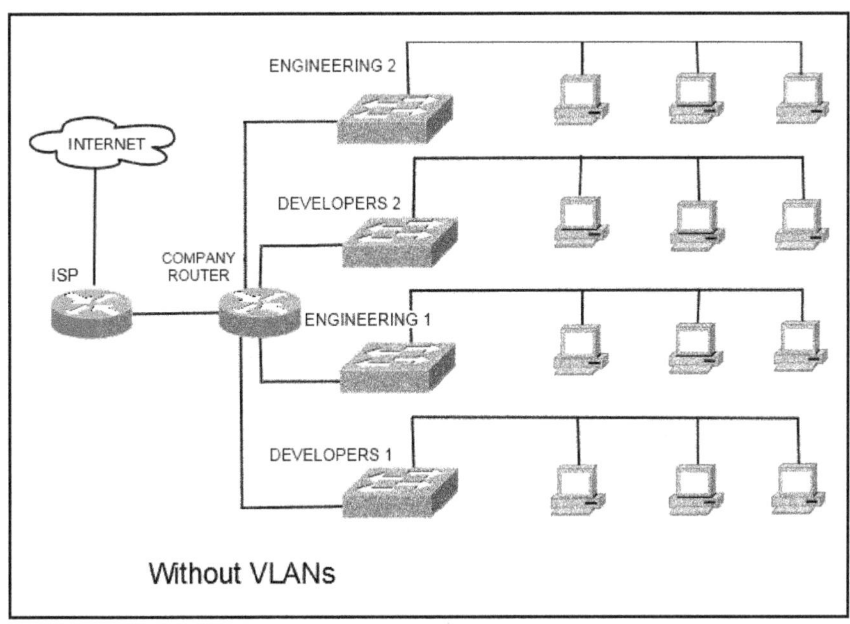

A possible method of segmenting our network using traditional network interfaces

As you can see, accomplishing our goal of having separate networks for developers and engineers in a traditional network is somewhat difficult. The developers are not all on the same interface, and neither are the engineers. One possibility is to continue having a subnet for each floor: we could call the first floor network **DEVELOPERS1**, the second floor network **ENGINEERING1**, the third floor network **DEVELOPERS2**, and the fourth floor network **ENGINEERING2**. Then we set up firewall rules to allow **DEVELOPERS1** to access **DEVELOPERS2** and vice versa, and do the same for **ENGINEERING1** and **ENGINEERING2**. This would be the easiest way of segregating the developers from the engineers with the current setup, but it still falls short of our goal of having one network for developers and one for engineers. What we have actually done is set up two network groupings with two networks in each of them. Moreover, if our setup gets more complex (for example, in addition to the first four floors, we add developers and engineers to the fifth floor), it is going to be challenging to reconfigure our network.

Another possibility is to connect the first and third floor switches, and connect the second and fourth floor switches. In this scenario, each network has two switches, one of which is directly connected to the company router. The second switch will be connected to the first switch via the uplink port. As a result, the two switches will be on the same network, and we will achieve our goal of having separate networks for the developers and engineering. There are, however, some problems with this configuration:

- We will have to run cabling between the first and second switches for the developers' and engineering networks. In a small office, this may not be a big problem. For example, assume that in our hypothetical network in the preceding diagram the company router is on the second floor of the building, in the same wiring closet as the **ENGINEERING1** switch. The engineering network requires no additional cabling, as we can just disconnect **ENGINEERING2** from the router and connect it to **ENGINEERING1** (which will remain connected directly to the router). Thus, all we need to do is run cabling between **DEVELOPERS1** and **DEVELOPERS2**. Nevertheless, it is not difficult to see how this is not a very scalable configuration. If we double or triple the number of floors in our hypothetical, we can see how the time and cost of running additional cabling can add up.
- This solution is not very flexible, either. For example, if the company decides to move some of the developers onto the fourth floor, we will have to either put them on the same switch as the engineers (in which case they won't be on the developers' network), or we will have to add another switch for the developers.

Now, let's consider how we would go about setting up different developer and engineering networks using VLANs. Again, each floor will have its own switch, except that the switch will be a managed switch, capable of processing VLAN traffic. There will be trunk lines connecting each switch with the switch on the floor above it (except for the fourth floor switch) and the floor below it (except for the first floor). The switch on the first floor will be connected via the trunk port to the company router. Again, we have a diagram of this configuration, as follows:

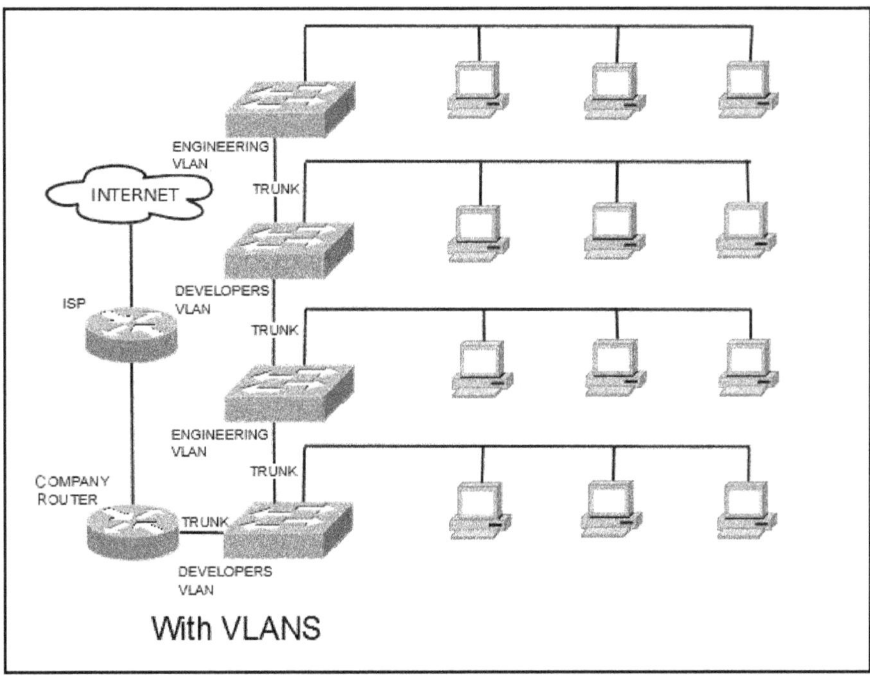

Our new and improved network, now with VLANs

The cost of setting up this VLAN may initially be higher, because we have to use managed switches, whereas in the non-VLAN scenario, we could have used unmanaged switches, which are typically cheaper than managed switches (although we will likely save some money on cabling). Our network is now much more scalable than before, as adding another floor to the network only requires (in addition to cabling to each node) an additional switch and trunk cabling to the switch on the previous floor. Moreover, on a managed switch, we can configure individual ports, so if management decides to move the software development and engineering departments around, we can just reconfigure ports on the switches. For a relatively small network, the benefits might not be that significant. But as you might have gathered, as our networks get bigger, using VLANs makes the task of configuring and maintaining networks much easier. And as we shall see later in the chapter, technologies such as Cisco's VLAN trunking protocol make administration even easier.

Example 2 – IoT network

Another example of judicious use of VLANs takes place when we consider accommodating IoT devices. IoT devices are devices embedded with electronics that enable them to connect to the internet and exchange data. An IoT device could be a heart monitor, an automobile, or even something as simple as a thermometer. These provide seemingly endless opportunities to integrate real world devices with computer networks, but they also, unsurprisingly, raise numerous security issues. It is not without reason that the IoT has come to be referred to as, somewhat humorously, as the internet of insecure things.

It is beyond the scope of this chapter to cover all of the security issues raised by IoT devices (for example, data privacy, the possibility that these devices could be hacked for malicious purposes, and the need to update the firmware on these devices). Even if you diligently secure all your IoT devices, however, you likely will not want to place these devices on your LAN network. Placing them in a DMZ network might seem like the prudent thing to do, and it is a good idea. It will prevent a hacker who compromises the security of a single IoT device from easily gaining access to the LAN:

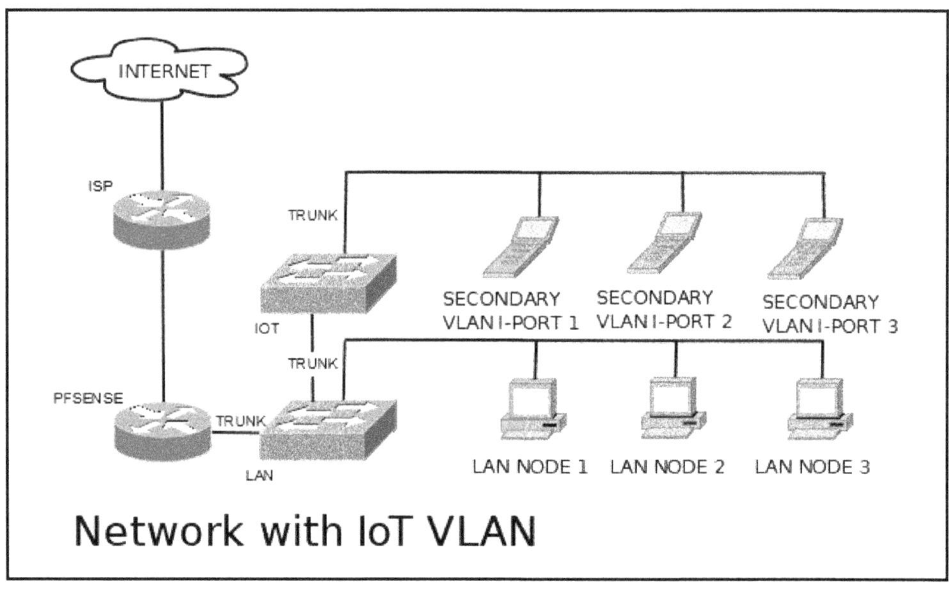

Using VLANs to secure the internet of insecure things

The one weakness of this approach, however, is that the hacker potentially could find other devices on the DMZ/IoT network, thus leaving them vulnerable to attack. We can mitigate this with by creating **private VLANs** (**PVLANs**), in which a subset of ports on a VLAN are isolated and are only permitted to communicate with an uplink port. In the IoT VLAN diagram shown, each IoT device is placed on a separate **I-Port** (**I** stands for **isolated**). I-Ports are only permitted to communicate with an uplink (also known as **P-Ports**, with the **P** standing for **promiscuous**); therefore, each IoT device can communicate only with its uplink and cannot communicate with the other IoT devices. However, if two or more IoT devices need to communicate with each other, we can designate these ports as **C-Ports** (**C** stands for **community**) and place them in the same community VLAN, in which case they will be able to communicate with other devices on the community VLAN and the VLAN's uplink, but not with I-Ports (or, for that matter, other community VLANs).

To summarize the most obvious advantages of VLANs, we have:

- The ability to easily segregate network traffic into different broadcast domains, which decreases bandwidth utilization and improves network performance
- Increased security from being able to easily segregate network traffic—even if two nodes are on the same switch, if they are on separate VLANs, they cannot talk to each other unless the router has been configured to grant them access
- The ability to create separate networks at a much lower cost than would be possible with traditional networks, and with a greatly reduced workload for those tasked with setting up the network

But VLANs also have many other features not available via traditional networking. They include:

- The ability to double tag traffic, referred to as QinQ.
- The ability to prevent a host from communicating with any other host on the network (hosts will only be able to communicate with the default gateway). As the example IoT network illustrated, PVLANs allow the network firewall to gain a more granular level of control over traffic. Otherwise, hosts could not be prevented from communicating with another host on the same subnet, as the traffic never reaches the firewall.

Hardware, configuration, and security considerations

VLANs are a layer 2 (data link layer) construct originally conceived of as a means of improving network bandwidth by allowing for multiple spanning trees on a network. This was accomplished by adding a special header, referred to as a tag, to every Ethernet frame. Each VLAN packet has a tag containing the VLAN ID for the VLAN to which it belongs, which switches and routers can then use to differentiate VLAN traffic. Several proprietary tagging mechanisms arose, but eventually the IEEE developed the 802.1Q standard for VLAN tagging. Although 802.1Q is not the sole encapsulation method for VLANs, it is the method supported by pfSense, and it is the tagging mechanism (sometimes referred to as the encapsulation method) with which we are primarily concerned in this chapter.

802.1ad is the IEEE standard for double tagging (QinQ). 802.1aq incorporates shortest-path bridging into VLANs. 802.3ac increased the maximum Ethernet frame size from 1518 bytes to 1522 bytes, to incorporate the four-byte VLAN tag.

Because each frame has this 4 byte 802.1Q tag attached to it, a VLAN Ethernet frame can be up to 1522 bytes. It can actually get even larger than this with QinQ tagging. This exceeds the usual maximum frame size for 1500 **maximum transmission unit** (**MTU**) Ethernet. Not all network cards work well with these larger frames, and some will drop them, resulting in decreased network performance when VLANs are implemented. Therefore, it is a good idea to make sure your network cards are VLAN-compatible. Even if the chipset supports longer frames, the network card's particular implementation of the chipset may not properly support them.

In addition, any switch on interfaces on which VLANs are implemented must be VLAN-aware. Any managed switch manufactured since 2000 should be, but unmanaged switches will not. As is the case with network cards, you will want to do some research into choosing which switches to deploy on your network.

Each VLAN has a number between 1 and 4094; this is used as an ID. In order to set up a VLAN on your network, you will need one or more managed switches. On a managed switch that has not been configured for VLANs, every port can talk to every other port. These switches tend to either have VLANs completely disabled, or enabled with a default VLAN of which every port is a member. VLAN1 is designated as the default VLAN, and therefore it is recommended that you not use VLAN1. If you do, then there are potential security issues, as someone with physical access to the switches could plug a device into an unused port and have access to all the hosts in VLAN1.

Even if a hacker doesn't have direct access to the switches, they will undoubtedly use the fact that VLAN1 is the default VLAN as a factor in formulating their attacks.

Which VLAN naming convention should you use? Other than not using VLAN1, you can use whatever convention you choose. One common convention is to start with VLAN2 and increment by one for each additional VLAN. It is also commonplace to use the third octet of the IP address to match the VLAN ID: for example, for VLAN 2 we could have `192.168.2.0`, for VLAN3, `192.168.3.0`, and so on. The same convention could be used with class A and class B private networks; for example, `172.16.2.0` or `10.1.2.0`. Another common convention is to increment by 10 for each VLAN, starting with VLAN10. In this scenario, we would have VLAN10 and subnet `192.168.10.0`; VLAN20 and subnet `192.168.20.0`, and so on.

Each VLAN resides on a physical interface, which is known as the parent interface. When VLANs are created, they are assigned a virtual interface, with names such as VLAN0, VLAN1, and so on, similar to the device names for physical interfaces. The virtual interface names do not correspond to the VLAN IDs. You should not assign the parent interface of a VLAN to an interface, although you can. It should only function as the parent interface for whatever VLANs reside on it. In one case, in which the author negligently assigned the parent interface to a pfSense subnet, the web GUI became inaccessible, and the issue was only resolved when all assigned interfaces were deleted and reconfigured from the console. It has also been known to cause problems with switch configuration and captive portal configurations.

There are also some security issues related to VLANs. VLAN misconfiguration may result in users gaining access to networks to which they should not have access. Because of this possibility, it is considered good practice to keep separate networks of different trust levels. For example, it is generally not a good idea to put the WAN and LAN networks on the same interface, even though it is possible.

Attacks that attempt to gain unauthorized access to VLANs are known as VLAN hopping. One method, known as **switch spoofing**, involves spoofing a trunking switch by using the trunking/tagging protocols. The other method, known as **double tagging**, involves the attacker placing two VLAN tags on a packet. The outermost tag is for VLAN1 (the native VLAN). The inner tag is for the VLAN the attacker wants to access (for example, VLAN2). The attacker sends the packet to a host on VLAN2, which can only be accessed by hosts on VLAN2. The first switch sees the VLAN1 header, removes it, and forwards the packet. The next switch sees the VLAN2 header (visible now that the VLAN1 header was removed) and sends the packet to the host on VLAN2. Thus, the attacker was able to trick the switch into thinking that the packet originated on VLAN2.

The good news is that most of the attack vectors involving VLANs can be mitigated—or even eliminated entirely—through proactive switch configuration. For example, disabling auto-negotiation can eliminate switch spoofing, and not placing hosts on the native VLAN can eliminate double tagging. Nonetheless, you should be aware of possible security issues related to your hardware and network configuration.

You will want to do some research to see what degree of security testing switches have undergone before making a purchase, and you should ensure that you are running the latest firmware.

VLAN configuration at the console

VLAN configuration can be done at the console; in fact, it can even be done on the initial setup, although many of the more esoteric features of VLANs (such as QinQ tagging) are not available from the console menu. Another disadvantage is that there does not seem to be a way of renaming the optional interfaces, although you could do so from the web GUI later.

To begin VLAN configuration from the console, use the **Assign Interfaces** option in the console mentioned (it should be option 1). pfSense will provide a list of available interfaces in a table which provides the interface device name, the MAC address, link status (up or down), and a description of the interface. For VLAN configuration at the console, perform the following steps:

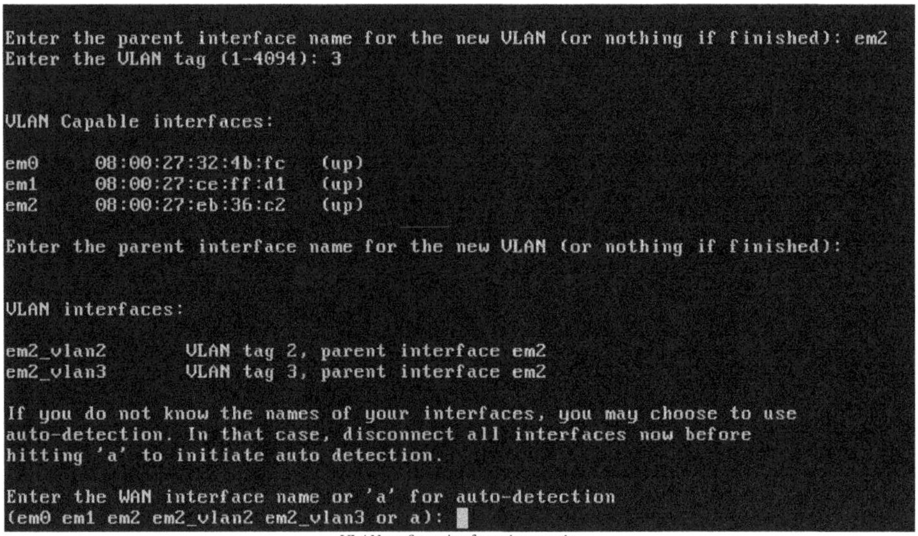

```
Enter the parent interface name for the new VLAN (or nothing if finished): em2
Enter the VLAN tag (1-4094): 3

VLAN Capable interfaces:

em0      08:00:27:32:4b:fc    (up)
em1      08:00:27:ce:ff:d1    (up)
em2      08:00:27:eb:36:c2    (up)

Enter the parent interface name for the new VLAN (or nothing if finished):

VLAN interfaces:

em2_vlan2        VLAN tag 2, parent interface em2
em2_vlan3        VLAN tag 3, parent interface em2

If you do not know the names of your interfaces, you may choose to use
auto-detection. In that case, disconnect all interfaces now before
hitting 'a' to initiate auto detection.

Enter the WAN interface name or 'a' for auto-detection
(em0 em1 em2 em2_vlan2 em2_vlan3 or a):
```

VLAN configuration from the console

1. When you select the **Assign Interfaces** option, the first prompt will be **Do you want to set up VLANs now [y|n]?**
2. At this prompt, type `y` and press *Enter* to begin VLAN configuration.
3. A confirmation prompt is presented next: **WARNING: All existing VLANs will be cleared if you proceed! Do you want to proceed [y|n]?**
4. Type `y` and press *Enter* to proceed.
5. Next, pfSense will provide a list of VLAN-capable interfaces and another prompt: **Enter the parent interface name for the new VLAN (or nothing if finished).**
6. Enter the parent interface name (the device name in the table) and press *Enter*. The next prompt is for the VLAN tag: **Enter the VLAN tag (1-4094)**.
7. Enter a VLAN tag other than `1` and press *Enter*.
8. After you enter the VLAN tag, you will be returned to the **Enter the parent interface** prompt, where you can repeat the process for as many VLANs you wish to set up, and then enter nothing when finished. When you are finished creating VLANs, you will be prompted to assign interfaces, starting with the WAN interface. If you have at least one interface that has not been partitioned into VLANs, you should probably assign one of these interfaces to the WAN. If you do assign a VLAN to the WAN, you will want to make sure the WAN is on a separate switch, for the reasons outlined in the previous section.
9. The next prompt will be for the LAN interface, and you can assign a VLAN to the LAN, although you should be aware of any security issues this creates. Enter the LAN interface and press *Enter*.
10. Once you have assigned the WAN and LAN interfaces, you can assign optional interfaces (OPT1, OPT2, and so on) to the newly-created VLANs. The convention for VLAN interface names is `parent_interface.vlan_number`. For example, if VLAN20's parent interface is **em3**, the interface name for VLAN20 would be **em3.20**.
11. When you are done assigning interfaces, press *Enter* at the prompt and you will be presented with a list of interfaces and their assignments.
12. After the list, you will see a confirmation prompt: **Do you want to proceed [y|n]?**
13. Type `y` and press *Enter*. pfSense will write and reload the configuration. Interface assignment is now complete.
14. You still need to assign an IP address to the VLANs, which you can do by selecting second option from the console menu, selecting the number corresponding to the desired VLAN interface, and typing in the IPv4 and/or IPv6 addresses, following the procedure outlined in `Chapter 1`, *Revisiting pfSense Basics*. You can also configure the DHCP server to work with VLANs using this menu option. Repeat this step for every VLAN you wish to configure.

If you have followed all of these steps, the pfSense portion of VLAN setup will be almost complete. You must still add firewall rules to give the VLANs access to other networks (since it cannot be done from the console, it will be covered in the next section) and configure one or more managed switches for the VLANs to work. We will cover switch configuration after we consider how to set up VLANs in the pfSense web GUI.

VLAN configuration in the web GUI

VLAN configuration can also be done within the web GUI, along with any other tasks related to the setup of VLANs (for example, DHCP and rule creation).

1. To get started with VLAN configuration in the web GUI, log in to pfSense in the web browser of your choice and navigate to **Interfaces | (assign)**.
2. From the **Interface assignments** page, click on the **VLANs** tab. From the **VLANs** tab, you will see a table with any previously created VLANs. Click on the **+Add** button to add a new VLAN:

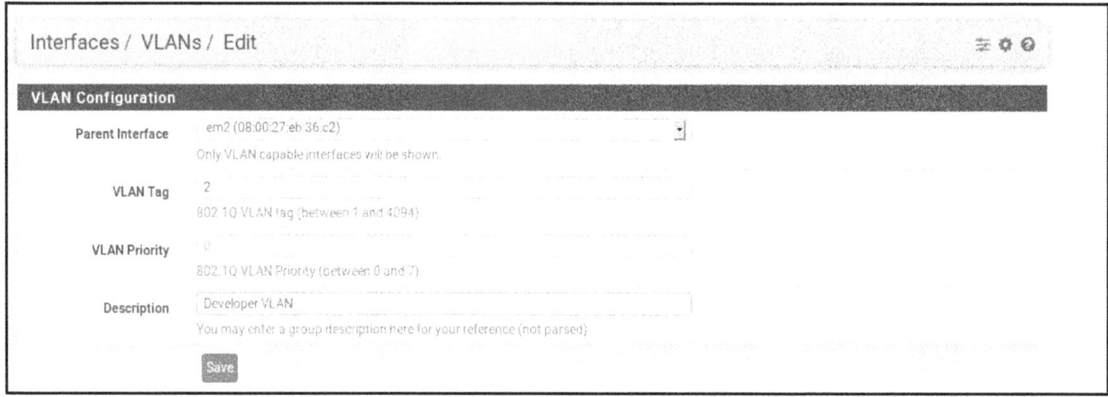

Adding a VLAN in the web GUI

3. On the **VLAN Configuration** page, the first setting is the **Parent Interface** drop-down box. Select the interface you want to be the parent interface of your VLANs. Next is the **VLAN Tag** edit box. Valid values for this field are `1` to `4094`; you shouldn't use `1`, but you can use any other values up to and including `4094`. Some low-end managed switches may have problems with larger numbers, so you may want to use low numbers (`2` to `8`) if you have one of these.

4. The **VLAN Priority** edit box was added with pfSense 2.3. This allows you to utilize the 802.1Q **priority code point** (**PCP**) field. This is a 3-bit field that makes reference to the IEEE 802.1p class of service. 802.1p defines how traffic should be treated based on the value of this field:

PCP value	**Priority level**	**Description**
0	1	Traffic gets best effort treatment.
1	0	Traffic is assigned the lowest priority. It is handled in the background.
2	2	Traffic gets excellent effort treatment, which is one step below best effort.
3	3	Suitable priority level for critical applications.
4	4	Suitable for video requiring < 100 milliseconds of latency and jitter.
5	5	Suitable for voice requiring < 10 milliseconds of latency and jitter.
6	6	Suitable for internetwork control.
7	7	Traffic gets highest priority.

5. As you can see, if you know what type of traffic is going to be prevalent on the VLANs you are creating, you can set the **VLAN Priority** value accordingly. Otherwise, you can set this value to **0**. The last field, **Description**, allows you to enter a non-parsed description of the VLAN. When you are done making changes, click on the **Save** button at the bottom.

In the first step, we have only created the VLANs and have not assigned them to interfaces, so in the next step, we must return to the **Interface assignments** tab. There will be a table on which all interface assignments up to this point will be shown, and you can add VLAN assignments by selecting one of the VLAN interfaces created in the previous step from the drop-down box in the last row (the one labeled **Available network ports:**) and clicking on the **Add** button. Repeat this process for as many VLANs as you created in the previous step.

1. Once interface assignment is complete, the next step is to configure each of the VLANs.
2. They will be given generic default names (**OPT1**, **OPT2**, and so on); click on the first VLAN in the **Interface** column. This will load the **Interface Configuration** page.

3. In the **General configuration** section, check the **Enable** check box. In the **Description** field, you can rename the interface.
4. In the **IPv4 Configuration Type** drop-down box, you will likely want to choose **Static IPv4**. If your VLAN is going to support IPv6, you will likely want to choose **Static IPv6** in the **IPv6 Configuration Type** drop-down box. Depending on whether you selected IPv4, IPv6, or both, you will have to enter IPv4 and/or IPv6 addresses in the sections below the **General configuration** section. Note that you must enter both the IP address of the interface and the CIDR.
5. For **IPv4 Upstream Gateway** and **IPv6 Upstream Gateway**, you can leave these drop-down boxes set to **None**.

The rest of the fields you can likely leave unchanged, but if you are having problems with dropped frames, you may want to enter a larger value in the **MTU** field.

When you are done making changes, click on the **Save** button at the bottom of the page. Once you have clicked on the **Save** button, you must click on the **Apply Changes** button at the top of the page for the changes to take effect. Repeat the interface configuration as many times as needed. You can reach the configuration page for each VLAN by accessing it from the drop-down menu at the top of the page, or by navigating to **Interfaces** | **(assign)** once again and clicking on the appropriate VLAN in the **Interface** column.

One of the bugs affecting the pfSense implementation of VLANs is that DHCP6c packets (packets from the DHCPv6 client daemon) were not being tagged with VLAN priority. This bug has been fixed with version 2.4.3.

QinQ

We have now covered the steps that are absolutely necessary for the initial VLAN configuration, but there are some additional features worth mentioning. pfSense supports QinQ tagging; you can configure QinQ by clicking on the **QinQs** tab on the **(assign)** page. This will take you to a table showing all the interfaces that have been configured for QinQ. You can add another QinQ interface by clicking on the **Add** button.

The first option on the QinQ configuration page is the **Parent Interface** drop-down box. As with VLAN configuration, the parent interface should be an interface that is not being used as an interface on pfSense (in other words, an interface that is being used solely as a parent interface for VLANs). The next option is **First level tag**. This is the tag on which all other tags are stacked; it is at the bottom of the nesting of tags. It cannot match any of the VLAN IDs for VLANs on this interface; for example, if VLAN2 is on this interface, the first level tag cannot be 2.

Next is the **Add interface to QinQ interface groups** check box. If enabled, an entry will be added on the **Interface Groups** tab for this QinQ interface. This will make rule creation somewhat easier, as once an interface group is created and configured, rules can be created based on that interface group. You can enter a brief, non-parsed description in the next edit box. Finally, in the **Tag(s)** edit box, you can enter a VLAN tag or range of tags, which will also be attached to traffic on this interface. Pressing the **Add** button allows you to add another tag or range of tags, while the **Delete** button deletes that tag. Press the **Save** button at the bottom of the page when you are done making changes.

If you added an interface group for the new QinQ entry, click on the **Interface Groups** tab. Find the newly created interface group and click on the edit icon that corresponds to the group. This will launch the **Interface Group Configuration** page. Here, you can edit the **Group Name** and enter a non-parsed group description. You can also select which interfaces will be members of this group in the **Group Members** listbox. When you are done making changes, click on the **Save** button.

You now have a QinQ VLAN, which you can add via the **Interface Assignments** tab just as you would an ordinary VLAN. The ability to nest tags in this way allows you to have even more VLANs on a single router than you would otherwise. With a single VLAN tag, you are limited to 4093 VLANs (you are allowed to use IDs of 1 to 4094, but VLAN1 is the default VLAN). With one level of nesting, this increases to 4093 * 4093 or 16,752,649 VLANs (you can have multiple levels of nesting, however, so you could have even more combinations than that).

Link aggregation

Another option we should consider addressing is link aggregation, which can be configured by clicking on the **LAGGs** tab on the **(assign)** page. Link aggregation (usually abbreviated as LAG) allows us to combine multiple ports in parallel, which accomplishes two goals. It increases the amount of throughput (for example, if you have two trunk ports per switch, you will have more throughput than you would with a single port), and it also provides some redundancy in case one or more ports go down. The **LAGGs** option does not refer to an interface; rather, it refers to LAGG, the FreeBSD link aggregation and link failover driver. Typically, trunk ports involve some form of link aggregation; with some switches, trunks have to be configured as pairs of ports.

To add a new LAGG interface, click on the **Add** button on the **LAGGs** tab. This will take you to the **LAGG Configuration** page. In the **Parent Interfaces** listbox, you can choose the interfaces that will be used for this link aggregation. In the **LAGG Protocol** drop-down box, you can select which protocol to use on the interface. The choices are as follows:

Protocol	**Description**
NONE	Disables traffic, but does not disable the interface.
LACP	The Link Aggregation Control Protocol, defined by IEEE 802.3ad. LACP provides a form of load balancing by automatically bundling together links.
FAILOVER	One port is designated as the active port; all other ports are used as failover ports. If the active port goes down, one of the failover ports becomes the new active port.
FEC	This protocol supports Cisco fast EtherChannel; unlike most of the other options, it is a static setup.
LOADBALANCE	This protocol balances all outgoing traffic on the member ports. This is also a static setup.
ROUNDROBIN	Distributes outgoing traffic in a round-robin fashion; in other words, in equal slices and in a circular pattern.

When you are done making changes to the new LAGG interface, click on the **Save** button. The new interface should now be listed in the table on the main **LAGGs** page.

Add firewall rules for VLANs

There are some additional steps needed before your VLANs are fully functional. At this point, your VLANs have been created and configured, but they will not be able to access the internet or other subnets, because the default in pfSense is to block all network traffic. The next chapter will have a detailed treatment of firewall rule creation, and you can reference it if you need more detailed information about firewall rules.

If you just want to create rules to allow your VLANs to access all other networks, however, there is an easy way to do this:

1. Navigate to **Firewall** | **Rules** and click on the **LAN** tab. There should be two rules that were created automatically when the LAN interface was created: the **Default allow LAN to any** rule and the **Default allow LAN IPv6 to any** rule.
2. Click on the copy icon for whichever rule you want to copy (the copy icon should be under the **Actions** column and is represented by two sheets with one on top of the other). This will take you to the **Edit** page for that rule.
3. Under the **Edit Firewall Rule** section, change the interface in the **Interface** drop-down box to one of the VLANs you created earlier.
4. In the **Source** section, change the source in the drop-down box to match the VLAN in the **Interface** drop-down box (be sure to select a net and not just a single address – for example, if you want to create a rule for VLAN2, you need to select **VLAN2 net** here, and not **VLAN2 address**).
5. Then, click on the **Save** button at the bottom of the page, which will take you to the **Rules** page for the VLAN that has just been configured.
6. On this page, click on the **Apply Changes** button, at the top right. Repeat this process for as many VLANs as you want to grant access to.

If you have a standard pfSense configuration, creating these rules should be enough to give the VLANs access to the internet. If you have enabled **Manual Outbound NAT rule generation**, however, you will have to add NAT rules in order for your VLANs to be able to reach the internet.

You may have enabled this mode in order to add rules needed to connect to an external VPN server or for other reasons. If so, follow these steps:

1. You should navigate to **Firewall** | **NAT** and click on the **Outbound** tab.
2. You need to create two NAT rules for each VLAN: a rule to enable NAT between the VLAN and the WAN on port `500` with a static port configuration (this is for **Internet Security Association and Key Management Protocol** (**ISAKMP**)), and a rule to enable NAT between the VLAN and WAN on all ports with a non-static port configuration.

   Fortunately, your outbound NAT rule set probably has similar rules for at least one interface (for example, the LAN interface), so you can easily copy these rules by clicking on the copy icon under the **Actions** column for the entry you want to copy, and then just changing the IP address listed in **Source** to correspond to the VLAN for which you want to create a NAT rule. You probably want to modify the **Description** as well. Click on the **Save** button when you are done.

There is an even easier way, however, to generate these rules:

1. From the **Outbound** tab, click on the **Automatic outbound NAT rule generation** radio button. Then click on the **Save** button, and when the page reloads, click on the **Apply Changes** button at the top right.
2. If you scroll down to the **Automatic Rules:** section of the page, you should see the VLAN subnets listed under the **Source** column for each rule. Now, click back on the **Manual Outbound NAT rule generation** radio button at the top and click on the **Save** button and then click on the **Apply Changes** button again when the page reloads.

The NAT rule listing on the page will now include rules for the VLANs. Furthermore, any rules that were manually created earlier will also be there. If you want your VLANs to be able to access the internet through your VPN server, you will still have to add NAT rules for the VPN, but you can do that easily by following the rule-copying procedure described previously.

Finally, you will have to configure any services you want to run on the VLANs. If you are using DHCP on your other interfaces, you will probably want to enable the DHCP server on the VLAN interfaces. Since we provided a detailed description of how to configure the DHCP server in the previous chapter, we will not repeat it here, but at a minimum, you will want to do the following:

1. Enable the DHCP server on the interface
2. Specify the IP address range for this interface
3. Add any static DHCP mappings that are needed

If you need to enable any other services on the VLAN interfaces, such as **Captive Portal** or **DHCP Relay**, you will want to do that as well.

Configuration at the switch

Before your VLAN configuration is complete, you must configure each of the switches that will be connected to the VLAN interfaces. The process will be different depending on which switch you are using; in this section, we will first discuss switch configuration in general, and then walk through a concrete example of VLAN switch configuration.

There will be differences in switch configuration depending on who the manufacturer is and what type of switch it is; however, all switch configurations include at least the following steps:

1. Trunk ports (the ports that connect the switch with the router and other switches) must be configured
2. The VLANs must be created
3. Ports must be assigned to the VLANs

Some switches also require you to configure a **Port VLAN ID** (**PVID**), which sets a default VLAN ID for each port.

Switches differ in the types of interfaces provided. Some provide only a command line interface; some provide a web-based interface; some provide both. Still others provide their own utilities for configuration. In cases where you have to use a vendor-provided utility to configure the switch, be aware that these utilities often do not have the ability to detect switches not on the current subnet, so you won't be able to configure the switch from another network.

Most switches support 802.1Q VLANs, but some also support port-based VLANs. With port-based VLANs, each port is statically assigned to a VLAN; any traffic that enters or exits the port does not have a VLAN tag. With 802.1Q VLANs, traffic entering a port assigned to a specific VLAN is tagged with an 802.1Q header. This allows for VLANs spanning multiple switches. Traffic between two nodes on the same VLAN and different switches can be sent out over a trunk port, which provides connectivity to other VLAN-capable switches. The switch on which the destination node resides will then recognize the destination port as a local switch port (by looking up the destination MAC address), and will send the traffic to the destination.

Since 802.1Q VLANs are supported by pfSense, we will use 802.1Q VLANs in the example. Assume that we have created two VLANs in pfSense: a **DEVELOPERS VLAN** (VLAN ID = 2) and an **ENGINEERING VLAN** (VLAN ID = 3). Our example demonstrates VLAN switch configuration with a Cisco switch. If you are deploying networks in a corporate environment, you are likely to encounter Cisco switches at some point, and they have even found their way into some SOHO networks.

VLAN configuration example 1 – TL-SG108E

The TL-SG108E comes with a resource CD, which contains a utility (the Easy Smart Configuration Utility) that you will need to install in order to configure the switch (there is no web-based interface available for this switch). Unfortunately, the utility only runs under Windows (it does not seem to work with Linux even with the WINE emulator), so a Windows computer running XP Service Pack 3 or later is required. For the rest of the configuration, you will need to have this computer connected to the switch via an Ethernet cable.

When you run the TP-LINK Easy Smart Configuration Utility for the first time, the utility will display a table called **discovered switches**, which will show any switches the utility was able to find. This will include any switches to which the computer is connected, as well as any switches that were uplinked to those switches. If you click on the entry for the switch you want to configure, you will be prompted for the login credentials of the switch. We enter the admin username and password and click on the **Login** button.

If the configuration utility found the switch, it is physically connected to the current subnet. The utility will not let you log in, however, unless the switch's IP address matches the current subnet. You can change the IP address of the switch by clicking on the gear icon in the IP Setting column. This will launch a dialog box where you can change the IP address and subnet mask. You can also change the default gateway here, although it is not necessary.

Once you are logged in to the switch, the configuration screen will have several tabs. The user interface defaults to the **System** tab, which displays the MAC address, IP address, and current firmware version of the switch. There are also options on the sidebar to change the IP address, password, backup and restore the switch, reboot and reset the switch, and upgrade the firmware. Clicking on the **Switching** tab, initially displays a table showing the status of each of the switch's eight ports. We first need to configure a trunk for the switch, so we click on **LAG** on the left sidebar menu.

The **LAG** option was called **Port Trunk** in earlier versions of the software.

On the **LAG** page, we can configure up to two trunks, each having a minimum of two ports and a maximum of four ports. Mirroring and mirrored ports cannot be added to a trunk group. We only need one trunk, so we select **Trunk1** in the **Trunk ID** drop-down box. Then, we click on ports **1** and **2** in the graphic below the drop-down box (you can select whichever ports you want for the trunk, as long as they don't conflict with any other port assignments) and then click on the **Apply** button. A confirmation dialog will appear, and we click on the **Yes** button in this dialog box. Trunk configuration is now complete.

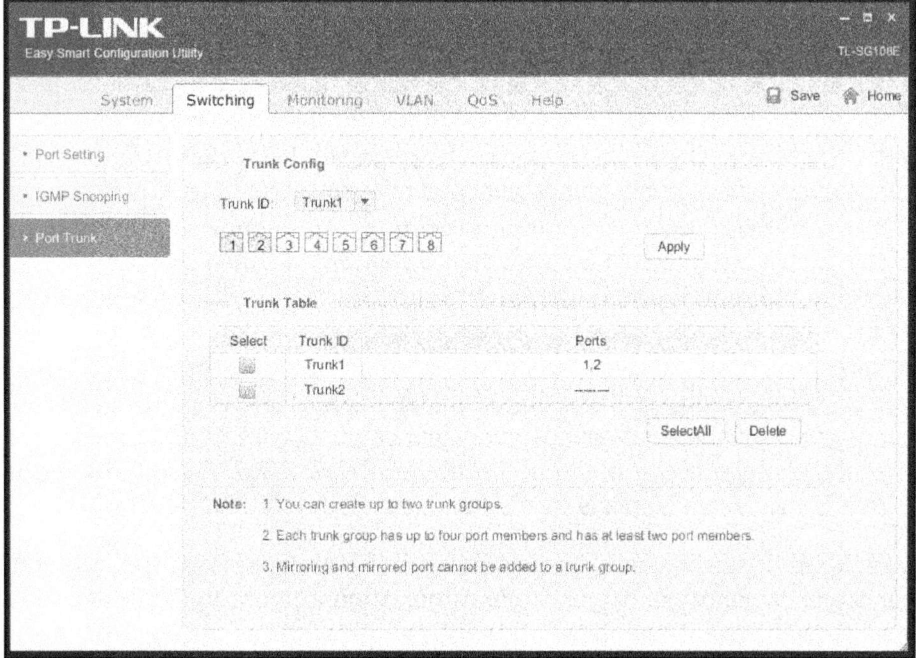

Now we can begin VLAN configuration, while being mindful of the fact that two of the eight ports have already been allocated for the trunk. We click on the **VLAN** tab at the top of the page. The three VLAN options offered on the sidebar menu are **MTU VLAN**, **Port Based VLAN**, and **802.1Q VLAN**. Since 802.1Q is the official IEEE standard for tagging VLAN traffic and is supported by pfSense, we will utilize this method and we click on the **802.1Q VLAN** option on the sidebar menu.

MTU VLAN is an option that allows us to have a single uplink port instead of having trunk ports, giving us an additional access port to which we can connect nodes. It is suitable if you want each port to be on its own VLAN. **Port Based VLAN** is a VLAN configuration option in which Ethernet frames entering and leaving the port are not tagged. The VLAN to which a port is assigned in the switch configuration is what determines which VLAN to which the traffic should be sent.

The **802.1Q configuration** page has two sections: **Global Config**, where the only option is to enable or disable 802.1Q VLANs, and the **802.1Q VLAN Setting** section, where we can enter information about our VLANs. Since we want to enable 802.1Q VLANs, we select **Enable** from the drop-down box and click on the **Apply** button, once again pressing the **Yes** button in the confirmation dialog box.

In the **802.1Q VLAN Setting** section, we enter several parameters. They are:

- **VLAN (1-4094)**: This should match the VLAN ID(s) of the VLANs you created during the pfSense portion of the configuration.
- **VLAN Name**: These can be any arbitrary names, but administration will be easier if the names match the names assigned to the VLANs in pfSense.
- **Tagged Ports**: These ports are the ports on which outbound traffic will have 802.1Q tags attached. Therefore, they should match the trunk ports assigned during the previous step. We select **1** and **2** as the tagged ports for both VLAN2 and VLAN3.
- **Untagged Ports**: These are the ports on which outbound traffic will have any 802.1Q tags removed. They should match the inbound ports for the VLANs. We are going to allocate three ports for each of our two VLANs, so we set ports **3** to **5** as the untagged ports for VLAN 2 (the **DEVELOPERS VLAN**), and we set ports **6** to **8** as the untagged ports for VLAN 3 (the **ENGINEERING VLAN**).

We enter **VLAN ID**, **VLAN Name**, **Tagged Ports**, and **Untagged Ports** for each of the VLANs, pressing the **Apply** button after the information for each VLAN is entered and clicking on **Yes** in the confirmation dialog box.

The next step is to click on **802.1Q PVID Setting** on the left sidebar, which sets the port **VLAN ID** (**PVID**) of the port. This ensures that when the switch receives a packet without a VLAN tag, it adds a VLAN tag for the VLAN matching the PVID before sending the packet to the trunk ports. On the TL-SG108E, setting the PVID is necessary for 802.1Q tagging to work, and setting the PVID also determines the broadcast domain for a port – broadcast packets received by a port will be sent to all ports with a matching PVID.

VLAN configuration example 2 – Cisco switches

Configuring VLANs on most Cisco switches is a fairly simple process. Cisco provides a command-line interface, which only requires a few commands. Moreover, Cisco provides three different ways of configuring a VLAN:

- Static VLAN creation
- VLAN creation with dynamic trunking protocol
- VLAN creation with VLAN trunking protocol

The commands utilized in this section were run via the serial interface on a Cisco SF 300-08 switch. The command syntax on other Cisco switches might vary slightly.

Static VLAN creation

A static VLAN is created when the administrator manually assigns switch ports to belong to a VLAN. Initially, the default is for all ports to be assigned to VLAN1. Static VLANs can be created in VLAN configuration mode. Creating our two VLANs involves only a few commands:

1. We move from privileged EXEC mode to configuration mode:

   ```
   Switch# configure terminal
   ```

2. Next, we create the first VLAN (VLAN2, the `DEVELOPERS` VLAN):

   ```
   Switch (config)# interface vlan 2
   ```

3. Now, we can assign it a name:

   ```
   Switch (config-vlan)# name DEVELOPERS
   ```

4. Next, we want to apply the changes, increase the revision number, and return to the global configuration mode:

```
Switch (config-vlan)# exit
```

5. We follow the same steps for the `ENGINEERING` VLAN, except for entering configuration mode, since we are already in that mode:

```
Switch (config)# interface vlan 3
Switch (config-vlan)# name ENGINEERING
Switch (config-vlan)# exit
```

6. Next, we need to assign ports to the VLANs. We can set up non-trunking access ports with a few commands. First, we move to interface configuration mode:

```
Switch (config)# interface range FastEthernet 3-5
```

In this command, `interface` indicates that we are entering interface configuration mode. `range` indicates that we are configuring a range of ports, not a single port. `FastEthernet` is the interface type. Other possible values include `ethernet`, `fddi` (for fiber connections), `token` or `tokenring` (for token ring networks), or **atm**. **3-5** indicates that we are configuring ports `3` to `5`. If you have a switch with more than one slot, you will have to specify the slot first, separated from the port range by the slash character (for example **FastEthernet 1/3-5**).

7. Next, we configure ports `3` to `5` as access ports:

```
Switch (config-if-range)# switchport mode access
```

8. Finally, we assign ports `3` to `5` to VLAN2 and return to the global configuration mode:

```
Switch (config-if-range)# switchport access vlan 2
Switch (config-if-range)# exit
```

9. Next, we will enter interface configuration mode for ports `6` to `8` and set up these ports as access ports for VLAN 3:

```
Switch (config)# interface range FastEthernet 6-8
Switch (config-if-range)# switchport mode access
Switch (config-if-range)# switchport access vlan 3
Switch (config-if-range)# exit
```

For both VLANs, we used the `range` command to select a range of ports. If you just want to configure a single port, the syntax is: `Switch (config)# interface FastEthernet 1`. This command would allow you to configure port `1`.

10. Next, we need to configure at least one port as a trunk port. First, we indicate the interface type, slot, and port:

```
Switch (config)# interface FastEthernet 1
```

11. Then, we set the mode to `trunk`:

```
Switch (config-if)# switchport mode trunk
```

This sets port `1` as a trunk port. By default, the native VLAN for this trunk port is the default VLAN (VLAN1).

12. We can change this with the following command:

```
Switch (config-if)# switchport trunk native vlan 2
```

This changes the native VLAN to VLAN2.

13. By default, a trunk port will carry traffic for any VLAN, but if we want, we can restrict the allowed VLANs for this trunk port:

```
Switch (config-if)# switchport trunk allowed vlan add 2-3
```

This will restrict the `trunk` port to allow only VLANs `2` and `3`, our `DEVELOPERS` and `ENGINEERING` VLANs. Other possible values for this command are `all` (to allow all VLANs), `none` (for no VLANs), a list of allowed VLANs, `remove` to remove a VLAN, or `add` to add a VLAN. For example, we could type:

```
Switch (config-if)# switchport trunk allowed vlan remove  2
```

This would remove access for VLAN `2` without affecting VLAN `3`. We could add VLAN `2` back again as well:

```
Switch (config-if)# switchport trunk allowed vlan add  2
```

14. To verify this configuration, we exit configuration mode and use the `show` command. For example, to verify the `DEVELOPERS` VLAN, we type:

```
Switch (config-if)# exit
Switch (config)# exit
Switch# show vlan name DEVELOPERS
```

15. This command will display configuration information for VLAN `2`. The following command will display all VLANs:

```
Switch# show vlans
```

Dynamic Trunking Protocol

Another approach is to use **Dynamic Trunking Protocol** (**DTP**). This protocol allows you to autoconfigure both the trunking and the type of trunking encapsulation on a Cisco switch:

1. First, enter switch configuration and interface configuration mode:

```
Switch# configure terminal
Switch (config)# interface fastethernet 1
```

2. Slot **0** port `1` can be statically converted into a trunk port with the following command:

```
Switch (config-if)# switchport mode trunk
```

3. Dynamic trunk configuration can be done in two different ways. If the neighboring interface is set to `trunk`, `desirable`, or `auto`, then the port will become a trunk if we issue this command:

```
Switch (config)# Switchport mode dynamic desirable
```

4. If the neighboring interface is set to `trunk` or `auto`, the port will become a trunk with the following command:

```
Switch (config-if)# switchport mode dynamic auto
```

Keep in mind, however, that enabling DTP can make your network vulnerable to VLAN hopping attacks. At the very least, you will want to make sure that only trunk ports are configured to use DTP.

VLAN Trunking Protocol

VLAN Trunking Protocol (**VTP**), like DTP, is a proprietary protocol for Cisco switches. The purpose of VTP is to make VLAN configuration easier by synchronizing VLAN configuration information throughout a VLAN domain. This is done by designating one switch as the VTP server, and letting it handle the addition, deletion, and renaming of VLANs throughout the domain.

The three available modes in a VTP domain are as follows:

- **Server**: This is the default mode. When changes are made on a VTP server, the changes propagate to all other switches on the domain. The VTP server is also responsible for creating VTP advertisements, which make this propagation possible.
- **Transparent**: If a switch is in transparent mode, changes made to the configuration will affect only that one switch. Transparent switches cannot create VTP advertisements, but they can forward VTP advertisements.
- **Client**: Switches in client mode cannot make any changes to the configuration, but they can send VLAN information in their databases to other switches. They can also forward VTP advertisements to other switches.

Obviously, the larger your network gets, the greater the potential is for VTP to make your life easier, since instead of configuring dozens or even hundreds of switches, you will only have to configure a single switch. In addition, VTP has a feature called **VTP pruning**, which forwards broadcast and unknown unicast messages to switches only if the switch has ports for the VLAN on which the broadcast/unicast messages are being sent. This makes for more efficient use of trunk bandwidth.

Configuring VTP requires only a few additional commands. Since we are making changes for the entire switch and not just a port or range of ports, we can use global configuration mode:

1. First, enter global configuration mode:

```
Switch# configure terminal
```

2. Next, set the switch as a VTP server, with the following command:

```
Switch (config)# vtp mode server
```

3. You can also put the switch in `client` mode or `transparent` mode:

```
Switch (config)# vtp mode client
Switch (config)# vtp mode transparent
```

4. To set the domain name, use this command:

```
Switch (config)# vtp domain <domain_name>
```

   Here, `<domain_name>` is the domain name to which you want to set the domain.

5. You can set a password with the following command:

```
Switch (config)# vtp password <password>
```

6. To set the VTP domain to VTP version two, type the following (the current version is version three):

```
Switch (config)# vtp v2-mode
```

7. Finally, to enable pruning, use this command:

```
Switch (config)# vtp pruning
```

The remainder of the configuration is identical to the steps outlined earlier. You must configure both the access ports and trunk ports, create the VLANs, and assign ports to them. By using VTP, however, configuration will be much easier, and it will be easier to make changes when necessary.

Troubleshooting VLANs

VLAN troubleshooting is somewhat different than troubleshooting other network problems in that if you have an enterprise-level switch, the manufacturer will have troubleshooting guidelines tailored to the switch. You still need to verify that the pfSense component of your configuration is correct, however, and there are some troubleshooting elements that are common to all brands of switches. We will begin by considering general configuration issues.

General troubleshooting tips

It is good practice to work our way down on the OSI network model, which means starting at the physical layer. You should check your cabling, and if necessary, you should replace suspect cabling with known good cabling. Having a working timedomain reflectometer, which can be used to locate discontinuities in a network cable, can be helpful in checking cabling.

The next step is to make sure that the ports are functioning. Even if they are physically functional, the layer 2 protocol (data link layer) may not be running on the ports you are using. On a Cisco switch, you can use the `no shutdown` command to restart a disabled port. You might also have a speed mismatch between the switch and the router; for example, the switch may be 1 Gbps, while the router might be 100 Mbps. For this reason, it is generally a good idea to have auto-negotiation set on both sides.

Verifying switch configuration

Once you have confirmed that you have physical connectivity, that the ports are enabled, and the port configuration is correct, you should confirm the following:

- Trunk ports are configured correctly and there is at least one connection between the trunk ports and the router. If you have a Cisco switch and are using DTP, you may want to switch to static port configuration until you confirm that the trunk ports are working correctly.
- Access ports are configured correctly and the nodes are connected to ports that are assigned to the VLANs to which they should belong.
- VLANs have been set up correctly and have been assigned VLAN IDs that correspond to the VLAN IDs assigned in pfSense.
- The correct encapsulation format is being used (for VLANs in pfSense, it should be 802.1Q encapsulation).

There are aspects of switch configuration that are peculiar to different brands and models of switches, so you will want to consult any documentation the switch manufacturer has provided. Doing a web search to see if there are any issues specific to your switch may be helpful. Cisco switches have copious amounts of documentation, and administration of these switches is a topic too involved to be fully addressed here. If you want to pursue it, though, there are books, tutorials, and even professional certifications you can obtain to demonstrate your proficiency in Cisco switch configuration.

Trunk port configuration is relatively easy. You need at least one trunk port per switch (some switches assign trunk ports in pairs), and these ports will be available for connections to the router and to other switches. With some switches, the trunk port configuration can be done after the VLAN is configured; in other cases, setting up the trunk ports is a prerequisite to setting up a VLAN. You should confirm that the VLAN is active on the trunk, and that packets from the VLAN are allowed on the trunk.

Configuring access ports should be simple as well. You need to assign the correct VLANs to the ports. In addition, you need to have the correct settings for VLAN tagging. Keep in mind that packets entering the access ports should be untagged – inbound packets should be ordinary Ethernet frames, unless they are double-tagged – whereas ports leaving the trunk ports should be tagged, so the router and switch know to which VLAN the packet belongs.

Another configuration element to consider is the PVID, which is the default VLAN ID for a port. Some managed switches require the PVID to be set in order for VLANs to work at all. If you cannot get your VLAN to work, and you have verified physical connectivity, you may try configuring the PVID for the ports you are using. The PVID settings for the access ports should mirror the access port VLAN assignments you made when you initially configured the VLAN on the switch.

Verifying pfSense configuration

Once you have confirmed that the switch is configured properly, you should log in to pfSense and confirm that pfSense's VLAN configuration is correct. First, go to **Interfaces** | **(assign)**, click on the **VLANs** tab, and confirm that the VLAN IDs for the created VLANs correspond to the VLAN IDs configured on the switch or switches. Then, click on the **Interface assignments** tab and confirm that the VLAN IDs are assigned to the correct interfaces.

If you are using DHCP or DHCPv6, you should confirm that the DHCP/DHCPv6 server is running on the VLAN interfaces and that they are configured correctly. If you have any doubts, you could try a static IP configuration on one of your nodes and see if you are able to access the VLAN (just remember to choose an IP address outside of the range of addresses assigned by the DHCP server). If you are using DHCPv6 and you have any doubts as to the IPv6 compatibility of either your switch or operating system, you might want to try DHCP first.

You may have a situation in which nodes can connect to the VLAN, but have no internet connectivity and may not be able to access other subnets at all. Keep in mind that VLANs, like traditional networks, need to be configured so that they have access to other networks. Other than the LAN, for which pfSense creates a default **allow LAN to any rule**, the default for any newly created network is to have all access to other networks blocked. Therefore, you must go to **Firewall** | **Rules** and create a rule to allow the VLAN to access the WAN interface. As mentioned earlier, an easy way of doing this is to use the rule **Copy** option and change a rule for another interface by changing the **Interface** and **Source** fields to match the VLAN for which you want to create the rule.

The default setting for NAT in pfSense is for automatic outbound rule generation. If you are in this mode of NAT rule configuration, the NAT outbound rules are created automatically and you don't have to configure any NAT rules. If you are using manual outbound rule generation, however, you will have to create rules for each of the VLANs you have created. You may be using manual outbound rule generation if you had to create outbound NAT rules in order to connect to a VPN server, so if you subscribe to a VPN service, you should check to make sure there are outbound NAT rules for your VLANs. You can do this by navigating to **Firewall** | **NAT**, clicking on the **Outbound** tab, and reviewing the rules there. One of the ways to avoid having to manually create rules is to utilize hybrid rule generation mode, in which pfSense still automatically generate rules, but you can also have manually created rules. To do this, select the **Hybrid Outbound NAT rule generation** radio button on the **NAT Outbound** tab and press the **Save** button below the radio buttons.

Here is a VLAN troubleshooting table that covers some of the common VLAN communication issues:

Problem	**Possible cause**	**Solution**
Node not able to communicate with other nodes on the same VLAN and the same switch	Possible cable fault or switch hardware failure; possible switch configuration error or misconfiguration on one or more nodes	Confirm cabling (possibly replacing cabling with known good cabling); confirm that the switch is functioning and configured properly
Nodes able to communicate with nodes on the same VLAN and switch, but not with nodes on the same VLAN/different switches	Possible cable fault; possible trunk port misconfiguration	Confirm cabling; check trunk port configuration on switches connected to affected nodes

Nodes able to communicate with nodes on the same VLAN, but cannot access the internet or other local networks	Rules to allow VLAN traffic not created or were created improperly	Confirm that pass-through rules have been created for the VLAN; confirm that outbound NAT rules have been created
Node is on the wrong VLAN	Node is connected to the wrong port or port is misconfigured	Confirm that the node is connected to the correct port and that the port has been configured correctly

Summary

In this chapter, we covered basic VLAN concepts while also considering two examples in which it would be advantageous to implement VLANs. We then covered the configuration of that example network, both in pfSense and in the switch itself. Finally, we covered VLAN troubleshooting, and walked through a hypothetical VLAN problem and how to solve it.

In the next chapter, we will cover pfSense as a firewall, which is one of the core functions of pfSense. The chapter will cover rule creation, NAT, scheduling, aliases, and virtual IPs. Traffic shaping, which is also part of pfSense's firewall functionality, gets its own chapter, and will be covered in `Chapter 5`, *Using pfSense as a Firewall*.

Questions

Answer the following questions:

1. What is the IEEE standard for VLAN tagging?
2. What are the minimum and maximum ID numbers for VLAN tags?
3. Name two methods used for VLAN hopping.
4. What should the priority code point (PCP) field be set to in order to ensure best effort treatment?
5. What is the main advantage of QinQ VLAN tagging?
6. Identify two advantages of using link aggregation.
7. What firewall rules does pfSense automatically create for an optional (such as OPT1) interface?
8. Identify two types of ports that must be configured on the switch before VLAN configuration is complete.
9. What is the default VLAN ID for a port called?
10. Identify a method of configuring VLANs on a Cisco switch.

4
Using pfSense as a Firewall

In computing, a firewall can mean one of two things—it can refer to a network appliance that has, as one of its functions, the ability to filter incoming and outgoing traffic (hardware) or a service running on a computer that has the ability to filter traffic (software). In this chapter, we will be using the latter sense of the term. We will be focused primarily on the ability to use pfSense as a means of filtering traffic on your network, which is likely to be one of the primary functions pfSense's performs on your network, unless you have a dedicated firewall appliance.

In previous chapters, we couldn't avoid talking about firewall rules, and in this chapter we will cover firewall rules and rule methodology in greater depth. We will also cover several services that are part of pfSense's core firewall functionality, such as aliases and scheduling.

Completing this chapter should enable you to master the following topics:

- Firewall fundamentals
- Firewall best practices
- Firewall rules and methodology
- Scheduling
- Aliases
- Virtual IPs
- Troubleshooting firewall rules

Technical requirements

There are no additional technical requirements for this chapter. A working pfSense firewall with at least a WAN and LAN interface (the WAN interface should provide internet access, so your internet connection should be somewhere upstream from it) and at least one node on the LAN network should be enough to work through the examples in this chapter. Working through the examples and seeing the results are useful in reinforcing the concepts learned in this chapter.

An example network

It often helps to use concrete examples to help illustrate concepts, so once again we will imagine a hypothetical network in order to understand how we would go about configuring firewall rules for a specific environment. Imagine a network with four subnets: SALES, MARKETING, DEVELOPERS, and a DMZ, and with the following requirements:

All subnets should be allowed to access the internet, subject to the restrictions outlined as follows:

- SALES should not be able to talk to MARKETING and DEVELOPERS; MARKETING should not be able to talk to SALES and DEVELOPERS; DEVELOPERS should not be able to talk to SALES and MARKETING.
- SALES, MARKETING and DEVELOPERS should be able to talk to the DMZ, but the DMZ should not be able to talk to any local subnets (other than DMZ).
- SALES and MARKETING share a printer that is on the MARKETING subnet, so SALES should have access to that printer, but not any other nodes on MARKETING.
- Developers waste too much time on recode, so `https://recode.net/` should be blocked on the DEVELOPERS subnet, although access should be allowed during lunch hour (Noon – 1 P.M.).
- The company wants to set up an FTP server for customers, which is to be placed on the DMZ subnet. For the FTP server to be accessible via the internet, access to port `21` must be allowed and traffic to port `21` must be forwarded to the FTP server.

As you might imagine, these requirements will figure prominently in what firewall/NAT rules we will implement. We can tentatively diagram our network in the following way:

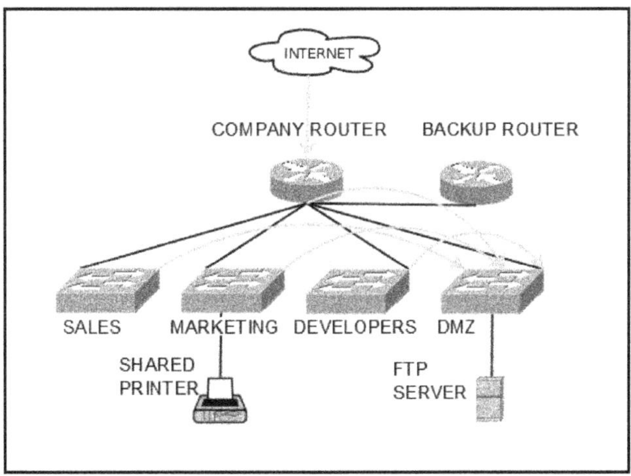

Network diagram for the example network, showing what traffic is allowed to pass

pfSense's firewall capabilities are more than enough to meet the requirements of our network. We will revisit this scenario in the next two chapters.

Firewall fundamentals

The fundamental purpose of a firewall is to establish a barrier between trusted internal networks and untrusted external networks. We may sometimes also refer to personal firewalls, which are firewalls placed on individual nodes, primarily to filter outgoing traffic. All networking firewalls have the ability to perform packet filtering, which is the ability to inspect packets and determine if they conform to the packet filter's filtering rules. If they do not match the rules, the packets will be dropped.

pfSense includes the following explicit rules:

- On the WAN interface, all RFC 1918 networks (private networks) and bogon networks (those not assigned by the IANA) are blocked.
- On the LAN interface, there are two *allow LAN to any* rules, one for IPv4 traffic and one for IPv6 networks. These rules allow users on the LAN network to access all other networks.

All other traffic by default is blocked, unless another rule allows it to pass. This includes traffic on other networks we create, which will not have the default rules the LAN interface does when it is created—therefore, if we want traffic to pass on these networks, we must create the rules ourselves. However, if a user behind the firewall requests a resource that resides on the other side of the firewall (for example, a web page), return traffic to send back that resource is allowed (in other words, pfSense is a stateful firewall – more on that later).

In pfSense, rules are evaluated on a top-down basis. Thus, if you read the ruleset (the list of rules) from the top to bottom, the first rule that matches the packet will be applied, and the remainder of the ruleset will not be applied for that packet. As a result, the order in which rules are placed within a list is significant, and the most permissive rules should be placed at the bottom of the list.

pfSense is a stateful firewall, which means that it records all packets passing through it, and determines whether the packet is part of a new connection, part of an existing connection, or neither of these. If the packet is part of an existing connection, the reply traffic is automatically allowed through the firewall. This is the case even if the packet uses a different protocol than the original connection, such as ICMP control packets. This is known as **stateful packet inspection**.

While stateful packet inspection has been an integral part of almost all firewalls since the early 1990s, it comes with a downside. Each connection represents a state, and each state requires an entry in the firewall's state table. In pfSense, each state requires about 1 KB of memory. The state table has a maximum size, which can be set under **System** | **Advanced** and clicking on the **Firewall & NAT** tab (**Firewall Maximum States**, which sets the maximum number of connections, and **Firewall Maximum Table Entries**, which sets the maximum number of entries, including entries for everything that creates entries, such as proxy servers, are the relevant settings here). If the number of connections exceeds **Firewall Maximum States**, then unpredictable behavior will occur, such as connections being dropped. This creates a potential attack vector, as some DoS attacks are based on bombarding the firewall with so many fake connection packets that the state table becomes overwhelmed, and starts dropping connections and preventing new connections from being made.

In addition, stateful firewalls raise the possibility that the host behind the firewall could be tricked into making outside connections. The return traffic from these connections then becomes a security vulnerability. The only way to defeat these exploits is to audit software running on your network. Also, protocol dissectors in stateful firewalls have had known security issues, highlighting the importance of keeping your firewall software up to date.

The two basic types of packet filtering are ingress filtering, which blocks traffic coming into your network from the internet, and egress filtering, which filters traffic initiated within your network whose destination is either the internet or another interface/subnet on your local network. It is easy to see why you would want to have ingress filtering, as we tend to want to protect our networks from nefarious forces outside of our networks. In fact, the default setting for pfSense is to block all incoming traffic, and there are no allow rules on the WAN interface by default (although as mentioned earlier, replies to connections already allowed by pfSense are allowed through the firewall). It is not as easy to see why egress filtering is necessary, as we tend to assume that all other things being equal, our local networks can be trusted.

There are, however, valid reasons for employing egress filtering. In spite of your best efforts, it is possible that malware may find its way onto your local network, and if you do not have some form of egress filtering, this malware will be able to phone home. The objectives of the malware may differ: the goal may be to send data back to a location controlled by the malware writer. The goal may be to use your computer as a bot which the malware writer controls for some purpose (for example, to send spam). It is also possible that compromising your network's security is the ultimate goal of the malware. Many of these programs use commonly allowed ports (for example, port `80`, the default HTTP port) to circumvent egress filtering, but many do not. If you block port `6667`, which is the default IRC port, you can cripple many bots that rely on IRC to function. Whatever the purpose is of the malware, lack of egress filtering will allow malware that is already running on your local network to achieve its purpose. Moreover, any reply traffic to the malware will also be allowed through the firewall. Thus, lack of egress filtering can result in harm being done to our networks.

Lack of egress filtering can also harm networks beyond our control. If malware or another party gains access to your local network, then your network can be used as a springboard to launch attacks on other networks. This includes attacks that involve IP spoofing, such DDoS attacks, or spam or phishing campaigns. This can become especially problematic if you have several connections to the internet. If you are running a DNS server on your network, someone might use it to host the zone data for a malicious domain. In short, you could unwittingly be an accomplice to criminal activities, which is definitely something we want to avoid doing.

Although in most cases, egress filtering will only minimize damage done once a network is compromised, in some cases it can prevent a network from being compromised at all. Some malware requires outbound access in order to succeed at all, and by using egress filtering judiciously, you can stop it in its tracks. The **Code Red** worm is a good example of this, and any malware that requires downloading a file from an external site controlled by the malware writer can be stopped in such a manner.

Another reason for employing egress filtering is to prevent use of unauthorized software on our own network. Many peer-to-peer programs use atypical ports, which can easily be blocked via egress filtering. Some of these programs have become more sophisticated and will hop from port to port until they find one they can use, but by blocking all ports except those which are essential, we can minimize the use of these programs. In addition, egress filtering can, in many cases, prevent users from using VPN software, which otherwise could be used to bypass firewall rules and access unauthorized sites.

Finally, egress filtering can be used to prevent traffic from passing through your firewall that should never have outbound access. SNMP traffic on ports `161` and `162` come to mind; not only should SMTP traffic never pass through to the internet, but allowing it to do so could compromise the security of your network by revealing information about what exists behind your firewall. You may also consider blocking DHCP traffic on ports `67` and `68` and SQL queries on port `118`.

Firewall best practices

From these fundamental principles, we can distil a set of best practices for implementing our firewall. Some of these practices are fairly obvious; some may not be quite so obvious:

- When you create your firewall rules, the principle of least privilege should apply. In many cases, firewall rules have been too permissive. You should try to avoid creating pass-through rules which have *any* in the destination field, or at least limit the range of ports to which these rules apply. pfSense blocks all network traffic by default, and you'll want to take advantage of that.
- You should periodically check your firewall rules and delete rules that are out of date. For example, in our example network, we had a printer on the MARKETING subnet that was to be shared and therefore a firewall rule would have to be created granting access to this printer. If the printer is subsequently decommissioned or moved to another subnet, then the rule granting access to the printer's IP address should be removed. In a corporate environment, finding out what rules should be removed may require network admins being proactive, as different departments may not make an effort to communicate this information. Still, it is an important practice, as deleting unnecessary firewall rules eliminates potential attack vectors.

- An important corollary to these two practices is that all firewall rule changes should be documented. Even if you remember why a rule change was made, others may not remember, especially if the rule change was made in response to an emergency. Documenting rule changes makes firewall management easier and can be helpful in a troubleshooting scenario.
- Firewall rules should be backed up on a regular basis. In a corporate environment, such backups should be maintained offsite. Such backups may prove to be of value if you ever have to recover from a firewall crash or some other catastrophe.
- You should create your rules in a manner that makes them consistent with your organizations written security policy, and when you are done creating them, you should review them to make sure they are consistent with such policy.
- Eliminate redundant and unnecessary firewall rules, and try to keep your ruleset as simple as possible.
- Patch the firewall with the latest updates on a regular basis.
- You should limit the number of applications running on the firewall in order to maximize CPU cycles and increase network throughput. Any applications that can be run on a dedicated machine (for example, a proxy server) should be moved to another system, either behind or in front of the firewall.
- It's a good idea to perform regular security tests on your firewall; new exploits are being found and the firewall should be tested on a regular basis. This should include testing every interface on both sides of the firewall.
- If your organization is required to comply with the **Payment Card Industry Data Security Standard** (**PCI DSS**), you will want to review your policies to make sure you are in compliance with this standard. For example, PCI requirement 1.1.6 requires a complete firewall review every six months. PCI DSS is constantly being updated – as of this writing, the latest version is 3.2, released in April 2016 – so you need to review the latest version of the standard to see if there are any new requirements that affect firewall implementation.
- Enable logging, but only if you are going to actually look at the logs; otherwise, maintaining logs is a waste of both disk space and CPU usage.
- If you have remote users, you should require that they run a personal firewall and/or intrusion detection system on their computer.
- You may also consider running a remote syslog server for logging, to make it more difficult for potential hackers to modify the log files and thus cover their tracks.

Obviously, some of these suggestions may be overkill for a home or SOHO user, so you'll have to decide how many of these suggestions you implement, but avoiding overly permissive rules, deleting outdated rules, and documenting rule changes are definitely good practices that we will want to employ even on home networks. Implementation of the other suggestions will depend on your security needs and level of paranoia.

Best practices for ingress filtering

Based on what we have already covered, we can articulate some best practices for ingress filtering. We want the default (block all traffic) to stand. We need to allow access to ports and nodes for certain services that we are providing. For example, in our example network, we are operating an FTP server. This requires leaving port `21` open on the FTP server's network. In addition, we want to use ingress filtering as a means of preventing denial of service attacks. The best practices for ingress filtering are described in the following **Internet Engineering Task Force** (**IETF**) documents:

- **Network ingress filtering:** Defeating DoS attacks which employ IP source address spoofing (**`https://tools.ietf.org/html/bcp38`**)
- **Ingress filtering for multihomed networks**: Discusses different strategies for ensuring that incoming packets are from the networks from which they claim to originate, both in general and from a multihomed (meaning the network has multiple points of access to the internet) perspective (**`https://tools.ietf.org/html/bcp84`**)

The aforementioned documents are not particularly long, and reading them in their entirety can be instructive. However, the most pertinent findings of these documents are as follows:

- Traffic which employs IP spoofing should be blocked by firewalls. Ingress filters should thus be configured to only allow traffic from valid source addresses.
- Automatic filtering should be used on remote access servers. If, for example, a user connects to a remote access server through an ISP, the only valid IP address for traffic from that user is the IP address assigned by the ISP.
- If DHCP or BOOTP is used, provision must be made on the relay agent for packets with a source IP address of `0.0.0.0` and a destination IP address of `255.255.255.255.`
- BCP 84 is aimed at ISPs and edge network operators, and describes different methods of **reverse path forwarding** (**RPF**) which can be used to thwart DDoS attacks. If RPF is employed, the router will check the source IP address of a packet, which will only be forwarded if they come from the router's best route to the source of the packet. Otherwise, the packet will be dropped.

Best practices for egress filtering

If you are configuring a home network or SOHO network, determining your egress filtering requirements begins with compiling a list of services to which you need access (this might include such services as DNS, SMTP, POP and/or IMAP, NTP, and HTTP/HTTPS). If you are configuring a corporate network, you probably want to begin by consulting your organization's security policy. You may also want to consult with those in charge of network security and perhaps other stakeholders within the organization.

You should make a list of remote servers that services running on your network have to access, and allow them through the filter. For example, if you are running a DNS server, it will undoubtedly have to communicate with other DNS servers. You may find it helpful to organize your interfaces into interface groups, with access being granted based on the interface group settings.

As mentioned previously, egress filtering should begin with a *deny all* outbound policy. From here, add access for the services identified when you first compiled a list of services. Then add rules that allow the admins access to network/security systems they need to get to in order to do their jobs. Finally, you should add rules to allow any servers you operate on your local network to communicate with externally hosted services.

You should also use your egress filtering policy to prevent IP spoofing. This means only allowing source addresses from the IP addresses you assign to nodes on your local networks to pass through the firewall. This will include addresses assigned via DHCP or statically, and subnets routed to the internet through the firewall, including VPN clients (if VPN is enabled). If you are only using a portion of the subnet to assign addresses (for example, you have `172.16.0.0` as one of your networks, and you are only using `172.16.1.0`), then allow only the addresses you are actually using and not the rest of the subnet.

You should block all connections from internal servers or workgroups that have no business establishing connections with external servers. Also, you should consult lists such as those maintained by The Spamhaus Project to determine which domains and IPs are used by spammers and botnets and therefore should be blocked. Spamhaus's **Don't Route or Peer** (**DROP**) List is particularly helpful, as it identifies IP blocks that have been hijacked or are otherwise totally controlled by spammers, and therefore should be blocked.

Creating and editing firewall rules

Now that we have covered some basic firewall principles, we can begin our firewall configuration with the following steps:

1. To create and/or edit firewall rules, log in to pfSense and navigate to **Firewall | Rules**. This should present you with a list of interfaces across the top of the page; you can see the ruleset for each interface by clicking on its name (initially, you will see the ruleset for the **WAN** interface, as shown):

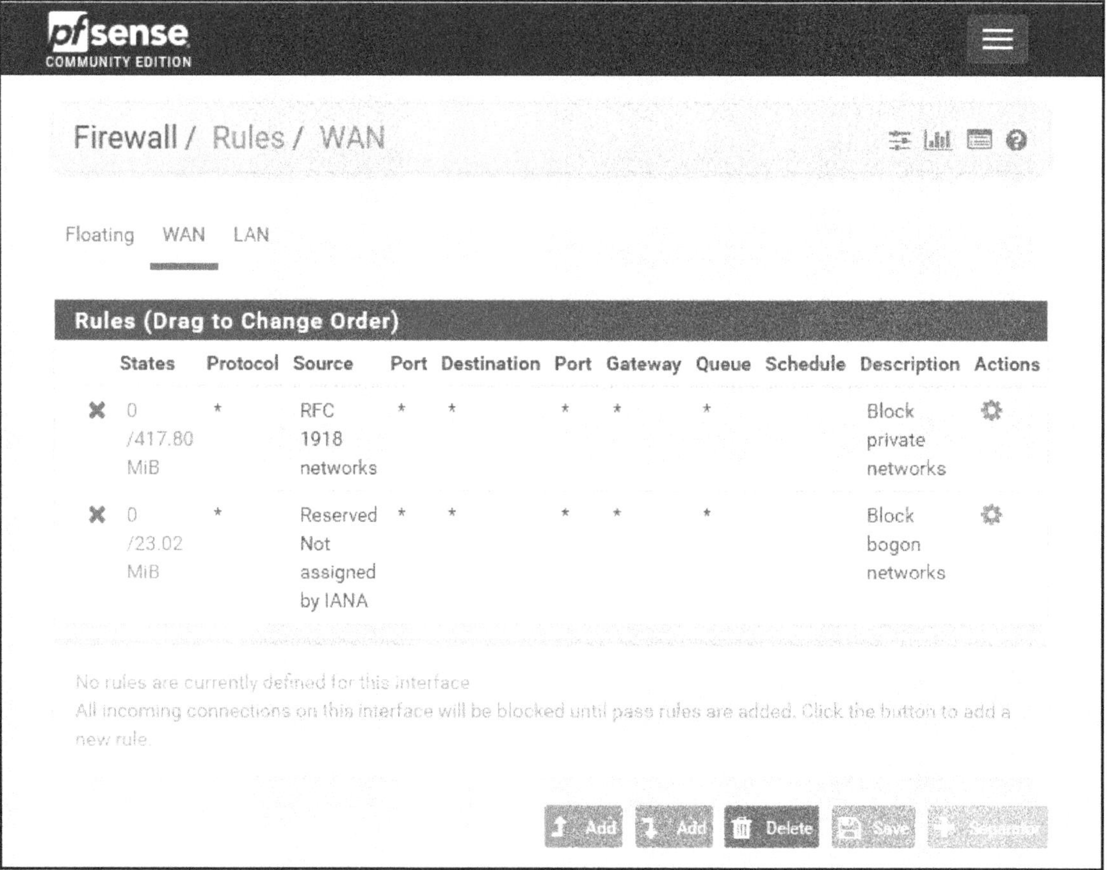

2. Usually, we will click on the tab for the interface for which we want to credit/edit rules, although this is technically unnecessary, since we can create rules for any interface from any tab—the rule edit page provides an **Interface** drop-down box that allows us to choose the interface to which the rule applies.

3. Click on the interface for which you want to add a rule and use one of the two **Add** buttons at the bottom of the page to create a rule.
4. The **Add** button with the up arrow will place the newly created rule at the top of the table, while the **Add** button with the down arrow will place the newly created rule at the bottom of the table.
5. Another helpful option is to use the **Copy** button, which can be seen on the right side of a table listing of a current rule. The **Copy** button (represented by an icon showing two sheets of paper) allows you to create a new rule based on an existing rule. When you press the **Copy** button, you will generate a new rule in which all the options are initially identical to the old rule.
6. Choosing any of the options outlined earlier will launch the **Edit** page for firewall rules, as shown:

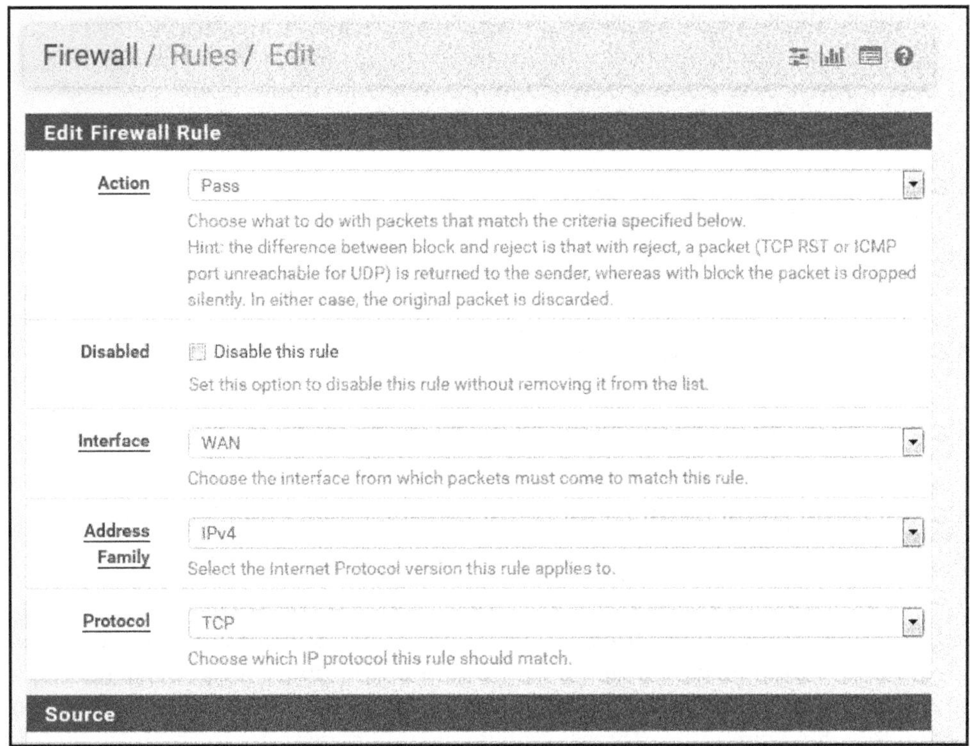
Firewall / Rules / Edit
Edit Firewall Rule
Action
Pass
Choose what to do with packets that match the criteria specified below.
Hint: the difference between block and reject is that with reject, a packet (TCP RST or ICMP port unreachable for UDP) is returned to the sender, whereas with block the packet is dropped silently. In either case, the original packet is discarded.
Disabled
Disable this rule
Set this option to disable this rule without removing it from the list.
Interface
WAN
Choose the interface from which packets must come to match this rule.
Address Family
IPv4
Select the Internet Protocol version this rule applies to.
Protocol
TCP
Choose which IP protocol this rule should match.
Source

The first section of the page is **Edit Firewall Rule**, and the first option is the **Action** drop-down box, which allows you to select what happens to packets that meet the rule criteria. The options for the rule are as follows:

- **Pass**: Let the traffic pass
- **Block**: The packet is dropped silently
- **Reject**: The packet is returned to the sender with a TCP RST or ICMP port unreachable message (TCP RST is for TCP traffic, ICMP port unreachable is for UDP traffic)

There is a split of authority on whether the best practice is to block traffic or reject it. The advantage of **Reject**, of course, is that the sender knows right away that access to the resource is not allowed, whereas with **Block**, the connection eventually times out. Generally, **Block** is a good choice if you do not want the user to know if a resource exists, since the result to the end user is identical to the result that would occur if a resource does not exist or is offline. For example, if a user tries to access your FTP server and access is prevented by a **Block** rule, the connection will time out and if the user is a hacker without knowledge of our network, the hacker may conclude that there's no FTP server there.

This **Disabled** checkbox, if checked, will result in the rule being disabled without removing it from the ruleset. The **Interface** drop-down box allows you to select the interface to which this rule applies (the interface from which packets must come in on for the rule to apply). The **Address Family** drop-down box lets you select which Internet Protocol version to which the rule applies: the choices are **IPv4**, **IPv6**, or both (**IPv4+IPv6**). Finally, the **Protocol** drop-down box allows you to select which Internet Protocol the rule should match. You should try to avoid using the any option here, and only allow the protocol or protocols you need to allow.

Another way to disable a rule is to click on the **No** symbol on the right side of the row of the rule you wish to disable in the **Rules** table. The **No** symbol icon will then become a checked checkbox icon, which you can then click to enable the rule.

The next section of the page is **Source**, which allows you to specify where the packets must originate if they are to match the rule. In the **Source** drop-down box, you can specify several options: **any** will result in any packet on the interface matching the rule; **Single host or alias** enables you to enter a single IP address or alias (we will cover how to create an alias later in the chapter). **Network** allows you to enter a subnet (if you select it, you must enter the network portion of the address and the CIDR). You can also select **PPPoE clients** (PPPoE stands for Point-to-Point over Ethernet) or **L2TP clients** (L2TP stands for Layer 2 Tunneling Protocol).

The remaining options allow you to select as the source, either an entire interface you previously created (for example, LAN) or an address on that interface. The **Invert match** checkbox, if checked, will result in the rule being applied to the opposite of what is selected for the source. For example, if you select **LAN net** and check **Invert match**, the rule will apply to everything but the **LAN net**. Clicking on the **Show advanced** button will reveal the **Source port range** options. You can select ports from the drop-down boxes or type them directly into the edit boxes.

The **Destination** section allows you to select the destination the packets must match for the rule to apply. It mirrors the **Source** section, with the exception of the fact that the **Destination port range** field is always visible and showing/hiding this option is not possible. As with **Source**, you can invert the match.

The next section is called **Extra Options**. The **Log** checkbox, if checked, will log packets that are handled by the rule. Usually you won't want to turn on logging for rules, since that's a good way to use up all remaining disk space, but if you need to log packets for an individual rule, you can do it here. You can also enter a brief description for future reference. Clicking on the **Advanced options** button will show the **Advanced Options** section of the page.

The **Source OS** drop-down box allows you to select the operating system from which the packets must come, if the rule is to be applied. There are many options (including **Any**), although there does not seem to be options for newer versions of Windows (there are no options for Windows 7, 8 , or 10, although there are options for older versions as well as a generic **Windows** option). The **Diffserv Code Point** option allows you to apply the rule only to certain **Diffserv Code Point** values; different Diffserv values are used for traffic filtering or queue assignments. Traffic shaping must be enabled for this option to work.

By default, pfSense blocks packets with IP options set; checking the **Allow IP options** checkbox allows these packets to pass. The **Disable reply-to** checkbox is designed for setups in which a non-WAN interface is the gateway for part of our network. If this is the case, reply-to traffic for a packet will be routed through the defined gateway rather than through the interface on which the packet arrived. This can result in the gateway forwarding the packet to the firewall, and the firewall sending it back, resulting in an eventual timeout. In cases such as this, we should enable the **Disable reply-to** option.

The **Tag** edit box allows you to mark a packet matching the rule. You can then use the *mark to match on NAT and/or filter* rules. The next option, **Tagged**, allows you to match a packet if a mark was placed on it by another rule.

The following options may be of some help in mitigating a DoS attack. **Max. states** defines the maximum number of state entries the rule can create, while **Max. src nodes** defines the maximum number of unique source hosts. **Max. connections** defines the maximum number of established connections per host. It only works on TCP (you have to have a connection for this rule to apply, so obviously it would not work with a connectionless protocol such as UDP). **Max. src. States** sets the maximum number of state entries per host. **Max. src. Conn. Rate** sets the maximum new connections per host. **Max. src. Conn. Rate** and **Max. src. Conn. Rates** together control the number of connections allowed per host per second(s). The first edit box specifies the number of connections and the second edit box specifies the time interval. For example, setting **Max. src. conn. Rate** to `25` and **Max.src. conn. Rates** to `60` will allow 25 connections per host per minute (60 seconds). Finally, **State timeout** specifies the amount of time before a state entry will expire. Obviously, this can help prevent the state table from filling up, thus potentially thwarting DoS attacks, but if the timeout is set for too short a time, legitimate traffic could be dropped. **Max src. Conn. Rate, Max.src. Conn. Rates,** and **State timeout** only apply to TCP connections.

The next setting, **TCP Flags**, can be used to choose which TCP flags need to be set or cleared in order for the rule to match. Check the flag in the **set** row to require that the flag be set; check the flag in the **out of** row to require that it be cleared. Check the **Any** flags checkbox for the rule to match if any flag is set or cleared.

The **No pfSync** checkbox, if checked, will result in states created by the rule not being synced over pfsync if **Common Address Redundancy Protocol** (**CARP**) is being used. The **State type** drop-down box allows you to choose which type of state tracking mechanism to use. The **Keep** option is the default option, and it works with all protocols. **Sloppy** also works with all protocols. It invokes a less stringent form of state tracking. This can be useful if asymmetric routing is used (like the situation with multiple gateways described earlier). **Synproxy** will automatically proxy incoming TCP connections. This is useful, because if it is invoked, pfSense will not create a new state table entry for a new TCP connection until it receives a **SYN ACK** packet. This will help protect your network from spoofed **SYN** flood attacks. As you probably have guessed, it only works on TCP connections. Finally, **None** results in no state entries being created for this rule.

The **No XMLRPC Sync** checkbox, if checked, will prevent this rule from syncing to other CARP members. Note that this only works between two or more master CARP members; it does not prevent the master from overwriting the rule on a slave CARP member. The **VLAN Prio** option allows you to choose an **802.1p** priority level that must be set for on a VLAN packet for the rule to match. These priority levels, which were discussed in `Chapter 3`, *VLANs*, are represented in the drop-down box as acronyms.

The following table describes each acronym:

Acronym	**Description**
BK	Background
BE	Best Effort
EE	Excellent Effort
CA	Critical Applications
VI	Video with less than 100 ms latency
VO	Voice with less than 10 ms latency
IC	Internetwork Control
NC	Network Control

The **VLAN priority set** drop-down box allows you to choose an **802.1p** priority to apply to the packets that match this rule. The abbreviations in this drop-down box are identical to the ones in the **VLAN Prio** drop-down box.

The **Schedule** drop-down box allows you to apply the rule only during a predefined time range. You can't create the time range on this page; you need to do this from **Firewall** | **Schedules**. The process will be detailed later in this chapter. The **none** option leaves the rule enabled all the time.

The **Gateway** drop-down box allows you to select a gateway for traffic matching the rule. If **default** is selected, then the system routing table is used. Otherwise, the traffic goes out on the selected gateway. This is useful if you want to set up policy-based routing.

The next option is **In/Out pipe**. This allows you to pipe traffic coming from a selected interface (the **In** interface), and send traffic leaving the interface to another interface (the **Out** interface). The **Ackqueue/Queue** option allows you to pipe traffic coming from a specific traffic shaping queue and send the **ACK** traffic to a specific **ack** queue.

When you are finished making changes, click on the **Save** button at the bottom of the page. This will return you to the main **Rules** page.

Floating rules

The first tab on the main **Rules** page is **Floating**, as shown, from which you can create floating firewall rules. These rules are different from other rules in three significant ways:

- They can be applied in either direction, or both directions (in other words, to traffic either leaving or entering an interface).
- They can apply to more than one interface.
- In addition to the **Pass**, **Block** and **Reject** options for **Action**, there is a fourth option called **Match**. If **Match** is selected, the rule will be invoked if the traffic matches the criteria specified by the rule, but the pass/block status of the traffic will not be affected. This option will be used in `Chapter 6`, *Traffic Shaping*, as it provides a means of diverting traffic into different queues:

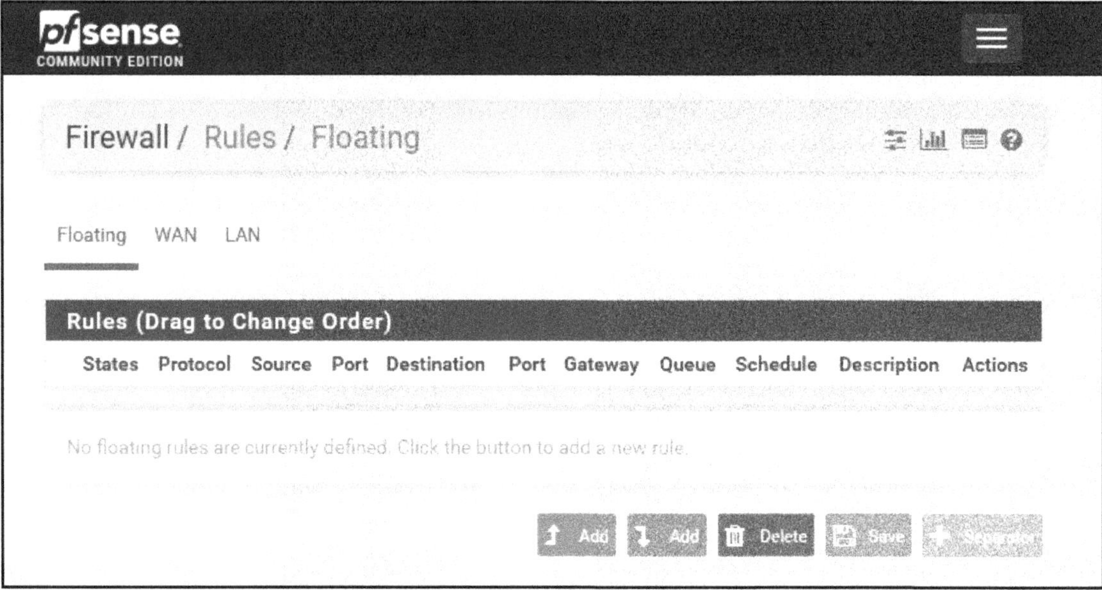

Floating rules can be created by clicking on the **Floating** tab on the **Rules** page and clicking on one of the **Add** buttons. The options are similar to those in the conventional rule **Edit** page, with the following exceptions:

- The **Quick** checkbox, if checked, will cause pfSense to apply the rule to packets matching the rule and pfSense will not attempt to filter the packets against any other rules
- In the **Interface** list box, more than one interface may be selected
- In the **Direction** drop-down box, you can choose to apply the rule to traffic coming into the interface (**in**), traffic leaving the interface (**out**), or both (**any**)

The **Quick** option is a significant one, and deserves further explanation. If the **Quick** option is enabled for a floating rule, then the rule will be enforced before any of the rules on the interface tabs, and they will be enforced in top-down order. If **Quick** is not enabled for a rule, however, and a rule on one of the interface tabs matches the traffic, the latter will be enforced. A floating rule without **Quick** enabled, therefore, is enforced on a "last match wins" basis – it is enforced only if none of the rules on the interface tabs and none of the rules above it on the **Floating** tab match the traffic first. This is a powerful option: if we need to enforce a rule before all other rules, we can enable **Quick**, whereas if we need to enforce default behavior on more than one interface, we can disable **Quick**.

An easy way to tell if the **Quick** option is enabled is to look at the left side of the rule's entry in the Floating Rules table. The fast forward icon (two adjacent green sideways triangles) indicates that the **Quick** option is enabled for that rule.

Regarding the **Direction** option, it should be noted that non-floating firewall rules are always enforced on traffic that is inbound to an interface. Thus, if we want to create a floating rule that behaves the same way as non-floating rules, we would set **Direction** to `In`. This is useful if you want to create a rule that acts the same as a non-floating rule, but applies to more than one interface. If we need to filter outbound traffic or traffic in both directions, we would select the **out** or **any** option.

Example rules

To illustrate the rule creation process, we will walk through the process by creating three new rules—two non-floating and a floating rule.

Example 1 – block a website

For our first non-floating rule, we will implement a rule blocking developers' access to `https://recode.net/`. The process is relatively simple:

1. We navigate to **Firewall** | **Rules**, and click on the **DEVELOPERS** tab. Then we can click on either **Add** button below the table to add a new rule.
2. On the **Edit** page, we change the **Action** value to **Reject**. For **Interface**, we keep **DEVELOPERS** as the interface from which packets must come in on to match this rule. We can set the **Address Family** field to **IPv4**, **IPv6**, or **IPv4+IPv6**, depending on whether or not our network supports IPv4 addresses, IPv6 addresses, or both. We only need to block TCP traffic, so we leave **Protocol** set to **TCP**.
3. The packets must come from the **DEVELOPERS** subnet for the rule to apply, so we set **Source** to **DEVELOPERS net**. We don't need to set a port range for this rule, so we will not click on the **Show Advanced** button.
4. We must block traffic to `www.recode.net`. A DNS lookup using nslookup returned an IP address of `151.101.21.52`. We set **Destination** to **Single host or alias** in the drop-down box, and in the adjacent edit box, we enter `151.101.21.52` (it's a single IP address, so we do not need to specify a subnet).
5. For **Description**, we type `Block Recode` for future reference. Then we click on the **Save** button. Once we are returned to the main **Rules** page, we need to click on the **Apply Changes** button to reload the firewall rules.

That's all there is to it – nodes on the **DEVELOPERS** subnet should now be blocked from accessing Recode. We still have not created a rule allowing the **DEVELOPERS** net access to other networks, and we need to do that, but if we want to test our new rule, we could copy it to the **LAN** subnet (remembering to change **Interface** to **LAN** and **Source** to **LAN net**). To confirm that the rule works, try accessing Recode with both the rule enabled and then with it disabled. Also, to confirm that the order of rules matters, try placing the new rule both at the beginning and end of the list of rules. If it is at the end of the list, one of the "Allow LAN to any" rules will match the traffic first and our rule will not have its intended effect, but if it is at the beginning of the list, it should work.

This rule could be improved upon—the IP address of recode could change, and perhaps we should have created an alias for the sake of clarity and so that if we copy the rule, we don't have to change the IP address in multiple locations. We will address the creation of aliases later in this chapter.

Example 2 – block all traffic from other networks

In our example network, we wanted to keep the SALES, MARKETING and DEVELOPERS networks separate, so that none of these networks had access to each other (with certain exceptions for shared resources), but all three networks should have access to the DMZ, which does not have access to other local networks. All of these networks should have access to the internet through the WAN interface. We can achieve this by creating two rules on each network:

1. Rules on each interface blocking access to non-DMZ networks.
2. A default rule such as the **Allow LAN to any** rule, for each specific interface.

This ruleset will block all incoming traffic that does not originate on the local network while still allowing access to the internet. We will address the creation of a default allow rule in the next section, but first let's create the block rule:

1. We again navigate to **Firewall | Rules**, and click on the **DEVELOPERS** tab. Then we can click on either **Add** button below the table to add a new rule.
2. On the **Edit** page, we change the **Action** value to **Block.** For **Interface**, we keep **DEVELOPERS** as the interface from which packets must come in on to match this rule. We can set the **Address Family** field to **IPv4**, **IPv6**, or **IPv4+IPv6**, depending on whether or not our network supports IPv4 addresses, IPv6 addresses, or both. We want to block all traffic, so we set the **Protocol** set to **Any**.
3. The packets must come from the **DEVELOPERS** subnet for the rule to apply, so we set **Source** to **DEVELOPERS net.** We don't need to set a port range for this rule, so we will not click on the **Show Advanced** button.
4. We will first create a rule to block access to **SALES**; thus, we set **Destination** to **SALES net**.
5. For the description, we enter something appropriate (for example, `Block access to SALES`) and click on the **Save** button. We also click **Apply Changes** to reload the firewall rules.

Our ruleset will not be complete until we create a rule to block access to **MARKETING** on **DEVELOPERS** and repeat the process on the **SALES** and **MARKETING** networks. Fortunately, this somewhat tedious process can be made easier by clicking on the **Copy** icon to make a copy of the rule and then changing the appropriate fields. Change the **Destination** to **MARKETING net** to finish the ruleset for **DEVELOPERS**, then duplicate these two rules on the other interfaces by copying them and changing **Interface** and **Destination** settings where appropriate. Note that we did not create a rule to block access to the **DMZ** network; we want other networks to have access to it.

Example 3 – the default allow rule

By implementing *Example 2 – block all traffic from other networks*, we have not really accomplished anything yet. We just blocked access to SALES, MARKETING, and DEVELOPERS from other networks, and pfSense blocks inter-network traffic by default anyway. We need to create a default allow rule for each network to make this work. If such a rule is evaluated after the previously created block rule, it will provide access to both the DMZ network and the internet through the WAN interface.

There are two ways to go about this. pfSense automatically creates *Allow LAN to any* rules for the LAN interface, which saves us the trouble of providing the LAN network access to other networks. If you have other subnets, most likely you will want to create similar rules for those interfaces. We could copy the *Allow LAN to any* rules easily enough and just change the **Interface**, **Source**, and **Description** to whatever interface to which we are applying the rule.

We can make the process a little easier, however, if we create a floating rule, because then we can create a single default *Allow X to any* rule where `X` is the interface to which we want the rule to apply. To do this, we follow these steps:

1. We navigate to **Firewall** | **Rules**, and click on the **Floating** tab. Then we can click on either **Add** button below the table to add a new rule.
2. Keep the **Action** set to **Pass**. We want this rule to be evaluated last, so we will also leave the **Quick** option disabled.

3. In the **Interface** list box, select all the interfaces to which you want the rule to apply. Unless you have a specific reason for not applying the rule to an interface, you should select every interface except the **WAN** interface and the **DMZ** interface.

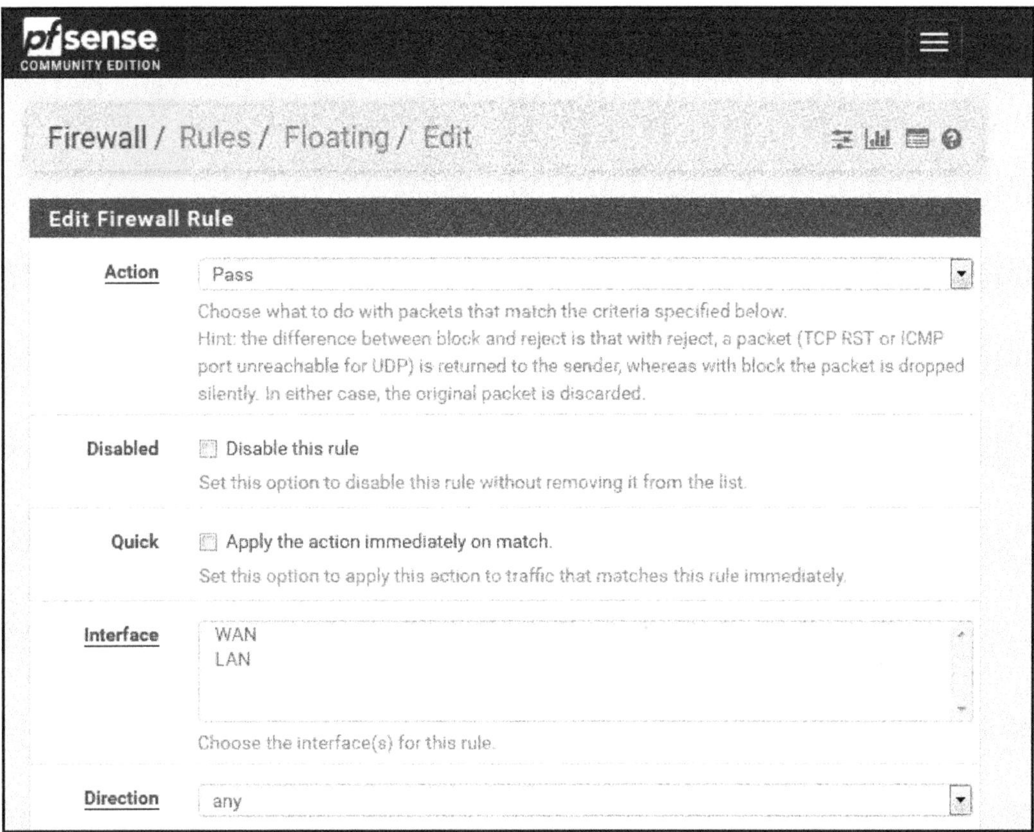

pfsense
COMMUNITY EDITION
Firewall / Rules / Floating / Edit
Edit Firewall Rule
Action
Pass
Choose what to do with packets that match the criteria specified below.
Hint: the difference between block and reject is that with reject, a packet (TCP RST or ICMP port unreachable for UDP) is returned to the sender, whereas with block the packet is dropped silently. In either case, the original packet is discarded.
Disabled
Disable this rule
Set this option to disable this rule without removing it from the list.
Quick
Apply the action immediately on match.
Set this option to apply this action to traffic that matches this rule immediately.
Interface
WAN
LAN
Choose the interface(s) for this rule.
Direction
any

4. We want the **Direction** to match that of rules on the interface tabs, so we select **In**.
5. As was the case in the previous example, we can set the **Address Family** field to **IPv4**, **IPv6**, or **IPv4+IPv6**. We want the default rule to apply to all protocols, so we set **Protocol** to **Any**.

6. **Source** and **Destination** should remain set to **Any**. In the **Description** edit box, enter an appropriate description (for example, `Default allow rule`).
7. Click on the **Save** button, which will return you to the main **Rules** page. Then click on the **Apply Changes** button to reload the firewall rules.

We now have a default allow rule, which also makes the "Allow LAN to any" rules redundant. We can disable these rules for the sake of clarity. If you want to confirm that the rule works, connect to one of the other networks and try to access another network. Then disable the rule and see what happens (taking care not to lock yourself out of the web GUI in the process).

Scheduling

Rules don't have to take effect all the time; we can define time ranges during which the rules apply, and the process is even easier than creating rules. Each schedule can have multiple time ranges, and, once defined, it can be applied to a rule. To get started with scheduling, follow these steps:

1. Navigate to **Firewall** | **Schedules**. There will be a table displaying all the previously created schedule entries; clicking on the **Add** button below the table allows you to create a new entry.
2. The **Edit** page for schedules has two sections: **Schedule Information**, in which you can configure options, and **Configured Ranges**, in which the already defined ranges for this rule appear.
3. You must create at least one time range per schedule, although you can create more.
4. The first option on the page is **Schedule Name**, where you enter the name, which can consist only of letters, numbers, and the underscore character. You may also enter a non-parsed, free-form description in the next field.
5. In the **Month** drop-down box, you can select the month that will appear in the **Date** section.

6. **Time ranges** can consist of individual dates (for example, April 15), or to days of the week (for example, Tuesdays). You can click on an individual date on the calendar to select only that date, or you can click on a weekday header to select all occurrences of that weekday.
   In the **Time** section, you can select a time range for the days selected on the calendar. The fields are **Start Hrs**, **Start Mins**, **Stop Hrs** and **Stop Mins**, and time is in 24-hour time. You can also enter a non-parsed **Time range description**. When you are done defining a time range, you can click on the **Add Time** button. Alternatively, you can click on the **Clear selection** button to clear the selection. Once you click on the **Add Time** button, the time range should appear in the **Configured Ranges** section of the page. You can create additional time ranges by selecting the appropriate dates/days of the week and time ranges, adding a description, and clicking the **Add Time** button again. You can also delete existing ranges by clicking on the **Delete** button to the right of each entry. When you are done configuring time ranges and editing other options, click on the **Save** button at the bottom of the page.

An example schedule entry

To illustrate the process of creating a schedule and using it in a rule, we will create a schedule for lunchtime (Noon – 1 P.M.) and create a rule using this schedule. This will allow us to implement a rule which allows access to Recode only during Noon to 1 P.M. on weekdays. To do this, we perform the following steps:

1. Navigate to **Firewall** | **Schedules**, and click on the **Add** button at the bottom of the page.

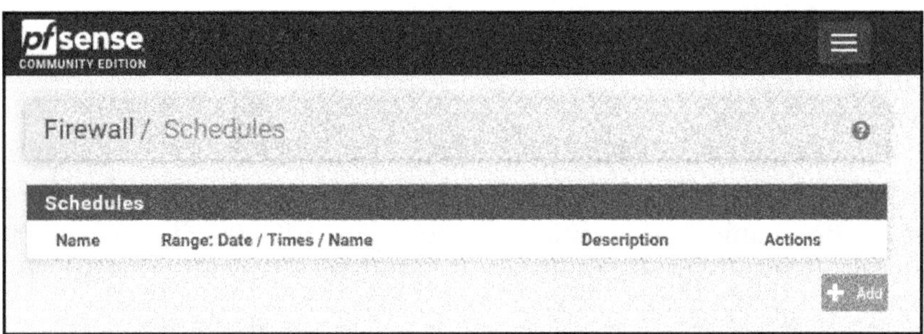

2. Set **Schedule Name** to **LUNCH_TIME** and add a brief description.

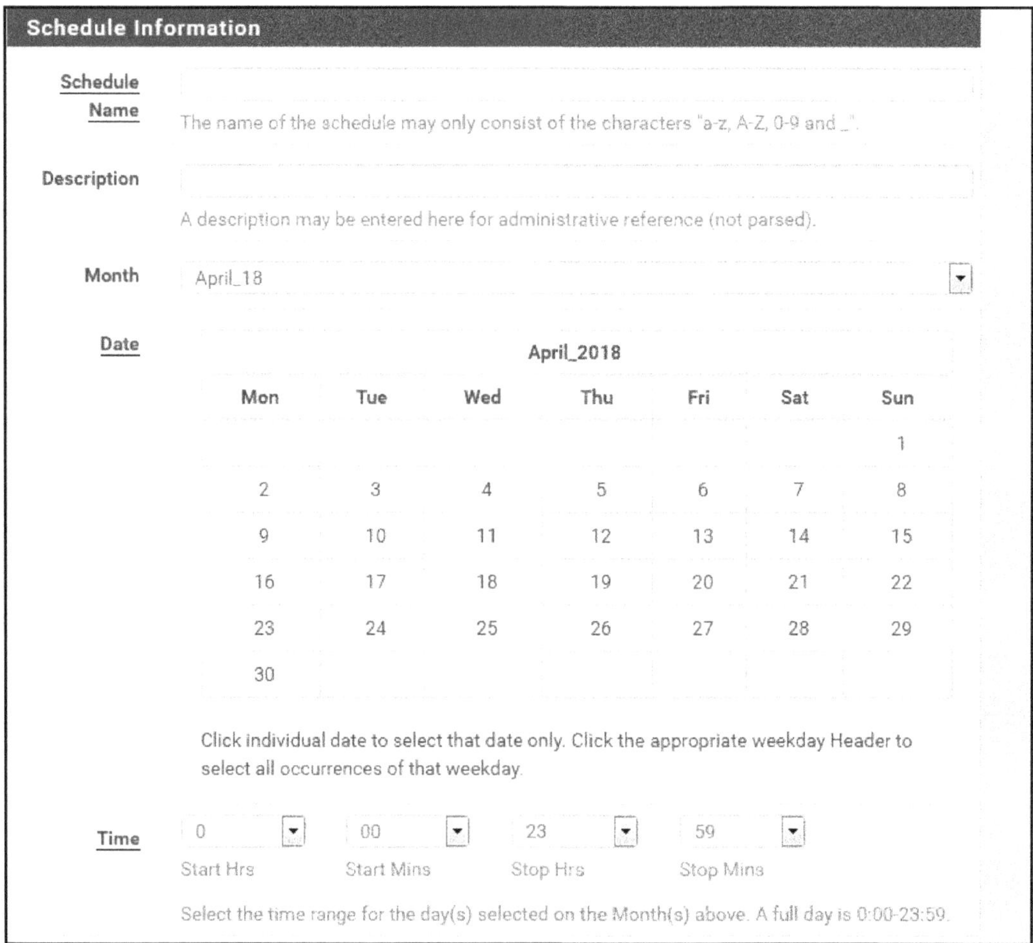

3. On the calendar, select **Mon**, **Tue**, **Wed**, **Thu**, and **Fri** by clicking on the top of each column.
4. Set the time range in the **Time** fields to begin at **12:00** and end at **13:00**. Enter a brief description (for example, `Lunchtime`), and click on the **Add Time** button. Then click on the **Save** button at the bottom of the page.

5. Now that the schedule has been added, we can navigate to **Firewall** | **Rules** and add a rule that utilizes it. We can use the previously created Block Recode rule as a template for the new rule, but instead of blocking access to Recode, we will allow access – but only during lunch hour. Click on the **Copy** icon in the row containing the rule for blocking Recode.
6. Change the **Action** for the new rule to **Pass**. Add an appropriate **Description** (for example, `Allow Recode during lunchtime`).
7. Click on the **Display Advanced** button at the bottom of the page and scroll down the page to the **Schedule** drop-down box. Select **LUNCH_TIME** in this box.
8. To configure scheduling options, we need to click on the **Advanced options** button. Once we do, the advanced options will appear on the page, and we can scroll down to the **Schedule** drop-down box. In this box, we can now select the **LUNCH_TIME** schedule we just created. Then click on the **Save** button at the bottom of the page. Our new rule is now created.
9. On the **DEVELOPERS** tab, you may notice that the new rule is lower in the table than the Block Recode rule. Thus, any traffic to Recode will be matched by the block rule first and the new allow rule will never be invoked. To change this, drag the new rule above the Block Recode rule. Click on the **Save** button at the bottom of the page to save the changes.
10. We still need to apply the rule changes, so click on the **Apply Changes** button at the top of the page.

We now have a rule to allow access to Recode during lunchtime, and it should work. Note that if you hover your mouse over **LUNCH_TIME** in the table, a pop-up window will appear with a description of the rule.

Aliases

Aliases enable you to group ports, hosts, or networks into named entities, which you can then refer to in firewall and NAT rules and traffic shaper configuration. This allows you to create more manageable rules; in addition, changes in IP addresses, ports or networks will not necessitate multiple configuration changes – you may be able to just change an alias.

Not all options available in the pfSense web GUI allow you to use aliases, but you will always know when you can use aliases. An edit box that is alias-friendly will have a red background, and if you start to type the alias name, pfSense's autocomplete functionality can complete the name.

1. To create an alias, navigate to **Firewall** | **Aliases**. The **Aliases** landing page has four separate tabs: **IP**, **Ports**, **URLs**, and **All**.

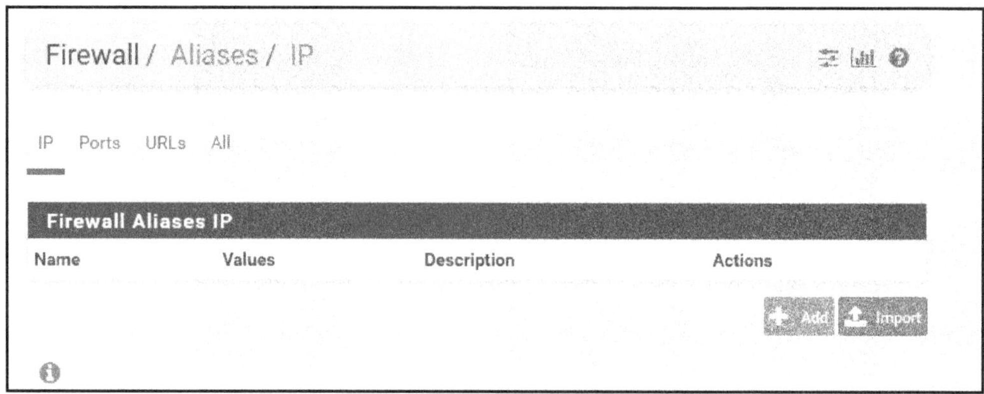

2. Clicking on one of the tabs will show a table with all of the previously created aliases in that category (for example, the **IP** tab displays a table with IP aliases).
3. If you want to create an alias of a specific type, you can click on the corresponding tab and then click the **Add** button below the table.

But selecting the right tab before clicking **Add** is not necessary – you can create an alias for any supported type from any tab, because selecting the corresponding tab before clicking on **Add** only changes the default value in the **Type** drop-down box.

4. Clicking on the **Add** button on any of the tabs will launch the **Aliases / Edit** page.

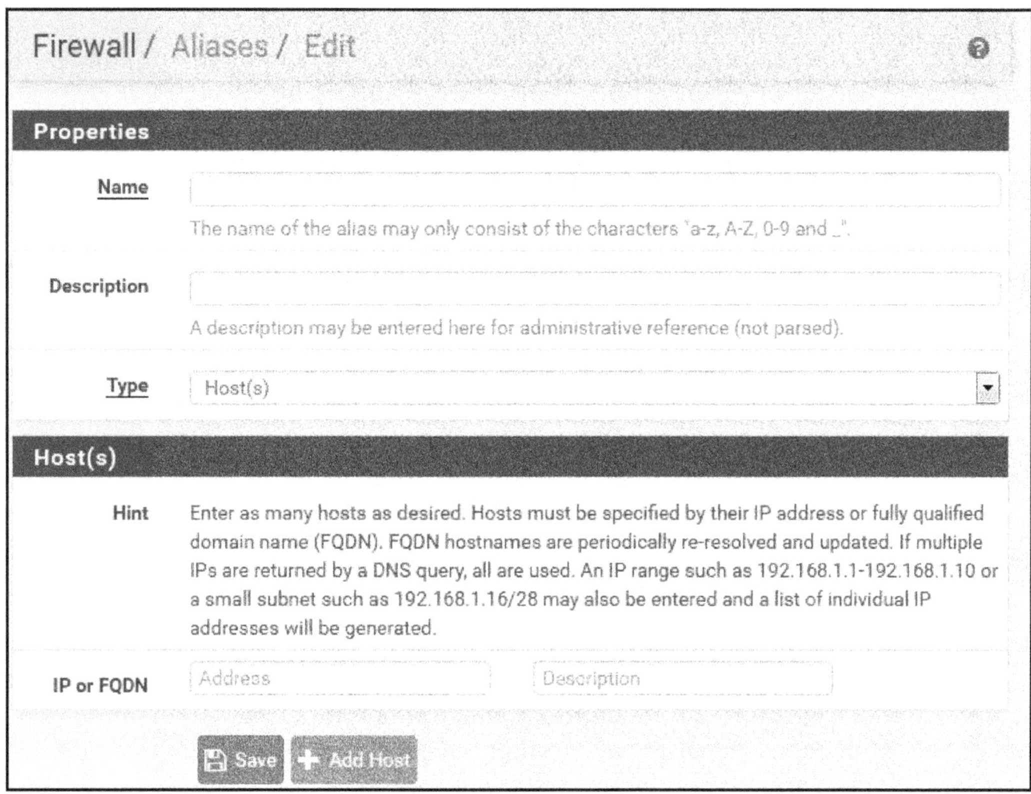
Firewall / Aliases / Edit
Properties
Name
The name of the alias may only consist of the characters "a-z, A-Z, 0-9 and _".
Description
A description may be entered here for administrative reference (not parsed).
Type
Host(s)
Host(s)
Hint
Enter as many hosts as desired. Hosts must be specified by their IP address or fully qualified domain name (FQDN). FQDN hostnames are periodically re-resolved and updated. If multiple IPs are returned by a DNS query, all are used. An IP range such as 192.168.1.1-192.168.1.10 or a small subnet such as 192.168.1.16/28 may also be entered and a list of individual IP addresses will be generated.
IP or FQDN
Address
Description
Save
Add Host

5. There are two sections on the **Edit** page. The first section is called **Properties**; the second section's name changes depending on what you select in the **Type** drop-down box. The first option in **Properties** is **Name**, where you enter the name which pfSense will use to identify the alias. It may only consist of letters, numbers, and the underscore character. You may also enter a free-form, non-parsed description in the next field. In the **Type** drop-down box, specify the type of alias you want. The options for **Type** are:
    - **Host(s)**: Selecting this option enables you to enter one or more hosts. The hosts must be specified by either their IP address or **fully qualified domain name** (**FQDN**). If you use an FQDN, the hostnames will periodically be reresolved and updated. If you use IP addresses, you may specify an IP range or a subnet. You can add more than one entry.

- **Network(s)**: Selecting this option allows you to specify one or more networks. The network prefix for each entry must be specified, along with the CIDR mask.
- **Port(s)**: Selecting this option allows you to specify one or more ports. Port ranges can be specified by separating the first and last port with a colon.
- **URL (IPs)**: Allows you to specify one or more URLs which point to text lists of IP addresses for which an alias will be created. Using this option causes pfSense to download the list, or lists, once and then convert it into a conventional alias. You can enter as many URLs as you wish, but each file should be limited to 3000 IP addresses/ranges or less.
- **URL (Ports)**: Allows you to specify one or more URLs which point to text lists of ports for which an alias will be created. As with URL (IPs), the list or lists are downloaded once and then converted into a conventional alias. You can enter as many URLs as you wish, but each file should be limited to 3,000 IP ports/ranges or less.
- **URL Table (IPs)**: Similar to **URL (IPs)**, but with this option, you can only specify a single URL containing IPs/ranges of IPs/subnets, and this list is downloaded and refreshed periodically. This option will work with large numbers of addresses/ranges/subnets (30,000 or more). With this option, in the second section of the page, you enter the URL of the list, the update frequency in days (selected in the drop-down box), and you can also enter a brief description in rightmost edit box.
- **URL Table (Ports)**: Similar to **URL (Ports)**, but you can only specify a single URL containing ports/ranges of ports, and this list is downloaded and refreshed periodically. As with **URL Table (IPs)**, in the second section of the page, you enter the URL of the list, the update frequency in days, and you may also enter a brief description.

As you may have surmised from our description of the different alias types, the second section of the page is where you enter information about what the alias stands for, which is one of the following:

- An FQDN
- An IP address/range of IP addresses/network
- A port or range of ports
- An URL

For all the types except the two **URL Table** options, multiple entries are allowed. You can add more than one entry by clicking on the green **Add** button at the bottom of the page after each new entry is defined (it will have the label **Add Host/Add Network/Add Port/Add URL**, depending on which option you choose). When you are done adding entries, click on the **Save** button at the bottom of the page and click on the **Apply Changes** button on the main **Aliases** page.

Creating aliases from a DNS lookup

There is another way of generating aliases that may be helpful in certain circumstances. Sometimes we want to create an alias for a website; however, that website may use multiple IP addresses (for example, Amazon uses six different IP addresses as of this writing). Rather than find out what these IP addresses are an input them manually, we can do this much more easily in pfSense.

To create an alias for a website, navigate to **Diagnostics** | **DNS Lookup**. On the **DNS Lookup** page, enter the hostname in the **Hostname** field and click on the **Lookup** button. When the results of the lookup are returned, there should be a button next to the **Lookup** button (before the **Results** section) labeled **Add Alias**. Click on the button, and an alias should be created, with any dots in the hostname converted to underscores (for example, if you did a DNS lookup on `www.amazon.com`, the corresponding alias would be **amazon_com**). Navigate back to **Firewall** | **Aliases**, and the newly created alias should be there.

The advantage of this method of creating an alias is that a DNS lookup should be effective in returning a list of valid IP addresses for a site, at least in the moment. A rule created based on such an alias should be effective, at least immediately after the DNS lookup was performed. But for popular websites, it may not be effective a day later, or even a few hours later, as such websites frequently add new IP addresses to the pool of addresses they use.

Bulk import

Another way of creating an alias for a site with a number of different IP addresses is to use pfSense's bulk import function. The bulk import function can be invoked by navigating to the main **Aliases** page (via **Firewall** | **Aliases**) and clicking on the blue **Import** button.

There are three fields on the **Bulk Import** page: **Alias Name**, **Description**, and **Aliases to import**. The first two fields are identical to the same-named fields on the **Aliases** page that appears when the **Add** button is pressed. In the **Aliases to import** edit box, enter a carriage return-delimited list of IP addresses, with or without a CIDR and a description. When done, press the **Save** button.

Using **Bulk Import** is easy; what is hard is finding a valid list of IP addresses for popular sites that is up to date. As with the DNS lookup method of creating aliases, the challenge is that many of these sites regularly add new IP addresses and ranges to the pool of IP addresses they utilize and retire other addresses/ranges. One (as of this writing) up-to-date list is a list of Facebook (`http://facebook.com/`) IP addresses at `https://gist.github.com/Whitexp/9591384`. Copying and pasting this list into your alias should enable you to block Facebook. Using this method to block popular social media sites, however, is generally not recommended, due to the administrative overhead associated with making sure that aliases maintain up to date lists of IP addresses. Rather, it is recommended that you use proxies, which will be discussed more fully in *Chapter 11, Extending pfSense with Packages*.

Virtual IPs

Virtual IPs (**VIPs**) refer to a situation where an IP address does not correspond to a single physical interface. They are used in many scenarios, including the following:

- NAT (including one-to-many NAT)
- Scenarios where fault tolerance is needed (for example CARP)
- Mobile usage scenarios, which allows a mobile user to maintain a consistent virtual IP address even as their actual IP address changes

To add a VIP, navigate to **Firewall** | **Virtual IPs** and click on the **Add** button at the bottom of the table. pfSense offers four options for virtual IPs:

- IP Alias
- CARP
- Proxy ARP
- Other

Of these four options, we can state the following:

- **CARP, Proxy ARP**, and **Other** were available with the earliest versions of pfSense. **IP Alias** is available with version 2.0 and higher.
- All current options can be used with NAT.
- **CARP** and **IP Alias** can be used by the firewall to bind and/or run services. **Proxy ARP** and **Other** cannot be used in such a way.
- All options except **Other** generate ARP (Layer 2) traffic. This makes the **Other** option useful in scenarios where ARP traffic is not needed.
- All options except **Proxy ARP** can be used for clustering. However, if **IP Alias** VIPs are used as part of a **CARP** VIP, then they must be inside the same subnet as the **CARP** VIP upon which they are placed.
- As of version 2.2, all available options allow you to generate a VIP that is in a different subnet from the real interface IP. However, **CARP** VIPs did not support this feature prior to version 2.2, and it is recommended that you keep **CARP** VIPs on the same subnet for better connectivity and fewer potential issues.
- For **CARP**, the subnet mask must match the interface IP's subnet mask. For **IP Alias**, the subnet mask should match the interface IP or be /32. If the IPs are in different subnets from the original IP address, then at least one **IP Alias** VIP must have the correct mask for the new subnet.
- **CARP** and **IP Alias** will respond to ICMP ping attempts if the firewall rules allow it; **Proxy ARP** and **Other** will not respond to ICMP ping attempts.
- **CARP** and **IP Alias** VIPs must be added individually; **Proxy ARP** and **Other** may be added individually or as a VIP subnet.

To create a VIP following are the steps:

1. First select one of the four options.
2. Then select a physical interface in the **Interface** drop-down box.
3. In the **Address type** drop-down box, you may select either **Single address** or **Network** with **Proxy ARP** or **Other**.
4. If you selected **CARP** or **IP Aliases**, you can only add a VIP individually, so this option will be disabled. In the **Address(es)** edit box, you enter the VIP or virtual subnet. You also need to specify the CIDR here. What follows are several options that are only available if you selected **CARP**.
    - For CARP VIPs, you must enter a **Virtual IP Password**, which can be whatever you like.

- The next option is the **VHID Group** drop-down box. Each VIP which is to be shared on multiple nodes must use a unique **Virtual Host ID group** (**VHID**), and it must also be different from any VHIDs in active use on any directly connected network interface. If you are not currently using CARP or Cisco's **Virtual Router Redundancy Protocol** (**VRRP**) on any other nodes, you can use **1** as your VHID. The next option is the **Advertising Frequency** drop-down box.
- The **Advertising Frequency** value should correspond to this node's role in the network. The master should be set to **1**; a backup should be set to **2** or higher.
- The next parameter is the **Skew** drop-down, which controls how often (in seconds) the node advertises that it is a member of the redundancy group. Specifying a lower number tends to ensure that this node, if it isn't a master already, will become master if the master node fails. This is the final option on the page that only applies to CARP VIPs.

5. In the **Description** edit box, you can enter a brief, non-parsed description.
6. When you are done, click on the **Save** button at the bottom of the page and then click on the **Apply Changes** on the main **Virtual IPs** page. We will cover CARP in greater depth in *Chapter 8, Redundancy and High Availability*.

Troubleshooting firewall rules

At some point, there will be a situation where your firewall rules aren't doing what you think they should be doing, and our firewall troubleshooting skills are put to the test. The first step is to diagnose the problem (for example, nodes on the DEVELOPERS network cannot access the internet). If we can easily identify the interface or interfaces which are affected, then we can focus on that interface's ruleset.

It is probably a good idea to check the **Floating Rules** tab first, since floating rules take precedence over rules for an individual interface, and if the problem is a misconfigured floating rule, then we can save a lot of time that we otherwise would spend double-checking an interface's ruleset. If you are running a proxy server on your firewall, you may want to check the settings on that, since a proxy server's allow and deny lists tend to supersede firewall rulesettings.

The next step is to check the firewall rules for the affected interfaces, keeping in mind that firewall rules are evaluated from the top down. If warranted, check the allowed/blocked protocols. For example, if a rule is set up to allow only TCP traffic to pass through to an interface, a video streaming client that uses UDP will not work.

A good way of finding out whether a **Pass** rule is effective is to look at the rules table and check the **States** column (the leftmost column). This column indicates the number of current states created, as well as the total amount of data that has passed through the firewall, as a result of traffic matching this rule. If you hover your mouse over this column, you will see even more information. If the rule has been enabled for some time and no data is passing in connection with the rule, then there is a good chance the rule is either misconfigured, or the traffic matches another rule before it gets to this rule.

pfSense makes it easy to disable and enable rules, and you should take advantage of this in your troubleshooting. Sometimes the easiest way to troubleshoot rules is to disable one or more rules, take note of network behavior after the rules are disabled, and then re-enable the rules one at a time, taking note of any network changes as you do so. This should help you pinpoint the rule or rules that are causing the problem, and bring you one step closer to solving the issue.

If you still cannot figure out what the problem is, it might be a good idea to enable logging for the rules you suspect may be causing the problem. This is usually not recommended, as enabling logging for rules tends to quickly use up disk space, but sometimes looking at the logs can be helpful. Once you have enabled logging for the rules, navigate to **Status** | **System Logs** and click on the **Firewall** tab. You can use the filtering options at the top of the page to help focus on the relevant log entries.

If logging doesn't provide enough information about the source of the problem, you might consider using `tcpdump`, a command-line utility including with pfSense. tcpdump is a packet analyzer usable which prints the contents of network packets. It is extremely useful, albeit somewhat difficult to use at first. It is beyond the scope of this chapter to provide a tutorial on tcpdump, but you should be aware that it is available. We will cover tcpdump in greater depth in the final chapter.

If you have made a recent change to the firewall rules, and some traffic is getting through that seems to violate the firewall rules, it is possible that the state table entries for the connections pre-date the rule change. Therefore, if you want the connections to be dropped, you will have to reset the state table. To do this, navigate to **Diagnostics** | **States** and click on the **Reset States** tab. Click on the **Reset** button, which will remove all entries from the state table. This will also reset any active connections, so take that into account.

Summary

In this chapter, we covered a subject that goes to the core of pfSense's functionality: firewall rules. The default behavior of pfSense is to block all traffic, so we require rules to access other networks. The number of rules you add will depend on the complexity and requirements of your network, and as you add rules, the ruleset will become increasingly difficult to maintain and troubleshoot. One principle that cannot be stressed too much is the fact that the order of rules matters; rules are evaluated on a top-down basis, with rules above other rules taking precedence. Floating rules are evaluated last unless the **Quick** option is set, in which case they are evaluated first.

Finally, we considered scheduling and aliases. Scheduling enables us to apply rules more selectively (only at certain times), while aliases enable us to do what would be extremely difficult to do otherwise by allowing us to represent multiple IP addresses as a single entity. This is extremely helpful if we choose to blacklist or whitelist a site or groups of sites.

In the next chapter, we will consider a network technology whose most common use has been to overcome the issue of IPv4 address exhaustion, but which provides utility in such a way that it should survive the transition to *IPv6: Network Address Translation (NAT)*.

Questions

Answer the following questions. For Questions 3 – 5, if the rulesetting is not specified in the question, assume the default value for that setting.

1. When we create firewall rules, what principle should apply?
2. What is the difference between **Block** and **Reject** in filtering traffic?
3. Our network has two interfaces: WAN and LAN. The only two rules created so far are the IPv4 and IPv6 "Allow LAN to any" rules that pfSense creates when the LAN interface is initially assigned. We create a rule to block Recode with the following settings: **Action** = **Reject**; **Interface** = **LAN**; **Address Family** = **IPv4 + IPv6**; **Protocol** = **TCP**; **Source** = **LAN net**; **Destination** = `151.101.21.52` (Recode's IP address). We place the rule at the bottom of the LAN rules table. What happens when we try to access Recode?

4. Assume we have created the same rule as the one in Question 2, but we place it at the top of the LAN rules table. Now what happens when we try to access Recode?
5. Assume we have the same ruleset as Question 2, but we also create a floating rule with the following settings; **Action** = **Pass**; **Quick** = **Disabled**; **Interface** = **LAN**; **Direction** = **in**; **Address Family** = **IPv4+IPv6**; **Protocol** = **Any**; **Source** = **Any**; **Destination** = **Any**. The Block Recode rule is at the top of the LAN rules table. (a) After we enable the new floating rule, what happens when we try to access Recode? (b) If we change the **Quick** setting on this rule to **Enabled** and reload the firewall rules, what happens when we try to access Recode? (c) After we change the **Quick** setting to **Enabled**, what effect do the "Allow LAN to any" rules have on traffic?
6. Name four types of aliases.
7. Describe three methods of creating aliases with multiple IP addresses.
8. Name a type of Virtual IP introduced with pfSense 2.0.

5
Network Address Translation

At some point, you will likely need to utilize **Network Address Translation (NAT)**, which, as the name implies, is a way of mapping one address space into another address space. When commonly referred to, NAT is often equated with **port forwarding**, a form of NAT that allows a computer on a public network (such as the internet) to connect to a computer on a private network by remapping the IP address and port. In reality, however, there are two broad categories of NAT. **1:1 NAT** is a form of remapping public IP addresses to private IP addresses in such a way that each public IP address corresponds to a single private IP address. **One-to-many NAT**, on the other hand, deals with the scenario in which there is a single public IP address shared by several nodes with private IP addresses.

The goal of this chapter is to demonstrate NAT in all its forms. If you have a SOHO network, you will almost certainly have occasion to use many-to-one NAT and port forwarding. But if you are an admin of a corporate network, you will likely implement 1:1 NAT at some point. And both SOHO and corporate networks will likely have to modify outbound NAT filtering at some point. Although NAT is commonly associated with IPv4 networks (and in fact NAT was a big factor in at least temporarily solving the problem of **IPv4 address exhaustion**), it can also be used with IPv6 networks, and we will demonstrate that as well.

This chapter will cover the following topics:

- NAT essentials
- Outbound NAT
- Port forwarding
- 1:1 NAT
- NPt
- Troubleshooting

Technical requirements

This chapter has no special requirements, other than a pfSense system with at least a **WAN** and a **LAN** interface to work through the examples in this chapter. It would be helpful if you have at least two separate nodes on the **LAN** network to test the examples. It would also be helpful to have a separate internet connection, such as a mobile connection, to confirm that any NAT changes made have the desired effect on the **WAN** side.

NAT essentials

NAT was a standard developed to deal with the depletion of IPv4 addresses. Since IPv4 addresses are 32-bit addresses, there are potentially 4.3 billion addresses available. But since IPv4 was initially divided into Class A networks (first octet = 1 to 126, 8-bit subnet, over 16 million nodes per network), Class B networks (first octet = 128 to 191, 16-bit subnet, 64K nodes per network) and Class C networks (first octet = 192 to 223, 24-bit subnet, 254 nodes per network), the situation was even worse. Class A and Class B networks were too large to be used efficiently even by large organizations, and many Class A networks were assigned to large corporations, thus further reducing the pool of available addresses. The next smallest size, Class C networks, was too small for many organizations. Many organizations ended up using multiple Class C networks, which created inefficiencies in both address use and routing. By the late 1980s, the issue was enough of an imminent threat to warrant concern, and in 1991, the Internet Engineering Task Force (IETF) formed the **Routing and Addressing Group (ROAD)** to deal with the issue.

The long-term solution to the problem was IPv6, which increases the length of an IP address to 128 bits. Several short-term solutions were also developed. One was the advent of **Classless Inter-Domain Routing (CIDR)** in 1993, which allows us to define arbitrary subnets; thus, if a Class A or B network is too large for our needs, we can divide it into smaller networks by changing the subnet mask. For example, assume we have a Class B network, which is too large for our needs, and what we actually need are several networks of 4,000 nodes each. A Class B address traditionally would have 16 bits for the network identifier and 16 bits for the host identifier. Doing the math, we realize that 2 to the power of 12 is 4096. Therefore, we only need 12 bits for the host identifier. By ceding the other 4 bits to the network identifier, we now have 20 bits for the network identifier. Our Class B network which originally supported 65534 nodes (65536 minus the first and last address) now has been divided into 16 networks of 4094 nodes each.

Another solution developed around the same time was the addition of private networks—a network that follows the standards defined in **RFC 1918**, the IETF document that describes address allocation for such networks. This document defined three different private address allocations, one each for Class A, B, and C networks:

- 10.x.x.x for Class A
- 172.16.x.x to 172.31.x.x for Class B
- 192.168.1.x to 192.168.255.x for Class C

Since private addresses, by definition, cannot be routed on the public internet, there must be some means of translating these addresses into public addresses and vice versa. Thus, along with private addresses, NAT was developed:

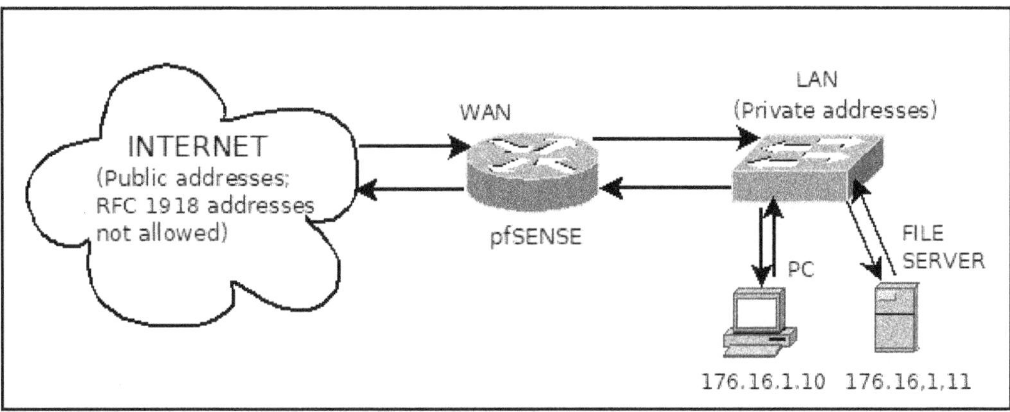

Illustration of issues presented by the existence of private addresses. Nodes with private addresses cannot directly access the internet, yet may want to access resources on the internet or may have resources that nodes on the internet want to access.

The preceding diagram suggests the different issues created by the existence of public addresses. A node on the private network may access a resource on the public network, and we need a way of making that possible; we also need a means of routing the return traffic. A node on the public internet may access a resource on the private network (such as, the file server shown), and there needs to be a way of making a socket connection to that resource. Finally, there may be a node on our network (such as a file or web server) that has its own public address that we want to be accessible on both the private network and the internet.

We will consider that last case first. 1:1 NAT is fairly straightforward; it is simply a way of connecting two networks that have incompatible addressing modes (a public network and a private network). This is not what NAT is mainly used for, but if you have multiple public IP addresses and can afford to use one for each publicly available resource, it is an option to consider.

One-to-many NAT may be more difficult to grasp, but it provides two distinct functions. It enables multiple nodes on a private network to access resources on the internet (**Outbound NAT**), and it enables nodes on the internet to access resources on the private network (port forwarding). Thus one-to-many NAT, also known as **Dynamic NAT**, performs the following functions:

- For outbound connections it, provides a means of mapping local IP addresses to the WAN address
- For outbound connections it, converts ports in the `0` to `1023` range, also known as well-known ports because they are commonly associated with certain services, to ports in the `49152` to `65535` range, also known as ephemeral ports
- For outbound connections it, keeps track to the source IP address and port so that return traffic is directed to the right location
- For inbound connections it, provides a means of mapping the WAN addresses to multiple local nodes (by directing traffic to different nodes based to their source port)

Dynamic NAT is in many ways analogous to an office with a PBX and several extensions. Outgoing calls seem to come from the same phone number, but incoming calls can be redirected to individual extensions. In this analogy, the public IP address of the network is like the phone number for the whole office, and port numbers are like extensions.

Although NAT has its advantages - it not only provides a solution to the problem of IPv4 address exhaustion, but it provides a way to hide entire private networks from the internet - it does have disadvantages as well:

- NAT traffic does not have end-to-end connectivity. Thus, services that require end-to-end connectivity can fail.
- Some protocols can work when one of the nodes uses NAT, but tend to fail when the nodes at both ends of the connection are behind a firewall that uses NAT. NAT tampers with IP headers, and this can break things such as FTP, internet telephony (SIP), SNMP, and others. IPsec, a network tunneling protocol, also sometimes has problems with the IP changes made by NAT.
- Since the advent of NAT in the 1990s, web-based content has become increasingly complex. As a result, when a web page is requested, it is rare that such a request requires only a single stateful connection. Embedded content in such pages increases the number of connections required, and web traffic alone on anything but the smallest private networks can result in port exhaustion.

- The problem with web traffic suggests a much larger issue: NAT adds complexity to networks and makes it much more difficult to troubleshoot networks.
- As a result of applications not having access to the actual IP addresses of nodes at the other end of connections, these applications may fail and thus may have to be rewritten to work with NAT.

Thus, NAT is hardly an ideal solution, but even as IPv6 makes inroads, NAT is not likely to go away soon, and we can implement it on our networks provided that we are cognizant of the drawbacks.

The advent of IPv6 makes NAT technically unnecessary, as we can now assign public IP addresses to each node on our private network without worrying about address space exhaustion. However, private address spaces do exist in IPv6, and we may want to make use of them for administrative and security reasons. Thus, there is a way of using NAT with IPv6 called **Network Prefix Translation (NPt)**, and we will discuss that later in this chapter.

This is not an exhaustive discussion of NAT and private addresses by any means; those sufficiently motivated may want to read the IETF documents related to these subjects. In particular, they are:

- RFC 1631 (the original NAT RFC, published in May 1994, describing one-to-many NAT)
- RFC 1918 (describing private networks)
- RFC 2663 (1:1 NAT)
- RFC 3022 (supersedes RFC 1631; describes one-to-many NAT, referred to in the document as **Traditional NAT**)

Outbound NAT

Outbound NAT configuration, as the name applies, covers traffic from our internal networks whose destination is an external network. The default NAT configuration in pfSense automatically translates outbound traffic to the WAN IP address. If there are multiple WAN interfaces, traffic leaving any WAN interface is automatically translated to the address of the WAN interface which is being used. If you navigate to **Firewall | NAT** and click on the **Outbound NAT** tab without having previously configured Outbound NAT, you will find that the default setting is **Automatic outbound NAT rule generation**.

The following screenshot demonstrates the default behavior of outbound NAT in pfSense on a relatively simple network with three interfaces: WAN, LAN (the `172.16.0.0` network), and DMZ (the `172.17.0.0` network). pfSense has generated two automatic rules. The first rule is an automatic rule for IPSec traffic. The second rule is the one that handles all other outbound NAT traffic. As you can see, outbound NAT takes all traffic that has as its source the loopback (`127.0.0.0/8`), the LAN and DMZ regardless of its destination and maps them to the WAN address. The sideways "X" in the static port column indicates that the outbound port is also translated to a random port. This makes sense, as it eliminates the possibility of a port conflict. For example, if a user requests a web page which uses the HTTPS protocol, and the outbound port was assigned the standard HTTPS port (443), then another user making a similar request would be unable to do so because the port is being used. By mapping the traffic to a random, unused port, pfSense avoids such problems:

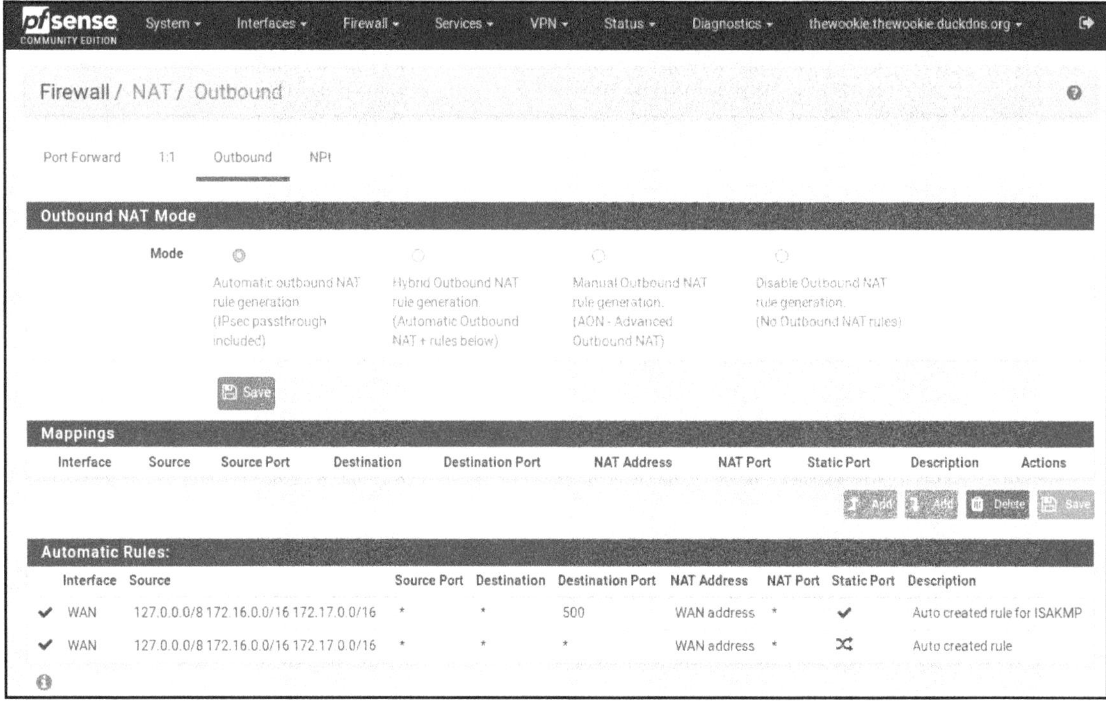

Automatic outbound NAT mode with automatically generated NAT rules for each non-WAN interface

If you want to confirm that NAT performs a necessary function on your network, select the **Disable Outbound NAT** radio button and then click on the blue **Save** button beneath the radio buttons. Unless you have configured your network so it is not dependent on NAT, you should find the internet is no longer accessible from nodes behind the pfSense box. Revert the setting back to **Automatic outbound rule generation** and the internet should be accessible again.

There are two other options for **Outbound NAT Mode**:

- **Hybrid Outbound NAT rule generation** will still automatically generate outbound NAT rules for each non-WAN interface, but you will also be able to create your own outbound NAT rules
- **Manual Outbound NAT rule generation**, if selected, will not automatically create any rules, although any previously created automatic rules will remain

It is good practice to document any changes we make to the settings, and this is especially the case if you select **Manual Outbound NAT rule generation**. If you select this, the previously created rules will remain, but if you add new interfaces, a NAT rule for the new interface will not be automatically created, which could cause bewilderment when you find the new subnet cannot access the internet. Nonetheless, this option could be useful if you want to filter certain traffic in order to make it easier to monitor.

To create or edit outbound NAT rules refer to, click on one of the **Add** buttons below the **Mappings** section. The first section of the page is **Edit Advanced Outbound NAT Entry**. The **Disabled** option just disables the rule, while **Do not NAT** completely disables NAT processing for traffic matching the rule. The **Interface** drop-down box allows you to select with **Interface** (as with almost every rule in which NAT is involved, this is usually set to **WAN**). **Protocol** allows you to specify the protocol the outbound rule applies to (usually we can keep it set to any, but you may want to create a more restrictive rule). **Source** is where you define where the traffic originates. This is almost always a subnet on your local network. For example, if we want to create an outbound rule for the DEVELOPERS network, and its subnet is `172.17.0.0/16`, we would choose **Network** in the **Type** drop-down box, and enter `172.17.0.0` in the adjacent edit box and set the **CIDR** in the drop-down box to `16`. Finally, **Destination** allows us to set a destination network for the outbound NAT mapping. Since we typically do not know the destination ahead of time, we usually set this to **Any**. The **Not** checkbox, if checked, inverts the sense of the destination match.

The **Translation** section of the page allows us to translate the IP address from the original internal address to another IP address. The default setting in the **Address** drop-down box is **Interface Address**, which just uses the IP address of the interface selected in the **Interface** drop-down box. We can also select **Other Subnet**, which will make additional options available. If we choose this option in the drop-down box, we can enter a different subnet in the **Other subnet** edit box; if we use this option, we need to define virtual IPs first, and use a subnet of virtual IPs.

The **Pool options** dropdown allows you to select how the subnet pool is used. The following options are available:

- **Round Robin**: This goes through the virtual IP addresses in a round-robin fashion; in other words, in a loop. It is the only option that works with host aliases.
- **Random**: This option will result in pfSense selecting an address from the virtual IP subnet randomly.
- **Source Hash**: This option will take the source IP address, hash it, and use the hash to determine the translation IP address. This guarantees that as long as the source IP address remains the same, the translation IP address will also remain the same.
- **Bitmask**: This option applies the subnet mask defined in **Other** subnet and keeps the last portion identical. Thus if we chose a virtual IP pool of `10.1.1.0/24` and the source IP is `192.168.1.12`, the translated address will be `10.1.1.12`.
- **Round Robin with Sticky Address/Random with Sticky Address**: These options invoke either **Round Robin** or **Random** addresses, but once an address is selected for a source IP address, it remains the same.

In the **Port** edit box, you can set the source port for the outbound NAT mapping. The **Static port** checkbox, if enabled, will prevent pfSense from rewriting the source port on outgoing packets. Rewriting the source port prevents other parties from finding out the original source port and thus thwarts fingerprinting nodes behind the firewall. Rewriting the source ports, however, breaks some applications, and in such cases, we can enable static ports for the rule.

The **No XMLRPC Sync** checkbox in the **Misc** section, if checked, will prevent the rule from syncing to other CARP members. You can also enter a brief description for future reference. When you are done, click on the **Save** button at the bottom of the page and the **Apply Changes** button on the main **NAT** page.

Example – filtering outbound NAT for a single network

To demonstrate how Outbound NAT can be used as a means to make it easier to monitor network traffic, consider a hypothetical example in which we suspect that users of a particular subnet are using a disproportionate amount of bandwidth. We want to monitor the traffic on the SALES net. There are several tools we could use to do this, but one of the easiest tools to use is pfTop, a utility built into pfSense that enables us to monitor bandwidth and traffic. We could filter the results to view only traffic whose source is the SALES net. However, this will show individual connections, whereas we might want to view the aggregate traffic for the interface. (We might even want to view aggregate traffic for each interface, but for now, we'll just focus on filtering a single interface.) We can filter traffic by source and/or destination IP address, and that method provides a potential solution. We could create a separate virtual IP address that is an alias for the WAN address, divert outbound NAT traffic for the SALES net to that virtual IP address, and then filter traffic that has as its source the virtual IP address, knowing that the traffic could only have originated on the SALES net. The process is relatively easy:

1. Using the information in `Chapter 4`, *pfSense as a Firewall*, we create a virtual IP for the WAN interface by navigating to **Firewall** | **Virtual IPs**, clicking on the Add button, and entering the appropriate information. **Keep IP Alias** as the **IP Type** and **WAN** as the **Interface**. Enter a unique IP address and CIDR for the virtual IP address, and enter an appropriate **Description** (such as "WAN Virtual IP address"). Then, click on the **Save** button.
2. Navigate to **Firewall** | **NAT**. Click on the **Outbound** tab. Change the **Mode** to **Manual Outbound NAT** and click on the **Save** button. This will generate a set of manual outbound rules for each active interface.
3. Find **Auto created rule – SALES to WAN** and click on the edit icon for that rule.
4. In the **Translation** section, use the drop-down box to change Address to the virtual IP address created in step 1. Then, click on the **Save** button. Click on the **Apply Changes** button on the **Outbound NAT** page.

Now, you should be able to navigate to **Diagnostics** | **pfTop** and by typing **src** and the virtual IP address into the **Filter expression** edit box, you can readily view all outgoing traffic from SALES net. If it looks like the amount of traffic from SALES is abnormal, then we could focus on which nodes are generating the traffic.

1:1 NAT

1:1 NAT also known as **one-to-one NAT**, addresses a scenario somewhat opposite to the scenario covered by Outbound NAT. Whereas with Outbound NAT, we were concerned with network traffic flowing from the local network to the WAN, 1:1 NAT allows us to map one public IP address to one private IP address, thus making a resource that otherwise would only be available on the local network available on the WAN side (that is, via the internet). All traffic from that private IP to the internet will then be mapped to the public IP specified in the 1:1 NAT mapping. This will override the Outbound NAT settings. Conversely, all traffic initiated on the internet which is destined for the specified public IP address will then be translated to the private IP. Then it will be evaluated according to the WAN firewall ruleset, and if the traffic is permitted by the WAN rules, it will be passed to the internal node specified in the mapping. These are the steps:

1. To create a NAT 1:1 mapping, click on the **1:1** tab on the **NAT** page and click on the **Add** button below the table. Many of the options are similar to the options we covered in the **Port Forwarding** section.
2. **Negate** allows you to exclude the rule from the NAT, which could be useful if you are redirecting a range of addresses, and need to exclude a subset of the range.
3. **No BINAT** disables redirection for any traffic matching the rule. This way, you can exclude a subset of addresses from a larger range of translated addresses.
4. The **Interface** dropdown allows you to specify the interface to which this mapping applies; usually, you can leave it set to **WAN**.
5. The **External subnet ID** edit box is where you enter the external subnet's starting IP address for the 1:1 mapping.
6. In the **Internal IP** section, you specify the internal subnet for the 1:1 mapping. The subnet size for the internal subnet determines how many IP addresses are mapped. For example, assume we have set **External subnet IP** to `10.1.1.1` and **Internal IP** to `192.168.1.100/30` (with **Network** as the type specified in the **Type** drop-down box). This will map `10.1.1.1` to `192.168.1.100`, `10.1.1.2` to `192.168.1.101`, and so on up to and including `10.1.1.3/192.168.1.103`. **Destination** allows us to use the 1:1 mapping only for connection to or from the specified destination; usually, this is set as **Any**. Both **Internal IP** and **Destination** have **Not** checkboxes allowing us to invert the sense of the match.
7. You can enter a non-parsed description for future reference in the **Description** field. The **NAT reflection** drop-down box allows you to access the mapped nodes on the local network from the public IP address.

8. Unlike **Port Forwarding**, where there were several options for reflection, there are only two options here: **Enable** and **Disable**.
9. Click on the **Save** button when you are done making changes to the 1:1 entry and click on the **Apply Changes** button on the main **NAT** page to reload the rules.

Example – mapping a file server

Assume that we have a file server that must be accessible from the internet. We have a public IP address, which we obtained from our ISP. We follow this procedure:

1. Navigate to **Firewall** | **NAT**, and click on the **1:1** tab. On the **1:1** page, click on one of the **Add** buttons.
2. On the **Edit** page, add the **External subnet IP**, which in this case would be just a single IP address.
3. For **Internal IP**, select **Single host** in the drop-down box and enter the internal IP address. Click on the **Save** button when you are done. Click on **Apply Changes** on the **1:1** page.

This procedure can be used to map a single external IP address to a single internal IP address, or you could map a block of IP addresses by using the external block's subnet mask and mapping it to the internal block's subnet mask, as outlined in the description of 1:1 NAT previously. When you are done mapping the IP addresses, you will want to test the mapping by accessing the file server from the other side of your firewall. In such cases, a separate internet connection such as a mobile connection can be helpful.

Port forwarding

Port forwarding is probably the most commonly used form of NAT. It is commonly used when we have a single public IP address and several resources that must be made accessible to the internet. As a result, instead of assigning a single public IP address to every resource, instead we use one public IP address and assign a separate port to each resource.

Port forwarding is rarely used in corporate networks; in fact, higher-end routers do not have easily configurable ways of setting up port forwarding. Fortunately, however, pfSense is designed to be used on a variety of different networks. Port forwarding is usually a feature found on consumer grade routers, and the inclusion of port forwarding in pfSense is an acknowledgement that pfSense will often be deployed in home and SOHO networks.

Before we get started with port forwarding, we should mention the following:

- Port forwarding is applied before 1:1 NAT. Therefore, port forwarding can interfere with any 1:1 NAT mappings we may have.
- Port forwarding rules are applied before firewall rules.
- We can only map a port number to a single node. For example, we cannot SSH into multiple SSH servers via port `22`. We can, however, set up separate SSH servers on separate ports, even if it means using non-standard ports: for example, we could set up one SSH server on port `6000`, another on port `6001`, and so on. In any case, it may behoove you to always use non-standard ports even when the standard port for a service is available, since it then be more difficult for hackers to identify what services are running on your network.

When we add a port forwarding entry, the mere creation of a port forwarding rule does not necessarily make that port accessible from the WAN side. Keep in mind that pfSense will block all traffic on all interfaces and all ports by default. Fortunately, pfSense makes the process of setting up a corresponding firewall rule easy.

To configure inbound NAT settings, the following are the steps:

1. Navigate to **Firewall** | **NAT** and click on the **Port Forwarding** tab.
2. From this tab, click on one of the **Add** buttons to add a new rule. The first option is **Disable**, which allows you to disable a rule without deleting it. When **No RDR (NOT)** is enabled, **Redirect target IP**, **Redirect target port**, and **Filter rule association** have no effect. This option is rarely used, but may be useful if you have a transparent proxy running. It could also be used if you want to exclude a subset of ports from a larger range of ports.
3. The **Interface** drop-down box allows you to select the interface the rule applies to (in most cases, you want to leave this as **WAN**, since with inbound NAT, we are concerned with traffic originating on the internet).
4. The **Protocol** drop-down box allows you to select which protocol to which the NAT rule applies.
5. The **Source** and **Source port range** options are hidden, you have to click on the Display Advanced button on that section of the page to make them appear. This is because although we can change these settings, usually we don't care about the source of the incoming traffic - as a result, most of the time you will probably want to leave these set at the default values of **Any**.

6. For **Destination**, you probably want to leave this set to **WAN address**, since users on the internet will be targeting your WAN address, not one of your private network IP addresses. If you have a multi WAN setup, you may want to change the destination to one of your other WAN interfaces. **Destination port range** is the port, or range of ports, you want to forward to one of your private IP addresses.
7. In the **Redirect target IP** edit box, you enter the internal IP address of the node to which you want to map the port or range of ports. The **Redirect target port** option specifies the port to which you want to map the port specified in the **Destination** port range. This is usually identical to the port specified in the **Destination** port range, but you can specify a different port or ports here. This can be useful in some circumstances.

   For example, you may want to set up a private web server which is accessible from the internet on your home internet connection. However, most ISPs block port `80` (the default HTTP port) and port `443` (HTTPS). Using **Port Redirection**, you can choose a port other than ports `80` and `443` for **Destination** (for example, `1234`) and redirect traffic coming in on that port to your web server (which likely would be accepting traffic on port `80`).

8. In the **Description** edit box, you can enter a non-parsed description for future reference.
9. The **No XMLRPC Sync** checkbox, if checked, will result in this rule not being synced to other CARP members (this does not apply to CARP slaves, which can still have their NAT rules overwritten by a CARP master).
10. The **NAT Reflection** drop-down box allows you to access the service to which port forwarding is enabled using the public IP address of your network.
11. The **Use system default** option allows you to use whatever NAT reflection option was chosen in **System** | **Advanced** under the **NAT** tab.
12. The **Enable (NAT + Proxy)** option will set up a proxy daemon which will receive and reflect connections, but it will only work with TCP connections, and only with single port forwards, or with ranges of less than 500 ports. **Enable (Pure NAT)** just creates automatic NAT redirect rules to accomplish redirection without using an external daemon.
13. Finally, **Disable** will disable NAT reflection.
14. The **Filter rule association** drop-down box allows you to select what type of firewall rule is created corresponding to the NAT rule.

15. **Add associated filter rule** generates a new firewall rule that is updated whenever the NAT rule is updated. **Add unassociated filter rule** generates a new firewall rule that is not automatically updated when changes are made to the port forwarding entry; thus there is a corresponding firewall rule, but it is not attached to the port forwarding entry.
16. **Pass** will pass traffic that matches the NAT rule through the firewall, but does not create a new firewall rule for it. Thus, it essentially creates an implicit pass rule. This will allow the traffic to pass through the firewall, but if you have to do any troubleshooting, it won't be easy to match the traffic.
17. Finally, if the **None** option is selected, no firewall rule is created and, unless an existing firewall rule allows the traffic from this NAT rule to pass, the traffic will not pass.
18. When you are done making changes, you can click on the **Save** button at the bottom of the page and then click on the **Apply Changes** button on the main **Port Forwarding** page.

Example 1 – setting up DCC

In this example, we will create a **Port Forwarding** entry for **DCC** (**Direct Client-to-Client**), a file transfer method which is a sub-protocol of **Internet Relay Chat** (**IRC**). This enables IRC peers to exchange files or perform non-relayed chats. Most clients will allow you to use any arbitrary port range, but ports over 5000 are commonly used, and we will use these ports. DCC uses the TCP protocol.

1. Navigate to **Firewall | NAT**. **Port Forward** is the default tab, so you should not have to click on that tab. Click on one of the **Add** buttons to add a port forwarding entry.
2. For **Protocol**, keep the default of **TCP**. **Destination port range** should be set to `5200` for the **From** port and `5250` for the **To** port. Set **Redirect target IP** to the IP address of the computer on which the IRC client is running, and set **Redirect target port** to `5200`. (The end port will be calculated automatically.) All other settings can be kept at their default values. (Note that the default value for **Filter rule association** is **Add associated filter rule**, so a corresponding firewall rule will be created.)
3. Enter an appropriate description (such as `Port forwarding for DCC`) and click on the **Save** button. On the **Port Forwarding** page, click on **Apply Changes**.

You probably want to navigate to **Firewall | Rules** to confirm that a corresponding **WAN** firewall rule has been generated. Note that the rule will only allow **TCP** traffic to pass, so the protocol for the rule matches the protocol set in the port forwarding entry. Assuming the IRC client has been configured correctly, sending files via DCC should now be possible.

Example 2 – excluding a port

Assume we have created the DCC Port Forwarding entry described previously, but now we want to exclude a subset of these ports (`5215` to `5220`) from the range of allowed ports. Fortunately, pfSense makes this process easy:

1. Navigate to **Firewall | NAT**. **Port Forward** is the default tab, so you should not have to click on that tab. Click on the **Add** button with the up arrow to add a port forwarding entry at the top of the list.
2. Enable **No RDR (NOT)** to disable redirection for traffic matching the rule.
3. For **Protocol**, keep the default of **TCP**. **Destination port range** should be set to `5215` for the **From** port and `5220` for the **To** port. Note that **Redirect target IP**, **Redirect target port**, and **Filter rule association** go away when **No RDR (NOT)** is enabled.
4. Enter an appropriate description (such as `Port forwarding for DCC`) and click on the **Save** button. On the **Port Forwarding** page, click on **Apply Changes**.

You now should have a subset of the ports forwarded in the previous example blocked. Whether or not your IRC client supports multiple port ranges for DCC, however, is another issue. Keep in mind that NAT entries are evaluated on a top-down basis, so if the new entry appears after the earlier entry, you will want to drag it above the more permissive DCC rule, otherwise the traffic will match the first rule and never get to the second one.

Example 3 – setting up a personal web server

Usually, the Destination port range and Redirect target port are the same, but there are some cases where we might want to redirect incoming traffic to a different port. For example, we might want to run a web server for our own personal use. For example, we might be running the web front end for MythTV (a Linux-based open source PVR application), and we may want to access it from the internet.

There is a good chance that our ISP blocks port `80` and port `443` traffic (the default ports for HTTP and HTTPS respectively); therefore, if we want to run a web server on our home connection, we would have to use a different port:

1. Navigate to **Firewall** | **NAT**. Again, we don't have to click on **Port Forward**, since it is the default tab. Click on one of the **Add** buttons.
2. For Protocol, keep the default of TCP. **Destination port range** should be set to a single port. Any unused, unblocked port will do; the higher the port number, the better, as these ports are less likely to be used. Set **Redirect target IP** to the IP address of the computer on which the web server is running, and set **Redirect target port** to `80`. (We could instead reconfigure the web server to accept traffic on the port set in **Destination port range**, but redirecting the port is easier.) All other settings can be kept at their default values.
3. Enter an appropriate description (such as `Port forwarding for web server`) and click on the **Save** button. On the **Port Forwarding** page, click on **Apply Changes**.

Now, you should be able to access your web server from the internet by typing in the IP address of your **WAN** connection + a colon + the port you set as the **Destination port range**. If you set up **Dynamic DNS** per the instructions in `Chapter 2`, *Advanced pfSense Configuration*, you could use the domain name for your **WAN** address rather than the **WAN** IP address.

Network Prefix Translation

Network Prefix Translation (**NPt**) allows us to map an internal IPv6 prefix to an external IPv6 prefix. Normally, we try to avoid using NAT when we use IPv6, but there are some cases where being able to translate IPv6 prefixes is helpful:

- It provides a means of implementing multihoming (connecting a host or network to multiple networks) on small networks. Another method is DHCPv6.
- It potentially makes routing more efficient, as it makes addresses on edge networks independent of addresses on upstream networks, and the upstream networks can then work only with the contiguous ISP-allocated addresses, which will make route summarization easier (and our routing tables much smaller).

NPt functions similarly to **1**:1 NAT for IPv4 addresses, only in this case, we are translating prefixes, not complete addresses. We can also use NPt to translate addresses between two private IPv6 networks. In such cases, both networks could use ULA prefixes, or one network could have a ULA prefix and the other could use global unicast addresses.

It should be noted that the IETF recommends using DHCPv6 instead of NPt; the reasons for this were enumerated in RFC 7157. The most compelling reasons for avoiding use of NPt are as follows:

- IPv6 allows for end-to-end connectivity, but NPtv6 does not, and whenever possible, end-to-end connectivity is desirable
- DHCPv6 is a more suitable solution to solve many of the most likely multihoming issues

Nonetheless, NPt may be necessary as an intermediate solution, and fortunately, pfSense provides the capability of implementing NPt. To create an NPt entry following are the steps:

1. Click on the **NPt** tab and click on one of the **Add** buttons on the page.
2. There is only one section on the page: **Edit NAT NPt Entry**.
3. Checking the **Disable** checkbox will disable the rule. The **Interface** drop-down box allows you to select the interface to which the rule applies (once again, it's usually **WAN**).
4. The first **Address** edit box is where you enter the internal ULA IPv6 prefix that will be selected.
5. You also need to select the CIDR for the prefix.
6. In the second **Address** checkbox, you enter the external, global unicast routable IPv6 prefix (you must specify the CIDR of the prefix here as well). Both the internal and destination (external) prefixes have corresponding **Not** checkboxes you can use to invert the sense of the match.

Per RFC 6296, if the prefix lengths for the internal and external networks do not match, then the shorter of the two prefixes will be zero extended. They are then both zero extended to 64 for the purposes of a calculation.

7. The last option is the **Description** edit box, where you can enter a non-parsed description.
8. Once you have entered all the information, click on the **Save** button and the **Apply Changes** button on the **NAT** page.

Example – mapping an IPv6 network

Assume that we have received a block of IPv6 addresses from our ISP, and we want to map a set of local IPv6 addresses to this block. Our internal IPv6 subnet is `fd30::/48`. We can do the mapping with **NPt**:

1. Navigate to **Firewall** | **NAT**, and from there, click on the **NPt** tab. On the **NPt** page, click on one of the **Add** buttons.
2. On the **NPt** edit page, set the first **Address** to the local IPv6 prefix, which in this case is `fd30::/48`. You must enter both the prefix and the CIDR.
3. Set the second **Address** to the IPv6 public subnet, which is the contiguous block of addresses assigned by your ISP.
4. Click on the **Save** button when done, and on the NPt page, click on **Apply Changes**.

The mapping is complete, and it should function similarly to a **1:1 NAT** mapping.

Troubleshooting

If you have created a **1:1** NAT or Port Forwarding entry and it does not have the expected effect, then there are several possible causes:

- You may have misconfigured the NAT entry
- The NAT entry may be configured correctly, but something else necessary for NAT to work was misconfigured (such as a firewall rule or a virtual IP address)
- There may be a software misconfiguration (such as port forwarding for a web server may be configured correctly, but the web server itself may be misconfigured)
- The issue may be beyond your control (such as, your ISP blocking a port)

As an initial step, you may want to try to access the resource locally (keeping in mind that if we are remapping the port from one port number to another, use the port number of the port on the local node hosting the resource). Use the local IP address of the node, even if you have NAT reflection enabled. If you can access the resource on the local network, but not on the WAN side, then at least you know the software is configured correctly. If not, you need to check to ensure the software or service is running and that it is configured correctly.

If the software is running and is accessible on the local network, you should make sure that the NAT entry is configured correctly. Check the IP addresses and port settings, as they have to be correct for NAT to work. In the case of port forwarding, make sure that Filter rule association is either set to Pass, or that there is an associated firewall rule for the NAT entry. You will also want to check the associated firewall rule to make sure that it allows the NAT traffic to pass. For example, make sure that the protocol for the NAT entry and the firewall rule match.

When checking the firewall rule, keep in mind that the entry for the rule in the rules table will tell you how much traffic has passed that matches the rule. If no traffic has passed (that is 0 states and 0 bytes), this is a good sign that the either the NAT rule is misconfigured or the traffic is not matching the firewall rule (a rule misconfiguration). This is one of the reasons why when adding a Port Forwarding entry, it is generally a better option to use **Filter rule association** to create a firewall rule rather than use the **Pass** option.

Also, keep in mind that for inbound NAT, typically we only need to configure the destination IP address and port. The source could be virtually anywhere, so we can usually leave this set to `Any`. Make sure that these options are configured correctly.

If you have checked the functioning of the underlying software of service and cannot find anything wrong with the NAT and firewall rule configuration, you might also consider the possibility that the port is blocked by your ISP. If it is a Port Forwarding entry, try changing the **Destination port range** setting and see if it works. You may also want to contact your ISP to see if any ports are blocked.

Also consider that Port Forwarding only works on protocols that use ports (primarily TCP and UDP). With Port Forwarding, different hosts have the same WAN IP address, but different ports. Because only one connection can be handled at a time, the protocol must support the use of ports. For protocols that do not use ports, consider using **1:1** NAT or NAT traversal (creating a TCP or UDP tunnel through which the traffic will move).

Port Forwarding may also run out of ports if there are too many simultaneous connections (for example, we configure DCC to use ports `5198` to `5200`, we can only have three simultaneous DCC connections). To prevent this from happening, you can either increase the range of ports, or create NAT entries with different target IPs (making sure the port ranges for the different IPs do not overlap).

Make sure that the Redirect target IP used in a Port Forwarding entry does not conflict with another IP address in the local network. IP address conflicts are just as harmful in Port Forwarding entries as they are elsewhere.

If you are trying to configure Outbound NAT, then keep in mind that **Outbound NAT** should be set to **Automatic Outbound NAT** unless there is a specific need to configure outbound NAT rules manually. If **Outbound NAT** is set to **Manual Outbound NAT** or Hybrid Outbound NAT, then make sure that source of traffic is matched. If the NAT settings are incorrect and your network uses private IP addresses, then traffic will not reach the WAN.

If you are configuring Outbound NAT for VPN usage, then make sure the following hold true:

- Make sure the rule for VPN traffic (such as, the ISAKMP rule for IPsec traffic is above the general pass-through rule for the interface (NAT entries, like firewall rules, are evaluated on a top-down basis).
- Make sure there is a rule for each interface on which VPN traffic will pass.

If you are configuring pfSense to act as a VPN client, you will also want to check with your VPN provider to find out what NAT entries must be created.

One possible problem with NAT is that incoming traffic may be reaching the target node, but the host may have a different default gateway. The outbound traffic will thus go out on a different router than the pfSense router from which the incoming NAT traffic came. As a result, the gateway for outgoing traffic may drop the connection, since there is no corresponding state in the state table, or it might send the outgoing traffic to the system originating the request, but the system will ignore the reply traffic because it has a different IP address than the WAN address of the pfSense router to which the request was sent. Therefore, you need to make sure that the incoming and outgoing gateway are the same.

It may be the case that pfSense is configured correctly, but the target node is running a firewall which blocks the request. If the system is running a firewall and you suspect the firewall may be blocking the connection, check the logs for the firewall and check the firewall settings.

Summary

In this chapter, we covered NAT, the reasons it was implemented, and the issues that it raises. We also covered both Static NAT, or 1:1 NAT, and Dynamic NAT, which covers both Outbound NAT and Port Forwarding. Although understanding all of these types of NAT are key to a thorough understanding of the technology, we also acknowledged that Port Forwarding is most commonly equated with NAT, and is probably the most likely form of NAT you will utilize. We also covered NPt, which is a rarely used method of mapping IPv6 public addresses to IPv6 private addresses, but does have its applications, particularly with multihoming.

Understanding this chapter is important, as we will return to NAT in subsequent chapters. For example, in `Chapter 7`, *Virtual Private Networks (VPNs)*, we will use Outbound NAT to redirect traffic when setting up VPN tunnels. At the very least, you will want to try to configure a few applications to work with Port Forwarding.

Thus far, we have focused mainly on getting our networks to work, but in the next chapter, we will focus on getting our networks to work well. We will cover how to use pfSense to allocate bandwidth to different networks, prioritize certain types of traffic, and relegate other traffic to lower priority levels. Different queuing disciplines will be discussed, as well as what to do when the pfSense traffic shaper does not provide the functionality we need. If you aim to optimize the speed of your network, you'll look forward to the next chapter.

Questions

Answer the following questions:

1. Name any two technologies other than NAT developed to deal with the issue of IPv4 address exhaustion.
2. If we initially install pfSense and configure the interfaces with IPv4 addresses only, do we need to alter the Outbound NAT settings? Why or why not?

3. If Automatic Outbound NAT is selected, how many rules are created for each non-WAN interface?
4. We have an FTP server that must be made accessible to the internet and also must be accessible within our private network. We want to assign this server its own public IP address. What type of NAT should we use?
5. What will happen if we create a Port Forwarding entry and set Filter rule association to None, assuming we do not make any changes to the firewall rules?
6. Why do we normally leave **Source** set to **any** on a Port Forwarding entry?
7. Assume we want to create a Port Forwarding entry for Remote Desktop Protocol (which normally runs on port `3389`), but want to make RDP accessible from the internet on port `7000`. (a) What should the Destination port range be set to? (b) What should the Redirect port range be set to?
8. (a) Name at least one reason to implement NPt on an IPv6 network. (b) What alternative to NPt does the IETF recommend?

6
Traffic Shaping

Traffic shaping, also known as **Quality of Service** (**QoS**), is a means of prioritizing network traffic that meets certain criteria. Without traffic shaping, network traffic is processed on a **first-in, first-out** (**FIFO**) basis. While in many cases, processing network traffic in such a way may be adequate, in other cases, it may lead to links becoming saturated, which in turn can lead to buffering and increased latency. Traffic shaping provides us with a means of prioritizing certain network traffic, which guarantees that it will receive available bandwidth before lesser priority traffic.

pfSense has its own traffic shaper, which is not only useful, but is also extremely easy to use. The pfSense traffic shaper wizard is easy and quick to configure, and the process of setting up traffic shaping can be done in a matter of minutes. In this chapter, however, it is our objective to provide a basic understanding of traffic shaping before delving into the specifics of how to implement traffic shaping in pfSense. Sometimes, pfSense's built-in traffic shaping functionality is not enough to meet our requirements, and in those instances, we must rely on third-party packages. We will cover that scenario as well.

In this chapter, we will cover the following topics:

- Traffic shaping essentials, including a summary of different queuing disciplines
- Configuring traffic shaping in pfSense, including using the pfSense traffic shaping wizard, as well as manual queue and rule configuration
- Some real-world traffic shaping examples
- Using Snort for traffic shaping
- Troubleshooting traffic shaping

Technical requirements

Again, you should be able to work though the examples in this chapter with a working pfSense system with at least a WAN and LAN interface with at least one node on the LAN network. It is helpful to have different types of software with which different traffic shaping scenarios can be simulated (for example, VoIP software to simulate cases where low latency is important; peer-to-peer (p2p) software for cases where high levels of latency can be tolerated, but we may want to absorb as much excess bandwidth as possible).

Traffic shaping essentials

Traffic shaping allows us to prioritize some traffic over other traffic, in order to optimize/improve network performance, and in some cases, lower latency. The purpose of traffic shaping is to make network traffic conform to certain predefined constraints, generally known as either a traffic profile or contract. Your **service level agreement** (**SLA**) and/or **traffic conditioning agreement** (**TCA**) with your ISP defines what traffic your ISP will accept. One of the basic parameters of this is the data rate. If packets are sent from your local network to the ISP in such a way that violates these agreements, forwarding upstream may be denied. At the very least, forwarding may be not guaranteed. Thus, it is in our interests to make sure that the traffic leaving our network does not violate these agreements, and we utilize a traffic shaper to make sure our traffic does not get dropped or penalized.

The traffic shaper is able to do this because it examines packets; if the packets meet certain criteria, they are handled differently. In this sense, traffic shaping bears similarities to firewall rules. In the case of firewall rules, packets that meet rule criteria are either allowed, blocked, or rejected. In the case of traffic shaping, packets that meet certain criteria (we can call them traffic shaping rules) are put into different queues. These queues are implemented as FIFO buffers. Priority traffic is typically sent immediately, while lower-priority traffic is held until the higher-priority traffic has passed.

Traffic shaping has to be implemented where the router can control the flow of data. Therefore, in pfSense, traffic shaping is always applied when packets are leaving the router. For example, traffic shaping of incoming traffic to the LAN is actually applied when the traffic is leaving the LAN interface. Similarly, traffic shaping of outgoing traffic is applied when traffic is leaving the WAN interface.

Traffic shaping can be used for a variety of purposes. This includes the following:

- It can be used in a number of different scenarios where low latency is required. This includes VoIP traffic, which, if it is given the same priority as other traffic, may be affected by uploads and downloads. Similarly, if you are playing an online game, you want the response time to be as fast as possible, even if you are simultaneously downloading a file. Other applications can tolerate a higher level of latency. For example, with video streaming using online services, such as Netflix or Hulu, a certain amount of buffering is tolerable.
- It can be used to limit the amount of bandwidth used by peer-to-peer applications. It can do this in two different ways. One is by lowering the priority of traffic coming to and from well-known peer-to-peer ports. The second is by actually examining the packets and finding out what application is generating them. The latter is known as Layer 7 inspection, or deep packet inspection. Both approaches have strengths and weaknesses. A port-based approach is easy to implement and will work in most cases, but users may be able to circumvent such an approach by using different ports. Layer 7 inspection is generally more effective in identifying peer-to-peer traffic, but it is also CPU-intensive, and it is of no help on encrypted traffic. In addition, small changes to the peer-to-peer protocol can result in Layer 7 inspection not working.
- It can be used to make asymmetric internet connections work more smoothly. If your download bandwidth is significantly larger than your upload bandwidth, the maximum download speed may seem unattainable because you won't be able to send enough ACK packets back to the target host to keep the traffic flowing. This is most likely as the connection becomes more saturated, for example, if you are downloading a file while simultaneously loading a web page. In these situations, pfSense can prioritize ACK packets, ensuring that traffic flows and that you are able to reach the maximum download speed.
- In business environments, traffic shaping can be used to prioritize business-related traffic.
- ISPs have sometimes used traffic shaping to limit bandwidth consumption of certain programs (for example BitTorrent traffic) so they can take on additional customers. This is often controversial, because such connections are often advertised as *unlimited* connections. Nonetheless, it is yet another example of traffic shaping being used for a specific outcome.

Traffic shaping is a large component of the current debate on **net neutrality**. Proponents of net neutrality argue (among other things) that internet data should be treated equally, while opponents of net neutrality argue for a two-tier or multi-tiered internet, in effect arguing that there have always been different levels of service and that less regulation would promote greater freedom of choice for the consumer. It is not within the scope of this chapter to deal with the potential impact of net neutrality, which seems in any case to primarily impact the public internet and not private networks, which are the main focus of our discussion.

Queuing policies

No discussion of traffic shaping would be complete without mentioning the different types of queues that can be utilized. The most basic queuing policy is a FIFO queue, sometimes also referred to as **first come, first served** (**FCFS**) queuing. With FIFO queuing, no packet is given priority; nor are there different classes of traffic. All packets are treated equally within the FIFO queue and packets are sent out in the order that they arrive.

Obviously, this makes for a very easy to implement policy. But when implemented, it can result in some users and applications consuming all the bandwidth. Even when they are not consuming bandwidth constantly, their usage may spike at inopportune times, delaying time-sensitive and important traffic. Worse yet, important traffic may be dropped because there is less important traffic in the queue.

Nonetheless, if you have congestion-free internet connection on which users and applications have as much bandwidth as they need, FIFO queuing may be appropriate. It is easy to implement and also guarantees that your access to bandwidth is delay-free. If this is not the case, however, it is time to consider one of the many alternatives to FIFO queuing.

Fair queuing represented the first improvement over FIFO queuing. In it, each program process is given its own FIFO queue. This prevents a badly behaving process from monopolizing the bandwidth. A further refinement of fair queuing is **weighted fair queuing** (**WFQ**), which provides a form of priority management. Packets are ultimately classified into high-bandwidth traffic and low-bandwidth traffic, and low-bandwidth traffic is given priority over high-bandwidth traffic. In turn, high-bandwidth traffic shares the connection proportionally based on assigned weights. This ensures that low-bandwidth streams, which represent the bulk of network traffic, are transmitted in a timely manner. One of the drawbacks of WFQ is that it relies on examining the packets, so it does not work on encrypted connections.

There are three queuing disciplines supported by the current version of pfSense: **priority queuing** (PRIQ), **class-based queuing** (CBQ), and **Hierarchical Fair Service Curve** (HFSC). Each of these policies has advantages and disadvantages, as we will soon see.

Priority queuing

Priority queuing (PRIQ) is a queuing policy that divides traffic into different priority levels. At an abstract level, it is essentially the same as the priority queue you may have learned about when studying data structures in computer science. Items are being pushed into the queue; when an item is pulled from the queue, it is always the highest priority item. This continues until the queue is empty.

Implementations of priority queuing differ in the number of levels, but in pfSense, there are seven levels, with seven being the highest priority. This is a flat hierarchy of priority levels. On each interface, priority queues are scanned for packets in descending order of priority. The highest priority queue is scanned first, then the next highest priority queue, and so forth. The packet at the head of the highest queue is chosen for sending. This procedure is repeated each time the traffic shaper chooses a packet to be sent.

A priority queue's behavior is defined by a set of rules that describe how packets should be assigned to priority queues. Packets can be classified by protocol or subprotocol type, which interface they come from, packet size, and so on. The advantage of PRIQ is that it is easy to configure and also easy to understand. It also ensures that absolute priority is given to traffic that is in the highest priority queue. The main disadvantage is that because priority always goes to higher level traffic and there is no way of circumventing this policy or for moving traffic to a higher level once it has been assigned a lower level of priority, lower priority traffic can be completely starved of bandwidth. In addition, having only seven priority levels limits the granularity of traffic shaping; an interface which relies solely on priority queuing can have at most seven separate queues.

Class-based queuing

Class-based queuing(CBQ) allows a bit more control than PRIQ. In CBQ, each class gets a percentage of bandwidth, after being grouped by classes. It divides traffic into a hierarchy of classes and thus allows you to classify traffic into a hierarchy. Criteria for prioritization can include protocol, the application being used, the IP address of the sender, and many other factors. It operates at the IP network layer (Layer 3). An additional appeal of CBQ is that it is in the public domain.

Each class is assigned a bandwidth limit, and packets within the class are processed until the bandwidth limit for the class is reached. This tends to ensure that even low-priority packets get some bandwidth. The first goal of CBQ is quantitative bandwidth sharing, but a secondary goal is that when some class is not using its allocated bandwidth, the distribution of excess bandwidth should not be arbitrary. Rather, the distribution of such bandwidth should follow a set of guidelines.

As a simple example of PRIQ and CBQ in practice, consider a company in which the ISP guarantees 150 Mbps of download bandwidth and 50 Mbps of upload bandwidth and four networks: developers, engineering, sales, and DMZ. We want two-thirds of the download bandwidth and half the upload bandwidth to go to the developers and engineering networks. We also want 60% of this share of the bandwidth to go to the developers network. This means that developers should get 60 Mbps of download bandwidth and 15 Mbps of upload bandwidth; engineering should get 40 Mbps of download bandwidth and 10 Mbps of upload bandwidth; the rest is allocated to sales and DMZ.

With PRIQ, we have no way of guaranteeing a fixed share of bandwidth to developers and engineering. We could assign higher priority levels to developers and engineering, so that developers have a higher priority than engineering, which in turn has a higher priority than sales and DMZ. However, this could result in sales and DMZ ultimately being starved of bandwidth, as a packet from either DEVELOPER or engineering will always win out over one from sales or DMZ.

With CBQ, however, each subnet could be assigned a percentage of bandwidth. Even better, CBQ can be hierarchical, so that developers and engineering share a percentage of bandwidth, with engineering being assigned a greater portion of their shared bandwidth.

Hierarchical Fair Service Curve

The third queuing discipline supported by pfSense is **Hierarchical Fair Service Curve** (**HFSC**). An HFSC can be thought of as a form of bandwidth allocation in which guarantees are made about latency. An HFSC queue is defined by a nonlinear curve with two parts. The first part, `m1`, determines the amount of bandwidth the queue gets up to `p` milliseconds. After `p` milliseconds, the second part of the curve (`m2`) determines the behavior of the queue. This is the amount of bandwidth guaranteed to the queue.

To illustrate HFSC, imagine two services competing for bandwidth: a VoIP connection and a file download. Assume a linear service curve such that the VoIP connection requires that a packet be sent every 30 ms, while for the file download, a packet must be sent every 9 ms. Assume that it takes 7 ms to transmit a packet. If packets are sent according to these deadlines, the delay for a video packet will be approximately 21 ms. Such a policy ensures that the deadlines are met, but the latency for VoIP packets is high.

Now imagine a different service curve such that the VoIP connection gets the bulk of the bandwidth up until 10 ms (for example, 75% of available bandwidth). The inflection point is at 10 ms, and after that the VoIP connection only gets 25% of the available bandwidth. With this policy, the delay for any VoIP is no more than 10 ms. The result is a lower latency for VoIP traffic, but a higher latency for the file download traffic, but this is acceptable, since throughput is more important than latency with respect to file downloads.

The main drawbacks of HFSC is that unlike PRIQ and CBQ, which are defined by very simple criteria (priority levels in the case of priority queuing, and amount of bandwidth allocated to a class in the case of CBQ), HFSC queues are defined by nonlinear curves, and thus are inherently more complex. There will be times when the traffic shaper cannot guarantee service to all curves at the same time, and/or it cannot do so fairly. Nonetheless, HFSC is a good choice for an algorithm if we are utilizing services that benefit from decoupling latency from bandwidth.

Configuring traffic shaping in pfSense

Traffic shaping in pfSense can be a challenge to configure, partially because of the number of options and the complexity of the shaper rules and shaper queues. It is generally recommended that you begin with the web GUI's traffic shaper wizard. You can access the wizard by clicking on **Firewall** | **Traffic Shaper** and then clicking on the **Wizards** tab. There are currently two wizards available: **Multiple Lan/Wan** and **Dedicated Links**. **Multiple Lan/Wan** can be used in a variety of scenarios in which there are one or more LAN-type interfaces, and one or more WAN interfaces. Dedicated Links, on the other hand, is designed for cases in which specific LAN/ WAN pairings do not mix with other traffic. For example, users on one subnet may have a different internet connection than users on another subnet. Therefore, there are two separate WAN interfaces (one for each internet provider). Traffic from one LAN interface goes to WAN, while traffic from another LAN interfaces goes to WAN2. Each LAN-WAN link has its own traffic shaping requirements, and this is where the Dedicated Links wizard helps. In most cases, however, you will not have dedicated WAN links, so Multiple Lan/Wan will be the correct choice.

The Multiple LAN/WAN Configuration wizard

The first page on the **Multiple Lan/Wan Configuration** wizard asks for the number of WAN-type connections and the number of LAN-type connections in two separate edit boxes. Since the wizard detects the number of each type of interface automatically, you can usually leave these numbers unchanged, and click on the **Next** button at the bottom of the page. You may not want to apply the traffic shaper to all interfaces, however, in which case you will want to enter fewer than the total number of WAN and LAN interfaces. You cannot, however, enter more than the total number of interfaces, or you will receive an error message. When you are done making changes, press the **Next** button.

The next page, **Shaper configuration**, is where you set up each of the individual interfaces. The page will have different sections, each labeled **Setup connection and scheduler information for interface X** where X is LAN #1, LAN #2, and so on, or WAN #1, WAN #2 and so on. In each section for the LAN interfaces, there are two drop-down boxes. In the first drop-down box, you select the interface; in the second drop-down box, you select the queuing discipline. Note that in subsequent pages of the wizard, the interfaces will not be specified by name, but instead will identified based on the assignments made on this page (for example, if you have a DMZ interface, and you specified it as the LAN #1 connection on the previous page, then on subsequent pages, Connection LAN #1 will refer to the DMZ interface). This is an aspect of the wizard that is not very user-friendly, and you want to make note of the assignments you make here. Otherwise, you will find yourself constantly hitting the back button on your browser to remind yourself what the assignments are.

The different queuing disciplines have been discussed previously in this chapter, so we won't discuss them in detail here, but here is a summary of their advantages and disadvantages:

- **PRIQ**: The simplest of all queuing algorithms. Packets are assigned different priority levels, with higher priority levels always being favored over lower priority levels. This guarantees lower latency for higher priority packets, but it also means packets with a lower level of priority can get starved for bandwidth.
- **CBQ**: Packets belong to classes, and each class is assigned an upper and lower bound for bandwidth. Classes can be hierarchical; therefore, a class can be divided into subclasses. This is a good queuing discipline for guaranteeing a minimum bandwidth, but no guarantees are made regarding latency.

- **HFSC**: A queuing discipline in which each queue has a curve with two portions: a fairness curve and a service curve. The fairness portion of the curve is designed to provide a minimum level of latency for each queue. There is no guarantee that all the goals of HFSC will be met under all circumstances, but HFSC is the best option for many purposes.

Once you have selected the queuing discipline for each of the LAN-type interfaces, you can set up your WAN connections. For each WAN interface, you can also select the queuing discipline (the same three options – **PRIQ**, **CBQ**, and **HFSC** – are offered). In addition, the wizard will prompt you for the upload and download bandwidth of each WAN interface. The numbers entered in these edit boxes should be a close approximation for your upload and download speeds, in order to ensure the traffic shaper works properly. When you are done making changes, click on the **Next** button at the bottom of the page.

- **VoicePulse**: A company that offers VoIP services to residential and business customers. They also offer trunking using the **Session Initiation Protocol** (**SIP**) for VoIP gateways and PBX systems.
- **Asterisk/Vonage**: You have probably heard of Asterisk, which provides you a means of setting up a PBX with software that has both an open source (GNU GPL) and a proprietary component. With Asterisk, you can implement many features previously only available in proprietary PBX systems, such as voice mail and conference calling. Asterisk also supports such VoIP protocols as SIP, the **Media Gateway Control Protocol** (**MGCP**), and H.323. Vonage is a VoIP company that offers both residential and business plans, as well as cloud services for enterprise-level customers.
- **PanasonicTDA**: The Panasonic KX-TDA series of phones supports both H.323 and SIP trunking, with the KX-TDA600 supporting up to 640 trunks.
- **Generic (lowdelay)**: Use this option if your VoIP service does not fall into any of the aforementioned categories.

The next option, **Upstream SIP Server**, allows you to enter the IP address of a remote PBX or SIP trunk to prioritize. If this option is used, the **Provider** field will be ignored. The value entered in this field can be an alias.

The rest of the page, **Connection WAN #1**, **Connection LAN #1**, and so on, allows you to enter the upload bandwidth for your WAN connections and the download bandwidth for your LAN connections. This allows you to specify the minimum bandwidth to be allocated to VoIP traffic. This will vary, based on the amount of bandwidth required per VoIP connection, and the total number of VoIP phones/devices, so you'll want to do your homework before entering this information. When you are done making changes, click on the **Next** button on the bottom of the page.

The next page, **Penalty Box**, contains two sections: **Penalty Box** and **Penalty Box specific settings**. The **Penalty Box** section has one option: the **Penalize IP or Alias** checkbox. If enabled, the priority of traffic from the IP (or alias) specified in the **Address** field in **Penalty Box specific settings** will be lowered. You must also specify a bandwidth percentage to which the specified host will be limited (only values between 2 and 15% are allowed). Note that although the drop-down box in this section allows you to select different options (percentage, bits/s, kilobits/s, megabits/s, and gigabits/s), if you select anything other than percentage, the entry will not be validated – when you click on **Next**, you will get a **Only percentage bandwidth specification is allowed** error message.

The next page, **Peer to Peer networking**, allows you to configure the peer-to-peer (commonly known as **P2P**) networking options. P2P networking protocols are designed to utilize all available bandwidth, unless you set limits. Often P2P clients allow you to set limits on the amount of bandwidth to be used, but if you expect P2P traffic on your network, you should ensure that other traffic will not be degraded as a result. Checking the **Lower priority of Peer-to-Peer traffic** at the top of this page allows you to configure other P2P options on the page.

The next option is the **p2p Catch All** checkbox, which, if checked, will feed all uncategorized traffic into the p2p queue. This addresses a common problem with traffic shaping with respect to P2P traffic. Many P2P protocols and technologies try deliberately to avoid detection, often by utilizing non-standard or random ports, or even ports associated with other protocols. The **p2p Catch All** option deals with this problem, sending all unrecognized traffic to the p2p queue, where its priority is accordingly lowered. As with **Penalty Box**, you must specify a percentage of bandwidth to allocate to the P2P queue, and once again, you are limited to specifying a value between 2 and 15%.

The next section, **Enable/Disable specific P2P protocols**, allows you to specify which P2P protocols will be recognized by pfSense. Check the corresponding checkbox for each service you want to be recognized. There are over 20 in total, including many well-known protocols, such as BitTorrent, DCC, Gnutella and Napster. When you are finished making your selections on this page, click on the **Next** button.

The next page of the wizard, **Network Games**, allows you to specify settings for network games. Since many online games rely on low latency for a good experience, you will want to check the **Prioritize network gaming traffic** checkbox if you or other users are going to play online games. Gaming can be affected by other users downloading large files, or even by gamers downloading game patches while playing. Enabling the prioritization of network gaming here raises the priority of network gaming so that game traffic will be transferred first and also given a guaranteed chunk of bandwidth.

The next section of the page, **Enable/Disable specific game consoles and services**, allows you to enable the game consoles/services you will be using. All the major game consoles are represented here (PlayStation, Wii and Xbox), and a few popular gaming services (such as Games for Windows Live). The last section of the page is **Enable/Disable specific games**. Quite a few popular games are represented here, including Doom 3, Minecraft, and World of Warcraft. If a game you play is not on the list, you may want to choose a game (preferably a similar one) so you can configure a reference rule later on. When you are done selecting games, click on the **Next** button.

The next page of the wizard, **Raise or lower other Applications**, provides a list of over 25 applications/services for which you can raise or lower the priority level. Each application or service has its own drop-down box with three options: **Default priority**, which keeps the priority level the same, **Higher priority**, and **Lower priority**. Your specific network configuration and requirements will dictate which applications, and services, for which you manipulate the priority levels. The applications and services are generally grouped with those that would need a higher priority closer to the top of the page and those whose priority can be lowered closer to the bottom of the page. For example, the **Remote Service / Terminal emulation** section of the page has **VNC** (**Virtual Network Computing**) listed. If you are using **VNC**, you probably want to choose **Highest priority**, since a poor-quality network connection will make it difficult to remotely control another computer (keep in mind that not just bandwidth but latency is a factor here, with keyboard and mouse events need to be transmitted to the remote computer for it to work).

On the other hand, there are services where nobody will notice if the priority level is lowered. Mail services such as SMTP, POP3 and IMAP come to mind, as well as applications such as MySQL Server. If you enabled **p2p Catch All** earlier in the wizard, you want to specify protocols here, so they are not penalized by the **p2p Catch All** rule. When you are done making changes, click on the **Next** button.

Once you click on the **Next** button, you will be on the final page of the wizard. At this point, all the rules and queues are created, but not yet in use. By clicking on the **Finish** button at the bottom of the page, the new rules will load and will be active.

Traffic shaping will now be active, but it will only be applied to new connections. In order for the traffic shaper to take effect on all connections, you must clear the state table. To do this, navigate to **Diagnostics** | **States**, click on the **Reset States** tab, and then click on the **Reset** button at the bottom of the page.

The Dedicated Links wizard

pfSense also provides an wizard for setting up dedicated links. To use this wizard, navigate to **Firewall** | **Traffic Shaper**, click on the **Wizards** tab and click on the second option (**traffic_shaper_wizard_dedicated.xml**). On the first page, **pfSense Traffic Shaper**, you will be warned that custom links should not exceed 30% of the interface link/bandwidth. There is also an edit box where you must enter the number of WAN connections. As with the **Multiple Lan/Wan** wizard, the wizard will automatically fill in the number of WAN connections, so unless you want to use this traffic shaper on less than the total number of WAN interfaces, you can leave this value as it is and click on the **Next** button.

On the next few pages, the **Shaper configuration** pages, you will enter the parameters for each connection. There are two **Local interface** drop-down boxes. In the first drop-down box, you will specify the interface which will use this connection, and in the second drop-down box, you will specify the queuing discipline (again, the choices are **PRIQ**, **CBQ** and **HFSC**). The two **WAN Interface** drop-down boxes are set up in the same way, with the actual interface specified in the first drop-down box and the queuing discipline specified in the second one. The next options on the page are **Upload**, where you specify the upload bandwidth for the connection, and **Download**, where you specify the download bandwidth.

Both options have an edit box and a drop-down box; in the edit box you specify the bandwidth, and in the corresponding drop-down box, you specify the unit of measure for the edit box (**Kbps**, **Mbps**, or **Gbps**). When you are done, click on the **Next** button at the bottom. This page will repeat itself for as many WAN connections as you specified on the first page of the wizard. Thus, if you entered `3` on the first page, the next page will prompt you for the settings for **Connection #2**, and the next page after that will prompt you for the settings for **Connection #3**.

The next page, **Voice over IP**, allows you to configure the VoIP settings. Since the options here are identical to the options in the **Multiple Lan/Wan** wizard, we will not cover them in detail here, but instead refer to the **Voice over IP** subsection in the previous section. In fact, the next few pages of the wizard (**Penalty Box**, **Peer to Peer Networking**, **Network Games**, and **Raise or lower other Applications**, are all identical to corresponding pages in the **Multiple Lan/Wan** wizard, so refer to the previous section for those options as well.

As with the **Multiple Lan/Wan** wizard, at the end of the process, you will be presented with a final page. The rules and queues have been created, but will not be loaded until you click on the **Finish** button. Once you have done this, the traffic shaper will be active, but will only apply to new connections. If you want it to apply to all connections, you have to empty the state table using the **Reset States** option in **Diagnostics | States**.

Advanced traffic shaping configuration

After the initial traffic shaping configuration using the traffic shaper wizard, you may find that the rules the wizard do not entirely fit your needs. This may be as a result of issues you knew about when you were using the wizard (for example, you are using a game not on the list of games) or there may be other issues, such as a service or application that needs to be limited. This should not be a major problem; now that the basic rules have been created, you can edit or copy those rules and create custom rules that suit your needs. There are two broad categories of changes you might want to make: changes to queues and changes to traffic shaping rules.

Changes to queues

To begin configuration, navigate to **Firewall | Traffic Shaper** and click on either the **By Interface** or **By Queue** tab. If you choose **By Interface**, you will see a list of interfaces at the root level, along with a list of queues available on each interface. If you choose **By Queue**, you will instead see a list of queues at the root level, and when you click on each queue, you will see a list of interfaces which utilize that queue. You can edit queues from either tab; which tab you use for such editing is a matter of preference. If you are creating queues, you will find that the easiest way to do so is to create a queue on a single interface on the **By Interface** tab, and then make the queue available on other interfaces by clicking on the **By Queue** tab and using the **Clone Shaper to this Interface** button.

Once you have selected a queue on an interface to edit, you will be presented with several options. The **Enable/Disable** checkbox, if unchecked, will disable the queue and any children queues. The **Name** edit box allows you to change the name, assuming you would want to do that. The **Priority** edit box allows you to set a priority level from `0` to `7`. Higher-numbered priority levels take precedence over lower-numbered priority levels. Keep in mind, however, that if the queue is a HFSC queue, the priority field will be ignored. HFSC queues are identifiable by the fact that their configuration pages have a section called **Service Curve (sc)**. We will cover HFSC configuration later in this section.

The **Queue Limit** edit box allows you to enter the queue limit (expressed in terms of packets). The next options are the **Scheduler options** checkboxes. These checkboxes allow you to apply additional traffic shaping algorithms to the queue. Checking the **Default Queue** checkbox will make this queue the default queue for the interface (it can only be selected on one queue per interface). The other options are as follows:

- **Random Early Detection**: A traffic shaping queue is essentially a buffer. Once the buffer is full, packets will be dropped (often referred to as tail drop). This can be problematic, as during times when the network is congested, all buffers can become full, and might alternate between being flooded and being under-utilized. **Random Early Detection** (**RED**) attempts to avoid this problem by randomly dropping packets as the buffer fills up. If the buffer is almost empty, all packets are accepted, but as the buffer fills up, the probability of a packet being dropped increases.
- **Random Early Detection In and Out**: This is a variation of RED. The RED algorithm is still employed, but there are separate in and out queues on the interface. The out queue is much more aggressive in dropping packets than the in queue. The advantage here is that the out traffic can be controlled before the queue grows to the point that any in traffic is dropped. We call this scheme **RED with In and Out**, or RIO.
- **Explicit Congestion Notification**: This is an extension to TCP/IP which provides for end-to-end notification of network congestion without dropping packets. It is defined in RFC 3168 (2001) and is supported by most modern network hardware.
- **CoDel Active Queue: CoDel**, or controlled delay, was developed to address perceived shortcomings in RED. Whereas RED/RIO are based on the assumption that average queue length is a sign of network congestion, CoDel is based on the assumption that average queue length actually tells us nothing about network conditions, and that a better metric is the minimum amount of delay experienced by any packet in the running buffer window. CoDel seeks to minimize this delay and keep it below `5` milliseconds. If the minimum delay rises to a higher value, packets are dropped from the window until the delay drops below this value. It is also based on the assumption that there are good queues (queues that handle bursts of traffic with only minor increases in delay) and bad queues (queues for which a burst of traffic cause them to fill and stay filled, with larger increase in delay), and that CoDel can safely ignore the good queues.

All of these algorithms are designed to deal with the problem of **bufferbloat**, an occurrence of excess buffering of packets, which causes high latency and packet delay variation. Network equipment manufacturers began to incorporate larger buffers into their routers. The problem with larger buffers is that the TCP algorithm uses the number of dropped packets to determine when a connection is saturated. But with large buffers, it may take several seconds for the buffers to fill and packets to drop. Thus, the buffer becomes a bottleneck until TCP adjusts. Then the buffer drains, the TCP connection ramps up again and floods the buffer. In other words, large buffers can actually break TCP's congestion avoidance algorithms to break and thus queues can be constantly congested unless appropriate countermeasures are taken.

The last option in the top section is the **Description** edit box. In this field, you can enter a description for your own reference, which is not parsed.

This covers options that are available for queues that employ PRIQ or CBQ. If **HFSC** was selected for the queue, however, there are additional options provided on a section of the page called **Service Curve (sc)**. The first option, **Bandwidth**, allows you to choose the amount of bandwidth of the queue. The remaining options allow you to configure the service curves for the queue. Each service curve has three parameters: **`m1`**, `d`, and `m2`. **`m1`** and `m2` represent two portions of the service curve, and `d` represents the dividing point between the two portions. For the first `d` milliseconds, the queue gets the bandwidth given as `m1`. After `d` milliseconds, the queue gets the value given in `m2`. You can configure three different service curves for each queue: **Max bandwidth for the queue**, **Min bandwidth for the queue**, and **B/W share of a backlogged queue**. The significance of these three curves is as follows:

- **Max bandwidth for the queue (Upper Limit)**:The upper limit service curve limits HFSC bandwidth to bandwidth available on the upstream router/ interface.
- **Min bandwidth for the queue (Real Time)**: The real-time service curve ignores any class hierarchy and guarantees precise bandwidth as well as delay allocation.
- **B/W share of a backlogged queue (Link Share)**: The opposite of the realtime service curve, link share distributes bandwidth according to a class hierarchy.

When you are done making changes, click on the **Save** button at the bottom of the page. You can also choose **Add new queue** or **Delete this queue**. **Add new queue** allows you to create a brand-new queue (the options are the same as those outlined earlier), while **Delete this queue** results in the deletion of the currently selected queue.

Limiters

Another option for traffic shaping in pfSense is using limiters. The **Limiters** option allows you to set up a series of dummynet pipes; **dummynet** is a FreeBSD traffic shaper that was designed to simulate different types of connections. Bandwidth and queue size limitations can be imposed, as well as scheduling and queue management policies and delay/loss emulation.

To set up a limiter, navigate to **Firewall** | **Traffic Shaper,** and click on the **Limiters** tab. If you have set up limiters previously, you will see a tree showing the different queues. Otherwise, the page will be mostly blank, but there will be a new limiter button on the left of the page. Click on this button to set up a new limiter.

There are some things to consider when creating a new limiter:

- It is generally considered a good idea to create separate queues for the in and out traffic. *In* and *out* are always from the perspective of the interface. Thus, the in queue is for upload traffic, and the out queue is for download traffic.
- Keep in mind that the newly created limiter will have no effect until a rule is created which assigns traffic to the limiter. We will cover creating rules that assign traffic to a queue later in this chapter.

The configuration page for limiters has two sections: **Limiters** and **Advanced**

Options. The first option on the page is the **Enable** checkbox. If checked, the limiter (and its children) will be enabled. Next, there is also a **Name** edit box where you must enter a name for the limiter.

The next section of the page is called **Bandwidth**. Here, you enter the upper limit for the bandwidth. The amount of bandwidth is entered in the **Bandwidth** edit box, and the unit of measure (**bps**, **Kbps**, or **Mbps**) can be selected in the **Bw type** drop-down box. The third option is **Schedule**. In this drop-down box, you can select a time frame in which the bandwidth limit will be imposed. The schedule has to be one that was defined by using the pfSense **Schedule** option, which can be found at **Firewall** | **Traffic Shaper**. (Detailed information about how to create a schedule can be found in `Chapter 4`, *pfSense as a Firewall*). If you do not want to use a schedule on this limiter, you can select **none** in the drop-down box. You can also create multiple bandwidth schedule entries by clicking on the **Add Schedule** button.

The next field is the **Mask** drop-down box. In this box, you can set up the limiter so that it only applies to either source or destination traffic. If you select either **Source addresses** or **Destination addresses**, then a dynamic pipe will be created for each source or destination IP address encountered. This dynamic pipe will have the bandwidth, delay, packet loss and queue size specified for the limiter. As a result, you can easily specify bandwidth limits per host with this option. If you utilize this option, you must specify the IPv4 mask or IPv6 mask in the appropriate drop-down boxes. You may also enter a brief non-parsed description in the **Description** field.

The next section is **Advanced Options**. These options are mainly useful if you want to simulate certain network conditions, and are not particularly useful in real-world situations. **Delay (ms)** allows you to specify a delay. **Packet loss rate** allows you to specify a rate of packet loss, expressed as a fraction of 1. For example, a value of 0.001 means that one packet in 1000 is dropped; 0.01 will drop one in 100, and so on. If a number is specified for **Queue size (slots)**, then the limiter will create a fix-sized queue into which packets in the pipe will be placed. They will then be delayed by the amount specified in **Delay (ms)**, and then they will be delivered to their destination. Finally, **Bucket size (slots)** allows you to specify the number of slots in the bucket array used for source or destination hashing. When you are done making changes, click on the **Save** button at the bottom of the page.

What is a limiter good for? You can use it for anything for which you would use a traffic shaper. One possible use of limiters is to set up a guaranteed minimum bandwidth queue. To do this, create two queues (one for uploading and one for downloading) with the upper bandwidth limit set to the amount you want as the guaranteed minimum bandwidth (for example, 1 Gbps up and 1 Gbps down). Then create two more queues with the upper bandwidth limit set to whatever bandwidth is left (for example, if your connection is 10 Gbps up and 20 Gbps down, set the upload queue limit to 9 Gbps and the download queue to 19 Gbps. Direct guaranteed service traffic into the 1 Gbps queues, and everything else into the other 2 queues. This will have the effect of guaranteeing bandwidth to an application or service using the 1 Gbps queues, since it will be able to have sole use of the queues.

Layer 7 traffic shaping

You probably noticed that the majority of traffic shaping rules use ports and/or protocols as matching criteria. This is an imperfect solution, since many applications use random ports, or have the ability to select different ports, and the protocol alone usually isn't enough to identify the traffic.

Layer 7 traffic shaping, also known as **deep packet Inspection** (**DPI**), attempts to address this shortcoming by identifying traffic based on the contents of the packets. Prior to version 2.3, pfSense had Layer 7 traffic shaping available as an option. As of version 2.3, however, Layer 7 support has been removed from pfSense. According to the release notes for 2.3, Layer 7 traffic shaping *had been broken for all of 2.2.x* and had high CPU usage. Instead, the notes recommend that we use Snort filters instead. Snort is a third-party package which we will cover in `Chapter 9`, *Extending pfSense with Packages*.

Adding and changing traffic shaping rules

We have demonstrated how queues can be added and how existing queues can be edited, but the traffic shaping rules control how network traffic is assigned into these queues. If a packet matches a rule, it will be assigned into the queue that the rule specifies. Thus traffic shaping rules are essentially a subset of the firewall rules covered in `Chapter 4`, *pfSense as a Firewall*.

In older versions of pfSense, traffic shaper had a separate tab called **Rules**. This tab showed all the rules generated by the traffic shaper. This is no longer the case. To see the traffic shaper rules, navigate to **Firewall** | **Rules** and click on the **Floating** tab. The traffic shaper rules will be listed here, mixed in with any other floating rules that you created yourself. Nonetheless, you should be able to distinguish the trafficshaper rules from the nontraffic-shaper rules by their description. In addition, all traffic-shaper rules will have a value specified for **Queue** (for example, **qOthersLow**, **qVoIP**, and so on), whereas other rules may not have a queue specified.

To edit a rule, click on the edit icon (represented by a pencil); to delete a rule, click on the *delete* icon (represented by a trash can). Both options can be found in the **Actions** column (the right most column in the table). You can also change the order of rules in two different ways. You can click on a rule in the table and drag it to a different position. If you need to move more than one rule, it may be more convenient to check the rules (the checkbox for each rule is in the left most column) and then click on the *Move checked rules above this one* icon in the **Actions** column for the rule, which the checked rules are to be moved ahead of. To add a new blank rule, click on one of the **Add** buttons at the bottom of the list (the **Add** button with the up arrow creates a new rule at the top of the list, while the one with the down arrow creates a new rule at the bottom of the list). To create a rule based on an existing rule, click on the c**opy** icon (represented by two sheets) in the Actions column of the rule you want to copy.

Each rule will have several matching criteria. These criteria are what ensure that traffic is fed into the proper queue. Traffic shaping rules can have separate inbound and outbound queues, but most of the rules generated by the pfSense traffic shaper wizard have the same queue for inbound and outbound traffic. This is because the wizard generates floating rules, which apply to traffic in both directions. This saves us from having to generate separate rules for inbound and outbound traffic, but it also means that inbound and outbound traffic must be fed into the same queue, since each rule can only assign traffic into one queue.

If we click on the **Edit** option for any traffic shaper rule, we can see that such a rule has much in common with any other firewall rule, although there are some significant differences. The first field is the **Action** drop-down box. Traffic shaping rules do not utilize the **Pass**, **Block** or **Reject** options used by most other firewall rules, but instead use the **Match** option. As mentioned in `Chapter 4`, *pfSense as a Firewall*, this option allows pfSense to match traffic without affecting its pass/block status. The interface selected in the **Interface** list box is usually the **WAN** interface. The **Direction** drop-down box determines whether the rule applies to inbound traffic, outbound traffic, or both. As mentioned previously, most of the rules generated by the pfSense traffic shaper wizard appear to take advantage of the fact that floating rules can apply to traffic in both directions; therefore, the traffic shaper rules are generally set to any.

The aforementioned settings are the same for all the autogenerated rules, but the elements that differentiate traffic are the core of traffic shaping rules. The two factors that seem to be used most often to filter traffic are protocol (TCP is most commonly used, but many VoIP and gaming services use UDP) and port number. Consider, for example, an autogenerated rule to divert DCC traffic into the P2P queue. **TCP** is selected as **Protocol** (which is not unusual), and **Destination port range** is set to `6666` to `6668`. This rule might not be that effective, since the end user can easily circumvent it by changing the port range on their DCC client (easy to circumvent in the case of receiving files; sending files via DCC requires adding a NAT port forwarding entry). On the other hand, our traffic shaper rules should work pretty well with services that always use the same ports. For example, our rule to send all port `25` traffic into the low-priority queue should be effective in ensuring that all SMTP traffic is given a lower priority.

A good example of a rule which uses both protocol and port as matching criteria is an autogenerated rule created by pfSense to assign a higher priority to Ventrilo voice traffic. Here, the protocol is UDP, so **UDP** is selected in the **Protocol** drop-down box. Port **6100** is also used, so it is specified as **Destination port range**.

Although they seldom seem to be used by the pfSense autogenerated rules, another way of matching traffic is to use the TCP flags. The TCP flags indicate various states of a connection, and they can be matched on whether or not they are set, cleared, or we can leave the checkboxes unchecked if we don't care whether they are set. Since we covered the TCP flags in detail in *Chapter 4*, we won't cover it here, other than to be aware that they may be used as matching criteria.

The last option in the **Advanced Options** section is **Ackqueue/Queue**, and this is where the matching traffic is assigned to a queue. The first drop-down box selects the queue for ACK traffic; the second drop-down box selects the queue for all other traffic. In practice, **Ackqueue** is often left undefined (set to **None**) and **Queue** is the only selection made, although it is good practice to set up a dedicated queue for ACK traffic to prevent delays caused by the remote node waiting for ACKs that are stuck in a queue with other traffic.

Armed with this information, we should now be able to make changes to traffic shaping rules if necessary. As always, you may want to make a backup before making any rule changes, in case the changes lead to unfavorable results and you want to revert back to your old ruleset.

Example 1 – modifying the penalty box

As an example of how we can change rules generated by the pfSense traffic shaper wizard to suit our needs, let's revisit the penalty box rule. As you might recall, the traffic shaper wizard lets us assign a single IP address to the low-priority queue (qOthersLow). Suppose we want to make two modifications to the penalty box:

- Instead of a single IP address, we want to ban a range of IP addresses.
- The only traffic we want to penalize is from a video streaming application that uses the **Real-time Transport Protocol** (**RTP**). RTP in turn uses UDP, so we only want to block UDP traffic.

The traffic shaper wizard does not allow us to do this. Fortunately, changing the existing penalty box rule is relatively easy to do. Assume that we want to assign `172.16.1.1` to `172.16.1.15` to the penalty box. Rather conveniently, the IP addresses all fall within a subnet that is defined by the subnet mask `255.255.255.240`, or a CIDR of `28`. Thus, we click on the edit icon for the penalty box rule and make the necessary changes:

1. **Protocol** is currently set to **Any**. Select **UDP** from the **Protocol** drop-down box.
2. **Source** is currently set to **Single host or alias** and to an **IP address** of `172.16.1.10`. Select **Network** from the **Source** drop-down box.

3. Set the network to `172.16.1.0`, and set the CIDR in the corresponding drop-down box to `28`.
4. Click on the **Save** button at the bottom of the page, and when the main **Floating rules** page loads, click on the **Apply Changes** button at the top of the page.

Now the entire subnet from `172.16.1.1` to `172.16.1.15` will be in the penalty box. But what if we want to assign an arbitrary set of IP addresses to the penalty box? For example, assume that we want to assign `172.17.1.10`, `172.18.1.12`, and `172.18.1.17` to the penalty box. Obviously, we cannot use the approach outlined earlier, since the nodes are on different networks. We could create three separate rules (one for each IP address), but we should try to avoid duplication when possible. Thus we revisit a concept *Aliases* introduced in the `Chapter 4`, *pfSense as a Firewall*, and utilize the following approach:

1. Navigate to **Firewall** | **Aliases** and click on the **Add** button.
2. In the **Name** edit box, type **PENALTYBOX**. You may also enter a brief description in the **Description** edit box (for example, **Nodes assigned to the low priority queue**). In the **Type** drop-down box, select **Host(s)**.
3. In the **Host(s)** section of the page, enter each IP address. Click on the **Add Host** button after entering the first and second IP address. The CIDR will be updated automatically.
4. Click on the **Save** button at the bottom of the page, then click on the **Apply Changes** button on the main **Aliases** page.
5. Now that we have an alias we can use, we will return to **Firewall** | **Rules** and click on the **Floating** tab. Click on the **Edit** icon on the penalty box rule.
6. For **Source**, select **Single host or alias** in the drop-down box. In the edit box, type **PENALTYBOX** (as soon as you start typing, the autocomplete feature should do the rest).
7. Click on the **Save** button at the bottom of the page, and click on the **Apply Changes** button on the main **Floating rules** page.

Example 2 – prioritizing EchoLink

We can also create rules for applications not covered by pfSense's traffic shaper wizard. For example, we may want to create a rule to prioritize traffic from EchoLink, a VoIP application that allows radio amateurs to communicate with each other.

EchoLink uses ports `5198` to `6000`, and uses UDP on ports `5198` and `5199`, and TCP on port `6000`. As a result, we will have to create two rules for EchoLink, but the process is still fairly simple:

1. From the **Floating** tab on the **Rules** page, click on one of the **Add** buttons at the bottom of the page.
2. In the **Action** drop-down box, select **Match**.
3. In the **Interface** listbox, select **WAN**.
4. Leave **Direction** set to **any**, so that the rule will be a bidirectional rule.
5. Change **Protocol** to **UDP**.
6. Set **Destination port range** to `5198` to `5199`. You may also enter a brief description (for example, **Prioritize EchoLink UDP rule**).
7. Click on the **Show Advanced** button and scroll down to **Ackqueue/Queue**.
8. Set **Queue** to **qOthersHigh**.
9. Click on the **Save** button. This will take you back to the main **Floating rules** page.
10. To save time, we'll copy this rule and make a rule for port **6000**. Click on the **Copy** icon on the newly created rule to make a new rule based on this rule.
11. In the new rule, change **Protocol** to **TCP**.
12. Change **Destination port range** to **6000**. You may also enter a brief description (for example, **Prioritize EchoLink TCP rule**).
13. Click on the **Save** button. On the **Floating rules** page, click on the **Apply Changes** button.

You'll probably want to check the firewall rules to make sure no existing rules conflict with the newly created ones. But as this example demonstrates, generating your own rules without the wizards is not necessarily difficult.

Traffic shaping examples

In the section covering traffic shaping essentials, we discussed an example network with four subnets - developers, engineering, sales, and DMZ - as well as some basic traffic shaping requirements. Now, we will attempt to implement traffic shaping using pfSense in a manner that matches these requirements as closely as possible.

Example 1 – adding limiters

Although it is generally recommended that you use the traffic shaper wizards when getting started with traffic shaping, for this exercise we will avoid using them, since the rules the wizard will implement would require significant modification. We will begin by navigating to **Firewall** | **Traffic Shaper** and selecting the **Limiters** tab.

We require that **developers** and engineering receive 100 Mbps of downstream bandwidth, with 60 Mbps going to developers. We also will gives developers and engineering 25 Mbps of upstream bandwidth, with 15 Mbps going to developers. To do this, we will set up two limiters: a limiter for download bandwidth and one for upload bandwidth. Each of these limiters will have two children (one for developers and one for engineering). We proceed as follows:

1. Click on the **New Limiter** button.
2. Check the **Enable** checkbox.
3. In the **Name** edit box, type **qDOWNLOAD**.
4. For **Bandwidth**, enter **100** in the edit box and select **Mbit/s** in the drop-down box.
5. We can leave **Mask** unchanged. You can enter a brief description (for example, **Download queue for developers/engineering**).
6. Click on the **Save** button; then click on the **Apply Changes** button.
7. Click on the **qDOWNLOAD** queue on the left sidebar; then click on the **Add new Queue** button to create the first of the child queues.
8. Click on the **Enable** checkbox.
9. In the **Name** field, type **qDLDEV**.
10. Again, **Mask** can be left unchanged; you may enter a brief description (for example, **Download queue for developers**).
11. Under **Advanced Options**, in the **Weight** field, type **60** (so that **developers** gets a 60% share of 100 Mbps, or 60 Mbps).
12. Click on the **Save** button and then click on **Apply Changes**.
13. Click on the **qDOWNLOAD** queue on the left sidebar and click on the **Add New Queue** button. Create a new child queue named **qDLENG** by checking the **Enable** checkbox and specifying **qDLENG** in the **Name** field.
14. Under **Advanced Options**, in the **Weight** field, type **40** (so that **engineering** gets a 40% share of 100 Mbps, or 40 Mbps).

15. Click on the **Save** button; then click on **Apply Changes**.
16. Follow the same procedure to create a queue called **qUPLOAD** with a total bandwidth of 25 Mbps. Create two child queues called **qULDEV** with a 60% share of bandwidth, and **qULENG** with a 40% share of bandwidth.

We now have a set of queues for the developers and engineering networks, but they are of no use until we create rules to send traffic to them. Navigate to **Firewall | Rules** and click on the **Floating** tab. We need to create four rules: an upload and download queue for each interface:

1. Click on one of the **Add** buttons at the bottom of the page.
2. In the **Action** drop-down box, select **Match**.
3. In the **Interface** listbox, select **developers**.
4. In the **Direction** drop-down box, select **out**.
5. All traffic to and from the interface is going to the queue, so in the **Protocol** drop-down box, select **any**.
6. You may enter a brief description in the **Description** edit box (for example, **developers download queue rule**).
7. Click on the **Show Advanced** button.
8. In **Advanced Options**, scroll down to the **In/Out** pipe drop-down boxes and select **qDLDEV** as the **In** pipe.
9. Click on the **Save** button at the bottom of the page; when the main **Floating rule** page reloads, click on the **Apply Changes** button.
10. Create a rule for the developers upload queue by clicking on the **Copy** icon for the previously created rule, changing the **Direction** to **in** and changing the **In** pipe to **qULDEV**. (You may also enter a brief description in the **Description** field.). Click on the **Save** button when done and then click on the **Apply Changes** button on the main **Floating rules** page.
11. Create rules for the engineering download and upload queues. Both queues should have engineering set as the **Interface** and **any** selected in the **Protocol** drop-down box. The download queue should have the **Direction** set to **out** and the **In** pipe set to **qDLENG**. The upload queue should have the **Direction** set to **in** and the **In** pipe set to **qULENG**.

We now have queues for both **developers** and **engineering** that meet our traffic shaping requirements for both networks.

Example 2 – penalizing peer-to-peer traffic

Dealing with P2P traffic is a bit more challenging. We are unlikely to be able to categorize every protocol and port used by P2P applications, and finding other matching criteria may be difficult. But if we can assume a certain range of ports is being used, we can create a rule. Moreover, we can at least create a queue for future use.

Once again, we begin by navigating to **Firewall** | **Traffic Shaper** and clicking on the **By Interface** tab. We then proceed as follows:

1. Click on **WAN** on the left sidebar.
2. If you have been following the examples sequentially, you won't have to create the parent queue for the WAN interface. Otherwise, see the previous example to see how to configure the parent queue on the WAN interface. If the WAN parent queue already exists, click on the **Add new Queue** button.
3. Check the **Enable/Disable** checkbox for the new queue.
4. In the **Name** field, type **qP2P**.
5. Set **Priority** to **1**. You can leave **Queue Limit** blank.
6. In **Scheduler** options, check **Explicit Congestion Notification**. You may enter a brief description in the **Description** field.
7. Click on the **Save** button, then when the page reloads click on the **Apply Changes** button.
8. Click on the **By Queue** tab. The **qP2P** queue should be listed on the left sidebar.
9. Click on **qP2P**. The right side of the page should display all interfaces, with a **Clone Shaper to this Interface** button for each interface. Click on each button to clone **qP2P** to each interface. Then click on the **Apply Changes** button at the top of the page.
10. Click on **By Interface** to confirm that the **qP2P** queue is available on all interfaces.
11. Navigate to **Firewall** | **Rules** and click on the **Floating** tab; we will now create a rule for P2P traffic. Assume that we are going to send traffic on ports `6881` to `6999` to `qP2P`.
12. Click on one of the **Add** buttons at the bottom of the page.
13. On the rule configuration page, select **Match** in the **Action** drop-down box.
14. In the **Interface** list, select **WAN**.
15. Leave **Direction** set to **any**. In the **Protocol** drop-down box, change the protocol to **TCP/UDP**.

16. In the **Destination** section, set **Destination** port range to **6881** to **6999**. Under **Extra Options**, you may enter a brief description.
17. Also under **Extra Options**, click on the **Display Advanced** button.
18. Scroll down to **Ackqueue/Queue** and set **Queue** to **qP2P**.
19. Click on the **Save** button, and on the main **Floating rules** page, click on the **Apply Changes** button.

We now have a queue for P2P traffic, and a corresponding rule. If our requirements change with respect to ports and/or protocols, we can always update the ruleset.

Using Snort for traffic shaping

As mentioned earlier in the chapter, Layer 7 (deep packet inspection) traffic shaping has been removed from pfSense's built-in traffic shaper, and it is now recommended that you use a third-party solution such as Snort for such purposes. Configuring Snort can be somewhat involved, but if your traffic shaping requirements include some form of deep packet inspection, Snort can do the job quite well.

Installing and configuring Snort

The initial installation of Snort is simple. Navigate to **System** | **Package Manager** and click on the Available Packages tab. Scroll down to the entry for Snort and click on the green **Install** button. Then click on the **Confirm** button to confirm installation. Once you do, the web GUI will automatically transfer you to the **Package Installer** tab, which will provide information on the progress of Snort's download and installation.

Once Snort is installed, there will be a new entry on the **Services** menu for it. Navigate to **Services** | **Snort** to begin configuration. Click on the **Global Settings** tab. Here, you will find a number of settings that will apply to all interfaces on which Snort is activated. Note that under **Snort Subscriber Rules**, if you check **Enable Snort VRT**, an edit box will appear into which you can enter a **Snort Oinkmaster Code**. Although not strictly necessary, you'll likely find that having a valid Oinkmaster code will be worthwhile, as it will enable you to download rules from the official Snort website. Registration is free, and it enables you to download the restricted rules (subscription to the Personal and Business tiers is not free).

To register at the official Snort website and thus receive an Oinkmaster code, navigate to `https://www.snort.org/subscribe` and fill out the registration form. The website will send an email confirmation. Once you receive the email and have confirmed your registration, log into the official Snort website and click on your email address in the upper right corner to see your account information. There should be a link on the menu on the left side of the page for the Oinkcode; click on it to generate the code. Once you have done this, you can enter your Oinkmaster code in the appropriate edit box in **Global Settings**.

What settings you choose will entirely depend on what your security needs are, but you will likely want to enable the download of **Snort GPLv2 Community rules**, as well as the **Emerging Threats Open rules**. Under **Rules Update Settings**, note that by default, Snort does not update the rules, so you will want to choose a reasonable value for the **Update Interval** (such as **1 DAY**). Also note that when Snort is first enabled, it does not automatically download the rules, so you should click on the **Updates** tab and click on the **Update Rules** button to make sure the rules are downloaded.

Snort is now installed and we have done some basic configuration, but nothing will happen until we enable Snort on one or more interfaces. To do this, click on the **Snort Interfaces** tab and then click on the **Add** button. When the page loads, under **General Settings**, you will be able to check the **Enable Interface** checkbox and then select an interface that has not been added to Snort yet in the **Interface** drop-down box. Most of the traffic that will be of interest to us is going to reach the **WAN** interface eventually, so in most cases you can just add **WAN** (we are assuming a single WAN setup). However, in some cases we might be interested in the traffic that reaches other interfaces. Malware may infect one of our networks and attack other local and remote networks. In such a case, you would want to monitor the local interfaces as well. But running Snort on multiple interfaces can be a resource intensive affair, so unless your use case dictates a need to monitor non-**WAN** traffic, you should only run Snort on **WAN**.

Troubleshooting traffic shaping

There's no doubt that troubleshooting traffic shaping issues can be challenging. Even if we set up the queues and rules the way we think they should be set up, it may not work the way we think it should, and in many cases, we might not get it to work right the first time. Often we must fall back on the tried and true troubleshooting steps: diagnosing the problem, forming a hypothesis, testing it, implementing a solution, verifying that the system works, and documenting the solution. But there are some common issues that we should also cover.

We may have problems keeping P2P traffic in the P2P queue. The main reason for this is that for the most part, pfSense relies on ports as matching criteria for the traffic shaping rules. Many P2P applications, including BitTorrent, rely on non-standard or random ports. There are several possible solutions to this. You could try to use Layer 7 DPI, which does not rely on ports but instead looks at the packets. However, Layer 7 traffic shaping is not available with the base pfSense installation; it is only available through third-party packages such as Snort.

If you don't want to use Layer 7 traffic shaping, another possibility is to make the default queue for all interfaces a low-priority queue. This approach, however, would require you to create rules for every type of traffic you don't want to be relegated to this queue.

If traffic is not being shaped correctly, there are several tools available to help you diagnose the problem. To get an overview of traffic on all queues, navigate to **Status** | **Queues**. This will reveal how much traffic is on each queue, both graphically (each queue has its own bar graph), and numerically in the form of **PPS** (**packets per second**), bandwidth, borrows (indicating whether bandwidth has been borrowed from a parent queue), suspends (indicating how many times a queue has been suspended), and drops (dropped packets). Also, length indicates how many packets are currently in the queue as well as the queue length (the default queue length is 50 slots, although the queue length can be changed). At the very least, this page will indicate what traffic if any is in the queues, which might be all you need to know to diagnose the problem.

The **Queues** page only shows traffic interactively, so what you see is a snapshot of the current traffic, rather than a summary of all the traffic in the queues. To see a cumulative summary of all traffic on the queues, navigate to **Diagnostics** | **pfTop** and select queue in the **View** drop-down box. This will provide similar information to that provided on the **Queues** page, only they are expressed in raw totals.

If you are using limiters, you can find information about their configuration by navigating to **Diagnostics** | **Limiter Info**. This will show configuration information and statistics for all limiters and any child queues they may have.

Finally, if none of these diagnostic tools are adequate, navigate to **Status** | **System Logs**. The **Firewall** tab is most likely to yield relevant results, so you'll want to click on that. Once you do, you can filter the results by clicking on the **+** button on the **Advanced Log Filter** bar. This will display the advanced filtering options. You can filter the logs by port, which can be helpful in finding out whether certain traffic is being passed into queues. If necessary, you can enable logging on the relevant rule. Generally, we try not to log every rule we create, since logging consumes disk space, but if you think enabling logging might help with troubleshooting, temporarily enable logging is always an option.

If your system is not deployed in a production environment and you can experiment with different settings, you might want to try different configurations and see what results you get. For example, it is generally recommended that you not alter the queue size settings (this is why in the examples, we left **Queue Limit** blank, which leaves the queue size at its default of 50). Some users have reported better results with larger queues, although too large of a queue will likely lead to bufferbloat. But, often the only way to find out is to test it on your router. Therefore, if you think that altering a setting might help optimize performance, and you can do it without breaking your network, feel free to make the changes and document the results.

Summary

In this chapter, we covered different forms of traffic shaping and introduced the pfSense traffic wizard. While the wizard is helpful in getting started using traffic shaping, this chapter showed some of the limitations of the traffic shaper. It also showed that creating queues and editing/creating our own traffic shaper rules is not that difficult. We also saw that limiters can sometimes be helpful in allocating bandwidth. We provided some concrete examples of implementing traffic shaping; finally, we covered what to do when traffic shaping doesn't work as it should.

In the next chapter, we will continue to build on our knowledge base and cover a subject that you are likely to encounter repeatedly, both with pfSense and in networking in general: virtual private networks (VPNs).

Questions

Answer the following questions:

1. What is the purpose of traffic shaping?
2. (a) Identify the three types of queuing supported by the pfSense traffic shaper. (b) Identify a queuing discipline that tends to ensure that low-priority traffic is not starved of bandwidth. (c) Identify a queuing discipline that uses a two-part nonlinear curve and decouples bandwidth from latency.
3. Can we implement Layer 7 traffic shaping with the built-in pfSense traffic shaper? Assume we are using the current version of pfSense.

4. Identify the two wizards with which we can implement traffic shaping in pfSense using the built-in traffic shaper.
5. Identify a type of queue which provides for end-to-end notification of network congestion without dropping packets.
6. Under which tab can you find the firewall rules generated by the built-in pfSense traffic shaping wizard? (Hint: It is the only rules category that has a Match option for Action.)
7. What interfaces are enabled by default when we install Snort?
8. How can we determine the length of a pfSense queue?

Further reading

- `Datacenter Traffic Control: Understanding Techniques and Trade-offs` – Mohammad Noormohammadpour and Cauligi S. Raghavendra. December 2017. 34 pages. Retrieved 15 March 2018. This provides a good overview of traffic control techniques in general (of which traffic shaping is a subset).
- `A Hierarchical Fair Service Curve Algorithm for Link-Sharing, Real-Time and Priority Services` – Ion Stoica, Hui Zhang, T. S. Eugene Ng. 18 September 1997. 16 pages. Retrieved 15 March 2018. This is the paper in which Hierarchical Fair-Service Curve (HFSC) was original defined and explained.
- `Blue: A New Class of Active Queue Management Algorithms` – Wu-chang Fengy, Dilip D. Kandlurz, Debanjan Sahaz and Kang G. Shiny. April 1999. 27 pages. Retrieved 15 March 2018. A paper in which the authors describe a new queuing discipline that is purported to be an improvement over Random Early Detection (RED). The paper provides a good explanation of RED and explicit congestion notification as well.

7
Virtual Private Networks

Virtual private networks (**VPNs**) provide a means of accessing a private network over a shared public network such as the internet. Access to the private network is provided via an encrypted tunnel, and connecting to the network in such a way emulates a point-to-point link between the remote node and the network. Since the tunnel is encrypted, any packets that are intercepted are indecipherable without the encryption keys. Thus, VPNs provide a secure means of accessing a private network remotely.

Prior to the advent of VPNs, the only way of providing remote connections to a private network was through private WAN circuits. Private WAN circuits provide low latency, and in some cases, they may still be the best solution for connecting to a private network, but they also have high monthly costs. VPN solutions have grown in popularity, in spite of the fact that they often have somewhat higher latency than private WAN circuits, because they provide the same point-to-point connectivity at a much lower cost.

pfSense is one such means by which you can implement low-cost VPN connectivity. While establishing and maintaining a VPN tunnel is somewhat CPU-intensive—a computer that barely meets the minimum specifications for pfSense will be hard-pressed to maintain a VPN connection—with pfSense, you will be able to set up VPN connections much more cheaply than you would be able to with commercial equipment.

In this chapter, we will cover the following topics:

- VPN fundamentals
- Configuring a VPN tunnel in pfSense (IPsec, L2TP, and OpenVPN)
- Troubleshooting VPNs

Technical requirements

To follow along with the examples provided in this chapter, you will need two fully functional pfSense firewalls (with one or more nodes behind each firewall), either on real physical networks or in a lab/virtualization environment. Installation and configuration of the ShrewSoft VPN client, described in the section on IPsec, requires a system running Microsoft Windows (Windows 2000, XP, Vista, 7, 8, or 10 will do). The examples presented in this chapter should not be particularly resource-intensive; however, setting up an encrypted VPN tunnel does tax the CPU somewhat. Therefore, running pfSense on hardware that barely meets the minimum specifications for pfSense is not recommended.

VPN fundamentals

VPNs enable a remote user to securely connect to a private network or server over a remote connection. To the end user, it is as if data sent is being sent over a dedicated private link. Another common usage is for network-to-network communication. For example, a branch office of a corporation may need to connect their local network with the network at corporate headquarters. In this case, the internet is logically equivalent to a WAN. In both cases, those using the VPN benefit from the fact that the connection is implemented as an encrypted tunnel. This enables end users to use the public internet as a private tunnel for a virtual point-to-point connection.

As noted earlier, private WAN circuits were the only way of connecting to a private network securely before there were VPNs, and in some cases, such private circuits may still be the only way to meet bandwidth and/or latency requirements. Latency is a big factor. A private WAN circuit will usually provide latency of 3 ms or less, whereas with VPNs, you will get that much latency just with the first hop through your ISP. Running ping tests will allow you to get a better idea of the latency of VPN connections, but in general, VPN connections have latencies of 30-60 ms. This can vary greatly based on two factors: the type of connection being used, and the distance between the remote node and the private network being accessed. One of the ways of minimizing latency is to use the same ISP on both ends of the connection, although this is not always possible. In some unusual cases, using a VPN may decrease latency rather than increase it. For example, if your ISP employs traffic shaping, encrypting traffic may result in the ISP not throttling it, and therefore latency will decrease.

Otherwise, you may find it necessary to research the types of applications you are likely to use over a VPN connection and find out how well they perform over connections with latency. Online games, for example, can be affected by higher latency. Microsoft file sharing (SMB) and Microsoft **Remote Desktop Protocol** (**RDP**) are also latency sensitive. Obviously, there is a cost-benefit analysis involved. You may find that the performance improvement justifies spending money on a private WAN circuit. Or you may find that the performance degradation involved in using a VPN is justified by the savings. In addition, it may be possible to alter your network settings to improve VPN performance.

If you decide to implement a VPN, you can choose from several different forms of VPN deployments. The most common ones are the following:

- **Client-server**: In this scenario, a VPN tunnel is used to connect one or more mobile clients to the local networks. The encryption provided by the VPN guarantees that data privacy is maintained. This is probably the most likely deployment scenario that you will be using if you configure a VPN with pfSense.
- **Peer-to-peer**: In this scenario, a VPN tunnel is created between two networks; for example, the main corporate office and a satellite office location. The general idea is that setting up a VPN is cheaper than a leased line between the two locations. Instead of having a router on one end and a mobile client on the other end, there is a router on each end of the tunnel. We will demonstrate an example of peer-to-peer by showing how to configure a site-to-site VPN with IPsec.
- **Hidden network**: This is not as common as a deployment scenario, but is nonetheless worth mentioning. In some cases, data may be too sensitive to place on the main corporate network, and this data may reside on a subnet that is physically disconnected from the rest of the network. If this is the case, a VPN can provide us with a means of connecting to this subnet.

We can also use VPNs to provide an additional level of security on wireless connections. By requiring wireless clients to log in through a VPN, we can force these clients to provide additional authentication, and the VPN connection itself will provide another layer of encryption in addition to the encryption that the wireless protocol provides.

There are several VPN protocols that can be used, and each VPN technology has its own advantages and disadvantages. In this section, we will focus on the VPN protocols currently supported by pfSense: IPsec, L2TP, and OpenVPN.

IPsec

IPsec, as the name implies, is a protocol suite that operates on the Internet layer of the four-layer network model (and the Network layer of the OSI model). It is the only protocol of the three discussed here that operates on this layer. Because it operates on the Internet/Network layer, it is capable of encrypting and authenticating the entire IP packet, thus not only ensuring privacy for our data, but also ensuring that the packet's final destination is kept private as well. Thus it differs from both OpenVPN (which offers encryption, but operates on the Application layer) and the Layer 2 Tunneling Protocol (which does not encrypt data at all).

As a protocol suite, IPsec is actually a group of protocols, which in combination provide the functionality we require. These protocols can be divided into three groups:

- **Authentication Headers (AH)**: This header is 32-bits long and provides authentication and connectionless data integrity.
- **Encapsulating Security Payload (ESP)**: This portion of the IPsec protocol suite provides authentication, as well as encryption and data integrity. It also exists in authentication-only and encryption-only modes, which provide either authentication or encryption, but not both. ESP is responsible for encrypting at least the payload (transport mode), and in some cases, the entire packet (tunnel mode).
- **Security Association (SA)**: The Security Association is the set of security attributes (for example, encryption algorithm, encryption key, and other parameters) that are used in a connection.

SAs are established through the **Internet Security and Key Management Protocol** (**ISAKMP**). Key exchange is typically done through **Internet Key Exchange** (**IKE**) versions 1 or 2, but other protocols are available, such as **Kerberized Internet Negotiation of Keys** (**KINK**), which uses the Kerberos protocol for key negotiation. Currently, the only methods supported by pfSense are IKE and IKEv2.

There are two different modes for establishing an IPsec connection:

- **Transport mode**: In this mode, the payload of the IPsec packet is encrypted, but not the header. This mode does not support NAT traversal, so if you are configuring an IPsec connection that must traverse more than one router, it is not a good choice.

- **Tunnel mode**: In this mode, the entire packet is encrypted. This mode supports NAT traversal.

IPsec supports a number of encryption algorithms. Advanced Encryption Standard with a key size of 256 bits (AES-256) is the most commonly used option, but other options are available. Since some systems only support DES, 3DES is offered as an option. If you need a bigger key, SHA-2 (with a 512-bit key size) is available. For more information about the cryptographic options available with IPsec, see RFC 7321 (`https://tools.ietf.org/html/rfc7321`).

L2TP

L2TP, or **Layer 2 Tunneling Protocol**, is a tunneling protocol that (not surprisingly) operates on the Link layer of the seven-layer OSI model. Unlike IPsec, it does not provide any encryption or confidentiality by itself, but instead relies on whatever encryption protocol is passing through its tunnel. As a result, it is often used in conjunction with IPsec.

The client end of an L2TP tunnel is known as the **L2TP Access Concentrator** (**LAC**). The server end is known as the **L2TP Network Server** (**LNS**). The LNS end, once configured, waits for new connections. A connection is established through the exchange of several control packets, for which L2TP provides reliability. No reliability is provided for data packets, although reliability may be provided by protocols running within the L2TP tunnel.

Because L2TP does not have any confidentiality or encryption, it is often implemented in conjunction with IPsec. This combination is known as L2TP/IPsec. Establishing an L2TP/IPsec connection involves negotiation of an IPsec security association (usually with IKE or IKEv2), establishment of ESP communication in transport mode, and negotiation of an L2TP tunnel. L2TP uses UDP; the default port is `1701`.

L2TP, without any other protocols nested within it, is generally referred to as native L2TP. You are unlikely to implement L2TP in native mode; however, L2TP/IPsec is a common option for VPN tunnels, and L2TP can be combined with other protocols to provide confidentiality and encryption (for example, L2TP/PPP).

OpenVPN

OpenVPN is an open source VPN protocol (published under the GNU General Public License, or GPL). Since it is based on SSL, and SSL operates just above the Transport layer, we can say that it exists between the Application and Transport layers in the four layer network model, and between the Session and Transport layers in the OSI model. OpenVPN client software is now available for Linux, Windows, and macOS.

OpenVPN uses the OpenSSL library for encryption. Thus, all the cryptographic algorithms available in OpenSSL are available in OpenVPN. It can also use HMAC packet authentication, and support for the mbed TLS (formerly PolarSSL) SSL library has been added.

Authentication in OpenVPN can be accomplished either through certificates, or a user/password combination, or both. Another one of the advantages of using OpenVPN is that it can be implemented with TCP or UDP. In either case, the official IANA assigned port number for OpenVPN is port `1194`. Version 2.0 and later of OpenVPN support several simultaneous tunnels per process.

OpenVPN uses the universal TUN/TAP driver for networking. Thus, it can create either a layer 3 (Network layer of the OSI model) TUN tunnel, or a layer 2 (Data link layer of the OSI model) TAP connection.

Although OpenVPN seems to be most heavily supported with Linux (not to mention UNIX variants such as FreeBSD), there are clients available for Windows (XP and later), as well as macOS X. Mobile devices are also supported, with clients available for iOS and Android.

AES-NI

With the release of pfSense 2.4, OpenVPN 2.4.3 has been incorporated into pfSense. As a result, OpenVPN can use AES-NI acceleration for AES-GCM tunnels. AES-NI is a form of hardware acceleration designed to speed up encryption and decryption in routines implementing **Advanced Encryption Standard** (**AES**). Utilizing AES-GCM encryption on a CPU supporting AES-NI should improve throughput on OpenVPN tunnels in pfSense by 30 to 50%.

With the release of pfSense 2.5, you will have an additional incentive to ensure that the CPU on which you are running is AES-NI-compatible, as version 2.5 will only run on CPUs that support AES-NI encryption or another hardware crypto offload. While this will prevent running pfSense 2.5 and up on some lower-end systems (such as many Celeron-based systems), it is supported by all AMD pCPUs since the release of the Bulldozer family of processors in late 2011, and by all Intel CPUs since the Skylake family (initially released in August 2015). AES-NI is also supported by a number of ARM CPUs, where it has the additional advantage of offloading AES instructions to on-die cryptographic accelerators. Examples of ARM CPUs supporting AES-NI include the ARM processors used in pfSense embedded systems produced by Netgate such as the TI AM3352 (SG-1000) and the Cortex-A9 (SG-3100).

Choosing a VPN protocol

Which VPN protocol you choose will likely be based on a number of factors. Interoperability is one factor to consider. If you need a VPN solution that is interoperable with another firewall or router, especially one from another vendor, then IPsec may be the ideal protocol to use, since it is included with every VPN-capable device. Using IPsec will also prevent you from being locked into a particular product or vendor, is easier to configure than L2TP, and is about as easy to configure as OpenVPN. If interoperability is your main concern, you might consider OpenVPN, which is rapidly gaining traction, although it is not as ubiquitous as IPsec.

Another consideration is what type of authentication the protocol uses. IPsec allows you to use a pre-shared key or certificates, as well as username/password combinations. L2TP does not provide for any authentication, while OpenVPN supports pre-shared keys and certificates.

Ease of configuration is another consideration. All of the VPN protocol options available under the current version of pfSense (IPsec, L2TP, and OpenVPN) are fairly easy to configure, but some are easier than others. OpenVPN requires the use of certificates for remote access in many environments but is otherwise relatively easy to configure. IPsec, on the other hand, can be somewhat difficult for the uninitiated, although IPsec may be preferable because of its near-universal acceptance.

More often than not, your choice will be dictated by what operating systems you will be supporting and what clients are available for these operating systems. If your network is Windows-centric, you may consider using IPsec. Support for IPsec is built directly into Windows and has been since Windows Vista. As a result, connecting to a VPN with IPsec under Windows can be as easy as navigating to **Settings** | **Control Panel**, clicking on **Network and Sharing Center**, clicking on **Set up a new connection** or network, and then using the wizard to set up an IPsec/L2TP connection. You can also use third-party VPN clients, such as the Shrew Soft VPN Client.

On the other hand, most Linux distributions do not have built-in VPN support. Ubuntu and distributions that are derivative of Ubuntu (for example, Linux Mint) have built-in support for PPTP, a protocol that is no longer supported by pfSense. Third-party clients are available, and in some cases, can be downloaded from repositories, and these clients involve varying degrees of configuration. If your network is Linux-centric, you should be able to support IPsec, although OpenVPN is probably a better option in such cases.

macOS X has had IPsec support for years, and now even has a user-friendly interface for IPsec. OS X 10.6 (Snow Leopard) and later has a built-in Cisco IPsec VPN client that provides an easy-to-use graphical interface for connecting to a network that supports IPsec. Earlier versions of macOS X do not have the Cisco built-in VPN client, but you can install the Cisco Remote Access IPsec client on them. You can also use the Cisco AnyConnect Secure Mobility Client on earlier versions, although you should be aware that support for macOS X 10.5 (Leopard) was dropped with version 3.1 of AnyConnect.

For a network that is likely to have a variety of platforms, L2TP is a good choice. Because of the inherent lack of encryption and confidentiality in L2TP, it is usually implemented in conjunction with IPsec. Still, there are several clients on different platforms that support L2TP without IPsec. Beginning with Windows Vista, Windows has built-in support for L2TP without IPsec. One of the utilities provided for L2TP configuration is a **Microsoft Management Console** (**MMC**) snap-in called **Windows Firewall with Advanced Security (WFwAS)** and it can be found in **Control Panel** | **Administrative Tools**. The other is a command-line tool called `netsh advfirewall`.

Support for L2TP is not built into Linux, but there are third-party clients available. They are available for most popular distributions such as Arch Linux and Ubuntu, and configuration for most of these clients is relatively easy.

The Cisco IPsec client for macOS X supports L2TP, but it appears that it supports only L2TP over IPsec. At the time of writing, there does not appear to be a third-party client for macOS that supports native L2TP without IPsec. Thus L2TP is a poor choice if your network must support computers running macOS.

OpenVPN has been ported to several operating systems. Windows does not have built-in support for OpenVPN, but there are several third-party clients for Windows. In fact, the OpenVPN project has a client for Windows that works on XP or later, and it is easy to install and configure.

Linux not only supports OpenVPN, but OpenVPN support is built into many popular Linux distributions. OpenVPN configuration through the Network Connections applet in Ubuntu and its variants is rather easy, and it supports authentication with both certificates and with a pre-shared key. This makes OpenVPN an excellent choice if you are mainly supporting Linux clients.

If you are running Linux and the ability to create an OpenVPN connection does not appear as one of the VPN options, you may have to install OpenVPN. In most cases, you should be able to install OpenVPN from your distribution's repositories with the following command: `sudo apt-get install openvpn`

This should install OpenVPN and all dependencies. If this does not work, consult the official OpenVPN site at `http://openvpn.net/` or your distribution's documentation.

macOS X does not have built-in support for OpenVPN. The OpenVPN project does not provide a macOS version of their client, and, to my knowledge, no one has successfully compiled the source code of the client under macOS. There is an open source project called **Tunnelblick**, which provides the necessary drivers for implementing OpenVPN under OS X. It has a graphical interface that provides a way to control either server or client connections. It can be used on its own or in conjunction with commercial software such as Viscosity. For more information, see the Tunnelblick website at `http://tunnelblick.net.`

If your network setup is fairly complex, your choice of protocol may be dictated at least in part by how well the protocol works behind multiple firewalls. Some of these firewalls may be beyond your control, and their configurations and capabilities may differ substantially.

IPsec uses both UDP port `500` (for IKE) and the ESP protocol. Not all firewalls handle ESP traffic well when NAT is used, because the ESP protocol does not have port numbers that make it easily trackable by NAT devices. IPsec clients behind firewalls may require NAT-T to function, which encapsulates ESP traffic over port `4500` using the UDP protocol. Versions 2.0 and later of pfSense support NAT-T, so you should be able to utilize NAT traversal with IPsec if necessary.

OpenVPN is generally more firewall friendly than IPsec. It uses TCP or UDP and thus is not affected by NAT behavior such as the rewriting of source ports. As a result, it is rare that a firewall won't work with OpenVPN. One possible issue is that the protocol and port may be blocked. OpenVPN uses port `1194` by default; if that port is blocked, you may want to switch to a port commonly used for something else to evade egress filtering. For example, ports `80` and `443` are assigned for HTTP and HTTPS respectively, but any TCP traffic should pass through these ports, so you could use them.

Since L2TP uses UDP, it shouldn't create any especially challenging issues with firewalls. It is often used with IPsec, however, so all of the issues related to IPsec come into play when you are using L2TP/IPsec.

One of the justifications for using VPNs is cryptographic security, so this is another factor to consider. **Point-to-Point Tunneling Protocol** (**PPTP**), which has been removed from the current version of pfSense, has numerous security vulnerabilities, and thus became a poor choice for the security-conscious administrator long ago. L2TP has no encryption capability; if you want encryption, you'll have to use it in combination with another protocol (usually IPsec). Therefore, the choice essentially comes down to either IPsec or OpenVPN.

OpenVPN uses the SSL encryption library, which provides a number of different ciphers. To find out what ciphers the version of OpenVPN installed with pfSense supports, execute the following command, either at the pfSense console's Command Prompt or from **Diagnostics** | **Command Prompt**:

```
openvpn --show-ciphers
```

Shell Output - openvpn --show-ciphers

```
The following ciphers and cipher modes are available for use
with OpenVPN.  Each cipher shown below may be use as a
parameter to the --cipher option.  The default key size is
shown as well as whether or not it can be changed with the
--keysize directive.  Using a CBC or GCM mode is recommended.
In static key mode only CBC mode is allowed.

AES-128-CBC  (128 bit key, 128 bit block)
AES-128-CFB  (128 bit key, 128 bit block, TLS client/server mode only)
AES-128-CFB1  (128 bit key, 128 bit block, TLS client/server mode only)
AES-128-CFB8  (128 bit key, 128 bit block, TLS client/server mode only)
AES-128-GCM  (128 bit key, 128 bit block, TLS client/server mode only)
AES-128-OFB  (128 bit key, 128 bit block, TLS client/server mode only)
AES-192-CBC  (192 bit key, 128 bit block)
AES-192-CFB  (192 bit key, 128 bit block, TLS client/server mode only)
AES-192-CFB1  (192 bit key, 128 bit block, TLS client/server mode only)
AES-192-CFB8  (192 bit key, 128 bit block, TLS client/server mode only)
AES-192-GCM  (192 bit key, 128 bit block, TLS client/server mode only)
AES-192-OFB  (192 bit key, 128 bit block, TLS client/server mode only)
AES-256-CBC  (256 bit key, 128 bit block)
AES-256-CFB  (256 bit key, 128 bit block, TLS client/server mode only)
AES-256-CFB1  (256 bit key, 128 bit block, TLS client/server mode only)
AES-256-CFB8  (256 bit key, 128 bit block, TLS client/server mode only)
AES-256-GCM  (256 bit key, 128 bit block, TLS client/server mode only)
AES-256-OFB  (256 bit key, 128 bit block, TLS client/server mode only)
CAMELLIA-128-CBC  (128 bit key, 128 bit block)
CAMELLIA-128-CFB  (128 bit key, 128 bit block, TLS client/server mode only)
CAMELLIA-128-CFB1  (128 bit key, 128 bit block, TLS client/server mode only)
CAMELLIA-128-CFB8  (128 bit key, 128 bit block, TLS client/server mode only)
CAMELLIA-128-OFB  (128 bit key, 128 bit block, TLS client/server mode only)
CAMELLIA-192-CBC  (192 bit key, 128 bit block)
CAMELLIA-192-CFB  (192 bit key, 128 bit block, TLS client/server mode only)
CAMELLIA-192-CFB1  (192 bit key, 128 bit block, TLS client/server mode only)
CAMELLIA-192-CFB8  (192 bit key, 128 bit block, TLS client/server mode only)
CAMELLIA-192-OFB  (192 bit key, 128 bit block, TLS client/server mode only)
CAMELLIA-256-CBC  (256 bit key, 128 bit block)
CAMELLIA-256-CFB  (256 bit key, 128 bit block, TLS client/server mode only)
CAMELLIA-256-CFB1  (256 bit key, 128 bit block, TLS client/server mode only)
CAMELLIA-256-CFB8  (256 bit key, 128 bit block, TLS client/server mode only)
CAMELLIA-256-OFB  (256 bit key, 128 bit block, TLS client/server mode only)
SEED-CBC  (128 bit key, 128 bit block)
```

Some of the ciphers available with OpenVPN

As you can see from the screenshot, there are quite a few options. OpenVPN's default encryption algorithm is BF-CBC, or Blowfish, block cipher, with a 128-bit (variable) key size. While this is not a terrible cipher, it may be beneficial to choose a stronger cipher, such as AES-256-CBC.

OpenVPN also offers a number of different digests for message authentication, including many of the digests supported by IPsec (for example, SHA512). To see a list of digests supported by OpenVPN, use the following command:

```
openvpn --show-digests
```

One factor working against OpenVPN is that it seems that OpenVPN developers have generally given priority to backward compatibility over security. This and the fact that IPsec operates at Layer 3 of the OSI model and therefore provides encryption on the IP level would seem to give IPsec a slight advantage over OpenVPN in cryptographic security.

It might prove useful to provide a summary of some of the features of each VPN protocol currently supported by pfSense, so with that in mind, here it is:

Protocol	**Client included in OS**	**Client available for OS**	**Supports multi-WAN**	**Firewall friendliness**	**Cryptographically secure**
IPsec	Windows, macOS X	Windows, Linux, macOS X	Yes	Only with NAT-T	Yes
L2TP	None of the major desktop OSes have clients that support native L2TP. Both Windows and macOS X have clients that support L2TP/ IPsec	Windows, Linux	Yes	Yes	No (no encryption at all)
OpenVPN	Linux	Windows, Linux, macOS X	Yes	Yes	Yes

Configuring a VPN tunnel

Now that we have covered the basics of VPNs and considered the pros and cons of each of the pfSense-supported protocols, it's time to cover configuration of a VPN connection, both under pfSense and on the client side. IPsec is the most difficult to configure on both sides, and you may not get it to work on your first try. OpenVPN is probably the easiest to configure, in part because it does not have as many options as IPsec.

IPsec

When you configure an IPsec tunnel in pfSense, you are likely envisioning one of two deployment scenarios. One is to configure IPsec as a peer, which can connect to and/or accept a connection from another peer, establishing an IPsec tunnel between the two devices. Another is to set up an IPsec server as a server and accept connections from remote clients. This section will cover both scenarios.

If you want to set up IPsec to act as a server with multiple mobile clients, you should begin at the **Mobile Clients** tab. The mobile clients configuration process will then autogenerate a Phase 1 IPsec entry, which you can then configure. If this is your IPsec deployment scenario, you might consider skipping to the *IPsec mobile client configuration* section.

IPsec peer/server configuration

To begin IPsec configuration, navigate to **VPN** | **IPsec**. You can configure an IPsec tunnel from the default tab, **Tunnels**. This tab displays a table of all existing IPsec tunnels. Each IPsec tunnel requires a Phase 1 configuration, and one or more Phase 2 configurations. To begin Phase 1 configuration, click on the **Add P1** button below the table on the right side.

The Phase 1 configuration page has four sections: **General Information**, **Phase 1 Proposal (Authentication)**, **Phase 1 Proposal (Algorithms)**, and **Advanced Options**. The first option under **General Information** is the **Disabled** check box. If checked, the Phase 1 entry is disabled, but will still be in the table. The next option is the **Key Exchange version** drop-down box. This allows you to choose between IKEv1 (**V1**), IKEv2 (**V2**), or **Auto**. If **Auto** is chosen, IKEv2 will be used when initiating a connection, but either IKEv1 or IKEv2 will be accepted when pfSense is responding to a request to initiate a connection. **Auto** is the more foolproof option, as it will work unless the responder requires IKEv1; if you are setting up a VPN tunnel in a corporate environment, however, your choice may be dictated by company policy.

Next is the **Internet Protocol** drop-down box. This allows you to choose between **IPv4**, **IPv6**, or Both (Dual Stack). In the **Interface** drop-down box, you select the interface that is the local endpoint of the tunnel. Typically, you'll want to leave this as **WAN** since you will be accepting connections from the WAN side, but you can set it to any interface. In the **Remote Gateway** edit box, you must enter the public IP address or hostname of the remote gateway. If you are configuring IPsec on a pfSense box that sits at the boundary between the internet and your local network, then the value entered here should match the IP address of the WAN interface, or the domain name that matches that IP address. If you are configuring IPsec on a router that is behind one or more other routers, however, the value entered here may be different. You may enter a brief, non-parsed description in the **Description** edit box.

Version 2.4.3 added support for choosing both IPv4 and IPv6 at the same time, thus allowing a pfSense IPsec server/peer to accept inbound connections from either address family.

The first option in the next section is the **Authentication Method** drop-down box. The options are **Mutual PSK** and **Mutual RSA**. **Mutual PSK** allows for authentication using a **pre-shared key** (**PSK**), whereas **Mutual RSA** allows for authentication using certificates. The **Negotiation Mode** drop-down box allows you to choose the type of authentication security that will be used. What differentiates the two is what happens when the VPN tunnel needs to be rebuilt. **Main** will force the peer to re-authenticate, which is more secure, but will take longer, while **Aggressive** will rebuild the tunnel quickly, sacrificing security. The **Aggressive** mode is generally recommended, since it will ensure that if the VPN tunnel is down, it will be able to rebuild itself quickly. **My identifier** identifies the pfSense router to the far side of the connection. It can usually be left as **My IP address**. **Peer identifier** identifies the router on the far side; this can usually be left as **Peer IP address**.

If you selected **Mutual PSK** as your **Authentication Method**, then the next field will be **Pre-Shared Key**, where you enter the PSK string. You should choose a long key (at least 10 characters), and since special characters are supported, it might be a good idea to use them as well. If you chose **Mutual RSA**, then the next two options will be the **My Certificate** drop-down box, where you select a certificate previously configured in the pfSense certificate manager, and the **Peer Certificate Authority** drop-down box, where you select a **Certificate Authority** (**CA**) (also previously configured in the certificate manager).

The next section deals with encryption options. The **Encryption Algorithm** drop-down box allows you to choose an encryption method. Both **AES** and **Blowfish** allow you to choose between **128 bit**, **192 bit**, and **256-bit** encryption using an adjacent drop-down box, while **3DES** and **CAST128** do not have this option. The default option is **AES-256**, which is a good choice, but if a peer on the other end can only support DES encryption, you can choose **3DES**. IPsec employs a hash function to ensure the integrity of its data, and the **Hash Algorithm** drop-down box allows you to choose which one is used. **SHA1** is considered stronger and more reliable than **MD5**, but some devices only support MD5, so it is included as an option. If you require a more secure hash function, several are available (for example, **SHA512**).

Version 2.4.3 added the ability to use more than one encryption algorithm. To select additional algorithms, click on the **Add Algorithm** button in the **Encryption Algorithm** section, and select the desired **Algorithm**, **Key Length**, **Hash**, and **DH Group**.

The **DH Group** drop-down box allows you to select the **Diffie-Hellman** (DH) group that is used to generate session keys. The default value is `1024` bits, which is generally considered safe, especially for keys that have a relatively short lifetime. You can use a greater number of bits, but this potentially comes at a cost in performance. The **Lifetime (Seconds)** edit box allows you to choose how long pfSense will wait for Phase 1 to complete. The default value is `28800` seconds, but you may want to increase this value.

The **Advanced Options** section's first option is the **Disable Rekey** checkbox. By default, pfSense will renegotiate an IPsec connection if it is about to expire, but checking this box disables this behavior. The **Responder Only** checkbox, if checked, will cause pfSense to only respond to incoming IPsec requests, and never initiate a connection.

The **NAT Traversal** drop-down box allows you to enable the encapsulation of ESP in UDP packets on port **4500**, also known as NAT-T. This should only be set if one side or both sides of the connection are behind restrictive firewalls. If necessary, choose **Force** to enable NAT-T.

The **DPD (Dead Peer Detection)** checkbox, if checked, will help detect if the other side is having a problem, and if so, will try to rebuild the tunnel. If this option is checked, you must also set values in the **Delay** (the delay between requesting peer acknowledgement) and **Max failures** (the number of consecutive failures allowed before disconnect). The default values of **10** and **5** are suitable in most cases, although you may need to change these later. Click on **Save** when you are done making changes, and then click on **Apply Changes** on the main IPsec page.

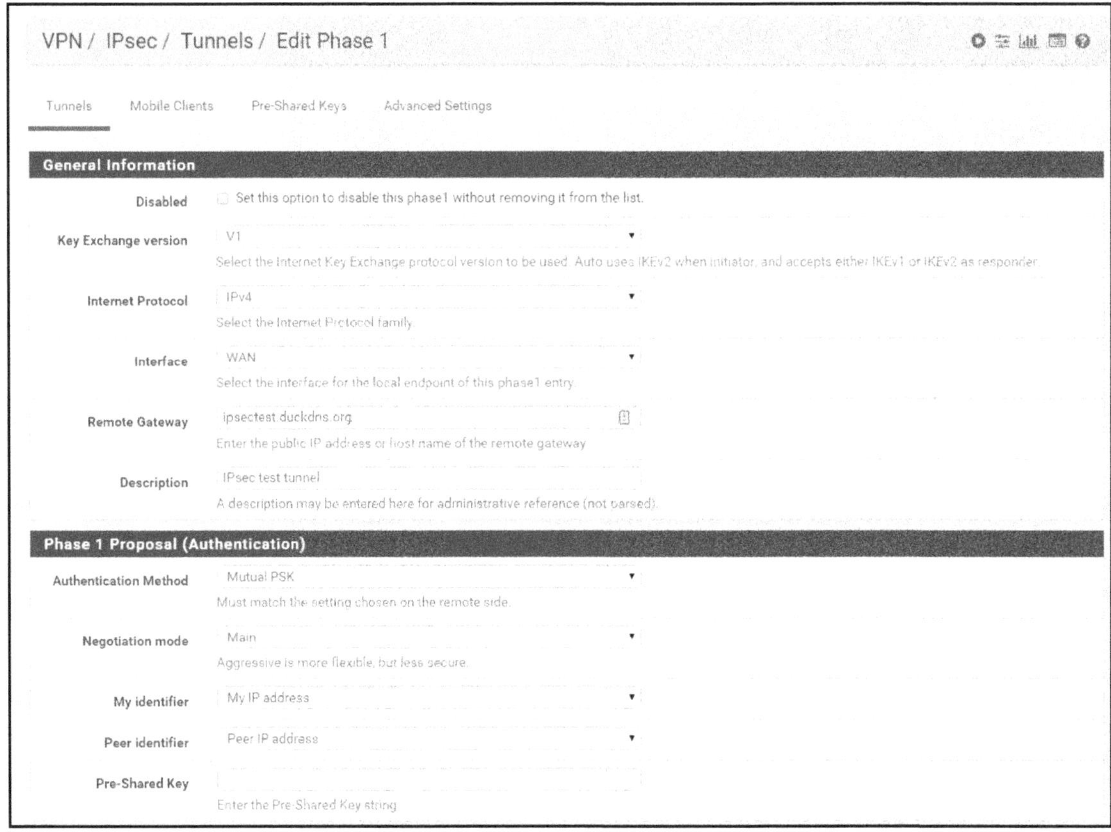

Phase 1 IPsec configuration.

You have now configured Phase 1, but you have to create one or more Phase 2 entries to complete the process. In the table on the main IPsec page, there should be an entry for the Phase 1 connection you just configured. Click on the **Show Phase 2** Entries to show any Phase 2 entries; this subsection should be empty, but there should be an **Add P2** button. Click on this button to begin Phase 2 configuration.

There are three sections on the Phase 2 configuration page: **General Information**, **Phase 2 Proposal (SA/Key Exchange)**, and **Advanced Configuration**. The first option in **General Information** is the **Disabled** checkbox, which allows you to disable this entry without removing it from the table. The **Mode** drop-down box allows you to choose between **Tunnel IPv4**, **Tunnel IPv6**, and **Transport**. The tunnel mode encrypts the entire IP packet and adds a new IP header, whereas the transport mode encrypts the payload, but not the IP header. If you choose tunnel mode, your choice between IPv4 and IPv6 will be dictated by what you set in the **Internet Protocol** drop-down box during Phase 1 configuration.

The **Local Network** drop-down box allows you to define which subnet or host can be accessed from the other side of the VPN tunnel. For example, if you select **LAN subnet**, the entire LAN will be accessible from the other side of the VPN tunnel. The other end of the tunnel's VPN settings will have the same setting, only the setting will be **Remote Network** or **Remote Subnet**. The settings must match on both sides for it to work.

The next setting is the **NAT/BINAT translation** drop-down box. This allows you to specify the settings that will be presented to the other side of the tunnel in cases where the actual local network is hidden. If you choose **Address or Network**, you can specify the IP address or subnet in the adjacent edit box. Next is the **Remote Network** drop-down. Here you specify the network or address on the other side of the tunnel, which will be accessible from this side of the tunnel. It must match the setting in the **Local Network** setting for the peer, or the connection will fail. You may enter a brief non-parsed description in the Description field.

The next section is Phase 2 Proposal (SA/Key Exchange). The first option is the **Protocol** drop-down, where you can select the protocol (for key exchange only). The options are **ESP** and **AH**. The de facto standard is **ESP**, and it is the recommended setting. ESP uses port **50** and AH uses port **51**. pfSense should autogenerate a rule to allow ESP or AH to the endpoint of the IPsec tunnel (the rules should appear under the **Floating** tab). If it does not, you will have to create a rule.

The next option is **Encryption Algorithm**. The default is **AES**, but you can choose more than one algorithm. It is recommended, however, that you only check the one that is to be used. The algorithm must match the setting of the remote peer. The recommended algorithm is **AES-256**.

Next are the **Hash Algorithms** checkboxes. You can choose more than one hash algorithm, although it is recommended that you only select the one being used. As mentioned before, some devices only support **MD5**, so check that if the remote peer is such a device. **SHA1** is the default setting.

The **PFS Key Group** is similar to the DH group in Phase 1. The default setting is **off**; as with the Phase 1 DH Group setting, there is a trade-off between security and performance. The **Lifetime** edit box sets the lifetime of the negotiated keys. The value should not be too high, or hackers will have more time to crack the key.

The last section, **Advanced Configuration**, has only one setting. The **Automatically ping host** edit box allows you enter an IP address for a remote Phase 2 network to ping to keep the tunnel alive. When you are done changing settings, click on the **Save** button at the bottom of the page, then click on **Apply Changes** when the main IPsec page loads.

Now that Phase 1 and Phase 2 configuration is complete, you may still need to add firewall rules (although there should be automatically-generated rules for most of these). IPsec requires the following ports to be open, so navigate to **Firewall | Rules**, click on the **Floating** tab, and confirm that the following rules (or at least the ones necessary for your configuration) exist:

Port	**Protocol**	**Notes**
`50`	ESP	Required if ESP is used for Phase 2 key exchange
`51`	AH	Required if AH is used for Phase 2 key exchange
`500`	UDP	For IKE
`4500`	UDP	Required if NAT traversal is used

Port `500` must be open in all configurations. The other rules may or may not have to be created, depending on which options you use. If you use NAT-T, port `4500` must have a NAT rule and corresponding firewall rule. For Phase 2 key exchange, you are going to use either `ESP` or `AH`. If you choose `ESP`, you don't need to open port `51`, and if you use `AH`, you don't need to open port `50`. The NAT entry must be created on the WAN interface, to allow port forwarding from the WAN to the IPsec tunnel.

If you used the traffic shaping wizard, the wizard may have already created a rule to allow port `500` IPsec traffic. Nonetheless, you'll probably want to navigate to the **Floating Rules** tab to confirm that the rule exists.

IPsec mobile client configuration

In the previous section, we configured an IPsec tunnel in which authentication is done though either a PSK or certificates. This is acceptable for connecting two routers, but what if there are multiple mobile clients? In such scenarios, it makes sense to configure settings for each individual user, and we can do that via the **Mobile Clients** tab.

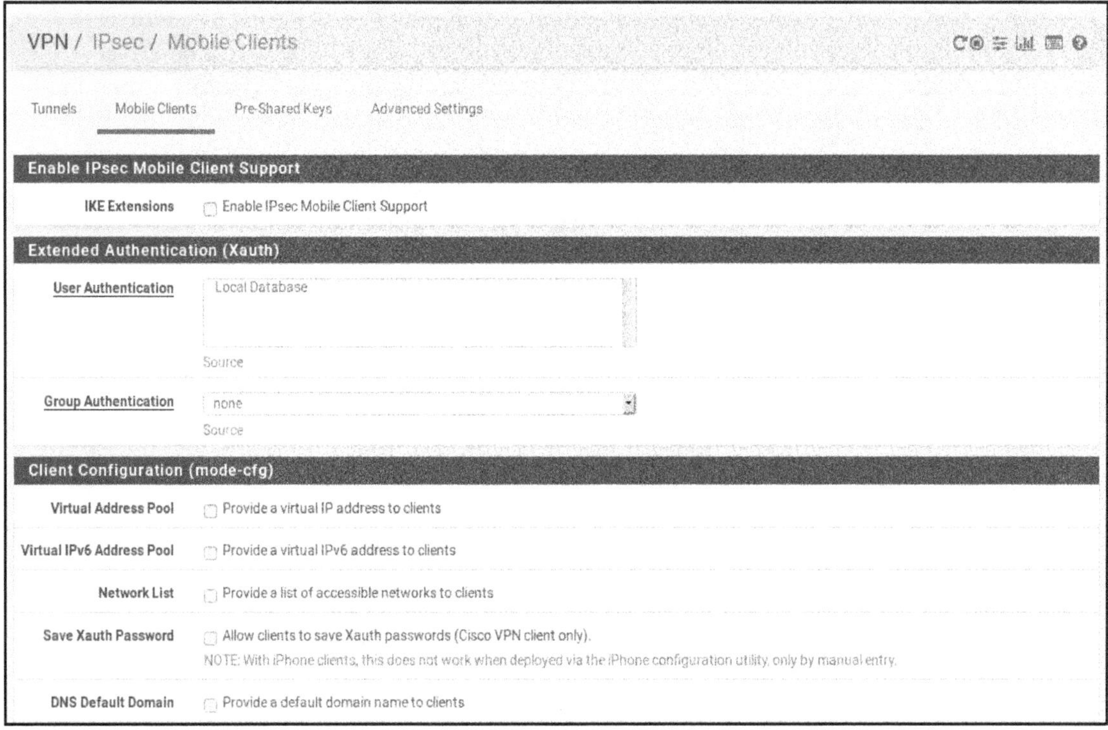

The IPsec Mobile Clients tab.

The first option on the **Mobile Clients** tab is the **IKE Extensions** checkbox. If checked, IPsec mobile client support will be enabled. The next section is **Extended Authentication** (**Xauth**). The **User Authentication** listbox allows you to choose what database is used for authentication. The only option seems to be **Local Database** and this will allow for authentication through the pfSense user manager. Next is the **Group Authentication** drop-down box; select **system** for user manager authentication.

The last section is **Client Configuration (mode-cfg)**. The first option is the **Virtual Address Pool** checkbox, which, if checked, provides virtual IP addresses to clients. If checked, you must enter a network mask (and the corresponding CIDR) in the edit box that will appear below the checkbox. The **Virtual IPv6 Address Pool** option also allows you to provide virtual IP addresses, but they will be IPv6 addresses instead of IPv4 addresses.

The **Network List** checkbox, if checked, will provide a list of accessible networks to mobile clients. The **Save Xauth password** option will allow clients to save Xauth passwords if checked, but will only work if the mobile user is using a Cisco VPN client. The **DNS Default Domain** checkbox will, if checked, cause pfSense to provide a default domain to clients; if checked, you must specify a DNS domain in the edit box that will appear below the checkbox. **Split DNS**, if checked, will enable you to provide a list of split DNS domain names to the mobile clients; this allows you to provide different sets of DNS information based on the source address of the DNS request. The domain names should be entered in the edit box below the checkbox and should be separated by commas.

The **DNS Servers** checkbox, if checked, allows you to provide a DNS server list to clients, which you will then have to enter in edit boxes below the checkbox. The **WINS Servers** checkbox is similar, only you are providing IP addresses to WINS servers. Checking **Phase 2 PFS Group** allows you to set a PFS group for mobile clients using the **Group** drop-down box. This will override whatever was set during Phase 2 configuration. Finally, the **Login Banner** checkbox, if checked, will allow you to provide a login banner to clients, which you can then enter in the edit box below the checkbox. When you are done, click on the **Save** button and click on the **Apply Changes** button on the main IPsec page.

The next tab under IPsec is **Pre-Shared Keys**. This tab allows you to add new keys and edit existing ones. If you click on this tab, you will see a table containing any previously entered keys. To add a new key, click on the **Add** button below the table on the right side.

The first option on the **Pre-Shared Keys** configuration page is the **Identifier** edit box. You can enter an IP address here, a FQDN (fully qualified domain name), or an email address. The next option is the **Secret type** drop-down box; you can select PSK or **Extensible Authentication Protocol** (**EAP**), a protocol commonly used for wireless networks) here. Finally, in the **Pre-Shared Key** edit box, you can enter a PSK. Note that you can create a PSK that can be used by anyone by entering `any` in the **Identifier** field. When you are done, click on the **Save** button and then click on **Apply Changes** on the main IPsec page.

The last tab is **Advanced Settings**, which presents a single page divided into two sections: **IPsec Logging Controls** and **Advanced IPsec Settings**. **IPsec Logging Controls** allows you to set different levels of logging for different components of IPsec (for example, **Daemon**, **SA Manager**, **Job Processing**, and so on). Each component has a corresponding drop-down box, which allows you to set the levels of logging. These are:

- **Silent**: There will be no logging.
- **Audit**: Logs audit events, which are generated when a service is accessed.
- **Control**: Logs access control events. This is the default logging level.
- **Diag**: Logs all diagnostic messages.
- **Raw**: Displays the contents of log files as-is without any parsing from the GUI.
- **Highest**: Displays all logs.

The next section of the page is **Advanced IPsec Settings**. The first option in this section is the **Configure Unique IDs** as drop-down box. This value determines whether a participant IKE ID should be kept unique.

The **IP Compression** checkbox, if checked, will enable IPComp compression of content. The **Strict interface binding** checkbox will enable strong Swan's interface use option to bind specific interfaces only. The unencrypted payloads in IKEv1 Main mode checkbox allows you to enable unencrypted ID and HASH payloads in IKEv1 Main Mode. Some implementations send the third Main Mode message unencrypted, and if you need to send unencrypted ID and HASH payloads to maintain compatibility with them, you can enable this option, but you should only do so if absolutely necessary.

The **Enable Maximum MSS** checkbox enables MSS clamping if checked. This is useful if you are having problems with **Path MTU Discovery** (**PMTUD**), which can be the case if large packets have problems being transmitted over the IPsec tunnel. **Enable Cisco Extensions**, if checked, will enable the Cisco Unity plugin, which provides Cisco extension support.

The **Strict CRL Checking** checkbox will, if checked, require availability of a fresh **Certificate Revocation List** (**CRL**) for peer authentication. If the **Make before Break** checkbox is checked, pfSense will create new SAs during re-authentication before deleting the old SAs. This is the reverse of the default behavior, in which SAs are deleted before new ones are created. This is advantageous in that it can help avoid connectivity gaps, but it must be supported by the peer if it is to work.

Finally, the **Auto-exclude LAN address** checkbox is designed to address cases in which the remote subnet overlaps with the local subnet. If this box is checked, traffic from the LAN subnet to the LAN IP address will be excluded from IPsec. Click on **Save** when done and then click on **Apply Changes** on the main IPsec page.

Example 1 – Site-to-site IPsec configuration

In this first example, we will create a tunnel between two networks separated by the internet. This simulates a VPN tunnel that might be set up if we had to connect two facilities run by the same company, but separated by some distance. The endpoints for the tunnels will be the WAN interfaces of two separate pfSense firewalls, and we will have to perform essentially identical configurations on both ends.

We begin by navigating to **VPN** | **IPsec**. On the default tab, **Tunnels**, we set up the Phase 1 entry first, which we begin by clicking on the **Add P1** button. In the **General Information** section, we change the **Key Exchange version** to **IKEv2**. We set the **Remote gateway** to the IP address of the second pfSense firewall. Enter a brief **Description** in the corresponding edit box. In the Phase 1 Proposal (Authentication) section, we enter a key into the **Pre-Shared Key** edit box. In the **Phase 1 Proposal** (**Algorithm**) section, we set the **Hash Algorithm** to **SHA256** for added security. All other values can be kept at their default values. Click on the **Save** button to save the Phase 1 configuration.

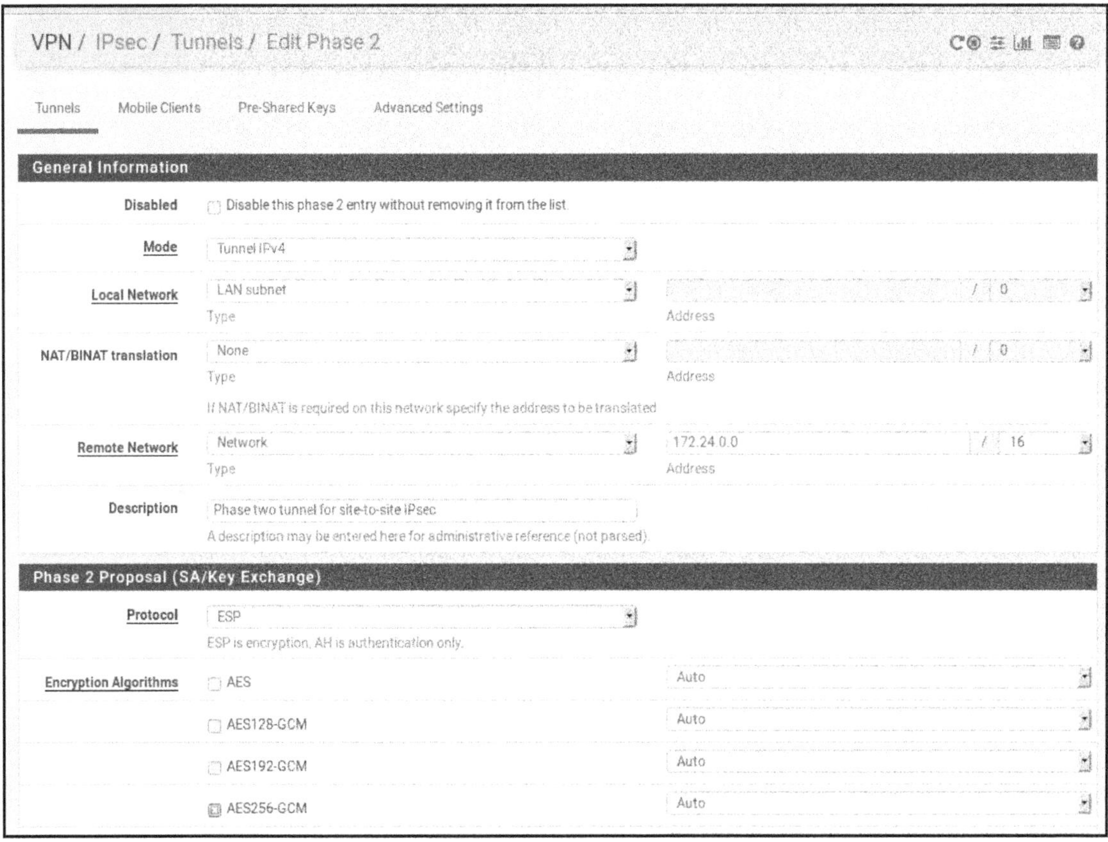

Phase 2 IPsec configuration.

On the **Tunnels** page, click on the **Show Phase 2 Entries** button that corresponds to the Phase 1 entry we just created. The Phase 2 section will be empty, but we can click on the **Add P2** button to create the Phase 2 entry for this connection. In the **General Information** section, **Local Network** will be set to LAN subnet, which in most cases is what we want. We need to enter the LAN subnet and CIDR of the remote network (the network behind the second pfSense firewall) for the **Remote Network** (we can also change the setting in the **Remote Network** drop-down box to **Address** and enter a single address). You can enter a brief **Description** in the corresponding edit box. In the **Phase 2 Configuration (SA/Key Exchange)**, make sure **AES256-GCM** is selected. For **Hash Algorithms**, select **SHA256**. All other values can be kept at their default values. Click on the **Save** button to save the Phase 2 configuration.

Before the IPsec connection can be used, we must add a firewall rule to allow IPsec traffic. Navigate to **Firewall** | **Rules** and click on the **IPsec** tab. On this page, click on one of the **Add** buttons to add a rule. Under **Source**, select **Network** in the drop-down box and enter the subnet and CIDR of the remote network (this should be identical to the information entered for **Remote Network** in the Phase 2 configuration). All other values can be kept at their default values. Click on the **Save** button to save this rule.

You can make the firewall rule as permissive or as restrictive as you wish, so long as it's not so restrictive that it blocks traffic that needs to pass. For example, we could have left the **Source** set to **Any**; however, it is good practice to restrict traffic to traffic from the remote subnet.

Now we need to repeat this configuration on the second pfSense firewall. Starting by navigating to **VPN** | **IPsec** and setting up the Phase 1 configuration, create a Phase 1 setting identical to the one on the other firewall, but make sure **Remote gateway** is set to the first pfSense firewall (therefore, the Remote gateway setting on each firewall will be different). When you create the Phase 2 entry, the settings will be identical to the settings on the first pfSense firewall, but make sure **Remote Network** is set to the subnet and CIDR of the network behind the first pfSense firewall. Once you have completed Phase 1 and Phase 2 configuration, create an IPsec firewall rule; the rule can be identical to the rule created on the first pfSense firewall.

Some guides to setting up site-to-site IPsec connections on pfSense have stated that it is necessary to add a gateway for IPsec traffic on each firewall with the **Interface** set to **LAN** and the **Gateway** set to the IP address of the LAN interface. I have found that when setting up an IPsec tunnel with the current version of pfSense, this step is unnecessary; site-to-site IPsec tunnels seem to work equally well without it.

Now that we have configured our IPsec connection on both firewalls, we can establish a connection. From either firewall, navigate to **Status** | **IPsec**. There you will see a table showing all available IPsec configurations. Click on the **Connect VPN** button corresponding to the configuration we just created. The IPsec tunnel should now be up and the **Status** column should change from **Disconnected** to **ESTABLISHED** to reflect this. Navigate to **Status** | **IPsec** on the other firewall and the table there should also display an established connection.

You can initiate the connection from either firewall, but once the connection is established, it can only be terminated from the side on which it was initiated.

Now that we have set up an IPsec tunnel, what can we do with it? We can access resources on the **LAN** side of the remote connection as if they were local resources. For example, if there is an FTP server or Samba file share on the remote LAN, we would be able to access them, with the only real limitations being the bandwidth of our internet connection, the latency associated with accessing remote nodes, and the processing overhead of maintaining an encrypted tunnel.

Example 2 – IPsec tunnel for remote access

Another possible scenario is one in which we want to create an IPsec tunnel so that remote users can connect to the tunnel using an IPsec client on their computer. This is the scenario that would exist if we are a company that has to support workers who are not at one of the company's sites, but still need to access the company's network. This might be the case if they are on site at a client's workplace, if they are on a business trip, or perhaps working at home. Fortunately, there are IPsec clients for all the major desktop operating systems.

One of the more popular IPsec VPN clients for Windows is the ShrewSoft VPN Client. Although it hasn't been updated in a while (the last stable release of the client is 2.2.2, released in July 2013), it is a stable client with many options. You can download the client at `https://www.shrew.net/download/vpn`.

To show the ShrewSoft VPN Client in action, we will step through the process of setting up an IPsec tunnel, which we will then connect to as a mobile client using ShrewSoft's VPN Access Manager. We begin by navigating to **VPN | IPsec** and clicking on the **Mobile Clients** tab. To enable mobile clients, check the **Enable IPsec Mobile Client Support** checkbox.

The **Extended Authentication (Xauth)** section has two settings: **User Authentication** and **Group Authentication**. **User Authentication** has one option, **Local Database**, so we won't make any changes here. For **Group Authentication**, we will select **system**.

In the **Client Configuration** (`mode-cfg`) section, we will configure a virtual address pool for the remote client. Thus, we check the **Provide a virtual IP address to clients** checkbox, and enter a subnet and CIDR below the checkbox. For purposes of this exercise, we will set the network to `172.25.0.0/16`.

The next setting that we will alter is **Save Xauth Password**. We will check this checkbox. We will also check the **DNS Default Domain** checkbox, and enter **localdomain** as the default domain name. We will also check the **Provide a DNS server list to clients** checkbox. For Server #1, we will enter `8.8.8.8`, and for Server #2, we will enter `8.8.4.4`. We will also check the **Login banner** checkbox and enter a login banner to clients. We then click on the **Save** button at the bottom of the page.

As you can see, pfSense is prompting us to create a corresponding Phase 1 entry for the mobile client configuration. The Phase 1 and Phase 2 entry we create in this manner will be designated as the mobile client IPsec tunnel, which is why you want to complete mobile client configuration before creating an IPsec tunnel – it will make the process much easier. We click on the **Create Phase 1** button to begin IPsec tunnel configuration.

In the **Key Exchange version** drop-down box, we want to select **V1**, as the ShrewSoft Client will not work with **V2**; I was unsuccessful in getting it to work on the **Auto** setting as well. We will leave **Internet Protocol**, **Interface**, and **Description** unchanged. Since we are going to require mobile user authentication, we set the **Authentication Mode** drop-down to **Mutual PSK + Xauth**. We will leave the **Negotiation** mode set to **Aggressive** and **My identifier** set to **My IP address**. We will change **Peer identifier** to **User distinguished name** and enter `vpnuser@ipsectest. duckdns.org` in the corresponding edit box. In the **Pre-Shared Key** box, we will enter **betterthannothing**.

In the **Phase 1 Proposal (Algorithms)** section, the default values are acceptable, so we will not change them. In the **Advanced Options** section, we will change one setting: we will change the **NAT Traversal** setting to **Force** to force the use of NAT-T on port `4500`. Once we are done, we will press the **Save** button, which will take us back to the main IPsec page.

From the main IPsec page, we click on **Show Phase 2 Entries** in the mobile client entry. Then we click on the **Add P2** button to add a Phase 2 entry for this tunnel. In the **General Information** section, we will keep the default settings. In **Phase 2 Proposal (SA/Key Exchange)**, we will keep **Encryption Algorithms** as **AES**, but we will change the value in the drop-down box from **Auto** to `256. 3600` is a bit short for **Lifetime**, so we will change this value to `28800`. When done, we will click on the **Save** button; then we will click on the **Apply Changes** button on the main IPsec page.

We still haven't created a user group and users for the VPN tunnel, so we will next navigate to **System** | **User Manager** and click on the **Groups** tab. Then we click on the **Add** button below the table to the right to add a new group. We enter a group name of **vpnusers**, and in the **Scope** drop-down box, we set the scope to **Remote**. Then we click on the **Save** button.

We must assign privileges to **vpnusers**, so we click on the **Edit** icon for **vpnusers** in the table. On the configuration page for the group, there will now be a section called **Assigned Privileges**, and we click on the **Add** button. In the **Assigned Privileges** listbox, we select **User – VPN: IPsecxauthDialin** and click on **Save**. From the main configuration page, we click on **Save** again. The group is now configured.

Now all we have to do on the local side is to create at least one user for the newly created group. We click on the **Users** tab and click on the **Add** button to create a new user. We set the **Username** to `remoteuser` and the **Password** to `suPerseCret01`.

Under **Group Memberships**, we make **remoteuser** a member of vpnusers. For the **IPsec Pre-Shared Key**, we re-enter the key we entered earlier (`betterthannothing`). Then we click on the **Save** button.

We are now done with configuration on the local side, and only need to configure the remote client. We launch the ShrewSoft VPN Access Manager, and then click on the **Add** button on the toolbar to add a new configuration profile. The **General** tab has two sections: **Remote Host** and **Local Host**. Keep in mind that the remote host and local host are now the reverse of what they were when we were configuring the other end of the connection. For **Host Name or IP Address**, we generally want the WAN IP of the router on which the IPsec tunnel was set up in the previous step, unless this router is behind another router, in which case you would enter the internet IP address of your network. If you set up dynamic DNS, you can enter the DDNS hostname here. In this case, we created the domain name **ipsectest.duckdns.org**, which provides a domain name for the pfSense router. For **Auto Configuration**, we want to select **ikeconfig pull** from the drop-down box. Finally, since the remote peer will be assigning virtual IP addresses to clients, we select **Use a virtual adapter and assigned address** in the **Adapter Mode** drop-down box. The **Obtain Automatically** checkbox should be checked, since the remote peer will be assigning the IP addresses. **MTU** can be kept at **1380**.

The next tab is the **Client** tab. Here, we want to set **NAT Traversal** to **enable** to match the setting on the remote end; **NAT Traversal Port** should be set to **4500**, which is the default value. The default values for **Keep-alive packet rate**, **Ike Fragmentation**, and **Maximum packet size** should be fine. We will check the **Enable Dead Peer Detection**, **Enable ISAKMP Failure Notifications**, and the **Enable Client Login Banner** checkboxes.

The next tab is called **Name Resolution**. It has two tabs of its own: one is called **DNS** and the other is **WINS**. Since we are not dealing with WINS servers, we will focus only on the **DNS** tab and check the **Enable DNS** checkbox. We also check the **Obtain Automatically** checkbox for DNS, and the **Obtain Automatically** checkbox for **DNS Suffix**.

Next, we move to the **Authentication** tab, which has three of its own tabs: **Local Identity**, **Remote Identity**, and **Credentials**. The method selected in the **Authentication Method** drop-down box must match what we set during Phase 1 configuration of the IPsec tunnel in pfSense, so we set it to **Mutual PSK + XAuth**. **Local Identity** must match **Peer Identifier** in Phase 1, so we select **User Fully Qualified Domain Name** (meaning user + FQDN).

For **UFQDN String**, we enter `vpnuser@ipsectest.duckdns.org`, just as we did for **Peer Identifier** in pfSense. On the **Remote Identity** tab, we can keep the default **Identification Type** of **IP Address** and move on to the **Credentials** tab. We are using a PSK, and the PSK must match the one we entered during Phase 1, so in the **Pre Shared Key** edit box, we enter **betterthannothing**.

The last two tabs we must configure are **Phase 1** and **Phase 2**. Moving to **Phase 1**, we must match the settings with those entered during Phase 1 configuration on the other end, so we set **Exchange Type** to **aggressive** and **DH Exchange** to **group 2** (1024 bits). The next three options you could set as **auto**, but the software seems to work better if you match the settings on the other end of the tunnel exactly. Therefore, we set **Cipher Algorithm** to **aes**, **Cipher Key Length** to `256`, and **Hash Algorithm** to **sha1**. We set **Key Life Time** limit to `28800` secs, and we leave **Key Life Data Limit** at **0** Kbytes.

Moving on to the **Phase 2** tab, we set **Transform Algorithm** to **esp-aes** and **Transform Key Length** to `256`. **HMAC Algorithm** should be set to **sha1**, and **PFS Exchange** and **Compress Algorithm** should be kept at their default values of disabled. We set **Key Life Time limit** to **28800** secs and **Key Life Data limit** is kept at **0** Kbytes. On the **Policy** tab, we do not need to make any changes, so we click on the **Save** button at the bottom.

Our client configuration is complete, so we can now click on **Connect** on the menu bar to try it out. We will be presented with a dialog box that states **config loaded for site <this_site>**. Click on the **Connect** button to start connecting. The VPN Access Manager will prompt us for a username/password combination, so we enter the username and password for the user we created in the previous step (**remoteuser**, **suPerseCret01**). We click on **Connect** again. The client should take a minute or less to connect to the tunnel. Once we are connected, we will be able to access the LAN subnet on the remote end as if LAN is a local resource.

L2TP

Owing to the fact that L2TP lacks both authentication and encryption, it is unlikely that you will ever set up L2TP as a standalone VPN protocol. A more likely scenario is that you set an L2TP/IPsec tunnel in which users can connect to the IPsec tunnel directly, or connect via L2TP, with IPsec traffic taking place within the L2TP tunnel. Fortunately, L2TP configuration is much easier than IPsec configuration, and implementing in should ensure that our VPN will be accessible to a greater number of users.

To begin L2TP configuration, navigate to **VPN** | **L2TP**. This should take you to the **Configuration** tab. The **Enable** checkbox, when checked, enables the L2TP server. In the **Configuration** section, the **Interface** drop-down allows you to select the interface on which the L2TP server is listening for connections (almost always **WAN**).

In the **Server address** field, you must enter the gateway IP address of the L2TP server. It should be an unused IP address, usually on the same subnet as the client IP address subnet. The **Remote address range** field is where you enter the starting IP address of the client subnet. There is a drop-down box labeled **Number of L2TP users** where you select the number of clients allowed. The starting IP address plus the number of L2TP users minus one will be the ending IP address.

The **Secret** field is where you can enter a shared secret (there are two edit boxes, as the secret must be entered twice). Next is the **Authentication type** drop-down box; there are currently three different options for the protocol to use for authentication:

- **Challenge Handshake Authentication Protocol (CHAP)**: When a peer tries to establish a connection, the authenticator sends a challenge message to the peer. The peer replies with a value calculated using a one-way hash function in which the challenge and the secret are inputs to the function (the handshake). The authenticator checks the response, based on its own calculation of what the hash value should be, and if there is a match, the peer is authenticated. This is the default choice and it is considered relatively secure because the secret (or password) is encrypted before it is sent.
- **MS-CHAPv2**: This is Microsoft's version of CHAP, which differs from standard CHAP in several ways (for example, it uses CHAP Algorithm 0x80, and provides authenticator-control mechanisms for password change and authentication retry). It is also considered weak, since it uses 56-bit DES encryption, which is vulnerable to brute-force attacks using modern hardware, so take that into account.

- **Password Authentication Protocol (PAP)**: The least secure of all the protocols, this authentication protocol transmits unencrypted passwords over the network.

The next section, **RADIUS**, has a checkbox that allows you to enable RADIUS authentication. If you check this box, then you will have to enter a series of **RADIUS** options, including **server IP address** and **shared secret**. When you are done making changes, click on the **Save** button.

There is also a **Users** tab for adding L2TP clients. To add a user, click on this tab and click on the **Add** button below the table (which lists users already added). The **User** configuration page is pretty self-explanatory. You enter the username in the **Username** edit box and the password in the **Password** edit boxes (the password must be entered twice). The **IP Address** edit box is optional and you can use it to assign the user a specific IP address. When you are done, click on the **Save** button.

OpenVPN

The third VPN protocol supported by the current version of pfSense is OpenVPN. It is an excellent choice if you require a protocol that has cross-platform support, it is relatively secure, and is easy to configure. A relative newcomer (OpenVPN was initially released in 2001), it has been gaining in acceptance in recent years.

To begin OpenVPN configuration, navigate to **VPN | OpenVPN**. There are four tabs: **Servers**, **Clients**, **Client-Specific Overrides**, and **Wizards**. Note that whereas in IPsec, both ends of the tunnels can be configured as peers, OpenVPN tunnels always have one end defined as a client and the other as a server.

OpenVPN server configuration

To begin server configuration, click on the **Server** tab, and from there, click on the **Add** button below the table (listing already configured servers). The first option on the configuration page, the **Disable** checkbox, allows you to disable the server entry without removing it if checked. The **Server mode** drop-down box allows you to choose between several modes:

- **Peer-to-Peer (SSL/TLS)**: Either side can initiate the connection. A certificate will be used for authentication.
- **Peer-to-Peer (Shared Key)**: Either side can initiate the connection. A shared key is used for authentication.

- **Remote Access (SSL/TLS)**: The remote client initiates the connection. A certificate is used for authentication.
- **Remote Access (User Auth)**: The remote client initiates the connection. User authentication is through a username/password combination.
- **Remote Access (SSL/TLS + User Auth)**: The remote client initiates the connection. User authentication involves both a certificate and username/password.

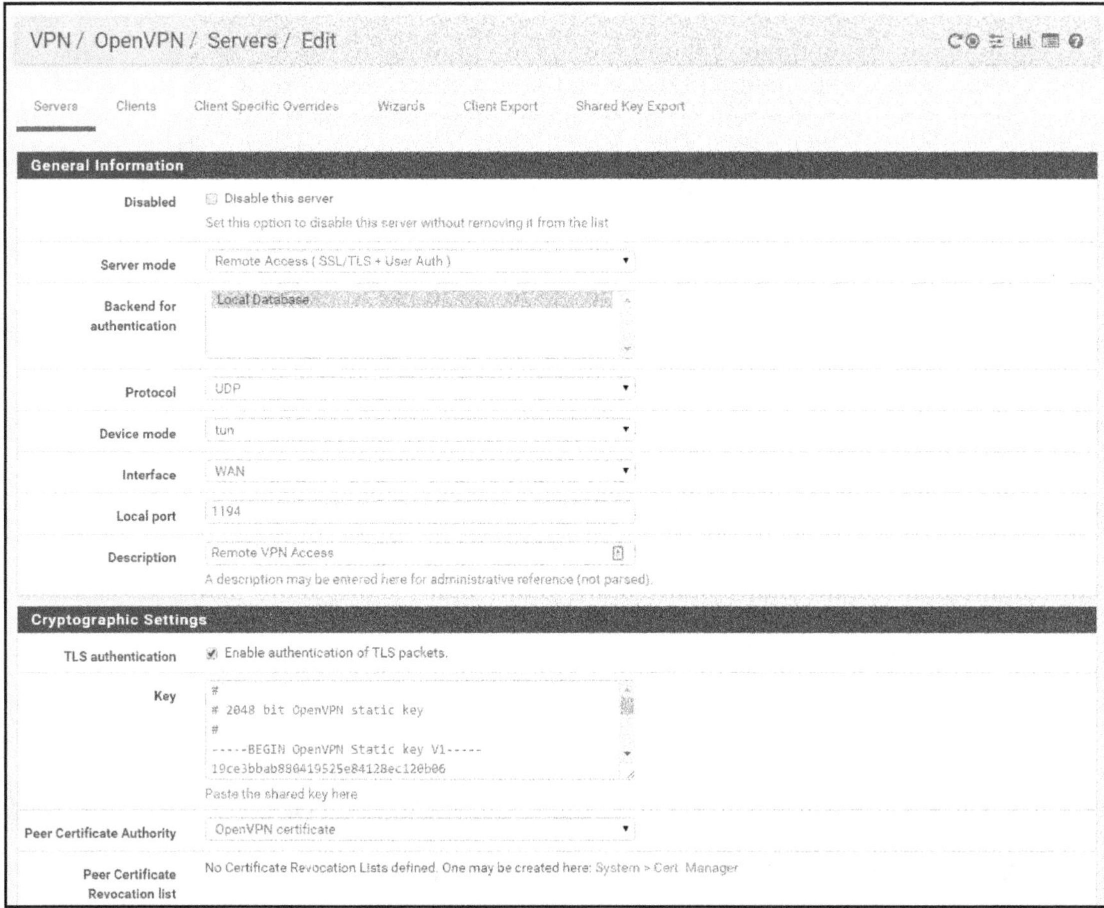

Adding an OpenVPN server

In the **Protocol** drop-down box, you can choose the protocol for this connection; both **UDP** and **TCP** are supported, as well as **UDP6** and **TCP6** for IPv6 connections. The **Device mode** drop-down box allows you to choose between **Tun** and **Tap**. A TAP device is a virtual Ethernet adapter; a TUN device is a virtual point-to-point IP link. This setting must match on both sides of the connection.

The **Local port** edit box lets you set the port for this OpenVPN connection. The default port for OpenVPN is **1194**. You may also enter a brief non-parsed description in the **Description** edit box.

Under **Cryptographic Settings**, you can configure a number of options for certificates. There are two checkboxes: **Use a TLS key** and **Automatically generate a TLS key**. If the latter is unchecked, a textbox will appear in which you can enter a TLS key. **Peer Certificate Authority** will allow you to choose from any defined certificate authorities. Similarly, if any certificate revocation lists have been created, you can choose one at the **Peer Certificate Revocation list**. The **DH Parameter Length** drop-down list allows you to set the size of the Diffie-Hellman key (or to use ECDH instead). You can also select the **Encryption Algorithm** and **Auth** (entication) digest algorithm (although you should leave the latter set to **SHA1**, since **SHA1** is the default for OpenVPN). You can enable hardware crypto acceleration in the **Hardware Crypto** drop-down box (the only option currently supported seems to be **BSD cryptodev engine**).

pfSense 2.4 has seen the addition of several new options for OpenVPN server configuration. One of these options is **ECDH Curve**. To enable use of ECDH, select **ECDH only** in the **DH Parameter Length** drop-down box. ECDH stands for **Elliptic-curve Diffie-Hellman**. Whereas standard Diffie-Hellman performs a modulus operation on a group of multiplicative integers in order to compute the secret key, ECDH uses a group of multiplicative points on a curve. The **Default** option uses the curve either from the server certificate or secp384r1, but you can choose from a variety of different curves in the drop-down box.

Another new option is the **Enable NCP** checkbox. NCP stands for **Negotiable Cryptographic Parameters**; when both peers support NCP and have it enabled, NCP overrides the algorithm set in **Encryption Algorithm**. Instead, the algorithm is chosen from the list of **Allowed NCP Algorithms**, which in turn is a subset of the **Available NCP Algorithms**. The **Available NCP Algorithms** and the **Allowed NCP Algorithms** textboxes are adjacent to each other and are below the **Enable NCP** checkbox. If one peer supports NCP and the other peer does not, pfSense will attempt to establish a connection using the algorithm requested by the non-NCP peer, so long as it is on the list of **Available NCP Algorithms**.

You can select the **Certificate Depth** as well; pfSense will not accept certificate-based logins from clients whose certificates are below the set depth. The certificate depth is the maximum number of intermediate certificate issuers that are allowed to be followed when verifying the client certificate. If the depth is set to **0**, then only self-signed certificates will be allowed. If the depth is set to **1**, the certificate may be self-signed or signed by a CA known to the system. Setting the certificate depth to a number higher than 1 allows for more intermediate certificate issuers.

Tunnel Settings determines what happens to the OpenVPN clients once they are authenticated. The **IPv4 Tunnel Network** and **IPv6 Tunnel Network** allow you to set the IPv4 and IPv6 virtual networks that will provide the address pools for the clients. For example, an **IPv4 Tunnel Network** setting of **192.168.3.0/24** will result in clients being assigned addresses of **192.168.3.1**, **192.168.3.2**, and so on. **Redirect Gateway**, if checked, will force all client-generated traffic through the VPN tunnel. The **IPv4 Local network(s)** and **IPv6 Local networks** allow you to set what local networks will be accessible from the remote end. These should be expressed as comma-separated lists of one or more CIDR ranges. **IPv4 Remote network(s)** and **IPv6 Remote network(s)** allow you to set what remote networks will be accessible from the remote end of the VPN.

The **Concurrent connections** edit box allows you to specify the maximum number of clients allowed to connect to the server concurrently. The **Compression** drop-down box allows you to set the compression option for this channel; the choices are: **No Preference**, **Disabled (no compression)**, **Enabled with Adaptive Compression** (dynamically disable compression for a time if OpenVPN determines compression is not being done efficiently), or **Enabled without Adaptive Compression** (compression always on). **Disable IPv6** will result in IPv6 traffic not being forwarded.

The **Advanced Configuration** section has two options. In the **Custom options** listbox, you can enter any additional options to add to the OpenVPN server. The **Verbosity** level drop-down box allows you to select the logging level (2 through 11, with 5 outputting R and W characters to the console for each read and write, and 6 through 11 providing debugging info) for OpenVPN. When you are done making changes, click on the **Save** button at the bottom of the page and the **Apply Changes** button on the main OpenVPN page.

OpenVPN client configuration

The **Client** tab under **OpenVPN** is for configuring pfSense to act as a client so it can connect to a remote OpenVPN server. This is an ideal option if you want to connect to a VPN service. Instead of connecting individual computers to a VPN, you can connect at the firewall, thus encrypting all traffic from nodes on your local network to the internet.

To begin configuration, click on the **Clients** tab and click on the **Add** button in the following table.

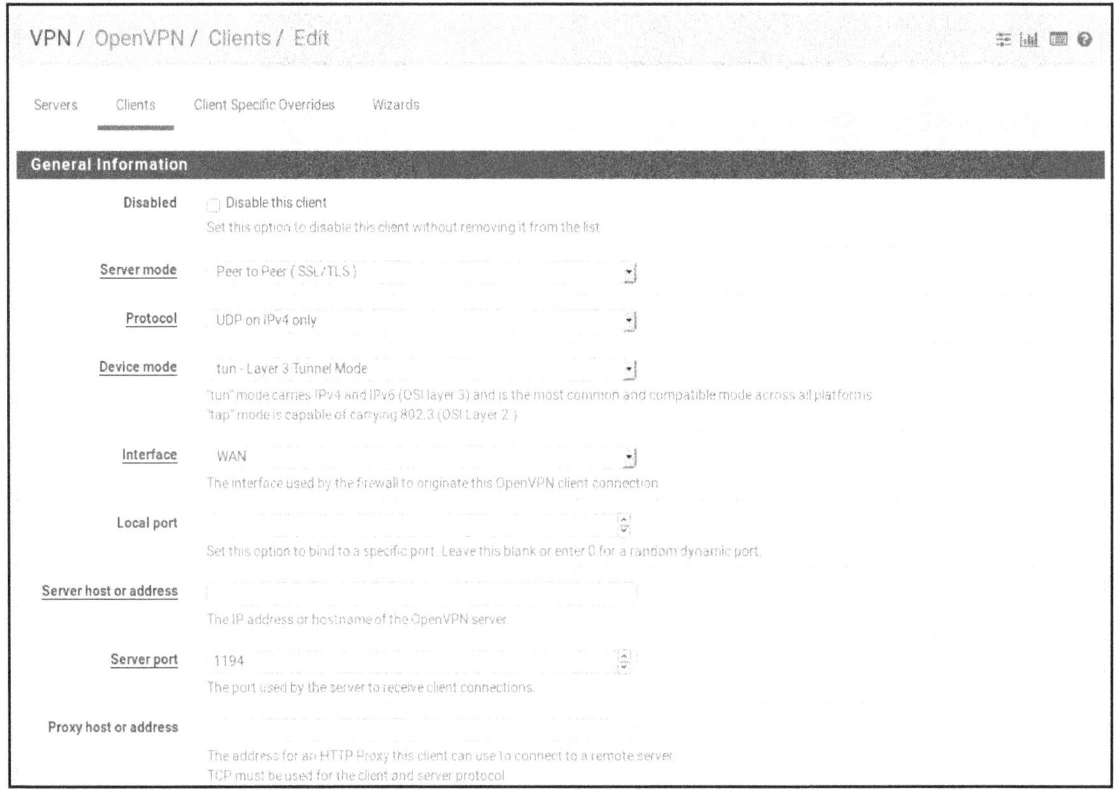

The OpenVPN client configuration tab.

Most of the options on the client configuration page are similar to options found on the server configuration page, with some notable exceptions. The **User Authentication Settings** section is where you set the username and password for the remote server. In the **Tunnel Configuration** section, the **Don't pull routes** checkbox, if checked, will bar the server from adding routes to your routing table. The **Don't add/remove routes** checkbox, if checked, will pass routes using environmental variables. Click on the **Save** button at the bottom to save the new client configuration and click on the **Apply Changes** button on the main **OpenVPN** page.

Client-specific overrides

If you are running an OpenVPN server and you need special settings for one or more clients, then the **Client Specific Overrides** tab is the place to configure such settings. To begin, click on **Client Specific Overrides** and click on the **Add** button below the table.

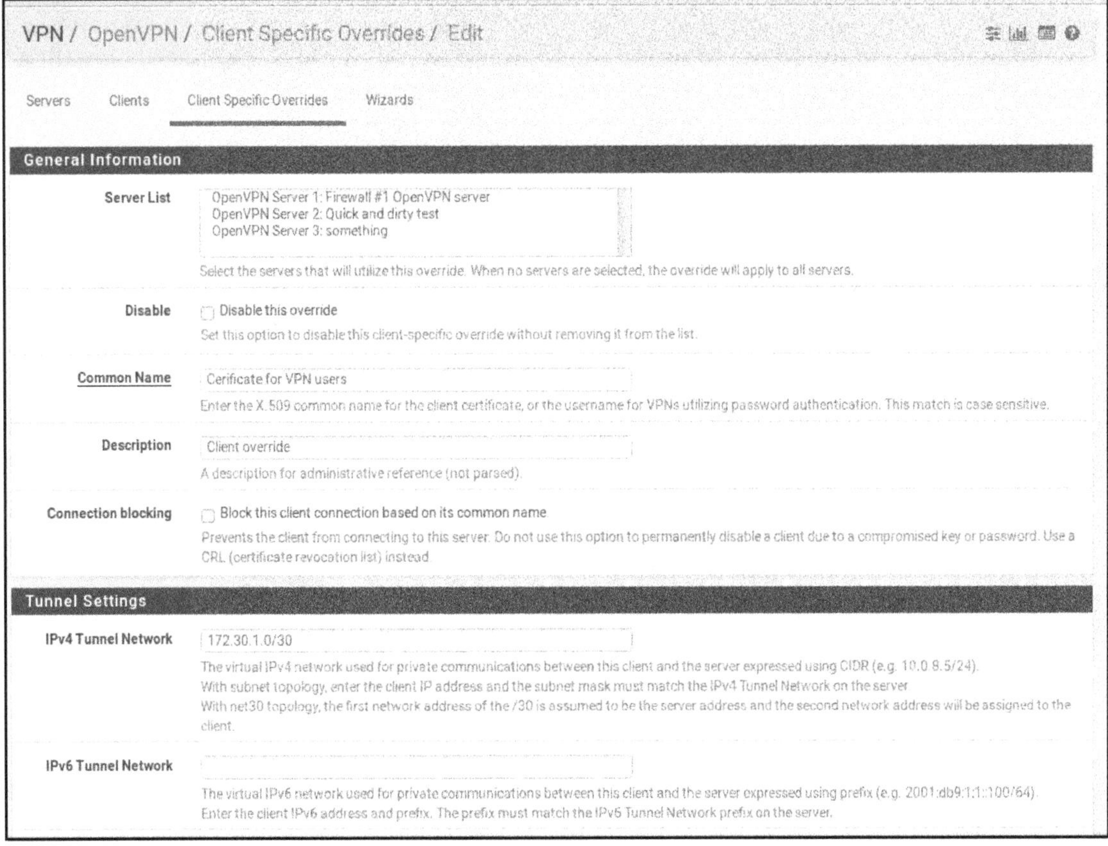

Configuring client-specific overrides for an OpenVPN server.

In the **General Information** section, you must specify both the server to which the override applies and the name of the client. In the **Server List** listbox, select a server for which the override will apply. Not selecting any servers will result in the override being applied to all servers. The **Disable** check box, if checked, will disable the override without removing it from the list. In the **Common name** edit box, you must enter the client's X.509 common name. In an X.509 certificate, the common name, or **CN**, is the field that must match the host being authenticated, and is typically used to identify a given user. You can enter a non-parsed description in the **Description** edit box. The **Connection blocking** check box will, if checked, block this client connection based on its common name.

In the next two sections, **Tunnel Settings** and **Client Settings**, most of the settings are similar to settings that are available on the server configuration page. The difference is, of course, that setting them here will cause them to be applied to the override only. For example, in **Tunnel Network**, you can define a virtual network to be used only by this client. In the **Client Settings** section, you can make changes such as providing a different DNS server list to this client. The **Server Definitions** checkbox, if checked, will prevent this particular client from receiving any server-defined client settings. Click on the **Save** button when you are done configuring the client-specific overrides for the client.

Server configuration with the wizard

One way you can set up an OpenVPN server easily is to use the server configuration wizard. To do so, click on the **Wizards** tab. The first option is the **Type of Server** drop-down box. The options are as follows:

- **Local User Access**: OpenVPN access with authentication through certificates, managed through the pfSense Certificate Authority Manager
- **LDAP**: Authentication through an **LDAP** (**Lightweight Directory Access Protocol**, a vendor-neutral protocol for directory services) server
- **RADIUS**: Authentication through a **RADIUS** (**Remote Authentication Dial-In User Service**) server

If you choose **Local User Access**, the wizard allows you to choose an existing CA/ server certificate (if any exist), or you can create a new CA in this step. If you opt for the latter, you must enter a non-parsed descriptive name, the **Key length** (in bits), **Lifetime** (in days), as well as the **Country Code**, **State** or **Province, City**, **Organization**, and **E-mail**. When you have entered all this information, click on the **Add new CA** button. On the next screen, the wizard will prompt you to create a new server certificate. The fields will be auto filled with the information you entered in the previous step. If you do not need to make any changes, you can click on the **Create new Certificate** button and move on to the next screen.

The final screen is the **Server Setup** screen. This screen mirrors the server configuration page we covered in the previous section, although it does have some options not available from that page. The **Inter-Client Communication** checkbox, if checked, allows communication between clients connected to the server. The **Duplicate Connections** checkbox, if checked, allows multiple concurrent connections using the same common name.

The **Client Settings** section has several more options not available on the server configuration page. The **Dynamic IP** option allows connected clients to retain their connections if their IP address changes. If you want to force reauthentication if the client changes IP addresses, uncheck this option. The **Address Pool** option provides a virtual IP address to clients (the IP subnet is defined in **Tunnel Network** in the previous page section). The **Topology** drop-down allows you to choose the method used to supply a virtual IP address to clients when using TUN mode on IPv4. There are two modes available:

- **Subnet – One IP address per client in a common subnet**: This is the default option.
- **net30 – Isolated /30 network per client**: This gives each client a subnet with two IP addresses (`2^2 - 2 = 4 - 2 = 2`). This may be necessary for older versions of OpenVPN (before 2.0.9) or some older clients.

In the **DNS Default Domain** edit box, you can provide a default domain to clients. There are four edit boxes where you can enter DNS server IP addresses. There are also two edit boxes where you can enter IP addresses for NTP servers. The **Enable NetBIOS over TCP/IP** checkbox, if checked, allows you to use NetBIOS over a TCP/IP network (if you intend to do so, you should choose TCP as your protocol).

The **NetBIOS Node Type** allows you to select the way pfSense resolves NetBIOS names to IP addresses. The options are:

- `b-node`: Broadcast
- `p-node`: Point-to-point, or peer, queries to a WINS server
- `m-node`: Mixed; broadcast first, then WINS
- `h-node`: Hybrid; WINS first, then broadcast

NetBIOS Scope ID allows you to provide an ID for an extended naming service, which isolates NetBIOS traffic onto a single network to only those nodes with the same scope ID. Finally, there are two edit boxes for WINS servers. You can click on the **Next** button when you are done making changes.

The next step of the wizard covers configuration of the firewall rules. You need two rules for an OpenVPN tunnel: a rule to permit connections on the OpenVPN port, and a rule to allow traffic to pass inside the VPN tunnel. This page enables you to easily create both rules, simply by checking the appropriate checkboxes. If you previously set up an OpenVPN tunnel, you probably don't need to create these rules. When you are done making changes, click on the **Next** button. You should see a message on the next page acknowledging that the configuration is complete; click on the **Finish** button on this page.

OpenVPN Client Export Utility

One of the advantages of using OpenVPN is that it has gotten popular enough to where there are third-party packages available to make the process of using OpenVPN easier. One of these packages is the OpenVPN Client Export Utility, which allows a pre-configured OpenVPN Windows client or macOS X's Viscosity configuration bundle to be exported directly from pfSense.

To install the OpenVPN Client Export Utility, navigate to **Packages** | **OpenVPN** and click on the **Available Packages** tab. Scroll down to `openvpn-client-export` and click on the **Install** button. The next page will prompt you to confirm installation; click on the **Confirm** button to complete the process. This will install `openvpn-client-export` and all its dependencies. The process should take less than a minute.

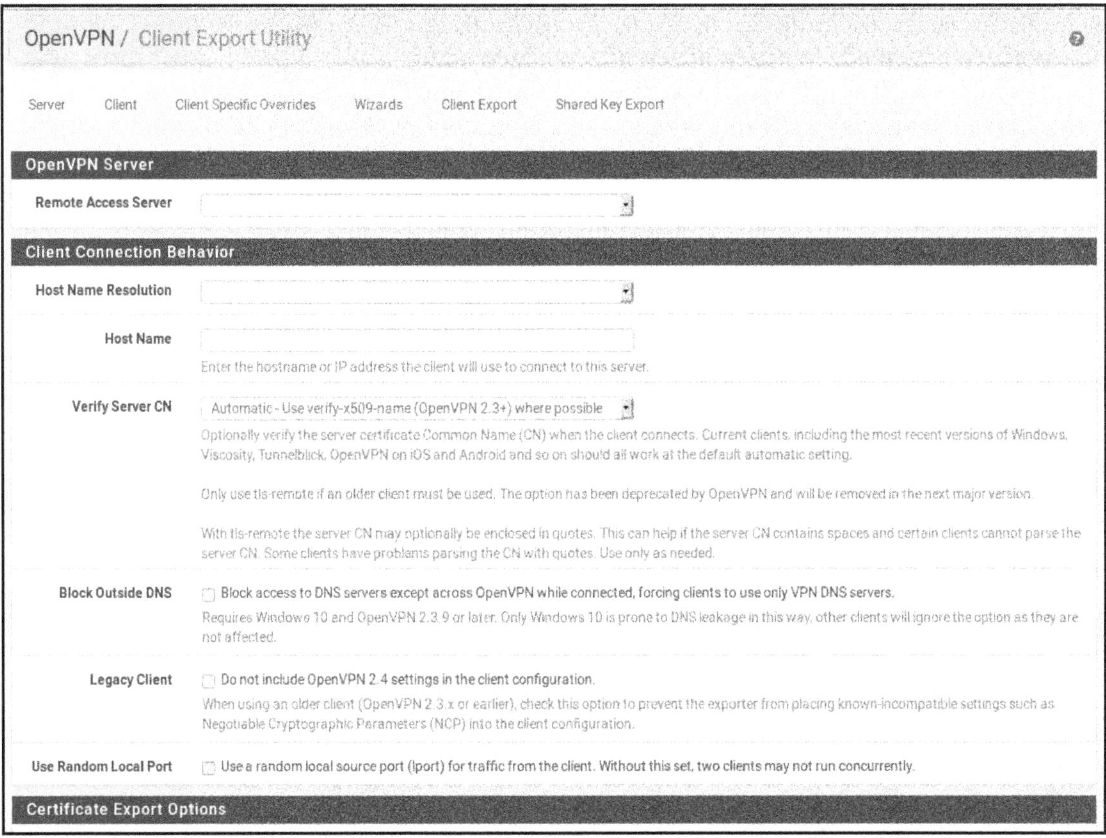
OpenVPN / Client Export Utility
Server
Client
Client Specific Overrides
Wizards
Client Export
Shared Key Export
OpenVPN Server
Remote Access Server
Client Connection Behavior
Host Name Resolution
Host Name
Enter the hostname or IP address the client will use to connect to this server.
Verify Server CN
Automatic - Use verify-x509-name (OpenVPN 2.3+) where possible
Optionally verify the server certificate Common Name (CN) when the client connects. Current clients, including the most recent versions of Windows, Viscosity, Tunnelblick, OpenVPN on iOS and Android and so on should all work at the default automatic setting.
Only use tls-remote if an older client must be used. The option has been deprecated by OpenVPN and will be removed in the next major version.
With tls-remote the server CN may optionally be enclosed in quotes. This can help if the server CN contains spaces and certain clients cannot parse the server CN. Some clients have problems parsing the CN with quotes. Use only as needed.
Block Outside DNS
Block access to DNS servers except across OpenVPN while connected, forcing clients to use only VPN DNS servers.
Requires Windows 10 and OpenVPN 2.3.9 or later. Only Windows 10 is prone to DNS leakage in this way, other clients will ignore the option as they are not affected.
Legacy Client
Do not include OpenVPN 2.4 settings in the client configuration.
When using an older client (OpenVPN 2.3.x or earlier), check this option to prevent the exporter from placing known-incompatible settings such as Negotiable Cryptographic Parameters (NCP) into the client configuration.
Use Random Local Port
Use a random local source port (lport) for traffic from the client. Without this set, two clients may not run concurrently.
Certificate Export Options

The OpenVPN Client Export Utility

Installation of the OpenVPN Client Export Utility will result in two additional tabs becoming available when you navigate back to **Protocols** | **OpenVPN**: **Client Export** and **Shared Key Export**. The **Client Export** tab allows you to generate configuration files for clients that can be used on various platforms, whereas **Shared Key Export** is geared towards peer-to-peer connections (for example, connecting two networks with an OpenVPN tunnel). The **Client Export** tab has a number of options. The **Remote Access Server** drop-down allows you to choose to which OpenVPN server the client will be connecting. Typically, the only available option will be the OpenVPN server on port **1194** using UDP, but if you have other OpenVPN servers configured on other ports (and possibly using TCP instead of UDP), these servers should appear in the drop-down box.

The **Verify Server** CN drop-down allows you to select how the server certificate **Common Name** (**CN**) is verified. The default selection of **Automatic** should work in most cases (it is compatible with OpenVPN v.2.3 and most modern clients), but there are other options available for backward compatibility. The **Use Random Local Port** checkbox allows you to enable using a random local source port, which is likely something you will want to enable, since the client end can send and receive on any port (only the server must send and receive on the same pre-defined port), and enabling this option allows more than one client to run on the same system. There are two options in **Certificate Export Options**: **Microsoft Certificate Storage** (instead of local storage) and **Password Protect Certificate** (for password protecting a certificate when using Viscosity with macOS X).

The **Use A Proxy** checkbox, if checked, will allow the client to use a proxy to communicate with the OpenVPN server. If this option is enabled, you must select **Proxy Type** (**HTTP** or **SOCKS**), **Proxy IP Address, and Proxy Port**. You can optionally choose a **Proxy Authentication** method. The options are **None**, **Basic**, and **NTLM** (NT LAN Manager).

The **Use the OpenVPN Manager Management Interface** option, if selected, will result in the management interface being activated in the generated configuration, allowing OpenVPN to be used by non-administrator users on Windows systems. Finally, the **Advanced configuration options** edit box allows you to add any additional options you require, separated by a line break or semicolon.

In the **OpenVPN Clients** section, there will be download links for different client configurations, assuming that you have added at least one client that uses the same CA as the OpenVPN server. There are configuration files available for Android, iOS, Windows XP and Vista, and Viscosity (both macOS X and Windows).

If you click on the **Shared Key Export** tab, you can export a shared key configuration. These are generally for site-to-site tunnels with other routers. To generate a shared key configuration, you must select a server in the **Shared Key Server** drop-down box. You must also select a resolution method in the **Host Name Resolution** drop-down box, and a hostname/address in the **Host Name** edit box.

In the **Proxy Options** section, you can opt to use a proxy to connect to the OpenVPN server and enter the proxy information. If so, you need to check the **Use a Proxy** edit box, and select a **Proxy Type** (**HTTP** or **SOCKS**), **Proxy IP Address**, **Proxy Port**, **Authentication Method** (again, the choices are **None**, **Basic**, and **NTLM**), and a username/password combination.

Example – site-to-site OpenVPN configuration

As with IPsec, it is possible to create a site-to-site connection between two pfSense firewalls, although the process is somewhat different than it is with IPsec. The steps in setting up a site-to-site OpenVPN connection are as follows:

- Create a Certificate Authority and Certificates for authentication
- Configure the OpenVPN server on the first firewall
- Create firewall rules to pass OpenVPN traffic on the first firewall
- Import the certificates into the second firewall
- Configure the OpenVPN server on the second firewall
- Create firewall rules to pass OpenVPN traffic on the second firewall

We begin by creating the certificates we will use for authentication. Navigate to **System** | **Certificate Manager**. On the **CAs** tab, click on the **Add** button. At the **Methods** drop-down box, select **Create an internal Certificate Authority**. Fill out the required fields and click on the **Save** button. We will need the newly-created CA on the server end, so click on the **Export CA** icon under the **Actions** column and save the CA somewhere so it can be copied to the server.

Now click on the **Certificates** tab so we can create the certificates. Click on the **Add/Sign** button. For **Method**, select **Create an internal Certificate** in the drop-down box. Fill out the required fields, and be sure to select **Server Certificate** as the **Certificate Type**. Click on **Save** to generate this certificate. We still need to create the user certificate, so click on the **Add/Sign** button again and once again select **Create an internal Certificate** as the **Method**. This time, select **User Certificate** as the **Certificate Type** and fill out the required fields. Click on **Save** to generate the certificate. We are going to need the user certificate on the client side, so click on the **Export Certificate** icon for this certificate and save the certificate. We will also need the key, so click on the **Export Key** icon and save the key.

Now we can configure the OpenVPN server. Navigate to **VPN** | **OpenVPN**, and on the **Servers** tab click **Add**. In the **General Information** section, we can keep all the default settings, although if you plan on setting up more than one OpenVPN tunnel, you may want to change **Local port** from the default port of **1194**. You can also add a brief **Description** (for example, "OpenVPN server on Firewall #1").

In the **Cryptographic Settings** section, we have to make some changes. In the **Peer Certificate Authority** drop-down box, select the CA we created earlier, if it isn't already selected. In the **Server Certificate** drop-down box, select the server certificate we created earlier. All other settings can remain the same, unless you want to select more secure settings for such parameters as **DH Parameter Length** and **Encryption Algorithm**.

In the **Tunnel Settings** section, we will also have to make some changes. **IPv4 Tunnel Network** is where we specify the virtual network used for private communications between the server and client. You can specify any private network you want, but it is customary to use 30 bits for the subnet, so the CIDR is usually /30. You can also set an **IPv6 Tunnel Network** if you are using IPv6. **IPv4 Local network(s)** is where we specify local networks that will be accessible from the remote endpoint, and **IPv4 Remote network(s)** is where we specify the remote LAN. Both of these settings have corresponding IPv6 settings that we can set if necessary.

All settings in the **Client Settings** and **Advanced Configuration** sections can remain unchanged. If you anticipate using this server with OpenVPN clients that require a /30 network for each client, you may want to change **Topology** from **Subnet** to **net30**. Click on **Save** when you are done. This will return you to the **Server** page, where you should now click on the **Edit** icon for the newly-created server entry, scroll down to the **TLS Key** textbox, and copy and paste the **TLS key** into a file - we are going to have to copy this on the client side.

The server configuration is complete, but we still need firewall rules to allow OpenVPN traffic to pass. Navigate to **Firewall | Rules** and on the WAN tab, click one of the **Add** buttons. For the **Protocol**, select **UDP** (the default protocol used by OpenVPN), and for **Source**, select **WAN address**. All other settings can remain the same. As with the firewall rules created for IPsec, you can make them as restrictive as you want, as long as they don't block traffic that needs to pass. Click on **Save** when you are done making changes. Next, click on the OpenVPN tab and click on one of the **Add** buttons. For the **Protocol**, select **UDP**, **TCP/UDP**, or **Any**; all other settings can remain the same. Click on **Save** when you are done.

Server-side configuration is now done, so we can go to the other firewall and begin client-side configuration. On the client side, navigate to **System | Certificate Manager** and on the **CAs** tab, click on the **Add** button. Keep the **Method** set to **Import an existing Certificate Authority**, and paste the CA certificate you created on the server into the **Certificate data** textbox. Enter a **Descriptive** name in the appropriate edit box and click on the **Save** button when done. Next, click on the **Certificates** tab and click on the **Add** button so we can add the user certificate. Keep the **Method** set to **Import an existing Certificate**, and paste both the user certificate and the private key into the appropriate textboxes. Click on the **Save** button when done.

Now we can begin OpenVPN client configuration. Navigate to **VPN | OpenVPN**, click on the **Client** tab, and click on the **Add** button. Settings under the **General Information** section can remain unchanged, unless you changed **Local Port** in the server configuration, in which case you will want to change **Server port** so they match. You can also enter a brief **Description** in the corresponding edit box.

In the **Cryptographic Settings** section, leave **Use a TLS Key** enabled, but disable **Automatically generate a TLS key**. An **TLS key** edit box will appear; here you must paste the TLS key from the server. Set the **Peer certificate authority** to the Certificate Authority previously imported. Set **Client certificate** to the user certificate previously imported. The rest of the settings in this section can remain the same, unless you altered the cryptographic options on the server side, in which case the client side settings must match.

In the **Tunnel Settings** section, set **IPv4 Tunnel Network** to match the **IPv4 Tunnel Network** setting on the server. Also, set **IPv6 Tunnel Network** if you are using IPv6. **IPv4 Remote networks** should match **IPv4 Local network(s)** on the server. Set **IPv6 Remote network(s)** if necessary. Again, all other settings in this section can remain the same unless you made changes to them on the server side; for example, if you changed **Topology**, make sure it matches on both sides. Click on the **Save** button when you are done.

Now, all that remains to be done on the client is to create the firewall rules. They are essentially the same rules as we created on the server, so I won't go into detail on their creation here. The first rule must allow UDP traffic to pass through the **WAN** interface, and the second rule must be created on the OpenVPN tab to allow traffic to pass.

Unlike with IPsec configuration, the OpenVPN tunnel should be up as soon as we have finished configuration. To confirm that the tunnel is up, navigate to **Status | OpenVPN** on either firewall; it should show that the newly-created OpenVPN tunnel is up, along with statistics such as the time the connection was established, the local IP address and port, the remote address and port, and the number of bytes sent and received. If the tunnel isn't up, try clicking on either the **Start** or **Restart icon** for the connection. If this does not work, it's time to start troubleshooting; for starters, make sure that the settings match on both sides and that you imported the correct certificates and keys.

Troubleshooting

Troubleshooting VPN connections can be challenging, because the process of establishing a VPN tunnel involves multiple steps, and a failure at any one of these steps will result in a failure to establish a tunnel. For that reason, it might be helpful to adopt a step-by-step approach in troubleshooting:

1. Is the remote client (or peer) able to connect to pfSense (acting either as a server or peer)? If not, then it's possible that either the VPN service is not running at the pfSense end, or, more likely, ports may be blocked that need to be unblocked. IPsec's port requirements differ depending on your configuration; consult the table included in the section of this chapter on IPsec configuration for more information. OpenVPN normally accepts connections on port **1194**; you can change this port, but if you are using OpenVPN, whichever port you use must be unblocked. If you are using IPsec, port **500** must be open for ISAKMP key exchange traffic, and port **50** or **51** must be kept open depending on your configuration (but not both); if NAT traversal is required, port **4500** must be open. L2TP uses UDP on port **1701**, so if you are using L2TP, make sure that port is open. Keep in mind that autogenerated rules created by pfSense are floating rules, so check the **Floating** tab to confirm that the necessary rules exist. If you are using OpenVPN, keep in mind that the autogenerated firewall rule for OpenVPN only allows UDP traffic. Therefore, if you are using OpenVPN over TCP, you may have to modify the rule to allow OpenVPN traffic on the WAN interface to allow TCP traffic.

2. If the remote client is able to make an initial connection to the server, but the connection ultimately fails, then often the best source for information as to why the connection failed is the log file. You can find the logs by navigating to **Status** | **System Logs**. Click on the **IPsec** tab to find IPsec log entries and click on the **OpenVPN** tab to find OpenVPN log entries. Very often, the source of the problem is a mismatch between the settings required by the server and the settings specified by the client in the client configuration.
3. For example, assume that there has been a failure of a mobile client to establish an IPsec connection, and you see the following log entry:

```
Charon: 13[IKE] Aggressive Mode PSK disabled for security reasons
```

Such an entry is a good sign that there was a mismatch in the negotiation mode between the client and server. The **Aggressive Mode PSK disabled** message indicates that the negotiation mode on the server is set to **main**. Sure enough, we discover that the client has set **Negotiation mode** to **Aggressive**, which is why the connection failed. Changing the setting on the client to **main** does not guarantee it will work, but at least we know a negotiation mode mismatch won't be the problem.

Some log entries are a little more cryptic. For example, a **pre-shared key** (**PSK**) mismatch may appear in the logs as follows:

```
charon: 09[ENC] invalid HASH_V1 payload length, decryption failed?
```

This doesn't exactly give us a clear indication of a PSK mismatch; still, if you see such a message, it's a good idea to check the PSK entry.

In addition, many of the IPsec log entries indicate whether the failure was at Phase 1 of the connection or Phase 2. Such an indication can help clue us in as to where we should be focusing our troubleshooting efforts. When the connection fails at Phase 2, often the problem is mismatched encryption methods.

Very often, the client side has **Auto** as an option for some settings – in other words, autonegotiate settings. For example, the ShrewSoft VPN Client has an Auto setting for Cipher Algorithm and Hash Algorithm. Sometimes a setting of Auto will work; however, I have generally found that the connection is more likely to succeed if all settings are set to match the settings on the other end of the tunnel. For example, I was unable to connect to an IPsec tunnel with **Auto** settings for **Cipher Algorithm** and **Hash Algorithm**, but by setting these to **AES-256** and **SHA1** (the IPsec server settings for these two parameters), I was able to successfully establish an IPsec tunnel.

There may be some cases in which even though the parameters match on both ends of the tunnel, you are unable to establish a tunnel. In many cases, this is because the client only supports one method of connecting. For example, the ShrewSoft VPN Client seems to require IKEv1 and **Negotiation mode** of **Aggressive**, while the Windows built-in VPN Client requires IKEv2. In such cases, consulting the client software documentation may help, and looking online for additional information is always a good idea.

One thing that is worth noting is that if you switch from IKEv1 to IKEv2 and then back to IKEv1, **Negotiation mode** will be set to **main**, even if you originally set it to **Aggressive**, so be sure you have the correct setting for **Negotiation mode** before saving your settings.

Summary

In this chapter, we began with some basic VPN concepts, with our focus being primarily on the three VPN protocols currently supported by pfSense: IPsec, L2TP, and OpenVPN. We weighed the advantages and disadvantages of each protocol with respect to security, cross-platform support, ease of configuration, and firewall-friendliness. We emphasized that since L2TP lacks confidentiality and encryption, you are not likely to ever implement L2TP in native mode; rather, it is more likely to be implemented in combination with IPsec, making your choice one between IPsec, L2TP/IPsec, and OpenVPN.

We then covered IPsec, L2TP, and OpenVPN configuration in some depth. We covered the OpenVPN Client Export Utility, which makes the process of generating OpenVPN configuration files for different platforms much easier. Finally, in the troubleshooting section, we covered what to do when we are unable to establish a tunnel between the remote and local ends.

In the next chapter, we will cover how to implement redundancy and high availability with pfSense. This is accomplished by implementing load balancing as well as the **Common Address Redundancy Protocol** (**CARP**).

Questions

Answer the following questions:

1. Name the two most common types of VPN deployments.
2. (a) Identify the three VPN protocols supported by the current version of pfSense. (b) Which protocol does not natively support encryption?

3. Identify the three protocols encompassed by IPsec.
4. If we are setting up an IPsec connection and **Key Exchange version** is set to **Auto**, what will happen if we try to initiate a site-to-site connection to (a) a firewall where the **Key Exchange version** is set to **IKEv1**? (b) a firewall where the **Key Exchange version** is set to **IKEv2**? (Assume that the rest of the configuration is correct.)
5. (a) Which port must always be unblocked for IPsec to function? (b) What is the default OpenVPN port?
6. What are the three authentication options for L2TP?
7. What option was added to the Diffie-Hellman key configuration in pfSense 2.4?
8. With OpenVPN, what alternatives are there to authentication through certificates managed through the pfSense Certificate Authority Manager?

8
Redundancy and High Availability

One of the primary selling points of pfSense is that deploying pfSense routers on our network enhances the overall reliability of the network. A single network component, however – for example, a single router or a single web server – still represents a single point of failure. Even in the absence of hardware failure, a single network component may not be adequate in accommodating the level of traffic on our network. For that reason, we need to consider eliminating single points of failure from our network whenever possible. This process is two-pronged, and involves incorporating both redundancy and high availability:

- **Redundancy** is defined as the duplication of critical components. Redundancy can be both active and passive. With passive redundancy, we incorporate excess capacity into the network, so that when an individual component fails, resources are still available. An example of this would be having two or more redundant web servers. If one server fails, the website should still be available. Active redundancy involves monitoring components and doing an automatic reconfiguration if a component fails. This might involve, for example, having a spare web server on the network, but not active. When the primary web server goes down, the failure is detected and the spare becomes active. As you may have guessed, both forms of redundancy are implemented in pfSense.
- **High availability** is defined as ensuring a specified level of operational performance over a prolonged period of time. In practice, it means incorporating some of the same elements as redundancy. Single points of failure are eliminated when possible, and we seek to detect failures when they occur and provide for reliable switch over to the redundant components. Again, we can use pfSense to provide high availability.

pfSense incorporates these functions via load balancing and the **Common Address Redundancy Protocol** (**CARP**), which are the main subjects in this chapter.

This chapter will cover the following topics:

- Basic load balancing and CARP concepts
- Server load balancing
- CARP configuration
- An example of both load balancing and CARP
- Troubleshooting

Technical requirements

Working through all the examples in this chapter will require at least three working pfSense systems, either in a real-world or virtualized environment. If you are implementing a CARP setup on your network and plan to have two or more redundant firewalls, be aware that this means two or more WAN interfaces, which will require either additional public internet addresses from your ISP, or a router to interconnect the WAN interfaces with your modem (or whatever internet connectivity device you use).

Basic concepts

In networking, load balancing is designed to distribute workloads across multiple network resources. Load balancing in pfSense has two types: gateway load balancing and server load balancing:

- The purpose of gateway load balancing is to distribute internet-bound traffic over more than one WAN interface. Thus, configuration is separate from server load balancing, and is done by configuring gateway groups by navigating to **System | Routing** and clicking on the **Gateway Groups** tab.
- The purpose of server load balancing is to distribute traffic among multiple internal servers. In some cases, we may also want to have redundant servers available for failover, and this is supported in pfSense as well. Server load balancing also ensures both reliability and high availability because it ensures that only servers that are online respond to client requests. A good load balancer will also direct traffic away from servers that already have high levels of traffic and toward servers that have lower levels of traffic. In this way, it tends to ensure that a single server is not taxed too heavily. A load balancer should also provide a means of adding and subtracting servers from the server pool as needed.

Gateway load balancing merits a separate discussion, and we will hold off on discussing it until we address various multi-WAN configurations in the next chapter. Instead, we will discuss load balancing as a means of distributing traffic among multiple servers.

Load balancing can be either hardware-based or software-based. If it is hardware-based, then the load balancing functionality is provided via firmware. Updating the firmware, whether it be to provide bug fixes, new features, or security patches, can be difficult, and in most cases is harder than a simple software update. The advantage, however, is that hardware load balancers tend to have dedicated circuits that can optimize load balancing for specific cases, and they also tend to support a certain number of connections and amount of traffic right out of the box. Load balancing was once done exclusively by hardware devices. It is possible to do load balancing via software now, however; in fact, pfSense is such an example of software-based load balancing. This form of load balancing can be much less expensive and easier to update, but they can be sensitive to changes made in the underlying operating system. When using software-based load balancing, we have to make sure that OS changes do not adversely affect the load balancer.

One way we can differentiate between forms of server load balancing is by the type of algorithm they use. Some of the common algorithms used are as follows:

- **Random**: Requests are directed to a randomly chosen server. Provided that there is a large enough number of requests, this should result in good load balancing.
- **Round-robin**: Requests are distributed across the pool of servers sequentially. This can lead to an uneven load if some requests are more demanding of resources than others, but it is a simple algorithm that provides good average case outcomes.
- **Weighted round-robin**: This is a variant of round-robin in which servers are assigned a greater weight. Servers with higher weights tend to service more requests than ones with lower weights.
- **Least connection**: This algorithm takes into account the number of requests a server is servicing. The server that is servicing the least number of requests (and therefore has the least number of connections) is chosen. There is also a weighted variation on this algorithm by which a weight is assigned to each server. In the case of a tie between two or more servers with an equally low number of connections, the request is serviced by the server with the higher/highest weight.
- **Least traffic**: With this algorithm, the system monitors the bit-rate of outgoing traffic from each server. The request is serviced by the server with the least outgoing traffic. As with the other algorithms, there is a weighted version.
- **Least latency**: In order to determine which server services a request, the system makes an additional request to servers in the pool. The first server to respond gets the request. There is a weighted version of this algorithm as well.

- **IP hash**: This algorithm uses the source and destination IP addresses to generate a hash number that determines which server services the request. One of the advantages of this method is that if the connection is interrupted, when it is resumed, requests will be directed to the same server as long as the source and destination IP addresses remain the same. Thus this algorithm is ideal for scenarios that demand that requests from the same source IP addresses (for example e-commerce sites in which resumed connections should be directed to the server with the customer's shopping cart).
- **URL hash**: Similar to IP hash, but the hash is done on the URL requested. This is a good choice for a pool of proxy servers, because it guarantees that requests for a certain URL are always directed to a specific server, thus eliminating duplicate caching.
- **SDN adaptive**: The SDN stands for **Software-Defined Networking**; this algorithm takes information about the network from layers 2 and 3 and combines in with information about the data from layers 4 and 7. It uses this information to make a decision as to which server will handle the request. The decision is based on the status of the network, the status of applications currently running, the overall health of the network and the health of the network's infrastructure.

Another way of differentiating between types of load balancing is to consider whether it is done on the client side or server side. **Client-side load balancing** relies on the client randomly choosing an internal server from a list of IP addresses provided to the client. This method relies on loads for each client being roughly equal. Although it might seem this would be an unreliable method of load balancing, it is surprisingly effective. Over time, clients will connect to different servers, and the load will be evenly distributed over the different servers. Moreover, this is a very simple method of configuration, since it doesn't require us to set up server pools.

Client-side load balancing relies on the law of large numbers, a probability theorem that states that the result from a large number of trials should be close to the expected value. In the same way that one side of a traditional die should come up roughly one-sixth of the time if we roll the die enough times, the load for each server in a server pool that generates significant traffic over a long enough period of time should be roughly equal if randomly chosen by the client.

Server-side load balancing uses software to listen on the port/IP address to which external clients connect. When a client connects, the software forwards the request to one or more backend servers. There are multiple advantages to this approach:

- Since the software decides which backend server to which the client is forwarded, server-side load balancing tends to be able to guarantee effective load balancing at all times.
- The load balancing process is transparent to the client, who has no idea of our network configuration.
- Since the client doesn't get to connect directly to the backend server, it tends to be more secure than client-side load balancing. For that matter, since the client doesn't know that we are utilizing backend servers, there is an added security through obscurity benefit.
- We can present a special message to users when all backend servers are down.

The method used in pfSense is server-side load balancing, so all the benefits of this method are available to us. This requires us to set up load balancing pools (containing the backend servers), and one or more virtual servers (to which clients will connect). We will also be required to set up firewall rules to allow traffic to pass to the backend servers, as we shall see when we configure load balancing.

Ideally, our load balancing setup should provide dynamic configuration. It should be easy to add and subtract servers as needed, so that we only use the server capacity that we actually need. Some web hosting and cloud computing services are particularly good in this respect, allowing capacity to scale up in response to traffic spikes without interrupting current connections. pfSense provides the capability to add and remove systems from both a load balancing pool and a CARP failover group.

CARP has a single purpose: to allow multiple hosts to share the same IP address or group of IP addresses. To understand how this works, we have to reintroduce a concept originally introduced in `Chapter 4`, *Using pfSense as a Firewall*. As you may recall, virtual IPs allow multiple devices to share the same (virtual) IP address. We can configure two routers to share the same virtual IP address (each must also have a unique non-virtual IP address). One of these routers is designated as the master, and the other is designated as the slave. The master router is the one which handles traffic and ARP requests for the shared virtual IP address, under normal circumstances. When the master goes down, the slave takes over. This ensures that the network is able to function normally even when there is a hardware failure.

CARP itself provides a means of ensuring that the slave router knows when the master is down. When the slave router stops receiving CARP advertisements from the master (or in some configurations, when the CARP advertisements from the master become less frequent than advertisements from the slave), then the slave router begins handling traffic for the CARP virtual IPs.

There are also two protocols to ensure synchronization between the two routers. pfsync is for state synchronization, and **Extensible Markup Language – Remote Procedure Call** (**XML-RPC**) is for configuration synchronization. The pfsync connection between the two routers is achieved via a crossover cable on a dedicated network interface.

Server load balancing

Configuring server load balancing in pfSense involves two steps. First, you must create one or more virtual-server pools. Second, you must create one or more virtual server (the server to which clients will actually connect).

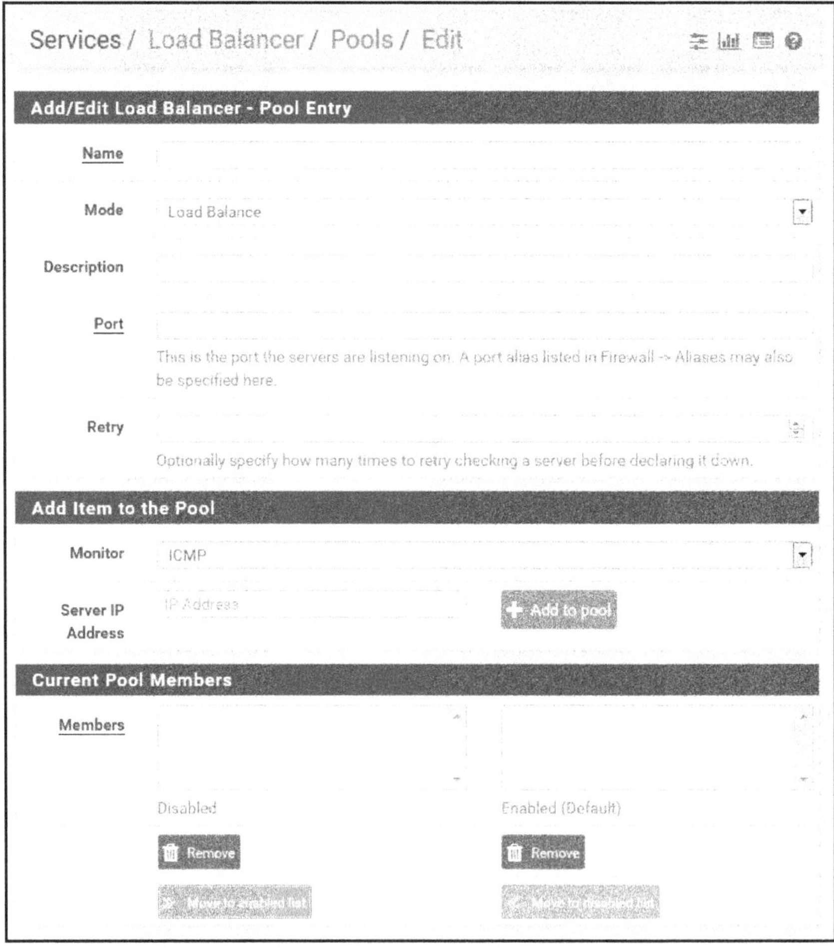

To begin server load balancing configuration, navigate to **Services** | **Load Balancer**. There are four tabs available: **Pools**, **Virtual Servers**, **Monitors**, and **Settings**. Configuration begins on the **Pools** tab; on this tab, click on the **Add** button to add a server pool.

On the pool configuration page, enter an appropriate name in the **Name** edit box. The next field is the **Mode** drop-down box; the choices are as follows:

- **Load Balancing**: This will balance the load across all servers in the pool
- **Failover**: The first server in the pool is used unless it fails; then it fails over to other servers in the pool

You may enter a brief, non-parsed description in the **Description** edit box. In the **Port** edit box, you must type the port on which the servers are listening (for example, port `80` for a web server). In the **Retry** edit box, you can specify how many times a server is to be retried before declaring it is down.

In the **Add item to the pool** section, you can add servers to the pool. The **Monitor** drop-down box allows you to choose the protocol used for monitoring the server (the default is **ICMP**), while the **Server IP Address** edit box is where you enter the IP address of each of the servers. Click the **Add to pool** button to add servers to the pool. As you do, the **Enabled (default)** listbox under **Current Pool Members** will become populated with servers. You can move pool members from the **Enabled (default)** box to the **Pool Disabled** box by selecting a server and clicking on the **Move to disabled** list button. Selecting a server in the **Pool Disabled** box and clicking on the **Move to enabled** list button does the opposite. You can remove a server from either list by selecting it and clicking on the **Remove** button underneath the corresponding box. When you are done configuring the server pool, click on the **Save** button.

The next step is virtual server configuration. Click on the **Virtual Server** tab, which will display a table with all of the configured virtual servers. Click on the **Add** button beneath the table to the right to add a new server.

On the virtual server configuration page, you must assign a name to the server in the **Name** edit box. The **Description** field allows you to enter a non-parsed description. The **IP Address** edit box is where you specify the address on which the server listens; this is normally the WAN IP address, but your configuration may be different. You can also specify an alias in this field.

The **Port** edit box is where you specify the port to which clients will connect. If it is blank, listening ports from the pool will be used. All connections made to this port will be forwarded to the server pool. As with the **IP address** field, you can specify an alias here.

The **Virtual Server Pool** drop-down box is where you specify the pool to which clients will be directed. You should specify the server configured during the first step. The **Fall Back Pool** allows you to specify a fall-back in case all the servers in the main server pool are down. It could contain another list of servers that serve the same content as servers in the main pool, but more likely, it will contain a server (or servers) that relay a **This server is down** message. Finally, the **Relay Protocol** drop-down box determines the protocol with which the virtual server communicates with the backend. **TCP** is the default choice, but **DNS** is also an option. Click on the **Save** button when you're done configuring the virtual server and click on the **Apply Changes** button on the main **Load Balancer** page.

Clicking on the **Settings** tabs reveals some global settings. The **Timeout** field represents the global timeout for checks (in milliseconds). If the field is left blank, the default value of `1` second is used. The **Interval** field allows you to set the interval at which a pool member will be checked (in seconds). The default is `10` seconds. Finally, **Prefork** allows you to set the number of processes forked in advance by the relayd daemon. The default is `5` processes.

Relayd is OpenBSD's load balancer. It can handle layers 3, 4, and 7; it can relay connections from a virtual IP address to actual IP addresses and distribute loads. In short, it makes possible much of pfSense's load balancing capabilities. For more information about relayd, check the relayd man page.

Now the server and server pool are configured, but you still need to create firewall rules to allow access to each of the servers in the server pool. This rule should be placed on whatever interface the server is waiting for connections on (usually the WAN interface). To make the process easier, you can create an alias for all the servers and then create a single rule for the entire server pool.

To do this, navigate to **Firewall | Aliases**, and click on the **Add** button. Enter a name for the alias in the **Name** field (for example, `SERVER_POOL`) and in the **Description** field, enter a brief description. Leave the type in the **Type** drop-down at its default value of **Host(s)**. Then begin entering the server IP addresses in the **IP or FQDN** field along with the CIDR, clicking on the **Add Host** button to add each server. Click on the **Save** button when you are done adding servers. Then click on the **Apply Changes** on the main **Aliases** page.

You still need to create a firewall rule, which you can do by navigating to **Firewall** | **Rules** and adding a rule for the interface which will accept incoming connections. The destination, for this rule, of course, should be the alias defined in the previous step (I used `SERVER_POOL`).

There are two options relevant to load balancing that can be found by navigating to **System** | **Advanced**. Both options are on the **Miscellaneous** tab. **Use sticky connections**, if checked, will alter the default behavior of pfSense when there are successive connections from the same client. Normally, these connections would be directed to different servers in the server pool in round-robin fashion, but if this option is checked, successive requests will be directed to the same server as the first. The adjacent edit box determines the timeout period for sticky connections, in seconds. The default is zero, in which case the sticky connection expires as soon as the last state that refers to the connection expires. Changing this option restarts the load balancing service. This is not a perfect solution for cases in which all requests from the same client must go to the same server; a request that takes place at a long enough interval (longer than the timeout period) after the last state expired will be directed to the next web server. As a result, pfSense may not be the ideal solution for these cases.

The second option is the **Enable default gateway switching** checkbox. If this is checked, then if the default gateway goes down, the default gateway will be switched to another available one. This is not necessary in most cases, as gateway groups ensure another gateway is available if the default gateway goes down.

If you want to monitor your load balancing pool, navigate to **Status** | **Load Balancer**. The **Pools** tab will show any configured load balancer pools. The table shows the name and mode (load balancing or failover) of each pool, the IP addresses of each server in the pool under **Servers**, the **Monitor type**, and the **Description** that was entered. The listing of servers under the **Servers** column will also show the percentage of the load covered by each server in the pool. There is also a checkbox corresponding to each server, unchecking the checkbox corresponding to a server and clicking on **Save** will remove the server from the pool, while clicking on **Reset** will result in connections to the server pool being reset.

Clicking on the **Virtual Servers** tab will display a different table. The table lists the name of each virtual server, the address of each virtual server, as well as the IP address of each of the servers in the server pool under **Servers**. The **Status** value of the virtual server will be displayed in the table (up or down), as well as the description.

Example – load balancer for a web server

In this example, we will use the pfSense load balancer to load balance three Apache web servers. We will assume that these servers handle requests on both port `80` (HTTP) and port `443` (HTTPS). Assume that our web servers are in the **DMZ** and that the IP addresses for the servers are `192.168.2.11`, `192.168.2.12`, and `192.168.2.13`.

The first step is to create an aliases for ports `80` and `443`, and an alias for the three servers. Navigate to **Firewall** | **Aliases** and click on the **Ports** tab. Click on the **Add** button to add a new entry. Enter an appropriate name (for example `WEB_SERVER_PORTS`); also enter a brief **Description** if desired. Enter `80` in the **Port** field and a description (for example `HTTP`). Click on the **Add Port** button. Enter `443` in the **Port** field and a description (for example `HTTPS`). Click on the **Add Port** button and then click on the **Save** button. On the main **Aliases** page, click on the **Apply Changes** button.

Next, click on the IP tab to create an alias for the servers. Click on the **Add** button. Enter an appropriate name and a brief description. In the **IP or FQDN** field, enter the first IP address (`192.168.2.11`) and a brief description in the adjacent edit box, then click **Add Host** and repeat the process for all three servers. Then click on the **Save** button, and on the main **Aliases** page, click on **Apply Changes**.

Next, navigate to **Services** | **Load Balancer** to begin load balancing configuration. Stay on the **Pools** tab and click on the **Add** button. This will load the **Edit** page for the load balancer. Enter an appropriate name (for example `WEB_SERVER_POOL`) and description. In the **Port** field, enter the alias we created in the previous step. In the **Retry** field, you can enter the number of times pfSense will retry a server before declaring it to be down.

In the **Add Item to Pool** section, enter the first Apache server IP address (`192.168.2.11`) and click on the **Add to pool** button. Repeat the process for the other two servers (`192.168.2.12` and `192.168.2.13`). You can change the **Monitor** protocol if necessary. Click on the **Save** button when you are done. On the main **Load Balancer** page, click on the **Apply Changes** button.

We need to set up the virtual server, so click on the **Virtual Servers** tab and then click on the **Add** button. Enter an appropriate name (for example `WEB_SERVER_IP`) and description. Enter the WAN IP address in the **IP Address** field. Unfortunately, the current version of pfSense does not allow us to enter an alias in the **Port** field (in spite of the fact that the description of this field on the page says that we can). Therefore, we are going to have to create two entries, one for port `80` and the other for port `443`.

For Port, enter `80`. For **Virtual Server Pool**, enter the web server pool we previously created. Leave **Fall Back Pool** set to **None** and Relay **Protocol** set to **TCP**. Click on the **Save** button when you are done and then click on the **Apply Changes** button on the next page.

Fortunately, creating the other virtual server is not difficult. On the main **Virtual Servers** tab, click on the copy icon for the virtual server we just created. On the **Edit** page for the new server, change **Port** to `443`. You may also want to change name to give this server a unique name. Click on the **Save** button when you are done and then the **Apply Changes** button.

You'll want to set up monitors for the web servers on both ports, so click on the **Monitors** tab and then click on the **Add** button. Enter an appropriate name (for example `HTTP_MONITOR`), a description, and select **HTTP** in the **Type** drop-down box. Set the **Path** to a web page that will return a **200 OK** code. For example, if you have a page called `index.html` in the root directory, you can set **Path** to `/index.html`. Set **Host** to the **IP Address** you set under **Virtual Servers** (this is likely the WAN IP address). Leave **HTTP Code** set to **200 OK** and click on the **Save** button. On the main **Monitors** page, click on **Apply Changes**. To set up an **HTTPS** monitor, repeat the process by clicking on the copy icon in the column for the monitor we just created, and change **Type** to **HTTPS**. Set **Path** to a valid HTTPS resource on your web server (for example `/index.php`). Click on **Save** when done and then click on **Apply Changes**.

Finally, we must add a firewall rule for the server pool. Navigate to **Firewall** | **Rules**, and on the **WAN** tab, click **Add**. The **Edit Firewall Rule** and **Source** sections can be kept at their default values. For **Destination**, select **Single host or alias** in the drop-down box and enter the server pool alias we previously created in the adjacent edit box. Since this rule is on an interface that faces the public internet, we want to make it as restrictive as possible. Therefore, set the **Destination Port Range** to the port alias we created previously. Enter an appropriate description, and click on the **Save** button; on the main **Firewall** page click on the **Apply Changes** button.

We have now completed configuration of the Apache web server pool. To check on the status of the pool, navigate to **Status** | **Load Balancer**. The **Pools** tab will show the status of each server in the pool. Servers that are up will be colored green, while servers that are down will be colored red. You can also use this page to manually deactivate individual servers in the pool. To do this, uncheck the checkbox in the column containing the server. Click on the **Save** and **Apply Changes** buttons to ensure that the changes take effect.

Click on the **Virtual Servers** tab to check on the status of the virtual server we defined. Again, if the server is up, it will be colored green, and if it is down, it will be colored red. For a virtual server to be down, all the servers which are members of the pool would have to be down.

Note that if we wanted to add or remove servers from the pool, it would be as easy as navigating back to **Services** | **Load Balancer** and editing the settings for the pool we created, adding and/or deleting IP addresses for the servers as needed. We could also easily convert this pool to a failover group by changing the **Mode** to **Manual Failover**. In such a case, the first IP address in the **Current List Members** list box would be the master web server, and all others would be backup web servers.

Remember that, if you add servers to, or remove them from the server pool, the alias we created in the first step will not be automatically updated. Thus, any servers subsequently added to the pool will be blocked on the WAN interface - unless we update the alias accordingly, so remember to do that.

HAProxy – a brief overview

The built-in pfSense load balancer may be perfectly adequate for many use cases, especially if you are setting up a load balancer for a home or small office/home office network. If you require a more enterprise-level solution for load balancing, however, you need not fret: **High Availability Proxy** (**HAProxy**), an open source program (covered by the GPL) which is advertised as *a fast and reliable solution offering high availability, [and] load balancing* is available as a third-party package.

It is not within the scope of this chapter to provide a detailed discussion of HAProxy- it will be covered in more depth in `Chapter 12`, *Extending pfSense with Packages*. Be aware that it is an option, however, and that installation is relatively easy. Just navigate to **System** | **Package Manager**, click on the **Available Packages** tab, scroll down to HAProxy on the list, click the **Install** button, and on the next page, click on the **Confirm** button. Once installation is complete, there will be a new entry on the **Services** menu called **HAProxy**. If you navigate to it, you can begin configuration.

There are several tabs on the **HAProxy configuration** page, but I will confine my overview to the first three tabs. The **Settings** tab has some global settings that define HAProxy's behavior. The first setting is the **Enable HAProxy** checkbox; upon installation, HAProxy is disabled by default and we must enable it if we want it to run. You may set **Maximum connections** and also enable the **Carp monitor** on this page. HAProxy can use CARP to update its settings within a CARP firewall failover group. The **HAProxy Sync** checkbox is at the very bottom of the page. You can also use this page to do such things as send log data to a remote syslog server, point HAProxy to a DNS server, and provide for email notifications of any change in the state of HAProxy.

On the **Frontend** tab, we see a table with all configured frontends. Click on the **Add** button to add a new frontend. This is where you specify the listen address and port for the virtual server (usually the network's public IP address). You can also configure such things as the **Type of server** (either **http/https**, **ssl/https**, or **tcp**), **access control lists** (**ACLs**), and logging options.

On the **Backend** tab, where we see a list of configured backends, we can click on the **Add** button to add a backend. The backend is where you specify the IP addresses of servers in the server pool. You can also specify the load balancing algorithm. Many of the algorithms discussed earlier in this chapter (for example round-robin, weighted round-robin, least connections, and so on) are available. You can also specify timeout settings, options for checking to see whether a server is up, email options, and many more options.

There is much more to HAProxy than this brief overview covers, but do not let that discourage you from installing HAProxy if it sounds like something that will better suit your load balancing requirements.

CARP configuration

Whereas pfSense's load balancing capabilities may leave something to be desired, pfSense's high availability capabilities are quite good, and pfSense offers an enterprise class CARP solution that provides for stateful failover. We will first consider a basic CARP group for firewall failover, but we will also consider other scenarios involving CARP, such as multi-WAN deployments.

Version 2.4.3 added support for **Point-to-Point Protocol over Ethernet** (**PPPoE**) on CARP virtual IPs. The PPPoE connection will only be active on the master node.

Example 1 – CARP with two firewalls

This is probably the most common deployment scenario in which CARP is involved. There are two common deployment scenarios you could employ for a two firewall setup in which one firewall is designated as the failover. Both of them involve a single virtual IP for the LAN interface, separate actual IPs for each LAN interface, and the LAN interface on each firewall connecting to a switch on the LAN side. Allocating additional IP addresses for the LAN is not a problem, since these are private addresses. The WAN side poses a problem. The WAN interface of a firewall would normally be connected directly to our modem (or whatever other internet connectivity device we have) and the WAN interface would be assigned a public IP address. In many cases, especially in a home or small office/home office scenario, we have a single public IP address allocated by our ISP. Both WAN interfaces need an IP address, and we need a virtual IP address to cover both of them, but we cannot just freely create public IP addresses. We therefore have two broad alternatives:

- Acquire two additional public IP addresses from our ISP. This is the most foolproof solution, but it is potentially expensive, depending on how much our ISP charges for public IP addresses.
- Place a router between the modem and the two WAN interfaces. This neatly solves the problem of needing additional public IP addresses. With the router in place, both WAN interfaces may have private IP addresses and a single virtual IP address that is also a private address. These addresses can be routed to the modem and the single public IP address we have. This is a less expensive solution, but it also adds a single point of failure to our setup. If the router fails, we have no internet connectivity, completely undermining the redundancy we were trying to incorporate into the network. (A simple router, however, is likely easier to replace and configure than a pfSense firewall.)

Fortunately, configuration for each setup is largely the same, with the only difference being that one uses public IP addresses for the WAN interfaces, and the other uses private IP addresses. Therefore, you should be able to follow along with this configuration regardless of which option we choose. As always, a diagram sometimes helps in clarifying where each component fits into the overall setup.

In order to create a firewall failover group, we need to synchronize data between the two firewalls. Synchronization does not need to be done via a dedicated interface - for example, it could be done via the LAN - but synchronization is generally more reliable if it is done via a dedicated interface. Thus, our example setup will have three interface: WAN, LAN, and a dedicated pfsync interface connected with a crossover cable. Setting up a CARP failover group involves several steps:

1. Configuration of virtual IP addresses
2. Configuration of a dedicated pfsync interface
3. Enabling pfsync and XML-RPC sync
4. Manual outbound NAT configuration
5. DHCP server configuration
6. Secondary firewall configuration

Once you have the concept of what your setup will look like and you have the required hardware, we can begin by determining what the virtual IP addresses will be. Keep in mind that each interface will require a virtual IP address, and the physical interface on each of the *N* firewalls will have its own IP address, for a total of *N + 1* IP addresses for each interface. Thus, in the case of a two firewall CARP group, each interface will have three IP addresses. It is generally a good idea to have a consistent convention for IP address assignment. One way to do this is to assign the first address on an interface's subnet to the virtual IP address for that interface, with subsequent addresses being used for the interfaces on each firewall. In our example setup, we have a LAN subnet of `192.168.1.0`. Thus, `192.168.1.1` will be the LAN interface's virtual IP, while the LAN interface's IP on first firewall will be `192.168.1.2` and the LAN interface's IP on second firewall will be `192.168.1.3`.

To begin configuration, we will make sure that everything is functioning on the primary firewall. Additional firewalls should be offline until this point. Configuring virtual IPs is the first step, so navigate to **Firewall | Virtual IPs**. Then click on the **Add** button below the **Virtual IP** table on the right to add a new virtual IP entry.

On the **Virtual IP** configuration page, set **Type** to **CARP**. Set the interface in the **Interface** drop-down box to whichever interface you wish to configure. You are going to have to create virtual IPs for both the WAN and LAN interfaces, so you will likely be starting with one of these two. In the **Address(es)** edit box, enter the virtual IP address. The mask specified in the adjacent drop-down box should be the network's subnet mask.

In the **Virtual IP Password** edit boxes, you need to enter a **Virtual Host ID** (**VHID**) group password, which can be whatever you want. You won't have to enter this on the other firewalls, as it will automatically propagate to them via the pfsync interface. You do need to enter the password a second time for confirmation, however.

In the **VHID Group** drop-down box, you need to select the VHID group for this interface. The only requirement is that the VHID must not already be in use, and the VHID must be unique on the entire interface's subnet. If there is no CARP or VHID traffic on your network, you can set this to **1**; otherwise set it to the next available VHID.

The **Advertising frequency** drop-down boxes allow you to set the frequency with which the machine will advertise its presence. The lowest combination of both values (**Base** and **Skew**) determines which firewall is the master. For this reason, you will want to set **Base** to **1** and **Skew** to **0** on the master firewall (the lowest allowed values for these fields). Keep in mind that the XML-RPC process will automatically add 100 to each skew when syncing virtual IPs to secondary nodes. Thus, if x is the skew on the master firewall, the first slave will have a skew of $x + 100$; the second slave will have a skew of $x + 200$, and so on. In addition, the skew has a maximum value of `255`, and XMLPRC will keep adding 100 to each skew when syncing VIPs to secondary nodes even if it results in values over `255`, which it will if there are three or more slaves. In such cases, you should uncheck the **Virtual IPs** checkbox in the **Select options to sync** subsection of **XMLPRC sync** (which can be found under **High Availability Sync**). In the **Description** field, you may enter a brief non-parsed description. When you are done making changes, click on **Save** at the bottom of the page.

From the main **Virtual IPs** page, click on the **Add** button again and repeat the process for each interface that requires a virtual IP address. At a minimum, you will have to create virtual IPs for both WAN and LAN, but you may have multiple other interfaces on your firewall that will have virtual IPs. Just change **Interface** option to the interface you want to configure, and enter the virtual IP address for the new interface. The **VHID group password** will be for a different VHID group, so it can be different than the VHID password you entered previously. The **VHID Group** should be set to the next available VHID; this is likely the previously entered value `+1`. Finally, since this system is the master, in **Advertising Frequency**, **Base** should be set to **1** and **Skew** to **0**. Enter a brief description and click on the **Save** button. When you have entered all the required virtual IPs, click on the **Apply Changes** button on the main **Virtual IPs** page.

If you have more than just a WAN and LAN interface (for example, a DMZ interface), be sure to create a virtual IP for each additional interface. Just repeat the process for creating virtual IPs outlined previously.

The next step is to set up a dedicated pfsync interface. Setting up a dedicated interface for synchronization is not strictly required, but there are benefits to such a configuration:

- **Increased security**: In a typical two interface (WAN and LAN) configuration, the alternative is to transmit sync data to between the primary and secondary firewalls via the LAN. Although it is less likely to happen in the era of switched ports, this traffic is potentially vulnerable to interception. Isolating pfsync traffic onto a separate network to which only other firewalls are connected eliminates this vulnerability.
- **Improved resource utilization**: The secondary firewalls must sync to the primary firewalls often to ensure their configuration is up to date, and the traffic generated can be considerable. Placing this traffic on a separate network thus reduces congestion on the LAN.

To set up an interface for pfsync, navigate to **Interfaces** | **(assign)**, select an unused interface in the **Available network ports** drop-down box, and click on the **Add** button. Then click on interface name and begin configuration. There isn't much required for the pfsync interface, except that all the pfsync interfaces should be on a shared subnet. Give the interface an appropriate name (for example, `SYNC`). Click on the **Save** button at the bottom of the page when you are done configuring the pfsync interface and, when the page reloads, click on **Apply Changes**.

Next, you must create a firewall rule for the pfsync interface. Navigate to **Firewall** | **Rules**, and click on the tab for the newly created interface. Click on the **Add** button to add an **allow pfsync interface to any** rule. The **Action** column should be set to **Pass** and the **Interface** should be kept set to the **pfsync** interface. The protocol in the **Protocol** drop-down box should be set to **PFSYNC**. The **Source** field should be set to the **pfsync** network and **Destination** should be set to **any**. Enter a brief description in the **Description** field, and click on the **Save** button. When the main **Firewall** page reloads, click on the **Apply Changes** button.

You may also want to create a rule to allow ICMP traffic on the pfsync interface; this will allow you to ping the interface and send pings from the interface, which is always useful in verifying connectivity. If so, click on the **Add** button again to create a new rule. Change the protocol to **ICMP**; you can leave the **ICMP Subtypes** list box set to any, but if you opt for a more restrictive rule, be sure to select both **Echo reply** and **Echo request**, or ping won't work. A more restrictive rule would also set **Destination to PFSYNC address**. Add an appropriate description (for example `Allow ICMP ping traffic`) and click on the **Save** button.

The next step is enabling pfsync and XML-RPC. Navigate to **System | High Availability Sync**. In the **State Synchronization Settings** section, make sure the **Synchronize states** checkbox is checked. In the **Synchronize Interface** drop-down box, select the **pfsync** interface. If you set up a dedicated interface, select it as the interface; otherwise, select whichever interface you are using to synchronize the firewalls (the most likely alternative is **LAN**). By default, pfsync data is sent via multicast, but by specifying an IP address in the **pfsync Synchronize Peer IP** edit box, you can force pfsync to synchronize its state table to the specified IP address. If we are setting up the primary firewall, this field should be set to the secondary firewall's IP address. For example, if we have a primary firewall on which the dedicated pfsync interface has an IP address of `192.168.2.1` and the secondary firewall's pfsync interface is `192.168.2.2`, this field should be set to `192.168.2.2` on the primary firewall (to sync the secondary firewall) and `192.168.2.1` on the secondary firewall.

Next, we must enable configuration synchronization for XML-RPC. On the same configuration page, scroll down to the **Configuration Synchronization Settings (XML-RPC Sync)** section. In the **Synchronize Config to IP** edit box, enter the IP address of the firewall to which the firewall should be synchronized. This should match the IP address entered in pfsync **Synchronize Peer IP**. The **Remote System Username** edit box should be set to admin (other usernames will not work) and then enter the password in the **Remote System Password** edit box (it should match on all firewalls). In the **Select options to sync** subsection, you should check all the checkboxes for items you want to synchronize. By default, only **Firewall schedules** and **Virtual IPs** are selected, but if you want to have truly redundant secondary firewalls, all checkboxes except **DHCP Server settings** (we handle the DHCP synchronization separately) should be checked (the **Toggle All** button at the bottom of this section lets you select everything). When you are done making changes, click on the **Save** button at the bottom of the page.

Note that **Select options to sync** does not have an option for packages. This is because the settings for packages often need different configurations on different hosts and in some cases may need to know the actual IP of physical interfaces rather than just the virtual ID. Some packages, such as HAProxy, are able to synchronize data across a failover group, but in such cases, you will still have to install the package on each machine and configure synchronization.

The next step is configuration of manual outbound NAT. Navigate to **Firewall | NAT** and click on the **Outbound** tab. If you haven't already, set **Mode** to either **Hybrid Outbound NAT rule generation** or **Manual Outbound NAT rule generation** and click on the **Save** button. In the **Mappings** table, find the autocreated LAN to WAN rule, and click on the edit icon for that rule. If you did not have any virtual IPs configured, then in the **Translation** section, **Address** is likely set to **Interface Address**. Change this setting to the WAN virtual IP that was added earlier for CARP. Then click on the **Save** button; click on **Apply Changes** on the main **NAT** page. If you configured everything correctly, connections leaving the WAN interface should be translated to the new WAN CARP IP. If you want to confirm this, one possible method is to access a website that displays the IP address from which the site is being accessed. Also, if you look at the **Mappings** table, the address in the NAT address column should be the virtual IP of the WAN interface. You should repeat this process for all local interfaces (non-WAN/non-pfsync) you have on the firewall.

Now, you need to update the DHCP settings. Navigate to **Services | DHCP Server** (these options are not available for DHCPv6) and scroll down to **Servers**. In the **DNS servers** subsection, set the first DNS server to the LAN virtual IP created earlier on in the process. In the **Other Options** section, set the **Gateway** field to the LAN virtual IP. Finally, enter the actual LAN IP address of the secondary firewall in the **Failover peer IP** edit box. This will allow the two firewalls to maintain a common set of DHCP leases. Then click on **Save** at the bottom of the page. Repeat this process for as many local interfaces you have on the firewall that are using DHCP.

This completes configuration of the primary firewall; we can now begin configuration of the secondary one. For the first phase of the secondary firewall configuration, keep the firewall offline. Assuming that pfSense is already installed and is working, you need to go through the interface assignment process. Set the **LAN** IP to whatever you previously designated as the backup LAN IP (for example, if we set the primary firewall's **LAN** IP to `192.168.1.1`, we might set the backup **LAN** IP to `192.168.1.2`). You need to assign an interface to pfsync, and set an IP address for that as well. The DHCP settings should be the same as they are on the primary firewall. Note that all of these configuration steps do not require use of the web GUI and can be done from the pfSense console. Once you have completed these steps, you should be able to put the secondary firewall online.

You can now log in to the secondary firewall via the web interface. If you haven't done so already, configure the WAN IP address (again, set it to the IP address you previously designated as the WAN IP). The admin password on the backup firewall must be set to the same value as that of the primary firewall, or synchronization will not work.

You need to create a firewall rule for the pfsync interface of the secondary firewall. This rule has two purposes. First, it will allow the initial synchronization data to pass from the pfsync interface to the primary firewall. Second, it will (hopefully) be overwritten by firewall rules from the primary firewall during the synchronization process, and thus will confirm that synchronization was successful. With this in mind, navigate to **Firewall** | **Rules** and create an *allow any to any* rule (**Source** should be set to **any** and **Destination** should be set to **any**). It may be helpful to use the **Description** field to flag this rule as one that will be overwritten. If you want to ping the second firewall, you may want to add a firewall rule to allow ICMP traffic as outlined in the configuration for the first firewall.

It will be necessary to set the CARP **LAN** virtual IP address as the gateway, and to set the primary firewall's LAN IP address as the failover peer. As with the primary firewall, this process must be repeated for each secondary firewall.

Note that you did not have to alter the NAT settings to redirect outbound NAT traffic to the WAN virtual IP, as we did with the primary firewall. This is not necessary because the NAT settings will be copied from the primary firewall to the secondary firewall once synchronization has taken place.

Now, you can bring the secondary firewall online. After you have done this, navigate to **System** | **High Availability Sync** on the secondary firewall, and make sure the synchronize states is enabled. The **Synchronize Interface** should be set to **PFSYNC**, and you likely want to enter the primary firewall's IP address in the **pfSync Synchronize Peer IP** edit box. The settings in the **Configuration Synchronization Settings (XMLRPC Sync)** section, however, should not be changed.

Now, all that is left to do is to activate CARP. Navigate to **Status** | **CARP (failover)** on both the primary and secondary firewall. If there is a button called **Enable CARP** on either firewall, click on it. Also, verify that the virtual IP for each interface is correct and that they show the correct status. On the primary firewall, the status should be **MASTER**. On the secondary firewall, the status should be **BACKUP**.

There are two additional buttons on this page that are useful, especially when troubleshooting. The **Temporarily Disable CARP** button disables CARP on the firewall on which it is invoked by removing the CARP virtual IPs from the system. If the firewall's status is **MASTER**, then the next available firewall whose status is **BACKUP** will take over.

This setting is not remembered through a reboot, and if you reboot a firewall that had been master before CARP was temporarily disabled, the firewall will regain its status as **MASTER**. The button toggles to **Enable CARP** when you press it, and pressing **Enable CARP** also enables a temporarily disabled master firewall to become master again.

Sometimes, you may need to keep CARP disabled through a reboot. This is where the other button, **Enter Persistent CARP Maintenance Mode**, comes in. If pressed, this button will disable CARP on the firewall, and this condition persists through a reboot, thus preventing the firewall from prematurely regaining the **MASTER** status. The button toggles to **Leave Persistent CARP Maintenance Mode**, and pressing this button is the only way to exit maintenance mode from within the web GUI.

If you have followed these steps, synchronization should take place. If not, you may want to navigate to **System** | **High Avail**. Sync on the primary firewall and confirm that the **Synchronize States** checkbox is checked. If not, you should check this box and save the settings. You may also want to navigate to **Status** | **System Logs** and check the logs to see if synchronization occurred. Successful synchronization will generate a series of log entries like these (as indicated in the log, pfsync screenshot shown below takes about 30 seconds to complete):

May 23 20:40:31	check_reload_status: Syncing firewall
May 23 20:40:33	php-fpm[42315]: /rc.filter_synchronize: Beginning XMLRPC sync to http://192.168.4.4:80.
May 23 20:40:40	php-fpm[42315]: /rc.filter_synchronize: XMLRPC sync successfully completed with http://192.168.4.4:80.
May 23 20:40:41	check_reload_status: Syncing firewall
May 23 20:40:42	php-fpm[20136]: /system_hasync.php: waiting for pfsync...
May 23 20:41:14	php-fpm[20136]: /system_hasync.php: pfsync done in 30 seconds.
May 23 20:41:14	php-fpm[20136]: /system_hasync.php: Configuring CARP settings finalize...

Log entries from a successful CARP operation

If not, the log entries may provide a clue as to why the sync failed, or you can navigate to **Diagnostics** | **Ping** and try to ping the pfsync interface of the other firewall. If the ping fails, then you have a connectivity issue with the pfsync connection, and you can start your diagnosis there. Check to make sure that the crossover cable is good, and also check to see if there is a link light on the pfsync interface on both sides of the connection.

If the settings synchronized, the CARP group should be active. To ensure that this is the case, navigate to **Status** | **CARP (failover)**.

At this stage, if you look at the **Status** column, the primary firewall's status should be designated as **MASTER** and the secondary should be **BACKUP**. If the secondary firewall's CARP status is **DISABLED,** and there is an **Enable CARP** button on the status page, click on that button, and it should activate CARP.

Once you have confirmed that CARP is running on both firewalls, you probably want to confirm that settings have been copied over from the primary firewall to the secondary firewall. Check the firewall rules, NAT rules and DHCP settings; the temporary firewall rule created during configuration of the secondary firewall should be overwritten by now.

Finally, you probably want to confirm that your CARP failover group actually works in a real-world scenario. At a minimum, you'll want to power down the primary firewall and confirm that the secondary firewall takes over. You may also want to test the failover group in a variety of scenarios. In all cases, you should still be able to access the internet.

At this point, we will have proven that the CARP group works, but depending on what your requirements are, you may want to test your CARP setup in different failure scenarios. For example, you may want to unplug the WAN or LAN cable and see what happens, or try downloading a file or streaming audio and/or video while one of the firewalls goes offline.

Once the failover group is up and running, you can force synchronization by navigating to **Status** | **Filter Reload** and clicking on the **Force Config Sync** button.

Example 2 – CARP with N firewalls

As I tested the two-firewall CARP configuration I began to wonder. Every demonstration of CARP on pfSense I have ever read about or seen involves two firewalls: a primary firewall (the master) and the failover (the backup). Is it possible to have more than one system as a failover? Some of the documentation refers to *a failover cluster*, so at the very least, it seems to have been contemplated. But I could not find anything in the documentation on the official pfSense site or in the existing literature that describes how to do this.

Nevertheless, I was able to successfully implement, in a virtualized environment, a setup that incorporated three firewalls. I call this setup CARP with *N* firewalls, because, at least in theory, it should be possible to add as many failover firewalls as you find practical. Implementing this setup requires the following:

- N pfSense firewalls (obviously)
- Either *N + 1* public IP addresses (one for each firewall + one for the virtual IP) or a router to go between your modem and WAN interfaces with at least *N* ports
- Since we are going to have at least three pfsync interfaces, we can no longer use a crossover cable, and we will need a dedicated switch for the pfsync network

There were two distinct problems that had to be solved in order for this setup to work. First, the order of priority must be clear so that when the master goes offline, pfSense knows which backup system gets promoted to master. Second, the synchronization data must propagate from the master to all backups. If both of these do not work, then the failover is not going to go smoothly. The following steps should ensure that the process works:

- While system is offline, configure interfaces on the pfSense system you want to add as a backup
- Configure virtual IPs on this system
- Configure firewall rules
- Bring the system online and finish configuring high availability sync

As with configuration of the secondary firewall in first example, you will want to begin configuration of the new firewall offline at first. At the very least, you will want to configure the WAN, LAN, and PFSYNC interfaces. A good convention to follow is to add one to the last octet of the IP address of the last previously configured backup firewall; for example, if the last backup firewall had a LAN IP address of `192.168.1.3`, set it to `192.168.1.4` on the new firewall.

Next, you must configure the virtual IP addresses on the new firewall. Set the WAN and LAN virtual IPs to the same IP as was set on the other firewalls. In addition, you should set the **Advertising frequency** for each virtual IP so that is different than the **Advertising frequency** for the same virtual IP on the other firewalls. This parameter sets the priority within each VHID group (higher totals for **Base** and **Skew** result in lower priorities), and you should set each firewall's virtual IPs to different totals. Otherwise, when the master firewall goes offline, two or more backups may become promoted to master at the same time. One possible convention is to set the **Skew** for the first backup firewall to 10, and then increase the **Skew** for each successive firewall by 10.

The next step is to configure the firewall rules. This means, at the very least, adding a firewall rule to the **PFSYNC** interface to pass all traffic (this rule will be overwritten when the firewall data is synchronized, so you probably want to put something like `Temporary rule` in the **Description**). You may also want to add a rule to pass ICMP traffic so you can ping the **PFSYNC** interface on this firewall if it doesn't work.

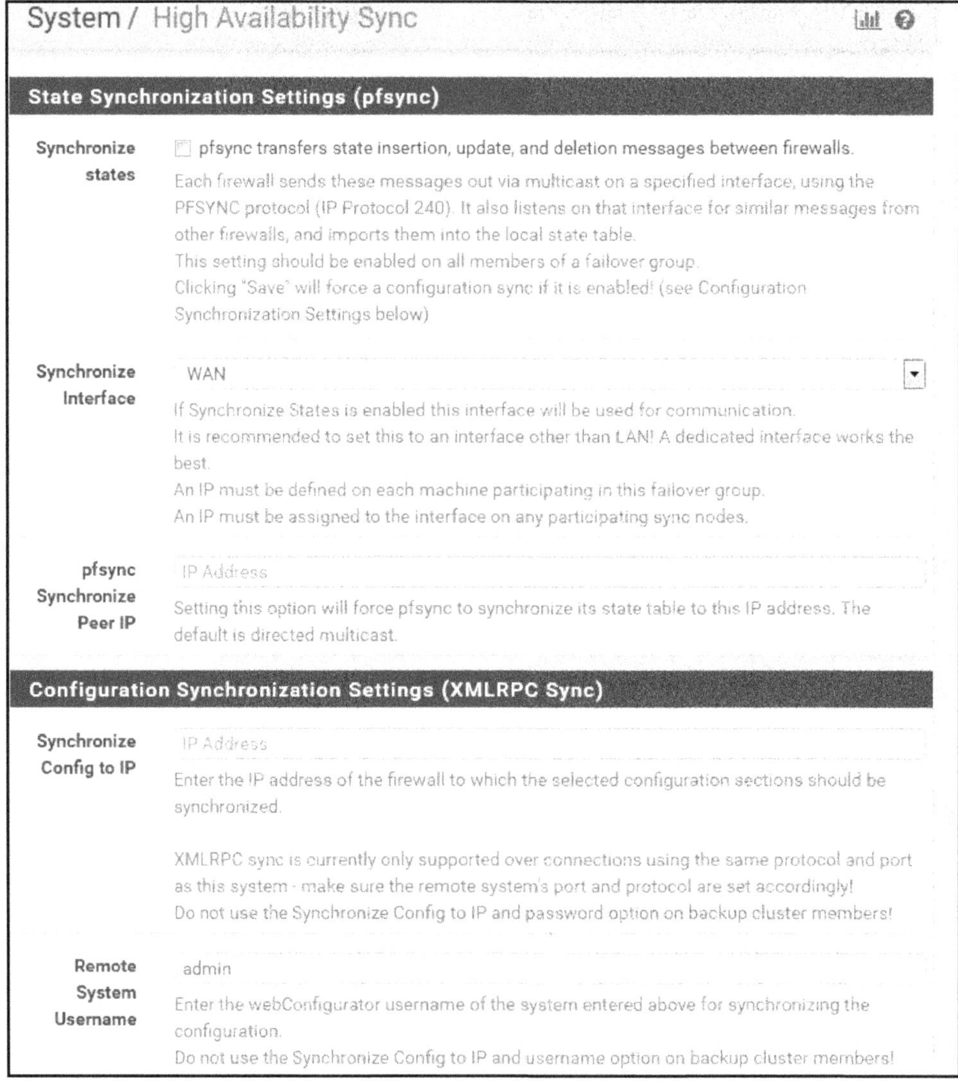

Next, you need to address the issue of how to synchronize firewall data. The **Synchronize Config to IP** setting, according to the notes on the **System** | **High Availability Sync** configuration page, should not be set on backup cluster members. But the setting only allows for a single IP address, which does not seem to make it possible to propagate synchronization data from the master to more than one backup. In order to get this setup to work, navigate to **System** | **High Availability Sync** on the last backup system added to the failover group, and set **Synchronize Config to IP** to the **PFSYNC** interface of the new firewall. In addition, set the **Remote System Username** and **Remote System Password** on this system. For Select options to sync, select everything you want to synchronize; I recommend disabling synchronization of **DHCP Server settings** and **Virtual IPs** (disabling synchronizing virtual IPs guarantees that the **Advertising frequency settings** we made previously will not be overwritten). I also recommend leaving **pfsync Synchronize Peer IP** blank (to cause the state table to be synchronized via directed multicast). Also check all other firewalls in the failover group, including the master, to make sure Virtual IP synchronization is disabled and **pfsync Synchronize Peer IP** is left blank.

Now, you can bring the new firewall online and complete the last step of configuration. Navigate to **System** | **High Availability Sync** and enable Synchronize states. Change the Synchronize Interface to PFSYNC, and leave the **Synchronize Config to IP** blank. All other settings on this page can be kept at their default values. Click on the **Save** button to save the settings.

The way we have set up this failover group, changes will propagate from the primary firewall to the secondary firewall, from the secondary firewall to the tertiary firewall, and so on to the Nth firewall. To confirm that it worked, first navigate to **Firewall** | **Rules**, click on the **PFSYNC** tab, and ensure that the temporary firewall rule previously created has been overwritten. To further confirm that this setup works as it should, take the master firewall offline and ensure that the backup firewall with the lowest **Advertising frequency** setting for its virtual IPs has now been promoted to master, and that all other backup firewalls remain as backups. You can do this by navigating to **Status** | **CARP (failover)** and checking the CARP status. Repeat this process, each time taking the master firewall offline, and checking to make sure there is only one new master firewall, until only one firewall in the failover group remains. Then, start bringing firewalls back online in reverse order and make sure the current master is demoted back to backup, and that each time there is only one master firewall, until all firewalls are back online.

One major weakness of this configuration is that synchronization data does not propagate from the primary to all the backups; instead, it propagates from the primary to the secondary, from the secondary to the tertiary and so on. Therefore, if a backup firewall goes down and it is not the last firewall in the chain, at least one firewall will not be receiving updates. If the firewall is only offline temporarily, this shouldn't be a problem; once it comes back online, synchronization will resume. If the system is going to be offline for more than a brief time, however, you'll probably want to update **Synchronize Config to IP** on the firewall that was sending synchronization data to the offline firewall. Instead, set this parameter to the **PFSYNC** IP of the firewall that was receiving synchronization data from the offline firewall. This will ensure that firewall settings propagate to all firewalls in the failover group. If and when you bring the offline firewall back online, of course, you should revert the back to the previous setting.

Another problem with this setup is that the way synchronization works within the failover group may cause unexpected results. If changes are made to a backup firewall, those changes can propagate to other backups, resulting in multiple firewalls being out of sync with the master firewall. This will persist until either a configuration change is made on the master firewall, which triggers synchronization, or synchronization is forced from the master firewall (this can be done by navigating to **Status** | **Filter Reload** and clicking on the **Force Config Sync** button). These problems can be avoided by taking care when making changes to the configuration of backup firewalls.

An example of both load balancing and CARP

To demonstrate how the concepts introduced might be implemented in a real-world scenario, we will return to the example network introduced in the beginning of the chapter. Some very specific requirements were outlined:

- We need redundant firewalls, and this requires implementing CARP.
- Finally, we wanted to introduce some redundancy into our FTP server, and have at least two separate servers. This requires implementing server load balancing.

Assume that we have a LAN network for local traffic, and also assume that we have a separate **DMZ** network for the FTP server.

Assume we have a subnet of `192.168.1.0` for the LAN network, and a subnet of `192.168.2.0` for the DMZ network. The FTP server's IP address is `192.168.2.10`.

There are various ways we could go about implementing the changes we want, but implementing a CARP group is more difficult than implementing either server load balancing, so a case can be made for implementing the CARP group last. Thus, we will implement the changes in the following order:

1. Server (FTP) load balancing
2. CARP setup

Our first step is to set up FTP server load balancing. As mentioned earlier, our DMZ has a subnet of `192.168.2.0` and the FTP server's IP is `192.168.2.10`. We have decided that the redundant FTP server will be assigned an IP of `192.168.2.11`, and additional redundant servers will be added as needed. We don't have to assign an IP address for the virtual server, as it will be the WAN IP address. Thus, our IP assignments look like this:

WAN IP address	**Virtual server**
`192.168.2.10`	FTP server number 1
`192.168.2.11`	FTP server number 2

One issue we should consider before we move ahead with configuring load balancing is how we are going to synchronize the redundant FTP servers. We have two broad alternatives:

- Cluster the redundant FTP servers
- Run a utility on the FTP servers to ensure that the file systems remain synchronized

Note that if we cluster the FTP servers, the cluster will appear to other entities as a single server. There are many FTP servers that support clustering, and they have their own load balancing and high availability capabilities. In this case, pfSense can deal with the FTP cluster as if it was a single server, and we don't have to implement load balancing in pfSense.

If we choose not to cluster the server, however, then we have to find a means of synchronizing the servers. Fortunately, if we're using Unix or Linux, there is a widely-used utility called **rsync** that can be used; rsync has also been ported over to Windows, so if our FTP server is running on Windows, it's a potential solution, although there are many other file synchronization programs available for Windows. For the purposes of this exercise, we'll assume we decided not to create an FTP server cluster and thus we will use pfSense's load balancing capabilities.

To begin load balancing configuration, navigate to **Services** | **Load Balancer**. On the **Pools** tab, click on the **Add** button. We enter an appropriate name in the **Name** field (for example, `FTPPOOL`). The **Mode** field should be set to **Load Balance**. The **Port** value will be set to `21` (the default port for FTP). Then, under **Add Item to the Pool**, we begin entering FTP servers in the **Server IP Address** edit box, clicking on **Add to pool** after we enter each IP address to add it to the pool. Since there are only two servers, `192.168.2.10` and `192.168.2.11`, this does not take long. After we have entered all the servers, we click on the **Save** button at the bottom of the page.

The next step is virtual server configuration. On the main **Load Balancer** page, we click on the **Virtual Servers** tab, and then click on the **Add** button. On the **Virtual Servers** configuration page, we type an appropriate name (for example, **FTP**), a brief description in the **Description** field, and we enter the WAN IP address in the **IP Address** field. We enter `21` in the **Port** field, and we specify `FTPPOOL` as the **Virtual Server Pool** (if `FTPPOOL` is the only pool, then it will be the default value and we don't have to change anything). Since we don't see any issue in using **TCP** as the **Relay Protocol**, we leave this unchanged and click on the **Save** button. Then, we click on **Apply Changes** on the main **Load Balancer** page.

We now need to create a firewall rule to allow traffic to pass through the WAN interface to the FTP server pool. First, we create an alias for the FTP servers, which should help if we add servers in the future. We navigate to **Firewall** | **Aliases** and click on the **Add** button. On the **Aliases** configuration page, we enter an appropriate name in the **Name** field (for example, `FTPSERVERS`). We leave the **Type** set to **Host(s)** and, under the **Host(s)** section, we enter the IP addresses for the FTP servers. Then we click on the **Save** button, and from the main **Aliases** page we click on **Apply Changes**.

To create the firewall rule, we navigate to **Firewall** | **Rules**. On the **WAN** tab, we click on one of the **Add** buttons. All of the default values in the first section can be kept as they are (unless we have an IPv6 network and want to change the **Address Family** to **IPv6 or IPv4 + IPv6**). We keep **Source** as **any**, but in **Destination**, we select **Single host or alias** in the **Destination** drop-down box and enter `FTPSERVERS` in the adjacent edit box. We enter a brief description in the **Description** field, and then click on the **Save** button and click on **Apply Changes** on the main **Rules** page.

This completes the pfSense portion of our FTP load balancing pool. We still need to implement synchronization so that the files (including user account data) are kept identical on both servers. It is beyond the scope of this discussion to cover this topic, but as mentioned earlier, rsync is one possible solution. By utilizing rsync, implementing synchronization can be done as easily as entering the following line in our `crontab` file:

```
1 0 * * * rsync -az 192.168.2.10::ftp/   /var/ftp/
```

If entered into the `crontab` file on `192.168.2.11`, this will cause the cron scheduler to execute rsync at one minute past midnight every day, and copy the FTP tree on `192.168.2.10` to `/var/ftp`.

Even if we haven't yet implemented synchronization, we will want to verify that the FTP server pool is functioning, so we navigate to **Status** | **Load Balancer** and check both the **Pools** and **Virtual Servers** tabs to verify that both servers are up and running.

The final task is the setup of a CARP failover group, and this requires some consideration. Three interfaces will require CARP virtual IPs: the LAN and DMZ interfaces. We are going to have to add an interface for pfsync on each firewall. Assume also that we are going to make the CARP virtual IPs match the original interface IP assignments (`192.168.1.1` for the LAN and `192.168.2.1` for the DMZ) to make the transition easier. pfsync will be on its own network. We can summarize the IP assignments for our failover group as follows:

Interface	Firewall number 1	Firewall number 2	Virtual IP
LAN	`192.168.1.2`	`192.168.1.3`	`192.168.1.1`
DMZ	`192.168.2.2`	`192.168.2.3`	`192.168.2.1`
PFSYNC	`172.16.1.1`	`172.16.1.2`	None

As you can see, **PFSYNC** is the only interface on the failover group that doesn't get a virtual IP, as it is not accessible by the outside world, but is only there to allow the firewalls to exchange configuration data.

Since the virtual IPs for the LAN and DMZ are identical to the current IPs for those interfaces, we must change them before we create the virtual IPs, since pfSense will not allow us to create virtual IPs that match currently assigned IPs. Thus, we navigate to **Interfaces | LAN**, scroll down to the **IPv4 Address** edit box, and change this value to `192.168.1.2`, clicking on the **Save** button when we are done. Then, repeat this process with the DMZ interface, only we change the **IPv4 Address** to `192.168.2.2`.

Since we are going to have to add the PFSYNC interface anyway, we navigate to **Interfaces | (assign),** select one of the available interfaces in the **Available network ports** drop-down box, and click on the **Add** button. We select **Static IPv4** as the **IPv4 Configuration Type** and set the **IP address** to `172.16.1.1`. The **Enable Interface** checkbox also needs to be checked. Then, we click on the **Save** button and now that we are done configuring interfaces, we click on the **Apply Changes** button.

We begin configuration by navigating to **Firewall | Virtual IPs** and clicking on the **Add** button to add the first of our virtual IPs. We will set up the LAN IPs first, so for **Type** we select the **CARP** radio button, and then select **LAN** in the **Interface** drop-down box. We type in `192.168.1.1` in the **Address(es)** edit box and select **24** for the subnet mask. We type in a password in **Virtual IP Password**; the **VHID Group** should be **1** if we haven't added any CARP virtual IPs before. The **Advertising Frequency** should be set to **1** and **0** for the **Base** and **Skew** respectively. We enter a brief description in the **Description** field and click on the **Save** button.

We then repeat this process for the three remaining interfaces. The IPs entered in the **Address(es)** field for each interface must correspond to the virtual IP listed in the table (`192.168.1.1` for LAN, and `192.168.2.1` for **DMZ**). The **Virtual IP Password** value can be different for each virtual IP, and the **VHID Group** must be unique for each one (it should automatically increment). On the primary firewall, the **Advertising Frequency Base** and **Skew** should always be **1** and **0**.

Next, we navigate to **System | High Availability Sync** to configure pfsync and XML-RPC. We make sure the **Synchronize states** checkbox is checked, and select **PFSYNC** as the **Synchronize Interface**. For the **pfsync Synchronize Peer IP**, we enter the **LAN** IP of second firewall number, or `192.168.1.3`. Under **XML-RPC Sync**, we enter this IP again, and in the **Remote System Password** fields, we enter the admin password. In the **Select options to sync** section, we check everything, and then click on **Save**.

Finally, we must alter the DHCP settings. Since the **DMZ** is primarily for resources that need to be accessible from the internet, such as the FTP server, and those resources tend to have static IP addresses, there's a good chance the DHCP server won't be activated on the **DMZ**; thus, we only have to be concerned with DHCP settings for the **LAN**. Thus, we navigate to **Services** | **DHCP Server** and click on the **LAN** tab. Under **Servers**, we set the first DNS server to the CARP LAN virtual IP. Under **Other Options**, we set **Gateway** to the **LAN** virtual IP as well. We set the **Failover peer IP** to the actual **LAN** IP address of the other firewall (`192.168.1.3`). Then, we click on the **Save** button at the bottom of the page.

Now, we have completed configuration on the primary firewall, but we must repeat the process on the secondary firewall. We need to create a **PFSYNC** interface and create the same virtual IPs on the secondary firewall. When we configure pfsync, we set the **pfsync Synchronize Peer IP** to the LAN IP of first firewall, or `192.168.1.2` (this IP should also be used in the first field under **XMLRPC Sync**). The NAT manual outbound rules should not have to be changed, because the primary server should overwrite the NAT settings later. The DHCP settings will have to be changed; the first DNS server and the gateway should be set to the LAN virtual IP, and the **Failover peer IP** should match the IP address of the primary firewall (`192.168.1.2`).

Once we complete configuration of the second firewall and connect it to the network (and to the first firewall), our CARP setup is complete, and all that remains is to verify the CARP group's functionality, using the steps outlined in section on CARP configuration. We navigate to **Status** | **CARP** and see CARP is up and running. There may be a button on one of the firewalls labeled **Enable CARP**. If so, we will need to click it to get CARP to run. If it is working, we likely still want to test it in some likely failure scenarios. If it is not working, then we need to do some troubleshooting; this is the topic of the next section.

Troubleshooting

There are several problems that may arise when implementing a load balancing pool or a CARP group. The two broad possibilities are:

- The load balancing pool or CARP group may not be functioning at all – for example, traffic might not be passing to or from the gateway or server pool, or the CARP firewalls may not be syncing
- The load balancing pool or CARP group is functioning, but performance is suboptimal – for example, the load balancing pool is not balancing, or the state table on the CARP group is not synchronized, resulting in lost connections when the group fails over to the backup firewall

If load balancing or CARP is not functioning at all, then there is a good possibility that it was improperly configured. Double-checking the configuration is recommended, and confirming the functioning of each element of the configuration is a good idea. For example, if your CARP configuration is not functioning, you should check to make sure the virtual IPs are configured properly, then make sure that the pfsync interface is working, and then make sure that the firewall rules are configured properly.

Virtual IP misconfiguration is cited as a common source of misconfiguration issues. This is where the adage *slow is smooth, and smooth is fast* is good advice, and double checking that the settings are correct when initially configuring the virtual IPs is good practice. Duplicate VHIDs are sometimes a source of errors, and you'll want to check to make sure this is not an issue. However, pfSense automatically increments the VHID number when you add a new virtual IP, and if there is only a single pair of systems running CARP, pfSense will not allow a VHID conflict. If there are multiple systems on the same broadcast domain running CARP - as is the case in our example setup using CARP to create a failover group with three or more firewalls - then there can be a conflict and you may want to check to make sure there isn't one.

Another common source of problems with virtual IPs is an incorrectly set subnet mask. It is easy to overlook the **CIDR** drop-down box and leave this unchanged, but if it is not set, then your virtual IPs won't work. Another common issue is creating a virtual IP that is not within the subnet for that interface. If you don't remember what the subnets are for each interface, you may want to navigate to **Status** | **Interfaces** and make note of what the IP address and subnet mask for each interface is.

Improper firewall rules configuration is a common error with both load balancing and CARP setups. Keep in mind that rules are evaluated from the top down and the first matching rule wins. If you have a policy-based rule that is below an **allow [interface] to any** rule, then the rule will never be invoked. If the rule ordering appears to be correct, but you still suspect the rules may be responsible for your setup not functioning, then it might help to enable logging on the relevant rules and then examine the logs.

The system logs, which can be found at **Status** | **System Logs**, are often useful in troubleshooting CARP problems, since these logs indicate whether CARP syncing was successful, and if syncing failed, it will usually indicate a reason. If you see an XMLRPC sync error, navigate to **System** | **High Avail**. Sync, and make sure the backup firewall (or firewalls) do not have any information entered under **XMLRPC Sync**. Entering **Synchronize Config to IP**, **Remote System Username**, and **Remote System Password** on backup firewalls will cause synchronization to fail.

For load balancing, you should ensure that the firewall rules are directing traffic to the load balancing pool (or that you have a floating rule that directs traffic to the pool). Aliases are always useful when creating such rules, so you will want to make sure that you have such an alias and that it contains the IP addresses of all the servers in the server pool. You also need to set up a virtual server entry that maps to the public (usually **WAN**) IP address, so check to make sure you did this. If the rules appear to be correct and you configured a virtual server for the pool, you should navigate to **Status** | **Load Balancer** and confirm that every server in the load balancing pool is online.

If you are load balancing a pool of web servers, one good way to verify that load balancing is working properly is to use cURL. The cURL computer software project produces two products: libcurl and cURL. libcurl is a client-side URL transfer library which supports many different protocols, while cURL is a command line tool for sending and receiving files using the URL syntax, for example, invoking cURL at the command line like this:

```
curl www.somerandomsite.com
```

This command will result in the source code of the site being sent to standard output (usually the Terminal window). When testing load balancing with cURL, you will want to retrieve a page which displays the actual IP address of the site so you know which server you are hitting. Running cURL consecutive times should result in you retrieving pages from different servers, unless you have sticky connections enabled and the interval between each cURL command being executed is less than the sticky connections timeout.

One thing you probably should consider before you implement a load balancing pool or a CARP group is whether implementing load balancing and/or CARP may break something. This is especially important if it might cause a resource upon which users on your network rely becomes non-functional. For example, if you have a firewall which is directly connected to the internet and you are running a VPN server on pfSense, if you place pfSense behind a router, this will break VPN functionality unless you make changes to your VPN server configuration.

Summary

In this chapter, we covered redundancy and high availability. To this end, we discussed different types of load balancing and the basics of CARP. We then covered how to set up server load balancing in pfSense. We moved on to CARP configuration and provided two examples of CARP setups. The first was the conventional example of a CARP failover group with two firewalls - a master and a single backup. The second showed how it is possible to use CARP with three or more firewalls, and without much more configuration than would be necessary for the two firewall group. You may never have occasion to implement such a failover group, but it is encouraging to know that such enterprise-level redundancy is available to us.

We combined our knowledge of load balancing and CARP in an example that implemented server load balancing and a firewall failover group in a single network. Finally, we covered troubleshooting for redundancy and high availability, and acknowledged that the most common issues are virtual IP misconfiguration and neglecting to create firewall rules to allow traffic from the outside.

In the next chapter, we will cover a topic we held off in discussing in this chapter - gateway groups - as part of our coverage of multiple WANs. We will also expand on the example network we discussed in this chapter, and incorporate a multi-WAN setup into our network.

Questions

Answer the following questions:

1. Identify any three types of load balancing algorithms.
2. (a) What are the advantages of client-side load balancing? (b) What are the advantages of server-side load balancing?
3. What are the two modes of load balancing supported by the built-in pfSense load balancer?
4. If I am using pfSense's load balancer and I add a server to a server pool but no traffic from outside the network is reaching the new server (and traffic from outside the network is reaching other servers within the pool), what is the likely cause? Assume that my server pool setup was functioning correctly before I added the server.
5. Identify which of the following can be synchronized using pfSense's High Availability Sync. (a) firewall rules; (b) packages; (c) virtual IPs; (d) system logs.

6. In a normal CARP configuration, do we need to create a virtual IP for the **PFSYNC** interface? Why or why not?
7. Assume we have a functioning CARP failover group in which all options are selected in **Select options to sync** on the **System** | **High Availability Sync** page. On the backup firewall, we create a new firewall rule. What happens to this rule when we navigate to **Status** | **Filter Reload** and on the master firewall and click on the **Force Config Sync** button?
8. Why is it important to set the **Advertising frequency** in a CARP setup with multiple backup firewalls?
9. Assume you are required to implement load balancing on a pfSense firewall using the Least Connections algorithm. What is the easiest way of achieving this?
10. Assume that we need to keep CARP disabled through a reboot. How do we do this?

Further reading

- F5, `Load Balancing 101: Nuts and Bolts`: 10 pages. 10 May 2017. Retrieved 18 March 2018. This is a very good, brief overview of load balancing terminology and how load balancing works. Reading it will reinforce the basic concepts discussed in this chapter and provide a good overview of load balancing technology.
- `Common Address Redundancy Protocol (CARP)`: A brief overview of CARP from the FreeBSD handbook.

9
Multiple WANs

In the previous chapter, we discussed how to incorporate redundancy and high availability into our networks by implementing server load balancing and a firewall failover group. One problem that we did not address, however, was how to ensure redundancy and high availability in our connection to the public internet. Businesses that want to ensure that access to the internet is always available will want to eliminate single points of failure. We do this through a multi-WAN setup, which is the main topic of this chapter. Fortunately, pfSense makes it easy to implement such a setup.

In this chapter, we will cover the following:

- The basic concepts of multi-WAN
- Setting up multiple WANs for load balancing/failover
- An example multi-WAN setup
- Troubleshooting

Technical requirements

As with the previous two chapters, working through the examples in this chapter requires at least two working pfSense firewalls, either in a real-world or virtualized environment. It will also help to have two separate internet connections. This can be simulated in a virtual environment; you can also use your home and mobile internet connections if you have both.

Basic concepts

Sometimes, we want higher uptime and a higher throughput with our internet connection, and when we do, multiple WAN interfaces providing multiple internet connections is a way of doing this. Before you implement multi-WAN, you must already have a working LAN and WAN interface. Additional WAN interfaces are referred to as OPT WAN interfaces, and pfSense can support several WAN interfaces.

In order to fully take advantage of a multi-WAN setup, however, you should have separate internet connections. Ideally, you should have separate internet connections from separate internet providers, because there is a higher likelihood of a connectivity issue between your network and a provider affecting all connections to that provider than there is that a connectivity issue would affect multiple providers at the same time. And of course, if you have two connections to the same ISP and there is a failure of the entire ISP, then both of your connections are down – a far cry from the redundancy we hoped to achieve, although such a setup will at least provide more bandwidth than a single connection.

There may be cases, however, where there is only one provider in your area. In such a case, if you opt for two connections from the same provider, you should try to obtain a second connection that has a different type and path of cabling from the first. This is good practice when using different providers as well, because often connections carried on the same cabling are subject to the same cable cut and therefore the same outage.

Your connections should not only use different cabling, but they also should have different paths to the internet. This is one aspect in which having the same provider may not be that much of a handicap. Often, different types of connections from the same provider (for example, broadband cable and DSL) might utilize completely different networks and therefore take completely different paths.

Service Level Agreement

Before making a final decision on what ISPs to use, you probably want to see each provider's **Service Level Agreement (SLA)**. The SLA is the official commitment between the ISP and the client which defines particular aspects of service that should be provided to the client per the service contract. An ISP is not required to have an SLA, but many do, and many of them make their SLA available on their website.

The SLA may be part of the contract between the ISP and the client, or might not be. Aspects of service defined by the SLA can include such things as throughput, mean time between failures, mean time between recovery, mean time between repair, and uptime, as well as which party is responsible for reporting faults and paying fees. A good SLA will also delineate the process for supervising and monitoring performance levels, who to contact when there are issues, the time frame in which problems will be responded to and resolved, and the consequences for a service provider not fulfilling its SLA obligations. In some cases, an ISP failing to abide by the SLA can lead to the client having the right to terminate the contract or receive a refund for the time during which connectivity is unavailable.

You may be configuring multi-WAN for a business environment; in such cases, T1 service has been held in high regard for many years. The SLA for a T1 connection is generally more favorable than SLAs for other types of connections, and T1 service is seen as more reliable. With pfSense, however, you can achieve a higher level of reliability at a lesser cost. Two low-cost broadband connections in a multi-WAN setup can give you greater bandwidth and the same or greater level of reliability. It is less likely, for example, that two broadband connections will go down at the same time than two T1 connections.

One of the advantages of a multi-WAN implementation is that it makes possible **policy-based routing**, which is a form of routing in which routing decisions are based on administrative policy rather than some other criteria. In a multi-WAN context, it means that we can divert traffic that matches a firewall rule to a specific gateway. A simple example of this would be directing outbound traffic from one subnet to a certain gateway. We can also direct traffic from a specific host or traffic that uses a certain protocol. You might also want to use policy-based routing to segregate certain services based on their priority. For example, you may have a high-quality connection that has little bandwidth (for example, a T1 connection with 1.544 Mbps), and a low-quality connection with a higher level of bandwidth (a broadband connection). Using policy-based routing, you could route high-priority traffic (for example, VoIP traffic) to the T1 connection, leaving other permitted but low-priority traffic (for example, file downloads) to the broadband connection.

As with server load balancing, multi-WAN provides for two forms of redundancy and high availability: failover and load balancing. With failover, some gateways have priority over other gateways, and only when all higher priority gateways fail do the lower priority gateways come online. Load balancing entails having multiple gateways online at the same time, handling some share of the total WAN traffic. This means that if we want to utilize multiple connections in order to increase our bandwidth, we can, but if we want to use additional connections only when our primary connection goes down, we can do that as well.

One caveat that should be mentioned in connection with bandwidth aggregation is that while we can use multiple connections in a load balancing gateway group to increase overall bandwidth, a single connection will still be routed through a single WAN interface. As a result, while we might have two connections, each providing *x* Mbps of bandwidth, our total bandwidth may be *2x*, an individual connection will still only be able to use *x* Mbps of bandwidth. If you have applications that use multiple connections (for example, a download client), such an application should be able to take advantage of multiple connections. Of course, if there are multiple users on your network, a load balancing gateway configuration will enable you to take advantage of the additional bandwidth.

There are many different algorithms that could define the behavior of a gateway group; pfSense load balancing uses a round-robin algorithm (requests distributed sequentially). Different weights can be assigned to each gateway; by default, they each handle an equal share of traffic, but if there is a need to change the share of traffic handled by a gateway, we can alter it by changing the weight assigned to it.

A multi-WAN setup requires a means of determining when a gateway is down. The way it is done in pfSense is that each WAN has its own monitor IP. pfSense will ping the monitor IP, and if it stops responding, the gateway is assumed to be down. If the monitor IP is for an OPT WAN interface, then pfSense will automatically add a static route to divert traffic to the correct gateway within the gateway group. Thus, each WAN interface within a gateway group must have a unique monitor IP; WAN interfaces in different gateway groups, however, can have the same monitor IP.

You may wonder what constitutes a ping failure for purposes of gateway monitoring. pfSense uses the following default parameters:

- If packet loss reaches 20% and packet loss is one of the criteria used for determining when a gateway is down, the gateway will go down
- If a packet is sent and does not receive a reply after 2 seconds, the packet is considered lost
- An ICMP probe will be sent every 0.5 seconds
- If latency (the time between when a packet is sent and a reply is received) averages 0.5 seconds and high latency is one of the criteria used for determining when a gateway is down, the gateway will go down

The criteria used to determine when a gateway is down is set by editing the settings for a gateway group, as will be shown later.

In addition, a gateway will reach alert status (the gateway will remain up but the background of its listing in **Status | Gateways** changes to yellow) when packet loss reaches 10% or latency reaches 0.2 seconds. If these default settings are unacceptable, you can adjust them by navigating to **System | Routing**, clicking on the **Gateways** tab and editing the gateway whose values you wish to change (click on the **Advanced** button on the **Edit** page to reveal these settings). We will cover this in greater detail in the next section.

Multi-WAN configuration

Gateway load balancing is accomplished by setting up gateway groups, which consist of two or more WAN interfaces. Configuring gateway load balancing involves several steps:

1. Adding and configuring additional WAN interfaces.
2. Configuring DNS servers for each of the new WAN interfaces.
3. Adding gateway groups which include the new interfaces.
4. Adding firewall rules for each of the new gateway groups.

The first step, adding and configuring additional WAN interfaces, is a fairly simple process. When you initially set up pfSense, the WAN interface was automatically configured, but configuring additional WAN interfaces isn't much different from configuring any other interfaces. Refer to the following steps:

1. Navigate to **Interfaces | (assign)**, and on the **Interface Assignments** tab, there should be a tab showing all the existing interface assignments (which should be, at a minimum, the WAN and LAN interfaces).
2. To add the second WAN interface, select an unused network interface in the **Available network ports** drop-down box and click on the **Add** button on the right side of the row. This will add the new interface (which will initially have a generic name like **OPT1**). Click on the new interface's name in the leftmost column in the table.
3. Alternately, you can select it from the **Interfaces** drop-down menu to begin configuration.
4. On the interface configuration page, check the **Enable** checkbox, and enter an appropriate description in the **Description** field (for example, `WAN2`).

5. In the **IPv4 Configuration Type** and **IPv6 Configuration Type** drop-down boxes, you must select the appropriate configuration type for the interface IP. If the interface will be receiving an IP address from your ISP, then the correct selection is **DHCP** (or **DHCP6** or **SLAAC** for IPv6). If you choose **DHCP** and/or **DHCP6** or **SLAAC**, then there isn't much more you have to do for interface configuration. pfSense will automatically set up the interface as a gateway, so you don't have to do this.
6. If you chose **Static IPv4** and/or **Static IPv6** as **Configuration Type**, however, you will have to manually configure this interface as a gateway.
7. Fortunately, all we have to do is scroll down to the **Static IPv4/IPv6 Configuration** section of the page and click on the **Add new gateway** button.
8. This will launch a dialog box which will allow you to configure the most basic options for the gateway.
9. You should leave the **Default gateway** checkbox unchecked, as the first WAN interface is already the default gateway. Give the gateway an appropriate name in the **Gateway name** edit box (for example, `GW2`), and enter a gateway IP address in the **Gateway IPv4** (or **Gateway IPv6**) edit box. This should be an address different to the interface's IP address, but on the same subnet.
10. Finally, you may enter a non-parsed description in the **Description** edit box. Click on **Add** when done. The screen for adding a gateway from the interface configuration page is shown here:

There isn't much more you have to do for interface configuration, unless you have some other options you need to enter for your connection (for example, if you need to configure advanced DHCP options, or if you have a PPP or PPPoE connection and must enter a username or password).

11. You probably should check the **Block bogon networks** checkbox to block non-IANA-assigned networks. Otherwise, you can click on the **Save** button at the bottom of the page and, when the page reloads, click on the **Apply Changes** button at the top of the page.
12. Repeat this process for as many **WAN**-type interfaces as you have.

The next step is DNS configuration for each of the new gateways. Perform the following steps:

1. Navigate to **System** | **General Setup** and enter a DNS server for each of the new gateways.

   There should be at least one unique DNS server per gateway in a multi-WAN step, as we are looking to eliminate single points of failure in our setup.

2. You enter the DNS server information by entering a DNS server IP address in one of the edit boxes (for **DNS Server 1–4**), and then selecting one of the gateways in the adjacent drop-down box, and then clicking on the **Add DNS Server** button. This process should be repeated for each of the gateways. When you have finished, click on the **Save** button at the bottom of the page.
3. Now that we have completed DNS configuration, we can navigate to **System** | **Routing** and begin gateway configuration.

4. On the **Gateway** tab, the newly created gateways should be listed in the table. If you configured the gateways manually in the previous step, they will have whatever names you assigned to them; otherwise, they will have names such as **WAN2_DHCP** or **WAN2_DHCP6**, and so on. The screen for editing a gateway from the Gateways tab is shown here:

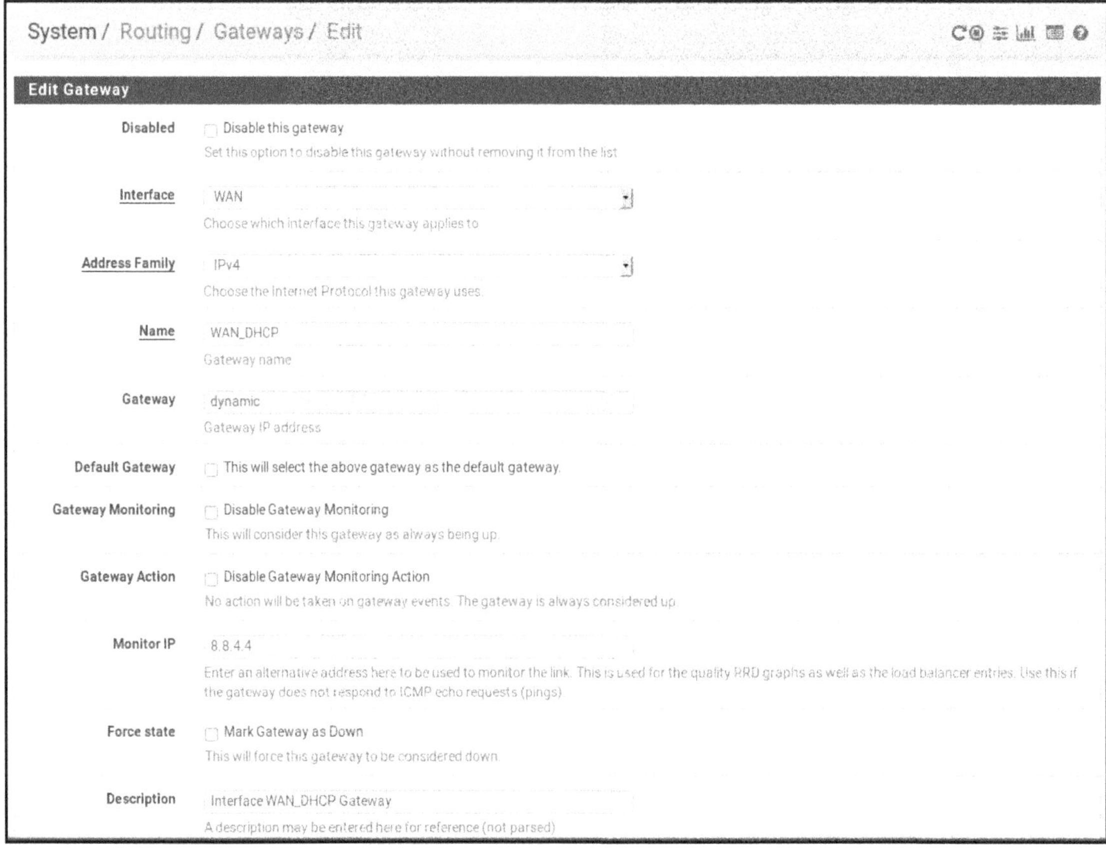

5. One thing you will notice if you click on the **Edit** icon (the pencil) for any of the gateways is that you have many more options than were presented in the dialog box that appears when you click on **Add new gateway** on the interface configuration page.
6. There is a **Disable this gateway** checkbox that allows you to save the gateway configuration while forcing the gateway offline, which can be useful in troubleshooting.

7. The **Interface** drop-down box allows you to change the interface being configured; the options for **Address Family** are **IPv4** or **IPv6**. **Gateway** allows you to specify the gateway IP address; if the interface is configured to use DHCP or DHCPv6, this field will be read-only.
8. As in the **Add new gateway** dialog box, there is a **Default Gateway** checkbox which allows you to set this gateway as the default. There is a **Disable Gateway Monitoring** checkbox, which, if checked, will cause pfSense to consider the gateway to always be up.
9. There is also a **Monitor IP** edit box, in which you can enter an alternative IP address to monitor the gateway. To determine whether a gateway is up or not, pfSense will first ping the gateway. Sometimes, however, having the gateway ping a remote address is a better measure of whether the gateway is actually up, so if the gateway fails to respond to a ping and a monitor IP is specified, pfSense will have the gateway ping the monitor IP. You should probably configure this option. To configure Monitor IP, enter a non-local IP address to ping (you can enter the DNS server IP address for the gateway if you can't think of another reliable site to ping).
10. The **Mark Gateway as Down** checkbox, if checked allows you to force pfSense to consider the gateway to be down.
11. There is also a **Description** field. Also of interest are the options available in the **Advanced** section (you need to click the **Display Advanced** button for these options to appear).
12. The **Weight** drop-down box allows you to select the weight for the gateway within a gateway group. Higher numbers mean the gateway has more weight. For example, if one gateway has a weight of 2 and another gateway has a weight of 1, the gateway with a weight of 2 will have twice as many connections going through it as the other gateway.
13. The **Data Payload** edit box allows us to set the -s parameter of the ping command, which in turn allows us to set the number of data bytes to send. The default is **1**.
14. The **Latency thresholds** edit boxes determine the low and high thresholds for latency (in milliseconds) in cases where latency is one of the criteria for determining if a gateway is up or down.
15. The **low threshold** value sends an alarm, while the **high threshold** value signifies the gateway is down. The defaults of **200/500** should be fine, although you may want to adjust this if you have a high latency connection (for example, a satellite connection).

The **Packet Loss** thresholds specify the low and high thresholds for how much packet loss is acceptable before the gateway is considered down in cases where packet loss is one of the criteria for determining if a gateway is functional. Again, the **low threshold** sends an alarm and the **high threshold** signifies the gateway is down. The **Probe Interval** edit box allows you to specify how often (in milliseconds) an ICMP (ping) probe is sent. The default is **500** ms. The **Loss Interval** is the allowed latency of replies; in other words, the time interval before packets are considered lost. The default is **2000** ms. The **Time Period** is the period over which results are averaged. The default is **60000** ms. The **Alert interval** edit box allows you to specify the time period between checking for an alert condition; the default is one second. There is also a **Use non-local gateway** checkbox which, if checked, allows use of a gateway outside of the interface's subnet.

16. Most of the settings in **Advanced** can be kept at their default values, although it is good to know that you can change them if needed. pfSense gateway pings were once hardcoded in such a way that a reply received 5 seconds after a ping request was considered successful, and a ping request was considered successful if at least 1 reply was received from every 5 requests. That means that pfSense tolerated up to 80% packet loss and a very high level of latency before it declared a gateway to be down. These settings undoubtedly eliminated a lot of false positives and **flapping** (when an interface is alternately advertised as up and down in rapid succession), but it also meant that a gateway could still be up when in practice the packet loss level would be so high that the connection would be unusable. Making these settings configurable allows us to make our own trade-offs. The value you will most likely have to adjust is **Latency thresholds**, and even then only for certain types of connections. Click on the **Save** button when you have finished making changes, and from the main **Routing** page, click on the **Apply Changes** button.

Now we can set up the actual gateway group for our multi-WAN connection, for which we can refer to the following steps:

1. Click on the **Gateway Groups** tab. This tab should display a table with all configured gateways.
2. Click on the **Add** button at the bottom of the table on the right to add a new gateway. The screen for adding a gateway group is shown here:

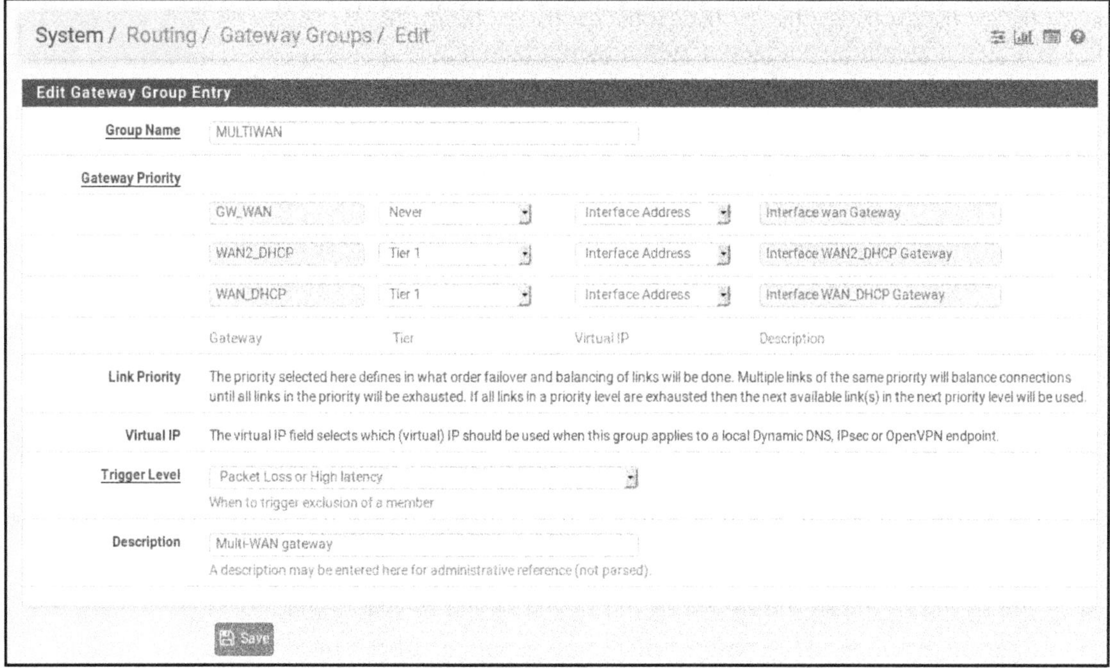
System / Routing / Gateway Groups / Edit
Edit Gateway Group Entry
Group Name
MULTIWAN
Gateway Priority
GW_WAN
Never
Interface Address
Interface wan Gateway
WAN2_DHCP
Tier 1
Interface Address
Interface WAN2_DHCP Gateway
WAN_DHCP
Tier 1
Interface Address
Interface WAN_DHCP Gateway
Gateway
Tier
Virtual IP
Description
Link Priority
The priority selected here defines in what order failover and balancing of links will be done. Multiple links of the same priority will balance connections until all links in the priority will be exhausted. If all links in a priority level are exhausted then the next available link(s) in the next priority level will be used.
Virtual IP
The virtual IP field selects which (virtual) IP should be used when this group applies to a local Dynamic DNS, IPsec or OpenVPN endpoint.
Trigger Level
Packet Loss or High latency
When to trigger exclusion of a member
Description
Multi-WAN gateway
A description may be entered here for administrative reference (not parsed).
Save

There are only a few options when configuring a gateway group:

1. In the **Group Name** edit box, enter the name of the group.
2. Under **Gateway Priority**, there are two configurable options. **Tier** allows you to select the tier on which a gateway exists. With tiers, lower numbers have priority over higher numbers.
3. Gateways on the same tier level are load balanced with each other, while gateways on a higher tier level only become invoked when all gateways on lower tiers are down.
4. Thus, if we set **WAN_DHCP** to **Tier 1** and **WAN2_DHCP** to **Tier 2**, then **WAN_DHCP** will get all the traffic for this gateway group, and **WAN2_DHCP** will not be used at all unless **WAN_DHCP** is down. But if both are set to **Tier 1**, then both gateways will be online at the same time and handle a share of the traffic.

This means that we can convert a gateway group from failover to load balancing very easily and vice-versa.

However, they will be load balanced. Since this is what we want, you should set all the gateways in the group to **Tier 1**.

5. The **Virtual IP** drop-down box allows you to select which virtual IP to use for each gateway. As this only applies to cases where the gateway group is used as an endpoint for a local **Dynamic DNS** (**DDNS**), IPsec or OpenVPN connection, you can leave it set to **Interface Address**.
6. The **Trigger Level** drop-down box allows you to specify when to trigger exclusion of a gateway member. The choices are as follows:
    - **Member down**: Member is excluded when it fails to respond to a ping attempt, or when it fails to ping the monitor IP.
    - **Packet Loss**: Member is excluded when packet loss is unacceptably high (the actual percentage value is set in **Advanced** in the gateway configuration).
    - **High Latency**: Member is excluded when latency is unacceptably high (the actual threshold is set in **Advanced** in the gateway configuration).
    - **Packet Loss or High Latency**: Member is excluded when either packet loss or high latency becomes unacceptably high.
7. Finally, in the **Description** field, you can enter a brief non-parsed description. Click on **Save** when you are finished making changes, and on the main **Routing** page, click on **Apply Changes**.

You may also want to configure failover groups for each of the gateways, the following are the steps to be performed:

1. Again, click on the **Add** button on the **Gateway Groups** tab.
2. Type an appropriate name in the **Group Name** field (for example, `FAILOVER1`). In the **Gateway priority Tier** drop-down box, set the first WAN connection to **Tier 1** and the second WAN connection to **Tier 2**.
3. Set the desired trigger level in the **Trigger Level** drop-down box, type an appropriate **Description** (for example, `WAN1 failover`), and then click on the **Save** button.
4. On the **Gateway Groups** tab, click on **Add** once again (or, to make life even easier, click on the **Copy** icon in the table entry for the first failover group, which will make a new gateway group with all values defaulting to the first failover group options), and configure another gateway group with an appropriate **Group Name**, only this time, set the second WAN connection to **Tier 1** and the first WAN connection to **Tier 2**.

5. When you are finished making changes, click on the **Save** button. On the **Gateway Groups** page, click on **Apply Changes**.

The gateway group is now configured, but without corresponding firewall rules, no network traffic will be directed through the group. You could create a rule for each interface that will be using the group, but if the group is going to be used on more than one network, it will be easier to create a floating rule. Refer to the following steps:

1. Navigate to **Firewall** | **Rules** and click on the **Floating** tab. Scroll down to the bottom of the table and click on one of the **Add** buttons to add a new rule.
2. The objective of this rule is to pass traffic, so the **Action** drop-down box should be left at its default value of **Pass**.
3. In the **Interface** listbox, you should select every interface that will be using the gateway group.
4. In the **Direction** drop-down box, select **out** (rules involving gateways can only be one-way rules).
5. In the **Protocol** drop-down box, select **any**. The **Source** field should be an alias which refers to all the interfaces selected in the **Interface** listbox (or **any** if you want to keep it simple); the **Destination** field can be left as **any**.
6. Then scroll down to **Advanced Options** (in the **Extra Options** section) and click on the **Show Advanced** button.
7. Scroll down further, and the third last option will be **Gateway**. In the **Gateway** drop-down box, select the newly created gateway group.
8. Then click on **Save** button at the bottom of the page.

Although it is easier to set up a floating rule to direct traffic to the gateway group, if you want to do per-interface policy-based routing, do not let this hinder you. The following are the steps:

1. Click on the tab for the interface for which you want to set the policy, then click on one of the **Add** buttons.
2. If you just want to make a general rule directing all interface traffic to a specific gateway, the only default values you have to change are **Protocol** (change this from **TCP** to **any**), and **Gateway** (found by clicking on the **Advanced Options** button and then scrolling down).
3. Change **Gateway** to the interface to which you want to direct traffic. If your policies are more granular, make the necessary changes so the rule only matches the traffic you want to direct to the gateway.

4. Enter a brief **Description** for each rule and then click on **Save** and click on **Apply Changes**.
5. Even though you are making specific rules for each interface, you may want to also have a floating rule as a fallback, so that all traffic that doesn't match the policy-based routing rules goes to the gateway group. If so, make sure the **Quick** option on the floating rule is disabled; otherwise the floating rule will take precedence over the policy rules. As always, make sure the ordering of the rules is correct.
6. You still need to create rules for the two failover gateway groups.
7. Click on the **Copy** icon in the table entry for the new rule, and create a new rule for each of the failover groups.
8. All you need to change is the **Description** field and the gateway in the **Gateway** drop-down box.
9. Click on **Save** when you have finished creating each rule, and when you have created all the necessary rules, click on **Apply Changes** on the main floating rules page.

Under most circumstances, you will not have to configure static routes, because when a route needs to change due to a gateway going offline, pfSense automatically creates a temporary static route to re-route traffic. There may be some cases, however, where you need to create static routes. One such case is with traffic that comes directly from pfSense, such as services, ping requests, and so on. Policy-based routing will work with traffic that enters a pfSense network interface from the outside, but it cannot be applied to traffic that originates from pfSense because it cannot be tagged for alternate routing. The solution is to set up a static route for such traffic. To do so, refer to the following steps:

1. Navigate to **System | Routing** and click on the **Static Routes** tab.
2. Click on the **Add** button to add a new route. On the **Edit** page for the route, choose the **Destination network** for the route (IP address and CIDR).
3. In the **Gateway** drop-down box, select the correct gateway (there is a link provided that enables you to add a new gateway, if necessary).
4. There is a **Disable this static route** checkbox, in case we need to do this, and in the last field, you may enter a brief **Description**.
5. Click on the **Save** button when you are finished making changes and then click on the **Apply Changes** button. The screen for adding a static route is shown here:

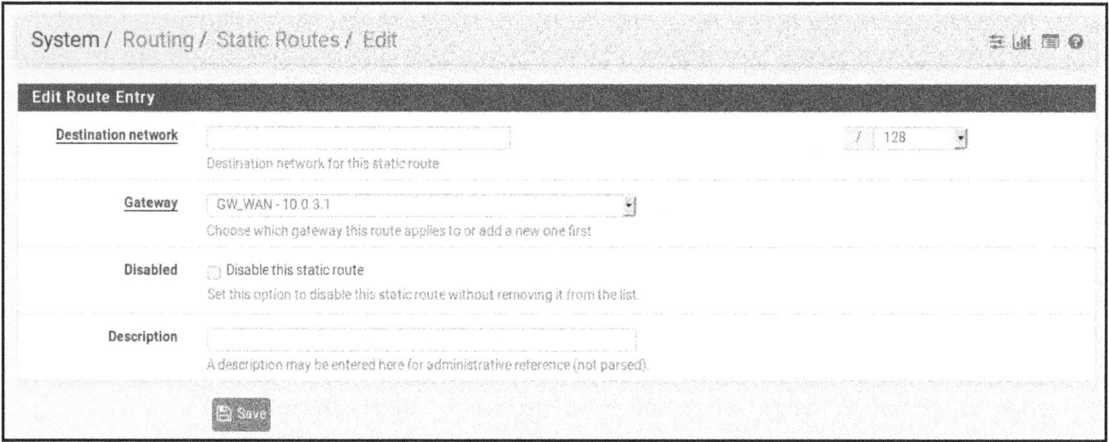

6. There are two options available from **System** | **Advanced** settings that are of interest in configuring gateway groups.
7. If you click on the **Miscellaneous** tab, there are two options in the **Gateway Monitoring** section.
8. The **State Killing on Gateway Failure** checkbox, if checked, will cause all states to be flushed when a gateway goes down. Otherwise, active states from the gateway that is now down will be transferred to other gateways in the gateway group. This may be undesirable if you don't want persistent connections to be transferred in such a way.
9. The **Skip rules when gateway is down** checkbox, when checked, will change the default behavior regarding what happens to a rule specifying a gateway when the gateway is down.

   By default, the rule will be created without the gateway which is down. This option changes that behavior so that if a rule specifies a gateway which is down, the rule is not created.

If you completed these steps, your gateway group should be up and running, but you will probably want to check to make sure it is functioning correctly. To do so the following steps will be helpful:

1. Navigate to **Status** | **Gateways**. There are two tabs on the **Gateways** page: **Gateways** and **Gateway Groups**. The **Gateways** tab has more useful information about configured gateways.

2. On this tab, there is a table showing all configured gateways. The meaning of the **Name**, **Gateway**, **Monitor** and **Description** fields are obvious, but there are also the following fields which convey crucial information about the gateways:
    - **RTT (Round Trip Time)**: The ping round trip time in milliseconds, averaged over the calculation interval
    - **RTTsd (Round Trip Time standard deviation)**: New to pfSense 2.3, this is the standard deviation of the round trip time over the calculation interval
    - **Loss**: Packet loss over the calculation interval
    - **Status**: Either online or offline

3. You can test the gateway group monitoring by unplugging each of the WAN interfaces in turn, and seeing how long it takes for this page to report the gateway as offline.
4. If the amount of time it takes is unacceptably high, you may have to adjust the **Trigger Level** setting in **Gateway Groups** or adjust the **Latency threshold** or **Packet Loss threshold** in the gateway settings.

DNS considerations

pfSense uses its internal routing table to determine the route to DNS servers (remember that policy-based routing does not apply to traffic generated by pfSense). As a result, if static routes are not configured, then pfSense will only use the primary WAN interface to access DNS servers. Therefore, you must configure static routes if you want pfSense to use the correct OPT_WAN interface for DNS queries. If you do not configure static routes for the OPT_WAN interfaces, there are two issues:

- If you are using your ISP's DNS servers, often ISPs will block recursive DNS queries from outside their network. This problem can be eliminated if you use alternative DNS servers such as the ones operated by OpenDNS.
- If no static routes are configured and the primary WAN interface goes down, then you will be left with no means of DNS resolution.

One of the ways to eliminate this problem is to use the DNS server for an OPT_WAN gateway as the monitor IP address for the gateway. If you do, pfSense will automatically add a static route for the gateway's DNS server.

If you need to add a static route for the DNS server, however, it's not difficult. For example, to add a static route to `8.8.8.8` for the OPT_WAN gateway, navigate to **System | Routing**, click on the **Static Routes** tab, and click on the **Add** button. For the **Destination network**, enter `8.8.8.8` with `32` for the **CIDR**. For the **Gateway**, select the **OPT_WAN** gateway in the drop-down box. Then click on **Save** and **Apply Changes** (enter a brief **Description** first if you wish), and you are done.

NAT considerations

If your setup relies on Network Address Translation (NAT), you must make sure that there is a set of outbound NAT rules for each OPT_WAN interface. If you have **Outbound NAT** set to **Automatic outbound NAT rule generation** or **Hybrid outbound NAT rule generation**, no worries: the necessary outbound NAT rules will be generated automatically. If you have it set to **Manual outbound NAT rule generation**, however, as would be the case if you have a CARP configuration and therefore must edit the rules in order to direct traffic to the WAN virtual IP, then you will have to create your own set of outbound NAT rules for each OPT_WAN interface. In such cases, you can use the existing rules as a template for the new rules with the **Copy** option; just change the **Interface** setting to the new OPT_WAN interface and the **Address** to the OPT_WAN virtual IP address.

Also, if you have any 1:1 NAT mappings, keep in mind that these mappings specify a unique WAN interface. Such 1:1 mappings also override any other outbound NAT settings for the interface on which it is configured. If you want the 1:1 mapping to work on the new OPT_WAN interface, you will have to add an entry for it.

If you have any Port Forwarding entries, take heed of the fact that, as with 1:1 NAT, these entries specify a unique WAN interface. If you want to open a port on multiple WAN interfaces, the easiest way to do this is to use the **Copy** option to create a new rule based on the old one. Change the interface to the new OPT_WAN interface; the **Destination** will automatically update to OPT_WAN address when you do so. Update the **Description** if desired. Then click on the **Save** button and when the page reloads, click on **Apply Changes**.

Third-party packages

There aren't many packages available that directly pertain to gateways (in fact, I found just one). **gwled** allows you to use the LEDs on certain embedded devices (for example, ALIX, WRAP, Soekris) to monitor gateways. After you install the gwled package, a new option will appear on the **Interfaces** menu called **Gateway Status LEDs**. Navigating to **Interfaces** | **Gateways Status LEDs** allows you to control the options for this package. Upon installation, gwled is not enabled by default, but by checking the **Enable gwled** checkbox, you can enable it. The package allows you to monitor the gateway using LEDs #2 and #3 on supported devices; you need to enable each LED individually using their respective checkboxes. There are also drop-down boxes for each LED which enable you to control which gateway each LED monitors.

Example – multi-WAN and CARP

In the previous chapter, we covered an example network in which we implemented both load balancing (for an FTP server) and a CARP failover group. In this section, we will add multi-WAN capabilities to this network. We don't want our second connection to go unused even when the first connection is up, so we want to make it part of a load balancing group. However, our second connection is a DSL connection with 1.544 Mbps up and 1.544 Mbps down, whereas our primary connection is a standard broadband connection. We will want to take this into account when setting up our gateway group and make sure the primary connection handles the lion's share of internet-bound traffic. Adding multi-WAN capabilities to a CARP setup is not particularly difficult, but it does involved several steps:

1. Add and configure the OPT_WAN interfaces.
2. Configure DNS settings for the OPT_WAN interfaces.
3. Add virtual IP addresses for each of the OPT_WAN interfaces.
4. Add outbound NAT rules for each of the OPT_WAN interfaces for each of the internal interfaces using them.
5. Add gateways for each OPT_WAN interface.
6. Create a gateway group containing the original WAN interface and every OPT_WAN interface we want in the multi-WAN setup.
7. Add firewall rules for the gateway group.

Now that all the OPT_WAN interfaces are installed and configured, we can move straight ahead and configure the DNS server settings for WAN and OPT_WAN. We navigate to **System** | **General Setup** and scroll down to **DNS Server Settings**. Since it is good practice to use different DNS servers for each WAN-type interface, we enter `208.67.220.220` (one of OpenDNS's DNS servers) in the **DNS server 1** listbox and then select **WAN** in the corresponding drop-down box. We enter `8.8.8.8` (one of Google's DNS servers) in the **DNS server 2** listbox and then select **WAN** in the corresponding drop-down box. We click on the **Save** button to save the settings.

Since this is a CARP failover group and there is an OPT_WAN interface on each firewall, we need to add virtual IPs for OPT_WAN. Navigate to **Firewall** | **Virtual IPs** and click on the **Add** button. On the **Edit** page, for the **Type** we select **CARP**. We select **OPT_WAN** as the **Interface**. **Address type** can be kept at the default of **Single address**. In the **Address(es)** edit box, we enter `10.2.1.1` – the virtual IP for OPT_WAN. We enter a **Virtual IP Password**; **VHID Group** automatically increments, so we do not have to change this setting. We enter a brief **Description** (for example "`OPT_WAN virtual IP`") and click on the **Save** button and then click the **Apply Changes** button. We repeat the process on the other firewall, remembering to make sure we adjust the **Skew** setting on the secondary firewall so it is higher than the **Skew** setting on the primary firewall.

As was the case with a single-WAN CARP setup, we need to create NAT rules for OPT_WAN, and make sure that these rules refer to the virtual IP and not the physical interface for OPT_WAN. This is because the NAT settings will be copied to the secondary firewall, and since the physical interface on the secondary firewall will be different, if we use the physical interface for these rules, NAT won't work on the secondary firewall. Since our initial CARP setup involved switching to manual outbound NAT rule generation, we have to manually create these rules. Our task will be easier, however, if we copy the WAN NAT rules. Thus, we find the **LAN to WAN virtual IP** rule, click on the copy icon, change the **Interface** setting to **OPT_WAN** and change the **Address** to `10.2.1.1` **(OPT_WAN virtual IP address)**. We then click on the **Save** button and the **Apply Changes** button. We click on the copy icon for the **DMZ to WAN virtual IP** rule and repeat the process, changing the **Interface** to **OPT_WAN** and **Address** to `10.2.1.1`.

Now we can move on to gateway configuration. We navigate to **System** | **Routing**, and on the **Gateway** tab, we click on the **Add** button. We enter a **Name** for the gateway (for example, `GATEWAY2`) and the **Gateway IP address**, taking care to make sure we use the physical interface's IP address and not the virtual IP address. In the **Monitor IP** edit box, we enter `8.8.8.8` (the same as the IP address for the DNS server). We also enter a brief **Description** (for example, `Gateway for OPT_WAN`) and click **Save**, then click **Apply Changes**.

Since our second connection is a DSL connection, we want to make sure the first gateway has a much higher weight than the new gateway. Therefore, we find the WAN gateway and click on the edit icon. On the **Edit** page for this gateway, we scroll down and click on the **Advanced** button. The first option in the **Advanced** section is **Weight**. Since we want the DSL connection to handle about 3% of the overall WAN-bound traffic, we select **30** in the drop-down box (higher numbers ensure that a gateway will receive a greater share of the traffic; with the **WAN** gateway set to `30` and the **OPT_WAN** left at its default of **1**, we will ensure that the WAN gateway gets most of the traffic). We click **Save** when we are finished and then click **Apply Changes**.

Next, we click on the **Gateway Groups** tab and click on the **Add** button. We give the gateway group an appropriate name (for example, `MULTIWAN`), and under **Gateway Priority**, we assign both **WAN** and **OPT_WAN** to **Tier 1** so they will be active. The **Trigger Level** for this group will be set to **Member down**. We enter a brief **Description** (for example, `Multi-WAN gateway group`) and click on **Save**.

It is good practice to create failover groups for each of the gateways, so we click on the **Add** button and add a group called **FAILOVER1** which has **WAN** on **Tier 1** and **OPT_WAN** on **Tier 2**. Thus, **OPT_WAN** only becomes invoked if WAN fails. Again, **Trigger Level** is set to **Member down**. We click on **Save** and then create another failover group called **FAILOVER2** which has **OPT_WAN** on **Tier 1** and **WAN** on **Tier2**. When we are finished configuring all the groups, we click on **Apply Changes** on the main **Routing** page.

Next, we must create firewall rules to pass traffic from the local interfaces to the gateway groups. In the section on load balancing in the previous chapter, I described a floating rule which covered all local interfaces. Because of the configuration of the network, we cannot use floating rules here. The LAN network has access to all local networks and the internet, but the DMZ, as its name suggests, only has access to the internet and has no access to local networks. Therefore, we cannot create a universal rule. Fortunately, it is not too difficult to modify the existing firewall rules for our needs.

First, we navigate to **Firewall | Rules** and click on the **LAN** tab. There should be a **Default allow LAN to any** rule. We click on the **Edit** option for this rule and, keeping all other settings the same, we scroll down to **Extra Options**, click on the **Show Advanced** button, and then scroll down to **Gateway** under **Advanced** options. In the **Gateway** drop-down box, we select the **MULTIWAN** gateway we created earlier. We change the description to reflect the change, and then click on the **Save** button.

We also need to create rules for each of the failover groups, so we click on the copy icon for the rule we just modified to create a new rule based on the old one. Again, keeping other settings the same, we scroll down to the **Gateway** drop-down box and set the gateway to **FAILOVER1.** We click on **Save** and repeat the process, only instead of **FAILOVER1**, **FAILOVER2** will be the gateway. Once we have created the rules, we look at the table to make sure the rule which set **MULTIWAN** as the gateway is closer to the top of the table than the other two rules, since rules are evaluated from the top down and we want traffic to be directed to the **MULTIWAN** group if it is functional. Once we have confirmed that the rules are correct and are in the right order, we click the **Apply Changes** button.

Now we have to create rules for the **DMZ**, so we click on the **DMZ** tab. There won't be an **Allow DMZ to any** rule, but if whoever set up the system set it up correctly, there should be an **Allow DMZ to WAN** rule. When we find this rule, we click on the **Edit** icon for the rule and repeat the process outlined earlier for the LAN interface – namely, we keep all other settings the same, but set the gateway in the **Gateway** drop-down box to **MULTIWAN** and alter the **Description** field accordingly. Then we click on **Save** and repeat the process, clicking on the **Copy** icon for the modified rule and create rules with **FAILOVER1** and **FAILOVER2**, making sure that the rule setting **MULTIWAN** is closer to the top of the table than the other rules. When we are done making changes, we click on the **Apply Changes** button.

Keep in mind that the firewall rules we created only cover the standard use case. If you want to alter or add to the rules to add policy-based routing to your setup, it is fairly easy to do so. When editing a firewall rule, choose the criteria for the traffic you want to match (for example, protocol or maybe only traffic that originates from certain IP addresses); then under **Advanced Options**, scroll down to **Gateway** and select the gateway to which you want to direct traffic. Save the rule, make sure the order of the firewall rules is correct, and then apply the changes. The **Gateway** option can be found in both per-interface firewall rules and floating rules, so this form of policy-based routing can be applied to the entire network or just a particular subnet quite easily.

Now that we have created the firewall rules, our gateway load balancing setup is complete. We may want to reset states in order to force all outbound traffic to use the newly configured groups (to do so, we would navigate to **Diagnostics** | **States**, click on the **Reset States** tab, and click on the **Reset** button), but otherwise, all we need to do is navigate to **Status** | **Gateways** and confirm that the gateways are up and running and that the gateway groups are working.

Thus, we have demonstrated that a multi-WAN setup can be added to a CARP failover group. The main considerations in such cases is that we add virtual IPs for each OPT_WAN interface we add to the group. If there are any special use cases within your setup, you will have to add a virtual IP for that as well. For example, you may have a mail server or FTP server for internal use that uses 1:1 NAT. In such a case, you will need a virtual IP so that the NAT rules work on both the primary and secondary firewalls. You will also have to create a NAT rule for each OPT_WAN interface and each internal interface you want to pass through the OPT_WAN interface. Finally, we must set up firewall rules that direct traffic to the gateway group.

Troubleshooting

In troubleshooting multi-WAN setups, we can group the problems we are likely to encounter into three broad categories:

- There may be a connectivity issue with either your primary or secondary connection.
- There may be a misconfiguration in your setup.
- pfSense thinks a gateway is up when it is actually down, or vice-versa.

The first point seems rather obvious, but you'll want to make sure that both connections are working independent of the gateway group. If the second connection accounts for a low percentage of our overall bandwidth (for example, our primary connection is broadband and our secondary connection is DSL), or is part of a failover group, then we might not notice it is not working until the primary connection fails. Ensuring that both connections work when we first set things up will potentially save us some grief; we wouldn't want to wait until our primary connection fails to find out that our secondary connection wasn't working either. If we are troubleshooting, ensuring that both connections work could save us a significant amount of time.

Before you declare your multi-WAN setup to be functional, you will want to perform a few tests. There are several ways you can simulate a WAN interface going down. In the first case (and for any type of connection), you should disconnect the cable between pfSense and your primary connection and confirm that you are still connected to the internet. Be sure to confirm that DNS resolution is also still working. Then reconnect the primary connection and disconnect the secondary connection, and perform the same test.

If you have a cable, DSL, or other connection with a modem, you should try unplugging the modem and unplugging the connection between the modem and the demarcation point (usually a coax or phone jack) and see what happens. For a T1 connection, unplug the internet connection from the router, and either unplug or power off the router. If you have more than two WAN interfaces in your setup, you may want to perform this test with different combinations of interfaces being down and up. As long as one interface in the gateway group is up, you should have some level of internet connectivity.

Such testing is valuable because sometimes you will uncover a configuration error that you would not have uncovered otherwise. For example, the OPT_WAN interface could use as its monitor IP the public IP address of the WAN connection. When you power off the modem connected to the WAN interface, OPT_WAN goes down, even though the secondary connection is solid and OPT_WAN should be up.

Misconfiguration is a likely issue; creating a gateway group is relatively easy, but there are many steps needed to make everything work as it should. Primarily, we need to remember that there must be NAT rules for each new OPT_WAN interface, and there must be firewall rules to direct traffic to the appropriate gateway group (or to a particular gateway, if desired). You will especially want to check the firewall rules. By default, the rules direct traffic to the default gateway, so when the primary WAN interface is up, everything might seem to be working. Then when the primary WAN interface goes down, internet connectivity will be lost even though there are still functioning interfaces in the gateway group. Double-check the NAT and firewall rules to make sure they are behaving as they should.

If the flow of traffic within your multi-WAN setup is working as it should, but DNS resolution does not work, the issue may be the fact that pfSense only uses its internal routing tables for traffic flowing in and out of interfaces. It does not apply them to internal pfSense traffic. Therefore, you may have to configure a static route for the OPT_WAN DNS server.

Sometimes there is a failure with gateway load balancing where there is a gateway group and one of the WAN connections no longer has internet connectivity, but still remains active. This may be because the monitor IP is still responding (for example, if you set it to an IP on your internal network), so pfSense thinks the connection is still good. If so, ensure that the monitor IP is correct.

Another issue with monitor IPs is the case where an external site is used for the monitor IP. The network administrator at the external site sees pfSense's pings to the site, and suspects this could be the beginning of a denial-of-service attack. The admin then blocks your monitor pings, and because the monitor pings fail, the gateway goes down, even though the network interface is still functioning and has internet connectivity. This potentially could happen whenever you set a monitor IP to a site you don't control. The solution, of course, is to use an external site you control for the monitor IP. In most cases, using the DNS server as your monitor IP should not result in your pings being blocked.

When you connect to certain websites, such as e-commerce sites, they will store session information, including your public IP address. If you subsequently connect to such a site through a different public IP address, the site might not function as it should. The **Use Sticky Connections** option is designed to eliminate this problem by directing traffic from such websites to the same WAN address so long as there are states that refer to the connection.

If your multi-WAN setup implements load balancing, you should verify that the load balancing works. One of the ways to do this is to visit websites that tell you what your public IP address is (just do a web search for "what is my IP address"), and keep refreshing the page. If you refresh the page multiple times, you should see your public IP address change. You may have to reload the page several times, however, since there may be other traffic on your network; in addition, you may have set the weights on your gateway group to heavily favor one interface above all others. Eventually, however, you should see your IP address change.

If your IP address never changes, make sure you are really reloading the page and not accessing the page from a cache (as may be the case if you are using a web proxy). Also, make sure that you don't have sticky connections enabled or some other option that enables persistent connections. Deleting your web cache, visiting different "what is my IP"-type sites, and trying different web browsers are good options to try before further troubleshooting load balancing.

Another way to test load balancing is to use the `traceroute` command. We will cover this command in greater detail in `Chapter 12`, *Troubleshooting pfSense*, but for now, you should know that it is a command that displays the route a packet takes to a site, while also displaying the transit delay at each step. It is available in Windows, Linux/BSD, and MacOS.

Finally, another possible issue is that your the default packet loss and latency settings are generating false positives (the opposite could also be true, and your connection could be down without pfSense detecting it, though this is less likely). In such cases, you need to navigate to **System | Routing**, and on the **Gateways** tab, edit the **Advanced Settings** for the gateway that is generating false positives. Increasing the **Time Period** over which results are averaged may help.

Summary

In this chapter, we discussed pfSense's multi-WAN capabilities, a continuation of our discussion of redundancy and high availability from the previous chapter. A multi-WAN setup with multiple internet connections enables us to achieve a level of reliability and bandwidth that would not be possible with a single connection. Moreover, pfSense makes it easy for us to switch between link aggregation/load balancing and failover. Setting up a multi-WAN gateway group entails several steps. In addition to creating the gateway groups, we must also configure DNS settings, create firewall rules to direct traffic to the gateway, and, if necessary, create NAT rules. In addition, special use cases may require additional steps; we covered one such use case (a multi-WAN setup with a CARP failover group).

In the next chapter, we will cover two basic concepts that you might not encounter in the typical home or small office/home office deployment, but become important in corporate deployments: routing and bridging, including a discussion of both static routing and dynamic routing via such protocols as the **Routing Information Protocol (RIP)** and the **Border Gateway Protocol (BGP)**.

Questions

Answer the following questions:

1. What document is provided by many ISPs that defines the aspects of service to be provided to the client?
2. What is policy-based routing?

3. (a) If we have two separate internet connections and we want to combine them for bandwidth aggregation, what form of redundancy and high availability should we use in our gateway group? (b) If we have two separate internet connections and we only want to use the secondary connection if the first one is down, what form of redundancy and high availability should we use?
4. What will happen if we configure a gateway group and do not add or change the firewall rules? Assume our setup is otherwise correct.
5. In a multi-WAN setup, under what circumstances must you add a static route for an external DNS server?
6. If we add multi-WAN capabilities to a CARP failover group, how many virtual IPs do we need to add?
7. What option can be used to ensure that all traffic to a certain website is routed through the same WAN interface as long as there are states that refer to the connection?
8. If you have set up a gateway group with load balancing and an external "what is my IP" website keeps reporting no change in your IP address, what could be the cause? Identify any three causes.

10
Routing and Bridging

Routing and bridging are functionally very similar, but they have significant differences. **Routing**, the process of moving packets between two or more networks, is one of the primary functions of a firewall, and most of them do a good enough job at it to make routing seem transparent. With a minimum of configuration, pfSense is able to route traffic between your local network (LAN) and the internet (WAN). Little additional configuration is needed to add other local networks. Firewalls, however, initially only know how to route traffic to the networks directly attached to them. For example, if you have a router connected to one of pfSense's internal networks, pfSense will not know how to route traffic to any nodes attached to the router unless you define a static route for it.

Bridging is not something that is done in typical network configurations. Bridges are connections between network segments. They allow us to extend a network beyond a single segment, while limiting broadcast traffic to a single segment so the network does not get overwhelmed by broadcast traffic. Normally, each interface is its own broadcast domain. It is often useful or necessary, however, to combine (or bridge) two interfaces so that they are within the same broadcast domain, similar to the way they would be if they were on the same switch. However, the difference between two bridged interfaces and a switch is that with bridged interfaces, firewall rules still apply. Thus, if you want traffic to pass between the two interfaces, you need to make sure the rules allow it.

This chapter will cover the following topics:

- Basic concepts
- Routing
- Bridging
- Troubleshooting

Technical requirements

To work through the examples in this chapter, you will need at least one fully functional pfSense router, and at least one other router. The other router does not have to be a pfSense router.

Basic concepts

This chapter deals with both bridging (which involves intra-network communications) and networking (which involves inter-network communications). Since bridging is the simpler concept, we will address this concept first.

Bridging

Network bridging takes place at layer 2 (the data link layer) of the OSI model. There are several different types of bridges. A simple bridge isn't much different from a repeater, except for the fact that the two network segments it connects may use different types of media (for example, one segment may use 100Base-T cabling and the other may use 1000Base-T) and the fact that bridges use a store-and-forward mechanism to forward packets, thus creating two separate collision domains.

A simple bridge forwards packets to the other side of the bridge, regardless of whether the destination host is on the other side. There are bridges known as transparent bridges, however, which are able to learn which side of the bridge hosts are on and use this information to decide whether or not to forward packets. Such bridges utilize a database which is initially empty. Packets are initially sent to both sides of the bridge regardless of the location of the target host. Gradually, however, a transparent bridge learns the location of hosts by observing which side of the bridge a host sends from, and as this information is entered into the database, the bridge will only forward packets to the other side of the bridge if the destination host is on the other side.

As an example of how a transparent bridge might work, imagine a bridge with three nodes: A, B, and C. Nodes A and B are on one side of the bridge, and C is on the other side. A begins a session with B. The bridge, not knowing initially that B is on the same side of the bridge as A, initially floods both sides of the bridge with B's packets.

When B replies, the bridge learns that B is on the same side of the bridge as A, and traffic will not be forwarded anymore. If B begins a session with C, the bridge will initially flood both sides with B's packets again, not knowing where C is. Once the bridge learns C's location, traffic between B and C will be sent across the bridge.

Bridges, though somewhat limited, are in the form of hubs and switches, still tremendously useful if we need to partition our networks. To demonstrate how this might work, let's revisit the example network from `Chapter 3`, *VLANs*. You might recall that we had separate DEVELOPERS and ENGINEERING departments, and we wanted to partition them into separate networks. In that chapter, we implemented separate developer and ENGINEERING networks as VLANs, as this option seemed to provide the greatest amount of flexibility, scalability and security. The following diagram shows how we might partition DEVELOPERS and ENGINEERING with stackable hubs or switches:

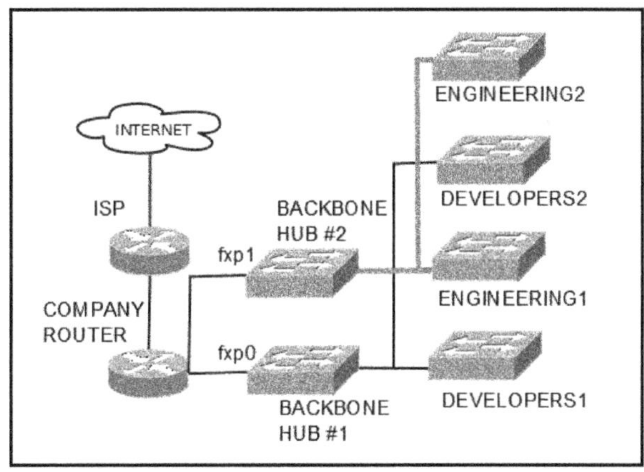

Network with stackable hubs

As you can see, the network has a multi-tier design. Instead of having DEVELOPERS and ENGINEERING on the same physical interface, but separate VLANs, in this setup, DEVELOPERS and ENGINEERING are on separate physical interfaces (**fxp0** and **fxp1**, respectively). Each network gets its own backbone hub, and each floor gets its own hub (or switch), and thus each floor forms a separate network segment.

This configuration isn't quite as good as the VLAN configuration we used earlier, but it does have several advantages:

- It can be implemented with unmanaged switches instead of managed switches. Unmanaged switches are typically far less expensive.

- It provides communication with nodes in the same department on different floors. At the same time, by partitioning the network in this way, we ensure that traffic between two nodes on the same floor does not reach the backbone hub. Thus, it does not affect users on different floors, which would not be the case if each network shared a single switch.
- Providing each network with its own backbone hub extends the total maximum distance between a node and the router. On a 1000BASE-T network, the maximum distance between devices is 100 meters. Thus, if a network has a single switch, and the switch connects to the router, then a node can be, at most, 200 meters from the router (100 meters to the switch and 100 meters between the switch and router). Adding a backbone hub extends the total possible distance between a node and the router by another 100 meters. Thus, it's like adding a repeater to the network.
- Another advantage of every network having its own hub is that if a hub/switch fails other than one of the backbones, the backbone hub will detect the problem and disable the port on the backbone to which it is connected. Thus the malfunctioning switch will not affect the rest of the network, while nodes on the same floor will still be able to communicate with each other.
- This setup is somewhat scalable; to add another network segment to one of the networks, we could plug another switch into the backbone hub for that network.
- This setup is relatively secure; DEVELOPERS and ENGINEERING are on separate networks and won't be able to communicate with each other unless we create firewall rules to allow it.

This setup still has its limitations. With VLANs, we could add another floor to our configuration simply by getting another managed switch and connecting it to one of the trunk ports on the previous floor's switch. In this setup, we can only add another floor if the total distance between the new switch and the backbone switch/hub is 100 meters or less. If not, we will have to add another backbone. Moreover, as you might recall, one of the advantages of VLANs is that we could make VLAN assignments based on MAC addresses, so we could move a node around, plug it into any available switch (as long as it's a managed switch), and the node will be assigned to the correct VLAN. With this setup, a node must be connected to a switch that is physically connected to the right interface for the network for the node to be assigned to the correct network. Still, it's a viable option if we don't anticipate much growth in our network and we don't have to move nodes around very often.

Our setup has a key weakness. The backbone hub for each network represents a single point of failure. For this reason, it is often desirable to introduce some redundancy into our network by adding backbones. The following diagram shows how this might work:

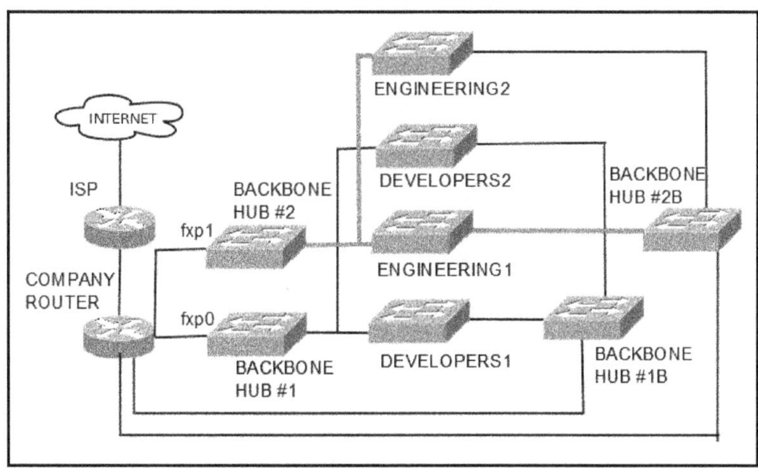

Improved network design with redundant backbone hubs

As you can see, we have added a redundant backbone hub to each network. This, however, creates a new problem. Assume that a node on **DEVELOPERS1** wants to start a session with a node on **DEVELOPERS2**. The switch for **DEVELOPERS1** generates two copies of each frame whose destination is the **DEVELOPERS2** node: one goes to **BACKBONE HUB #1** and the second to **BACKBONE HUB #1B**.

Then each of these hubs sends the frame to **DEVELOPERS2**. If there are only two segments on each network, it won't be too bad, but what if we add another segment (**DEVELOPERS3**)? The backbone hubs will not know whether the destination resides on **DEVELOPERS2** or **DEVELOPERS3**, so each of them will send a copy to both switches, generating a total of four frames. The number of frames generated from the original frame thus can grow exponentially fast, crashing the network. Even if the backbones are intelligent devices that have the capability of learning where nodes reside (for example, a transparent bridge), initially they don't know anything, at least until the destination node replies, so this problem exists whether our backbone is a simple hub, a switch, or a bridge.

Since we want to introduce redundancy into our network, but we don't want our network to crash, we are in need of a solution, and the solution in this case is a spanning tree protocol. With a spanning tree protocol, bridges communicate with each other in order to determine a spanning tree, a subset of the original network topology with no loops. The spanning tree algorithm is run, and certain interfaces are disconnected to create the spanning tree. If at some point one of the network devices fail, the spanning tree algorithm can be run again to determine which interfaces need to be activated to create a new spanning tree.

Since implementing a spanning tree is something you are likely to do if you implement multiple bridges on your network, it might be instructive to describe how **Spanning Tree Protocol** (**STP**), the oldest spanning tree protocol for bridges, works.

We will use the following network to illustrate the process:

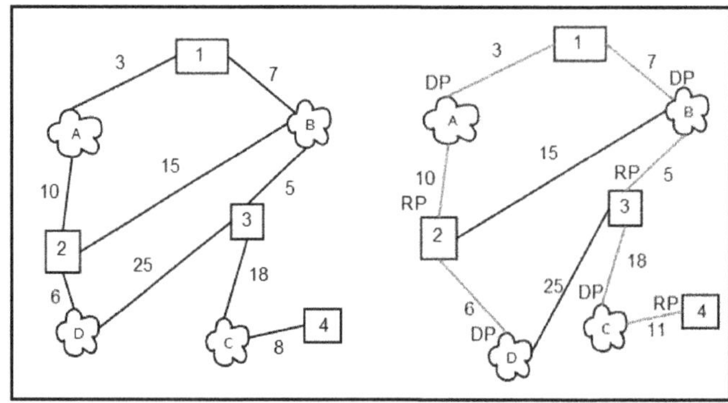

A simple network which illustrates STP. Digits represent bridges and letters represent nodes.

The diagram on the left represents the network before the spanning tree calculation. As you can see, we have a network with several bridges (represented by boxes) and several network segments (represented by clouds). The numbers in the boxes are the bridge IDs. Assume that each network segment has a cost metric of 1. A spanning tree is formed as follows:

1. First, a root bridge is chosen. The root bridge is the bridge with the lowest bridge ID. In our example network, it is bridge **1**.
2. Second, each bridge determines the least-cost path to the root bridge. The cost of traversing a path is the sum of the cost metrics of each segment on the path. The port, which provides a path to the least-cost path to the root bridge for each bridge, is designated the **root port** (**RP**).

3. Next, the bridges determine the least-cost path from each network segment to the root bridge. The port connecting each segment to each path is designated as the **designated port** (**DP**) for that network segment.
4. Finally, each port that is neither a RP nor a DP becomes a blocked port, and thus is not part of the spanning tree.

The diagram on the right illustrates the spanning tree after RPs and DPs have been determined. The spanning tree is outlined in red. All ports not connected to a red segment are blocked. We arrive at the spanning tree as follows:

1. We designate bridge **1** as the root bridge.
2. We determine the least-cost path from bridge **2** to bridge **1**. The path that runs through segment **A** has a cost of 13; the path that runs through segment **B** has a cost of 22; the path that runs through segment **D** has a cost of 38. We add the segments connecting 2 and **A** and **A** and 1 to the spanning tree.
3. We determine the least-cost path from bridge **3** to bridge **1**. The path that runs through segment **B** has a cost of 12; the path that runs through segment **D** has a cost of 44 (the cost of the segments we would have to add to the spanning tree, however, are what we are concerned with, and these add up to 31). We add the segments connecting **3** and **B** and **B** and **1** to the spanning tree.
4. We determine the least-cost path from bridge **4** to bridge **1**. Since there is only one active port on bridge **4**, our choice is forced, so we add the segment connecting **4** and **C** to the spanning tree. The only other port on connecting **C** to the rest of the network is the one that connects **C** to **3**, so we add the segment connecting **C** to **3** to the spanning tree.
5. The ports between **2** and **A**, **3** and **B**, and **4** and **C** are RPs.
6. We determine the least-cost paths from each network segment to bridge **1**. The least-cost path from **A** to **1**, **B** to **1**, and **C** to **1** are already part of the spanning tree. The ports connecting each network segment to bridge **1** are marked as designated ports. **D** is not in the spanning tree. The path that runs through bridge **2** has a cost of 19; the path that runs through bridge **3** has a cost of 37. We add the segment from **D** to **2** to the spanning tree and the port connecting **D** to **2** is marked as a DP.
7. All other ports are blocked. The spanning tree has been calculated.

Routing

Routing takes place on layer 3 (the network layer) of the OSI model. Whereas switches are store-and-forward devices that use MAC addresses, routers are store-and-forward devices that use IP addresses. Routers (and layer 3 switches, which also act as routers but lack some of the advanced functionality of routers) allow us to move data between networks. A router is responsible for maintaining tables of information about other routers on the network, and there are several different protocols available to enable a router to learn the topology of the network.

Often, the decision whether to use a hub/switch or a router is based on practical concerns. For example, in our hypothetical DEVELOPERS/ENGINEERING network, we could replace the backbone hubs with routers. Instead of dividing the networks into separate segments, now DEVELOPERS1 and DEVELOPERS2 and ENGINEERING1/2 are completely separate networks. A router can do everything a hub or a switch would, but it also has some additional functionality, such as firewall capabilities, and the ability to use the shortest path to a node. This can be useful in some cases. In our example network, we may want to allow traffic between DEVELOPERS1 and DEVELOPERS2, but each floor may have a printer that should only be accessible to users on the same floor. We could create a rule which only allows users on DEVELOPERS1 to access printers on DEVELOPERS1, and only allow users on DEVELOPERS2 to access printers on DEVELOPERS2, something we couldn't do with switches.

There are two types of routing with which we are concerned:

- **Static routing**: A static route is a routing entry which is manually entered into the routing table. Sometimes, it is necessary to add a static route. For example, we may have a network that is not directly connected to pfSense, in which case pfSense will not know where to send traffic which has this network as its destination. A router which relies solely on static routes is not very fault tolerant and cannot detect changes on the network. We thus seek something better, and that brings us to a second type of routing.
- **Dynamic routing**: As the name implies, this is implemented by dynamically configuring routing tables. The means by which this is done is through dynamic routing protocols such as **Routing Information Protocol** (**RIP**) and **Open Shortest Path First** (**OSPF**). Both of these protocols work on layer 3 of the OSI model. We can divide routing protocols into two categories:

- **Distance-vector routing protocols**: This class of routing protocols requires that a router inform only its neighbors of topology changes. Paths are calculated using algorithms such as the Bellman–Ford algorithm, the Ford–Fulkerson algorithm, or DUAL FSM. This method is effective in finding the shortest path to another router. One of the problems with this method, however, is that some of the paths could be infinite loops, as with a distance-vector protocol; there is no way to know if a path includes the router itself. Two ways of dealing with this problem are split-horizon and split-horizon with poison reverse. Split-horizon simply prevents a router from advertising a route back to the router from which it learned the route. Thus, if A is connected to B, and B is connected to both A and C, and if the link between B and C is down, we don't have to worry about B using A's route to C (which runs through B), because A learned the route from B. Thus, we are spared from packets being caught in an infinite loop between B and A (B sends packets whose destination is C to A, A sends the packets back to B, and the process repeats, resulting in an infinite loop.) Another method is split-horizon with poison-reverse, in which a router advertises a route back to the router from which it learned the route, but sets the route metric to infinity. Examples of distance-vector protocols are RIPv1 and RIPv2, and the **Interior Gateway Routing Protocol** (**IGRP**).
- **Link-state routing protocols**: This class of routing protocols involves every router constructing a map (in the form of a graph) of its connectivity to the network, not just its neighbors. Each router then independently calculates the best path from it to every other router, and these paths form the device's routing table. These protocols have some advantages over distance-vector protocols. Each router has a complete map of the network, so troubleshooting is much easier. Moreover, loops are less likely, since routers know which other routers through which a route runs. Changes in the network tend to be detected more quickly. There are several disadvantages to link-state protocols as well.

The database constructed of paths to other routers requires more memory and processor power than a distance-vector routing protocol table would, although the database size can be minimized with careful design. Furthermore, the initial discovery process generates a great deal of network traffic, and can significantly degrade network performance during this period. An example of a link-state routing protocol is OSPF.

There are several protocols available for dynamic routing. These include:

- **RIP**: This is one of the oldest and one of the most popular distance-vector routing protocols. The original specification (RIPv1) used classful routing, and since the routing updates had no subnet information, all subnets had to be the same size within a network class. The distance between routers was called a **hop**, and RIPv1 allowed a maximum of 15 hops. 16 hops represented infinity (an unreachable route). There was also no support for router authentication. Updates were done through broadcast packets. RIPv2 improved upon the original protocol in many respects, introducing support for classless routing, and using multicasts to send the routing table. MD5 authentication was also introduced. The maximum hop count, however, remained at 15, in order to maintain compatibility with RIPv1. The latest version of RIP, **RIP next generation** (**RIPng**), supports IPv6 networking.
- **OSPF**: This is a link-state protocol that monitors the network for routers whose link state has changed (turned on, turned off, or restarted). It uses the link-state information to construct a topology map of the network.
- **IGRP**: A proprietary distance-vector protocol developed by Cisco to deal with the limitations of RIP. The maximum hop count is 255, and there can be multiple metrics for each route. Like RIPv1, it is a classful routing protocol, and all addresses within a certain address class must have the same subnet mask.
- **Enhanced Interior Gateway Routing Protocol (EIGRP)**: An update to IGRP which supports classless routing. In addition, rather than sending the entire routing table to neighboring routers, EIGRP only sends incremental updates. EIGRP started out as a proprietary protocol, but parts of it were converted to an open standard in 2013.
- **Border Gateway Protocol (BGP)**: A distance-vector protocol used for routing within an autonomous system. It uses TCP as its transport protocol.

Routing

For the most part, pfSense does routing transparently. If a node on the local network is attempting to send a packet to a node on a local network, pfSense will send it to the right network, assuming that the network is directly attached to pfSense. If a node on the local network is attempting to send a packet to a remote network, pfSense will send it to a gateway. There are some special cases, however, and we will discuss them in this section.

Static routes

When we have local networks that are reachable through a router other than pfSense's default gateway, we need to configure a static route. A simple example of this situation is a router that is connected to the LAN network. The following diagram illustrates this scenario:

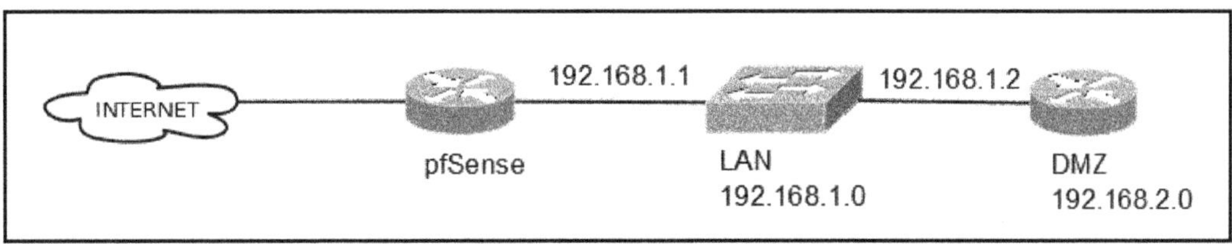

The DMZ network is not directly connected to pfSense and thus requires a static route

In this scenario, the LAN interface has a static IP address of `192.168.1.1`. The DMZ router is connected to the LAN switch and DMZ's WAN interface has an IP address of `192.168.1.2`. DMZ is not directly connected to pfSense, and the DMZ network is not reachable through pfSense's default gateway. Therefore, it is necessary to define a static route.

Setting up a static route for the `192.168.2.0` network involves first adding `192.168.1.2` as a new gateway, and then adding a new static route which has `192.168.1.2` as its gateway:

1. To begin, first navigate to **System** | **Routing**.
2. On the **Gateway** tab, click on the **Add** button. On the gateway configuration page, select the correct interface in the **Interface** drop-down box. This should match the interface on which the gateway resides (in our example, it would be **LAN**).
3. Type a name in the **Name** edit box.

4. In the **Gateway** edit box, enter the gateway IP address (again, in our example, it would be `192.168.1.2`).
5. Leave the **Default Gateway** checkbox unchecked.
6. You may want to enter an IP for monitoring the gateway in the **Monitor IP** edit box; this way, the gateway can be marked as down if it does not respond to pings from this address.
7. You can enter a brief description in the **Description** field; then click on **Save**.
8. And on the main **Routing** page, click on the **Apply Changes** button.
9. Next, click on the **Static Routes** tab and click on the **Add** button to add a new static route.
10. In the **Destination network** edit box, enter the network that will be reached by this static route (in this example, it would be `192.168.2.0`). Don't forget to select the appropriate CIDR in the adjacent drop-down box (in this example, it would be **24**).
11. In the **Gateway** drop-down box, select the gateway you created in the first step.
12. You can enter a description in the **Description** field, and then click on the **Save** button.

pfSense now knows a route to the DMZ router, but there is still a problem with our configuration. To illustrate this problem, imagine there is a node attached to the LAN switch. Assume that this node has an IP address of `192.168.1.3`. This node wants to establish a session with a node on the DMZ router (assume the destination node has an IP address of `192.168.2.3`).

The LAN node's default gateway is `192.168.1.1` (the LAN interface IP), so it sends packets destined for the DMZ node to pfSense, which in turn uses the static route to send the packets to the DMZ network via the `192.168.1.2` gateway. pfSense also adds a state table entry for this connection. The DMZ node receives the packets from the LAN node, and sends a reply, which is sent out through the DMZ router's gateway `(192.168.1.2)`. Since the destination is on the LAN network, the return traffic is never filtered by pfSense, as pfSense only filters traffic between networks, not intra-network traffic. Since as far as pfSense is concerned, the connection was never completed, the entry gets dropped from the state table, and the connection between the LAN node and the DMZ node is dropped.

Another scenario in which you may have a problem is with ICMP redirects, which are sent by a gateway when the gateway knows a more direct route to the destination host. If the sending node allows ICMP redirects, their routing table will temporarily add the new route. For example, NODE 1 tries to establish a session with NODE 2. This request goes through its default gateway (`192.168.1.1`) and reaches the pfSense box. pfSense, realizing there is a more direct route to NODE 2 via `192.168.1.2`, sends an ICMP redirect back to NODE 1, informing it of the more direct route, but sends the initial TCP SYN packet to NODE 2 via the static route, and creates a state table entry for the connection. However, all subsequent communication between NODE 1 and NODE 2 takes place through `192.168.1.2`, and pfSense does not see this traffic, since it is intra-network traffic. The state table entry created for the connection expires and is deleted. If the ICMP redirect-learned route of NODE 1 expires before the session ends, NODE 1 will send the next packet destined for NODE 2 to pfSense. Since it is not a packet establishing a new connection, pfSense will reject it, and the connection between NODE 1 and NODE 2 will be dropped.

There are two possible ways of dealing with these types of scenarios. The first is to navigate to **System** | **Advanced**, click on the **Firewall & NAT** tab, and under **Firewall Advanced**, check the **Static route filtering** checkbox. If this option is enabled, and one or more static routes have been defined, then traffic that enters and leaves through the same interface will not be checked by pfSense. This applies to our example, since traffic between NODE 1 and NODE 2 enters and leaves through the LAN interface.

Enabling this option will get the job done, but it will apply to all cases where traffic enters and leaves through the same interface, not just this one. Ideally, we want a rule that only applies to interfaces that have static routes to them. So, the second option is to create two rules: a rule on the interface through which the static route passes, and a floating rule to cover the return traffic.

To create the first rule, navigate to **Firewall** | **Rules** and click on the tab of whichever interface through which the static route passes (in the case of the example, **LAN**). Make sure the **Action** drop-down box is set to **Pass** and the **Protocol** drop-down box is set to **TCP**. **Source** should be set to match the setting in the **Interface** drop-down box (**LAN net**), since states only become an issue when the packets are sent and received through this interface. For **Destination**, choose **Single host or alias** in the drop-down box and in the adjacent edit box, specify the IP address of the static route's gateway (in this case, `192.168.1.2`). Scroll down to the **Extra Options** section and click on the **Show Advanced** button.

In the **Advanced** section, set the **TCP Flags** option to **Any Flags** (the rule will match regardless of what TCP flags are set or not set). In the **State type** drop-down box, select **Sloppy** (this performs a less strict state match on return traffic). When you have finished making changes, click on the **Save** button. This rule should be placed at the top of the firewall rules table for this interface to ensure it gets applied.

Next, you have to make a floating rule for the return traffic. Click on the **Floating** tab and click on the **Add** button. Make sure the **Action** column is set to **Pass** and in the **Interface** listbox, make sure the same interface selected in the first rule is selected (in our case, **LAN**). The direction set in the **Direction** drop-down box should be set to **out**, and **Protocol** should be set to **TCP**. Reversing source and destination from the previous rule, we set **Source** to `192.168.1.2` and **Destination** to **LAN net**. Again, scroll down to **Extra Options**, click on the **Show Advanced** button, scroll down, set **TCP Flags** to **Any Flags,** and set **State type** to **Sloppy**. When you have finished click on **Save**, and on the main floating rules page, click on the **Apply Changes** button. You now have rules covering traffic in both directions.

There is another potential issue with this setup that we haven't addressed yet. Once we set up the static route and add appropriate rules to take into account the asymmetrical nature of traffic between LAN and DMZ, nodes on the two networks should be able to connect to each other. But if a node on DMZ tries to access the internet, it will likely fail; because the default *allow LAN (or an alias with specifically defined networks) to any* rule only works for traffic whose source is the LAN net. While this result may be consistent with your intended policy (you may want to keep nodes on DMZ from accessing the internet), if you want to allow this network to access the Internet, you will have to alter the **Source** setting on the default *allow LAN (or alias) to any* rule to allow traffic with a source of any.

Public IP addresses behind a firewall

Another scenario that is common enough to warrant discussion is when you have one or more public IP addresses on an internal interface. In this scenario, you will have at least two public IP addresses: one for the WAN interface of your firewall, and another for the internal interface. More commonly, you might have an entire subnet allocated to you by your ISP, but the steps discussed here apply whether you are assigned a single IP address or a subnet. This configuration has four steps:

1. WAN configuration
2. Internal interface configuration
3. Outbound NAT configuration
4. Firewall rule configuration

As an example, assume that our ISP has assigned us several IPs: an IP for the ISP-provided router that is directly connected to the internet, an IP for the WAN interface of pfSense, and a block of eight IPs (six of which are usable) which can be used by an interface that is internal to our network. The IP assignment is as follows:

IP address	Description
`192.0.10.10`	ISP router IP address
`192.0.10.11`	pfSense WAN interface IP
`192.0.20.0/29`	Public IPs on an internal interface

1. The first step is to set up the WAN interface:
    1. This you can do by navigating to **Interfaces** | **WAN**. Your WAN interface may be directly connected to the internet, but more likely your ISP provided you a router, which is directly connected to the internet.
    2. In this case, the IP address of this router will be your WAN gateway IP. If your ISP assigned an IP address for pfSense's WAN interface, choose **Static IPv4** (or **Static IPv6** if it is an IPv6 address) as your configuration type, and enter the assigned IP address in the appropriate edit box.
    3. Specify the upstream router's IP address in the **IPv4 Upstream gateway** (and/or **IPv6 Upstream gateway**); you may have to use the **Add a new gateway** button if you have not yet added the upstream router as a gateway. If you haven't, then press this button and enter the information in the corresponding dialog box.
    4. Next, you need to configure the internal interface.
    5. If you haven't added it yet, navigate to **Interfaces** | **(assign)** and add an interface by selecting an available interface from the **Available network ports** drop-down box, and clicking on the **Add** button to the right of the drop-down box.
    6. Click on the name of the interface (for example, **OPT1**) and begin configuration. If you have already added the interface, you can navigate directly to its configuration page.

7. On the interface's configuration page, you must check the **Enable** checkbox, and you can optionally change the name of the interface in the **Description** edit box.
8. The configuration type should be set to **Static** (either **Static IPv4**, **Static IPv6**, or both).
9. Enter one of the public IP addresses assigned by your ISP in the appropriate edit box. In our example, this would be `192.0.20.1/29`. We were assigned a /29 subnet, which gives us six usable IP addresses (2^3 – 2 = 6). One IP address is assigned to the interface, and five IP addresses are available for internal hosts that require public IP addresses.
10. When you have finished making changes, click on the **Save** button at the bottom of the page and click on the **Apply Changes** button when the page reloads.

2. The next step is outbound NAT configuration. By default, outbound traffic on internal interfaces is translated to the WAN IP, and we want to disable this behavior:
   1. To do this, navigate to **Firewall** | **NAT** and click on the **Outbound** tab.
   2. Under **General Logging Options**, select the **Manual Outbound NAT** rule generation radio button, and click on the **Save** button.
   3. Now you should be able to add, edit and delete the mappings. In the **Mappings** tab, look for an autocreated rule for the internal interface to which a public IP address has been assigned (for example, **Autocreated rule – OPT1 to WAN**).
   4. Since we don't want to map outbound traffic on this interface to the WAN IP, delete this rule.
   5. Then click on **Apply Changes** on the main **NAT** page.
3. The last step is firewall rule configuration. Since users on the internet trying to reach the public IPs on the internal interface will be coming in through the WAN interface, at a minimum you will have to create a rule on the WAN interface to allow traffic to pass to one or more of the public IPs.

   For example, if we are hosting a web server on `192.0.20.2`, we would create a rule on the WAN interface with **Action** set to **Pass**, **Protocol** set to **TCP**, **Source** set to **any**, and **Destination** set to **Single Host or alias** with the source address set to `192.0.20.2` and **Port** set to `80`.

You will likely also want to create rules for the internal interface. For example, you'll probably want to block access to local networks, and possibly create a rule allowing access to the WAN interface, thus allowing connections to the internet. You could also create a more restrictive rule (for example, only allow outbound connections on port `80`).

Dynamic routing

Dynamic routing isn't natively supported in pfSense, but there are several third-party packages available, which provide dynamic routing capabilities. The following table lists these packages:

Package name	Routing protocol supported
OpenBGPD	BGP
Quagga OSPF	OSPF, BGP and RIP (via the Zebra daemon)
routed	RIP v1 and v2
FRR	BGP and OSPF (RIP supported by the Zebra daemon, but not directly configurable in the web GUI)

The Optimized Link State Routing Protocol had been available as a package, but it is no longer available as of version 2.3. Nonetheless, pfSense makes it possible to utilize both distance-vector protocols (OpenBGPD, routed, Quagga OSPF, and FRR) and link-state protocols (Quagga OSPF and FRR).

RIP

The routed package is actually just a frontend to the routed daemon for FreeBSD. To install routed in pfSense, navigate to **System** | **Packages**, scroll down to the table listing for routed, click on the **Add** icon for the package, and on the next page, click on the **Confirm** button. Routed should install in about two minutes or less.

To begin using routed, navigate to **Services** | **RIP**. There you will find a number of configuration options for the RIP daemon. Checking the **Enable RIP** checkbox enables the RIP daemon. The **Interfaces** listbox allows you to select the interfaces to which RIP will bind, so any interfaces that provide a path to another RIP-enabled router should be selected. The **RIP Version** drop-down box allows you to choose between **RIP Version 1** and **RIP Version 2**; the RIP daemon will advertise and listen using whichever version is selected. The **RIPv2 password** edit box allows you to specify an RIP v2 password. The **no_ag** checkbox, if checked, turns off aggregation of subnets in RIP responses, while **no_super_ag** turns off aggregation of networks into super-networks. When you have finished making changes, click on the **Save** button at the bottom of the page.

OpenBGPD

OpenBGPD is a daemon that implements BGP. To install it, navigate to **System** | **Packages**, click on the **Add** icon next to the OpenBGPD entry, and click on the **Confirm** button on the next page.

You can begin OpenBGPD configuration by navigating to **Services** | **OpenBGPD**. You should see several configuration tabs. The first one is **Settings**. The **Autonomous Systems (AS) Number** edit box allows you to set the local autonomous system number. The **Holdtime** edit box allows you to define the time (in seconds) a session with a neighboring OpenBGPD router is kept active without receiving either a KEEPALIVE or UPDATE message from the neighbor. The **fib-update** drop-down box allows you to choose whether to update the Forwarding Information Base (the kernel routing table).

In the **Listen on IP** edit box, you can specify the local IP address the BGP daemon should listen on. Leaving this field blank causes the daemon to bind to all IPs. In the **Router IP** edit box, you can set the router IP (it must be local to pfSense). In the **CARP Status IP** edit box, you can specify the IP address for determining the CARP status. If your router is in BACKUP status for the interface to which the IP address corresponds, then the BGP daemon will not start. Finally, in the **Networks** edit box, you can specify a network to be announced as belonging to the AS. You can set this field to (**inet** | **inet6**) connected to announce all IPv4 or IPv6 directly attached networks, or (**inet** | **inet6**) static to announce all IPv4 or IPv6 static routes.

The next tab, **Neighbors**, allows you to add neighboring routers. Clicking on the **Add** button below the table to the right allows you to add another router. On the configuration page, you can enter a description in the **Description** edit box. The **Neighbor** edit box is where you enter the neighbor's IP address. In the **TCP-MD5 key** edit box, enter the MD5 key for communicating with the peer. This does not work with Cisco routers, however; for Cisco routers, enter a value in the **TCP-MD5 password** edit box. The **Group** drop-down box allows you to add the neighbor to a BGP group; such a group must be defined by adding a group at the **Group** tab. Finally, the **Neighbor parameters setting** drop-down box allows you to set parameters on the neighbor router. Some of the parameters have associated numeric values that can be set; if they do, the **Value** edit box will become enabled when they are selected. To add a parameter to set, click on the **Add** button; you can add more than one parameter this way. When you have finished making changes, click on the **Save** button.

On the **Groups** tab, you can define groups into which neighboring routers can be placed. To add a group, click on the **Add** button below the table to the right. On the group configuration page, you must enter a name in the **Name** edit box. In the **Remote AS** edit box, you must enter an AS for the group. You can enter a brief non-parsed description in the **Description** edit box. Finally, there is a **Save** button for saving changes and a **Cancel** button for discarding changes.

The **Raw config** tab allows you to manually edit the `bgpd.conf` file. But be warned: whatever changes you make to `bgpd.conf` here will override any changes you make on the **Settings**, **Neighbors** and **Groups** tabs. At the bottom of the page, there are two buttons: the **Save** button saves `bgpd.conf`, while **Cancel** discards any changes. Finally, the **Status** tab provides information about the OpenBGP daemon as it runs.

Quagga OSPF

Another way of adding link-state routing capabilities to pfSense is to install Quagga OSPF. This OSPF implementation is available as a package and can be installed via **System | Packages** in the same manner as the other packages described in this chapter. One warning included in the package description, however, is that Quagga OSPF is installed in the same location as OpenBGPD; installing both will break things. Therefore, it is recommended that you not install OpenBGPD if you have Quagga OSPF installed, and if you are going to install Quagga OSPF and you have OpenBGPD installed, you should uninstall OpenBGPD first.

Once you have it installed, you can navigate to **Services** | **Quagga OSPFd** and begin configuration. The first tab is **Global Settings**. You must enter the password for the Zebra and OSPFd daemons in the **Master Password** edit box. The **Logging** checkbox, if checked, will cause OSPF information to be written to the syslog. The **Log Adjacency Changes** checkbox allows you to have the OSPF daemon write adjacency changes to the syslog. The **Router ID** edit box is where you specify the router ID for this router. The router ID is customarily written in the dotted decimal format in which IP addresses are written (for example, `1.1.1.1`). The router ID, although usually expressed in dotted decimal notation, does not represent an actual IP address. Moreover, expressing the router ID in dotted decimal notation is optional.

The **Area** edit box is where you enter the OSPFd area. What distinguishes an OSPF area is that it has its own link-state database. Areas, like Router ID, are usually expressed in IPv4 (dotted decimal) format, but they do not have to be formatted in this way. The **Disable FIB updates** checkbox, if checked, will turn the router into a stub router. Such routers only receive route advertisements within the **autonomous system** (**AS**).

Checking **Redistribute connected subnets** enables the redistribution of connected networks. The **Redistribute default route** checkbox, if checked, enables the redistribution of a default route to pfSense. Checking **Redistribute static** enables the redistribution of static routes if you are using Quagga static routes, whereas checking **Redistribute Kernel** enables redistribution of the kernel routing table and is required if you are using pfSense static routes.

The **SPF Hold Time** field is where you can specify the SPF hold time in milliseconds; this specifies the minimum time between two consecutive shortest path first calculations. The default value is 5 seconds. The **SPF Delay** field is where you can specify the SPF delay, also in milliseconds; this is the delay between receiving an update to the link-state database and starting the shortest path first calculation. The default value is **1** second.

Checking the **RFC 1583 compatible** checkbox will cause decisions regarding AS-external routes to be evaluated according to RFC 1583. Without RFC 1583 compatibility, intra-area routes will always be favored over inter-area routes, regardless of the metric costs. Enabling RFC 1583 compatibility will cause OSPF to learn routes based on costs.

The next section allows you to generate rules for certain areas that will take precedence over any redistribute options otherwise specified on the page. You need to specify the subnet to the route and the area ID, and for each entry, you can disable redistribution and disable acceptance. Click on the **Add** button to add an entry. Finally, the **CARP Status IP** edit box allows you to specify the IP address used to determine the CARP status. This is similar to the identical setting in OpenBGPD, where if the IP address specified has a status of BACKUP, then OSPF will be disabled. When you have finished making changes, click on the **Save** button.

The **Interface Settings** tab is where you specify which interfaces will send and receive OSPF data. Click on the **Add** button below the table and to the right to add a new interface. On the **Interface Settings** configuration page there are several settings. The **Interface** drop-down box is where you specify the desired participating interface. The **Network Type** drop-down box allows you to specify the OSPF network type of the interface. The allowed values are:

- **Broadcast**: This is the most efficient way of making OSPF data available to a large number of routers. Running OSPF in broadcast mode requires the election of a **designated router** (**DR**) and **backup designated router** (**BDR**) with which all non-designated routers will form an adjacency. This keeps the number of adjacencies from becoming too large.
- **Non-Broadcast**: This router will be able to receive OSPF data, but won't make it available to other routers.
- **Point-to-Multipoint**: This sends OSPF data to a collection of point-to-point networks. It does not require having a DR or BDR.
- **Point-to-Point**: This sends OSPF data to one router at a time.

Note that non-broadcast and point-to-multipoint are the only two modes officially supported by OSPF (defined in RFC 2328); broadcast and point-to-point modes were defined by Cisco for use in **non-broadcast** (**NMBA**) networks.

In the **Metric** edit box, you can enter the cost for the OSPF interface. In the **Area** edit box, you can specify the area for this interface. You may enter a brief description in the **Description** edit box. Checking the **Interface is Passive** checkbox prevents the transmission and receiving of OSPF packets on the interface, thus making the interface appear as a stub network. Checking the **Accept Filter** checkbox will result in the OSPF daemon not adding routes for this interface subnet from OSPF into the routing table, which is helpful in multi-WAN environments. The **Enable MD5 password** checkbox, if checked, will enable the use of an MD5 password on this interface. If it is checked, you will have to specify a password in the next field.

In the **Router Priority** edit box, you can specify the router priority in a DR election. The default is **1**. In the **Hello Interval** edit box, you can specify the interval (in seconds) at which *Hello* discovery packets are sent out. The default is **10** seconds. In the **Retransmit Interval** edit box, you can specify the retransmit interval in seconds. The default is **5** seconds. Finally, in the **Dead Timer** edit box, you can specify the dead timer, which is the interval at which OSPF will check to see if a neighbor is still alive. The default is **40** seconds.

As with OpenBGPD, there is a **Raw Config** tab where you can edit the OSPF config files manually. On this tab, you can also enter the physical IP address and virtual IP address of interfaces along with an MD5 password for each interface. Enter the physical address in the edit box labeled **Source Address (this FW)**; enter the CARP virtual IP for the interface in the edit box labeled **Peer Address**, and enter the password in the third edit box in the row (currently unlabeled). Click on the **Add** button when you have finished; repeat the process for as many CARP virtual IPs as you have. The textbox labeled **SAVED ospfd.conf** is where you can make changes to `ofpfd.conf`. The textbox labeled **RUNNING ospfd.conf** shows a copy of the current `ospfd.conf`. The **Copy OSPFd Running to Saved** button copies the contents of the first textbox into the second, which ensures any configuration changes you made are saved. In a similar way, there are textboxes for **SAVED ofpf6d.conf** and **RUNNING ospfd6.conf**, and a **Copy OSPF6d Running to Save** button to save changes. The `ospfd.conf` config file is for the Open Shortest Path First daemon that supports OSPF version 2, and the `ofpf6d.conf` config file is for the OSPF daemon that supports version 3 (which is currently the only version that supports IPv6). There are similar textboxes and buttons for `bgpd.conf` (the config file for the BGP daemon) and `zebra.conf` (the Zebra daemon, a routing daemon which supports RIP, BGP and OSPF).

Finally, the **Status** tab aggregates information about the OSPF daemon as it runs. It provides a summary of data for the OSPF Dameon, the BGP Dameon, and the Zebra daemon, including routes associated with each of them.

FRRouting

The **FRRouting** (**FRR**) package, available for pfSense since late 2017, supports BGP, OSPF, and OSPF6. It is intended as a replacement for both OpenBGPD and Quagga OSPF, and allows pfSense users to run both BGPD and OSPF simultaneously. It can be configured both from the web GUI and from the command line.

If you install FRR, pfSense will automatically uninstall OpenBGPD and Quagga OSPF, if either of these packages are already installed. Once FRR is installed, there will be four new options on the **Services** menu: **FRR BGP**, **FRR Global/Zebra**, **FRR OSPF**, and **FRR OSPF6**. The different menu options can also be accessed by clicking on the identically marked tabs on the pages for each option. For example, to access FRR Global/Zebra from FRR BGP, you can navigate to **Services** | **FRR Global/Zebra** or click on the **[Global]** tab. To navigate back to FRR BGP from FRR Global/Zebra, either navigate to **Services** | **FRR BGP** or click on the **[BGP]** tab.

FRRouting contains many of the functions of OpenBGPD and Quagga OSPF. It supports the same protocols, and allows you to edit the config files of each of the daemons. It also has some features not previously available. For example, the FRR BGP configuration page has a section called **Network Distribution**, which among other things, allows you to redistribute OSPF routes to BGP neighbors. There are also many advanced options, such as **Best Path Selection**. The OSPF options are similar to those found in Quagga OSPF. The **Global Settings**, however, support both access lists and prefix lists, which allow you to allow or deny certain networks or parts of networks in specific contexts used by the routing daemons. You can also view the status of each daemon on a separate page. FRRouting is an ideal choice if you anticipate running both BGP and OSPF at the same time.

Policy-based routing

Policy routing, also known as policy-based routing, refers to cases where the routing of traffic is based on criteria other than the destination network. A variety of criteria can be used to determine what route traffic takes, such as source or destination network, source or destination address or port, protocol, packet size, and many others. Basically, any criteria which can form the basis of a firewall rule can form the basis of policy routing. It is used often in multi-WAN setups, in cases where we want to direct traffic to a specific WAN interface based on certain criteria, but there are other cases where we might want to use policy routing as well.

You may recall in previous chapters, we sometimes had occasion to create a rule which directed traffic to a gateway other than the default gateway. We can use this ability to choose a gateway to implement policy routing. The process can be summarized as follows:

1. Create one or more alternate gateways
2. Create a firewall rule specifying certain criteria (the *policy* part of policy routing)
3. Select a gateway to which traffic matching the rule will be sent

Since we already discussed policy-based routing in the previous chapter, we will not get involved in a detailed discussion here, but it might be helpful to provide an example. Assume that we have a multi-WAN setup. WAN is our default gateway, but WAN2 provides a gateway to a secondary internet connection. We want to use WAN2 for video streaming with the **Real-Time Transport Protocol** (**RTP**) from the LAN network. The video streaming client will always be using port `554` to send video, and will utilize UDP only. We will also be using port `555` for the **Real-Time Control Protocol** (**RTCP**), which monitors the RTP session, but we do not need to re-route this traffic.

The first step is to navigate to **System** | **Routing** and confirm that WAN2 is already configured as a gateway (on the **Gateways** tab). As you may recall from our previous discussion of gateway groups, WAN-type interfaces that are configured to get their IP address from an upstream DHCP server are automatically configured as gateways. If not, we must click on the **Add** button and create a WAN2 gateway. The **Interface** drop-down box should be WAN2 and the interface's IP address should be entered in the **Gateway** edit box. You must also enter a name in the **Name** field; you may enter a brief description in the **Description** field as well. Click on **Save** when you have finished making changes and click on **Apply Changes** on the main routing page.

Next, navigate to **Firewall** | **Rules** and click on the **LAN** tab. In cases where we need to implement policy routing on multiple interfaces and/or in both directions, then creating a floating rule would be more appropriate. Since we only need to redirect traffic in one direction and on a single interface, however, we will not create a floating rule. Click on the **Add** button on the **LAN** tab to create a new rule.

On the rule configuration page, keep the **Action** column as **Pass** and **Interface** as **LAN**. Change **Protocol** to **UDP**. Since the traffic's source will be the LAN net, choose **LAN net** in the **Source** drop-down box. Set Destination port range to `554`.

We have correctly set the matching criteria; now we just have to select a gateway. Click on the **Show Advanced** button, then scroll down the page, and in the **Advanced Options** section, the **Gateway** option should be third from the bottom.

Select the **WAN2** gateway in the drop-down box. You could also use **Ackqueue/ Queue** to assign the traffic to a high-priority queue if you have traffic shaping configured. You can enter a description in the **Description** field for your own reference (for example, **Policy routing for video streaming client**), and click on the **Save** button). On the main rules page, make sure the newly created rule appears in the table before the `default allow LAN to any` rule, as well as any other rule which would match the traffic. If it does not appear before these rules, drag it above them, then click on the **Apply Changes** button. We have now implemented a form of policy routing for our video streaming client.

This is just a single example of policy routing; there are many other real-world applications for such routing. Another example might be if we had a web cache proxy on another router, and directed all of our HTTP and HTTPS traffic on ports `80` and `443` to this router. Also, our example demonstrated how to use pfSense for policy routing, but in a real-world scenario, such tasks might be delegated to a policy-based routing-aware level three switch.

Bridging

In some cases, a single broadcast domain is formed by combining two or more interfaces. Two ports on your pfSense router act as if they are on the same switch, except that the firewall rules are used to control the traffic between the interfaces. This can be achieved using bridging, but you need to be careful to avoid loops when employing bridging as mentioned earlier, the primary means of preventing looping on bridges is to use the STP, which is employed by managed switches and routers (including pfSense).

It should be noted that in the current version of pfSense, bridged interfaces are treated no differently than non-bridged interfaces. Therefore, firewall rules are applied to each interface that is a member of the bridge on an inbound basis. Older versions of pfSense had filtering turned off on bridges by default, and it had to be enabled to work. In the current version of pfSense, there is no way to selectively disable filtering on bridges; the only way to do so is to use the **Disable Firewall** checkbox in **System** | **Advanced**; (this disables all packet filtering).

Bridging two internal interfaces in pfSense is fairly easy, but there are some issues that you need to address:

- One interface will have an IP address (the main interface) and one will have no IP address (the bridged interface)
- You need to make sure that the DHCP server is running only on the main interface and not on the one being bridged
- In order to allow DHCP traffic on the interface, you need to create a firewall rule on the bridged interface

Bridging interfaces

To bridge interfaces in pfSense, navigate to **Interfaces** | **(assign)** and click on the **Bridges** tab. On this tab, a table displaying all configured bridges will be present. To add a new bridge, click on the **Add** button below the table and to the right.

On the **Bridge** configuration page, you must select at least two interfaces in the **Member Interfaces** listbox. These are the interfaces that will be bridged. You may also enter a brief non-parsed description in the **Description** edit box.

Setting up a bridge can be as simple as selecting the interfaces, but clicking on the **Show Advanced** button reveals a number of advanced options, many of them pertaining to spanning trees. The **Cache size** edit box allows you to set the size of the bridge address cache. The default size is **2000** entries. The **Cache expire time** edit box allows you to set the timeout (in seconds) of address cache entries. The address cache entries will not be expired if this field is set to zero. The default expire time is **1200** seconds.

The next setting is the **Span Port** listbox. If an interface is set as a span port, then that interface will transmit a copy of each frame received by the bridge. This can be useful for monitoring network traffic. Note that the span interface cannot be one of the bridge members.

Next is the **Edge ports** listbox. An edge port is a port that is only connected to one bridge. As such, it cannot create bridging loops in the network, and thus can transition straight to the forwarding state. The **Auto Edge Ports** listbox will cause the selected ports to automatically detect edge status, which is the default for bridge interfaces.

The **PTP Ports** listbox sets the selected interfaces as point-to-point links, which is necessary if the interface is to make a straight transition to forwarding. The **Auto PTP Ports** listbox allows you to select interfaces for which pfSense will automatically detect the point-to-point status by checking the **full duplex link** status. This is the default for bridged interfaces.

The **Sticky Ports** listbox allows you to mark an interface as sticky, which causes dynamically learned address entries from the interface to be treated as static once they enter the cache. These entries are never aged out of the cache or replaced, even if the learned address is seen on a different interface. Finally, the **Private Ports** listbox allows you to mark selected interfaces as private interfaces; these interfaces will not forward traffic to any other interface that is also private.

If you are going to use a spanning tree, you have to choose which STP to use. pfSense currently supports two protocols:

- **STP**: As described earlier, the original STP creates a spanning tree within a network of layer 2 bridges and disables links that are not part of the spanning tree, leaving a single path between any two nodes on the tree. This protocol was eventually standardized by the IEEE as 802.1D. STP is a relatively simple protocol, but it can take close to a minute for it to respond to a topology change.

- **Rapid Spanning Tree Protocol (RSTP)**: Standardized by the IEEE as 802.1w, RSTP reduces the convergence time for responding to a topology change to a matter of seconds, but at a cost of some added complexity. STP has three bridge port roles—root, designated, and disabled—and RSTP adds two (alternate, which provides an alternate path to the root bridge, and backup, which is a backup or redundant path to a segment) for a total of five bridge port roles. This, and the fact that the number of switch port states is reduced to three (discarding, learning, and forwarding), helps decrease the convergence time.

You can set the STP options by scrolling down to the **RSTP/STP** section. Right above this section is the **Enable RSTP/STP** checkbox which you must check to enable these protocols. Next is the **Protocol** drop-down box, where you can select the protocol. The **STP Interfaces** listbox allows you to select which interfaces on which STP/ RSTP is enabled. The **Valid time** field allows you to specify how long a spanning tree configuration will be valid, while in the **Forward time** field, you can specify a delay for forwarding packets when RSTP or STP is enabled. The defaults for **Valid time** and **Forward time** are **20** seconds and **30** seconds respectively. The **Hello Time** field allows you to set the time between broadcasting STP configuration messages (when STP mode is invoked). The **Priority** field is where you can enter the bridge priority, and the **Hold count** field represents the number of packets which will be sent before rate limiting is invoked.

The final series of edit boxes set the spanning tree priority for each of the interfaces. You can set them to anything from 0 to 240 (in increments of 16); the default is **128**. You can also set the path cost for each interface. By default, the path cost is calculated from the link speed. However, you can manually set it to anything from 1 to 200000000. Set it to **0** to change it back to the default behavior. When you are finished making changes, click on the **Save** button and from the main **Bridges** page, click on **Apply Changes**.

If you haven't done so already, you should disable DNS on the bridged interface. You can do this by navigating to **Services | DHCP Server** (or **DHCPv6 Server/RA**), clicking on the tab for the bridged interface, making sure the **Enable** checkbox is unchecked, and click on the **Save** button. This will ensure that DHCP continues to function properly.

You also need to create a firewall rule on the bridged interface to allow DHCP traffic. To do that, navigate to **Firewall | Rules**, click on the tab of the bridged interface, and click the **Add** button. Normally, the **Source** field is set to a network or IP address. DHCP is a special case, because a client does not yet have an IP address. Thus, you must set the **Source** to `0.0.0.0` (choose **Single host or alias** in the **Source** drop-down box).

Set the source port to `68`. In the **Destination** field, set the destination to `255.255.255.255` and set the destination port to `67`. In the **Protocol** drop-down box, select **UDP**. Make sure the **Action** drop-down box is set to **Allow**, and then click on the **Save** button, then click on **Apply Changes** on the main **Firewall** page. Make sure the new rule is at the top of the list of rules for the interface. Once this rule has been added, clients in the bridged segment should be able to receive DHCP leases.

Special issues

Bridged interfaces behave somewhat differently than non-bridged interfaces, and for that reason, you may find there are some things that cannot be done with bridges. In other cases, you may have to make modifications in order to get a pfSense feature to work with bridging.

Captive portal requires an IP on each interface on which it is active; this IP address is used to serve the portal contents. But bridged interfaces do not have an IP address. Therefore, captive portal does not work with bridging.

Another situation where bridged interfaces can be problematic is with multi-WAN setups. This is because the nodes on the bridged interfaces often have a different gateway than pfSense, and the router that is the default gateway for these nodes is the only device that can direct traffic from these nodes. However, multi-WAN can still work on a pfSense firewall in the following situations:

- Nodes on the bridged interfaces have pfSense as their default firewall
- Multi-WAN is being used only on non-bridged interfaces

CARP also does not work well with bridging. A standard CARP setup with two firewalls, one master and one backup will have both firewalls connected to the switch for each internal interface (for example, LAN and OPT1). This is acceptable, as there is still only one path to each of the switches for a node. The two network segments are essentially merged into a single larger network when they are bridged. A loop is formed when two paths are created between the switches for each interface. For example, in a CARP setup without looping, a node on LAN has one path to a node on OPT1—through the master firewall. If the interfaces are bridged, however, there will be two paths to OPT1—the bridge on the master firewall and the bridge on the backup firewall.

If the interface switch is a managed switch, we can handle it better by implementing STP or RSTP on the managed switch. Unmanaged switches, however, have no way of preventing looping, and looping can essentially crash a network.

There is another way of using bridged interfaces with CARP, although it is somewhat inelegant. It entails the following steps:

1. Configure your master and backup firewalls as you would with any CARP deployment, taking care to ensure the interface assignments are identical on all firewalls. This should carry over to the bridged interfaces; the bridges should be copied so they are also identical.
2. If you are using managed switches, use STP/RSTP to ensure the port connecting the switch to the master firewall has priority over the port connecting the switch to the backup firewall. When you have finished configuring the ports, confirm that the master firewall's port is forwarding traffic and the backup firewall's port is blocking traffic.
3. Another possible method is to use a script to ensure that a bridge on the firewall is up only if the firewall is designated as MASTER. This can be done by running the `ifconfig` command on the `carp0` interface, and checking the content of the command's output using a command such as `grep`. Once you have installed the script, you can run the script automatically using the cron daemon. You likely want to run the script fairly often—for example, every 60 seconds—to ensure that when there is a failover, it is as smooth as possible.
4. Yet another possible method is to use `devd` to catch when the actual CARP state transition happens. You can edit `/etc/devd.conf` on the master and backup firewalls so that the bridge (or bridges) is brought up and down whenever a CARP state transition is detected.

It is beyond the scope of this chapter to describe these procedures in detail. If you require implementing this solution on your network, you can find these methods described in a post at the official pfSense forum at `http://forum.pfsense.org/index.php/topic,4984.0.html`.

Bridging example

To provide an example of bridging, we'll use pfSense to bridge two interfaces—LAN and OPT1. We will also assume that there are downstream routers, and to prevent looping, we will run RSTP on the bridged interfaces. In this case, LAN1 will be the main interface and OPT1 will be the bridged interface. Assume that the LAN interface has an IP address of `172.16.1.1` and a subnet of `172.16.0.0`, and that the DHCP server is running on LAN.

To begin, we navigate to **Services** | **DHCP Server** and disable **DHCP** on **OPT1**. To do this, we uncheck the **Enable** checkbox, and click on the **Save** button. Now we can create our bridge. To do so, we navigate to **Interfaces** | **(assign)** and click on the **Bridges** tab. We click on the **Add** button on that page to add a new bridge.

Since we are bridging LAN and OPT1, we select these two interfaces in the **Member Interfaces** listbox. We also enter a brief description in the **Description** edit box (for example `LAN to OPT1 bridge)`. If all we wanted to do is create a simple bridge, we would be done with configuration, but we want to run RSTP on the bridged interfaces, so we click on the **Show Advanced** button and scroll down the page. We check the **Enable RSTP** checkbox, and then in the **RSTP/STP** section, we leave the protocol in the **Protocol** drop-down box set to **RSTP**. In the **STP interfaces** listbox, we select **LAN** and **OPT1**. Assume also that in spanning tree calculations, we want the **LAN** port to be favored over **OPT1**, so we scroll down and set **LAN Path cost** to **1** and **OPT1** to **1000**. Once we have finished setting these values, we click on the **Save** button and then click on **Apply Changes** on the main **Bridges** page.

We have now configured the bridge, but we still must create a firewall rule on the **OPT1** interface to allow for DHCP traffic. Thus, we navigate to **Firewall** | **Rules** and click on the **OPT1** tab, then click on the **Add** button. On the **Rules** configuration page, we set **Protocol** to **UDP**. In the **Source** drop-down box, we select **Single host or alias** and type `0.0.0.0` in the corresponding edit box. We click on the **Display Advanced** button, and in the **Source** port range edit box, we enter `68`. For **Destination**, we also select **Single host or alias** and type `255.255.255.255` in the corresponding edit box. In the **Destination port range** edit box, we enter `67`. We enter a brief description (for example, `Allow DHCP traffic`) then click on the **Save** button, and then click on the **Apply Changes** button on the main firewall rules page.

Once we confirm that the newly created rule is at the top of the list of rules for the OPT1 interface, our configuration is complete. Clients connecting to OPT1 should now be able to receive an address on the `172.16.0.0` subnet from the DHCP server on LAN.

Troubleshooting

Once you have learned the fundamentals of routing and bridging and begin to implement them in your network, it is almost inevitable that you will encounter a situation where you need to employ your troubleshooting skills. In this section, we will consider how to troubleshoot both routing and bridging.

The pfSense routing table, which can be found by navigating to **Diagnostics** | **Routes**, is a good starting point for learning about which routes exist, how they are configured, and the number of times a route has been used. The table is divided into two sections, one for IPv4 routes and the other for IPv6 routes. Each entry in the table has several columns: **Destination** is the route's destination, **Gateway** is the gateway through which the route travels, **Use** is the number of times the route has been used, **Mtu** is the maximum transmission unit, **Netif** is the gateway's interface, and **Expire** tells us if the route has expired (which may be the case for a temporary route such as an ICMP redirect). There is also a column called **Flags** which informs us of the flags that are set for this route. The netstat man page provides a complete listing of the flags and what they mean, but some of the more common ones are:

- **U = RTF_UP**: Route is usable
- **G = RTF_GATEWAY**: Destination requires forwarding by an intermediary
- **H = RTF_HOST**: Host entry
- **S = RTF_STATIC**: Manually added entry

Since routing encompasses both static routing and dynamic routing, we will first consider static routing. Let's consider a simple example, using the network we considered in the section on static routes. As you might recall, we had a DMZ network with a subnet of `192.168.2.0` which was connected to the LAN network. Assume we also have an OPT1 network directly connected to pfSense with a subnet of `192.168.3.0`. Thus, the LAN and OPT1 networks are known to pfSense, while the DMZ network is only known to pfSense via a static route (the DMZ router's IP address of `192.168.1.2` is configured as a gateway). A node on the DMZ network with an IP address of `192.168.2.10` is unable to establish a session with a node on OPT1 with an IP address of `192.168.3.10`.

First, we should consider obvious potential issues, such as an interface that is in shutdown mode, or a misconfigured interface. In this case, we begin at `192.168.2.10`. The router's WAN IP address is `192.168.1.2`, and the LAN-side IP address (not to be confused with the LAN network) is `192.168.2.1`. Therefore, the default gateway on `192.168.2.10` should be `192.168.2.1`. If it is not configured as such, we need to change it.

Now we need to confirm connectivity with the router, and we can do that by pinging `192.168.2.1` from `192.168.2.10`. If the ping fails, then the problem is likely a local issue, and either the router is malfunctioning or is misconfigured. If we can ping the router, however, we can begin to look elsewhere.

You could use the `traceroute` command (or `tracert` under Windows) to trace the route to `192.168.3.10`, which might be the better solution in a more complex networking scenario, but since our network is fairly simple, pinging the LAN address (`192.168.1.1`) will tell us a good deal. If the ping is unsuccessful, there are several possibilities:

- The LAN interface is down or is misconfigured
- The static route to the DMZ is misconfigured, and therefore pfSense doesn't know where to send the ping replies, or is sending them to the wrong address

One possible way of eliminating the first of these as a possibility is to try to ping `192.168.1.2` from pfSense, which we can do from the web GUI by navigating to **Diagnostics** | **Ping**. If we can ping the router in this manner, then we have proven that the LAN interface is up and running and that there is a path to the DMZ router from pfSense. If we can ping `192.168.1.2` from pfSense but not `192.168.2.1` or `192.168.2.10`, however, then there is a good possibility that the static route to the DMZ network is misconfigured.

If the pfSense firewall is reachable from `192.168.2.10`, however, then we may need to consider problems with the OPT1 interface. If we can ping `192.168.3.10` from pfSense, then OPT1 is up and running and there is connectivity with the node that `192.168.2.10` is trying to reach. If not, then we have isolated the problem to the OPT1 network.

But what if pfSense can be pinged from `192.168.2.10`, and pfSense can ping `192.168.3.10`? If so, we have proven both nodes have connectivity with pfSense, and that the static route to the DMZ network is configured correctly. Keep in mind, however, that this is inter-network traffic, and therefore firewall rules apply. We navigate to **Firewall** | **Rules**, and click on the **LAN** tab, since DMZ traffic is coming in through the LAN interface. It is here that we discover the problem: the *Allow LAN to any* rule only allows traffic to pass if its source is the LAN subnet. Since DMZ traffic doesn't match this requirement, the rule doesn't apply and traffic to OPT1 is not allowed to pass. We need to either modify this rule to allow traffic from the LAN interface to anywhere else to pass regardless of its source, or create another rule to allow traffic from the DMZ network (`192.168.2.0`) to pass.

Your network topology may be more complex than this, but the same basic troubleshooting techniques apply. Try to employ a divide and conquer approach; keep in mind that `ping` and `traceroute` are our friends, and if you are using Cisco switches, you have other command-line tools at your disposal, such as:

- `showip route`: This command shows, at the very least, the next hop, as well as other information such as the route metric, total delay, and reliability.
- `showip interface brief`: This command can be used to display a summary of the status information for each router interface.
- `showcdp neighbors`: This command can be used to display information about neighboring devices discovered during the **Cisco Discovery Protocol** (**CDP**). Adding detail to the command will cause it to display such information as network address, protocols, hold time, and the software version.

As our networks get more complex, static routing tends to prove inadequate and we opt for more elegant solutions, such as dynamic routing. But dynamic routing brings with it a whole set of issues which we have to consider. Keep in mind, however, that just as with static routes, we have to consider the obvious issues such as an incorrect gateway setting, or a port being down. Another common issue is that often there is connectivity between routers, but one or more routers (or more likely, specific ports on the router) are not configured to use the routing protocol being used by the rest of the network.

Another potential issue is that as your networks grow, your routers may require more CPU and RAM in order to hold routing tables and calculate dynamic routes. This can be avoided by choosing the right hardware for your network, and upgrading equipment as needed.

More likely, however, you may encounter a looping issue. This may be the case even if you are running STP or RSTP. A misconfigured or malfunctioning switch could still bring your network to its knees. You should make sure all devices are running the same version of STP (either legacy STP or RSTP, but not both). Once you have confirmed this, you can begin to look into other problems. If a switch recently went down, and you are having problems, perhaps the interval for calculating a new spanning tree is too long. It is also possible that there is an issue with convergence – the switch is not recognized as being down by all routers, hence the delay in incorporating this information into the spanning tree.

Another possibility is an incompatibility between versions of the routing protocol being used. For example, RIP v2 is backwards compatible with RIP v1, but not all subsequent versions of routing protocols may be backwards compatible with older versions. If you are running different versions of the same protocol, check your documentation to ensure they are compatible.

Bridging interfaces can cause a number of problems which require troubleshooting. There are several common problems with bridges:

- The bridge may not be forwarding traffic, or may only be forwarding traffic intermittently
- The opposite may occur—the bridge causes a storm of duplicate traffic, flooding the network
- After adding the bridge, the network seems unstable, and it might even cause pfSense to freeze

If the bridge is not forwarding traffic, then it's possible the bridge has not been created properly, or it was created, but one (or both) interfaces is disabled. Since firewall rules still apply to traffic between interfaces in a bridge, there is the possibility that the firewall rules are blocking traffic, so you need to consult the firewall rules for interfaces participating in the bridge.

If the bridge is forwarding traffic intermittently, then there are several possibilities. One is that STP is running on the bridge, and there are so many network topology changes that the spanning tree has to be constantly recalculated. Another possible reason is that there are equipment outages. The bridge forwarding delay adds at least 15 seconds to even the briefest of outages.

If there is a storm of traffic, then the cause is almost certainly a loop. One of the ways of solving this problem is to manually determine where the loops are and break them. The preferable way, however, would be to run STP or RSTP, but running these protocols can sometimes create pitfalls, as outlined above when discussing troubleshooting for static routes.

If the network is unstable and/or pfSense freezes, it is possible this happened because you are using one of the bridged interfaces for remote administration. There is also a possibility that it happened because users are relying on the bridged interfaces for essential network services, such as file sharing. Or it could be that it is a hardware issue with one or more of the bridged interfaces.

Bridging network interfaces usually is not a good idea, especially if there is a more elegant and straightforward solution available. But by employing some common sense troubleshooting techniques, you should be able to get your bridged interfaces to work.

Summary

In this chapter, we discussed routing and bridging, and the fact that while conceptually they are different, they often create the same issues; for example, in both cases we must take care to make sure looping does not take place, and both often involve firewall rule configuration. We discussed both static and dynamic routing, including policy-based routing, and covered four pfSense packages that implement dynamic routing: RIP, OpenBGPD, Quagga OSPF and FRR. We discussed how to implement bridging in pfSense and some of the issues associated with it. Finally, we covered troubleshooting for routing and bridging.

In `Chapter 11`, *Extending pfSense with Packages*, we will cover in greater depth something which we have already hinted at already: the extent to which pfSense's functionality can be enhanced with the addition of third-party packages.

Questions

Answer the following questions:

1. What is the key difference between routing and bridging?
2. (a) What class of routing protocols involves a router only informing its neighbors of topology changes? (b) What class of routing protocols involves each router constructing a map of its connectivity to the network?
3. Identify two methods we can use to deal with the problem of return traffic not following the same route as the traffic originally sent when configuring static routes.
4. (a) We want to utilize RIP v2 as our routing protocol. What pfSense package should we install? (b) We want to utilize OSPF as our routing protocol. What pfSense package can we use? (Identify either one.) (c) What is the best choice if we want to redistribute OSPF routes to BGP neighbors?
5. What is the first step in implementing policy-based routing?
6. Identify the two spanning tree protocols supported by pfSense bridging.
7. We have a CARP failover group and we want to bridge two interfaces on the failover group. What issue will this cause?
8. (a) What diagnostic tool found in the pfSense web GUI can we use to diagnose routing problems? (b) How are static routes denoted in this tool?

11
Extending pfSense with Packages

We have already demonstrated how packages can be used to extend the functionality of pfSense in previous chapters. For example, Snort is useful for blocking certain sites and for Layer 7 traffic shaping. HAProxy provides high availability and load balancing capabilities beyond what pfSense natively supports. Packages such as routed and FRRouting enable us to implement dynamic routing. These packages, however, only represent a fraction of what is available. The purpose of this chapter is to cover pfSense packages in greater depth. We will briefly discuss what issues package installation can raise, how to install packages from both the webGUI and the command line, and cover the most important packages. This includes some packages already mentioned, but many which we have not discussed previously.

It is impossible to do justice to all the packages available for pfSense within a single chapter, but we will cover the most important packages. The outline of this chapter is as follows:

- Basic considerations
- Installing packages
- The most important packages
- Other packages

Technical requirements

To follow along in this chapter, the main requirement will be a functioning pfSense system. Some packages may require greater resources than would be required by a barebones pfSense installation, and in such cases we will make note of the minimum requirements for these packages.

Basic considerations

For the most part, you can begin installing and configuring pfSense packages without worrying too much about the effects they will have on your pfSense system. Nonetheless, some caution is called for when installing packages on mission-critical systems. First, having some basic knowledge of the technologies underlying the packages you want to install is helpful. For example, it would be ill-advised to install routed (the Routing Information Protocol daemon) without having some basic knowledge of how dynamic protocols work in general and how RIPv1 and RIPv2 work (in this case, reviewing `Chapter 10`, *Routing and Bridging*, is a good starting point).

Beyond that, you should be mindful of the fact that installing additional packages may consume additional resources. Simple packages such as arping and cron can be installed on virtually any pfSense system without much consideration, but they are the exception to the rule. Installing and configuring a proxy server requires additional disk space to store cached web pages. Many packages require additional CPU resources. Any dynamic routing protocol requires CPU resources to calculate routes, as do many intrusion detection systems. If you did not foresee installing such packages when you initially came up with the specifications for your pfSense box, you may have to adjust these specifications accordingly.

Installing and using packages without consideration of resource utilization can result in the following:

- CPU resources being taxed heavily, bringing pfSense to a crawl
- Disk space being completely used up, so that the DHCP server stops functioning, and no more DHCP leases are assigned
- pfSense cannot update, because there is insufficient disk space
- In some cases, insufficient disk space/CPU resources can render pfSense unusable, requiring a complete reinstallation of pfSense

All of these are outcomes we want to avoid in a production environment, so obviously some caution is justified when installing and configuring packages.

Furthermore, you should take into consideration the way packages interact with existing pfSense functionality and other packages. For example, some packages are installed in the same location as other packages and thus cannot coexist with each other (OpenBGPD, Quagga OSPF and FRRouting come to mind; each of these packages are intended to be mutually exclusive and are not compatible with each other - and if you don't remember this, you quickly will if you install one when one of the others is already installed; the package installer will erase existing incompatible packages). If you already have firewall rules in place upon which you rely, be aware that installing a proxy can affect outcomes, and traffic that was assumed to be blocked may no longer be blocked, as we will see when we cover Squid later in this chapter.

Installing packages

Package installation can be done either within the web GUI or from the console. Since we already covered the steps involved in installing a package from the GUI, we will only provide a brief overview before discussing CLI installation.

To install a package using the pfSense web GUI, navigate to **System** | **Package Manager** and click on the **Available Packages** tab. This tab contains a table listing all the available packages. There is also a search box at the top of the page, so if you know at least part of the name and/or description of the package for which you are looking, you can type it into the search box. The adjacent drop-down box allows you to search the name, description, or both.

Each entry in the packages table has three columns: **Name**, **Version**, and **Description**:

- **Name**: The name of the package. This column also links to the package's official website, if one exists.
- **Version**: The current version of the package. This column links to the GitHub repository for the project, if available.
- **Description**: A brief description of the package, along with any notes and warnings. There is also a section in this column called **Package Dependencies**, which lists any dependencies the package has (each package is its own dependency, so there is at least one item listed for each package). Each dependency listed provides a link to the `www.freshports.org` entry for the package, which provides more information about it.

To install a particular package, refer to the following points:

1. Find the package's listing in the table and click on the **Install** button to the right of its description.
2. Once you do, you will be presented with a new page with a **Confirm** button.
3. Click this button to confirm installation, and the package will install. Most packages should take no more than a few minutes to install.

You can also install packages at the command line. To do so, type in the following at the command prompt:

```
pfSsh.php playback installpkg "some package"
```

This should result in the following command line output:

```
Starting the pfSense developer shell...
Installing package "some package" ... Done
```

It does not provide as much feedback about the status of package installation as you would get from installing packages within the web GUI, but it gets the job done, and you could easily write a script to install several packages at the same time to automate the process.

To uninstall a package at the command line, type the following:

```
pfSsh.php playback uninstallpkg "some package"
```

And to list available packages, type the following:

```
pfSsh.php playback listpkg
```

Once you have installed a package, it should appear on the **Installed Packages** tab of **Package Manager** in the web GUI. Each package's entry looks similar to its entry on the **Available Packages** tab, with a few significant differences:

- The **Name** column has an icon to the left of the name. A check mark icon indicates that the package is up to date, while circular arrows indicate that the package can be updated (in this case, clicking on the circular arrows icon updates the package).
- The **Actions** column has several options. Clicking on the trash can icon uninstalls the package, clicking on the arrows icon reinstalls the package, and clicking on the lowercase **i** icon (when available) redirects you to the package's website for more information.

Important packages

Since the publication of the first edition of this book, several new packages have been added. The most notable of these new packages are as follows:

- `acme`: A package which automates the process of generating Let's Encrypt certificates. The goal of Let's Encrypt is to encrypt the web by making it easier to obtain SSL certificates. acme stands for **Automated Certificate Management Environment**.
- `frr`: The FRR routing daemon for BGP, OSPF, and OSPF6. This package is intended to supersede Quagga OSPF, although the latter has not been removed from the package list or deprecated. It is not compatible with OpenBGPD or Quagga OSPF.
- `lldpd`: Provides support for the **Link Layer Discovery Protocol** (**LLDP**), which is specified in IEEE 802.1ab. It also provides support for several proprietary protocols, such as **Cisco Discovery Protocol (CDP)**, **Extreme Discovery Protocol** (**EDP**), **Foundry Discovery Protocol** (**FDP**), and **Nortel Discovery Protocol** (**NDP/SONMP**).
- `net-snmp`: A GUI for snmpd and snmptrapd which, unlike the built-in bsnmpd daemon, supports **Simple Network Management Protocol** (**SNMP**) version 3 as well as IPv6.
- `telegraf`: An agent written in Go (a compiled, statically-typed programming language similar to C) for collecting, processing, and writing metrics.
- `tftpd`: A package that installs and runs a TFTP (**Trivial File Transfer Protocol**) server.

To the best of my knowledge, no existing packages have been deleted or deprecated between the release of pfSense 2.3 and 2.4. Of the newer packages, FRR seems to be the most significant, and will be covered in this section.

Squid

Squid is a caching and forwarding web proxy which was originally designed to run as a daemon on Unix-like systems (Linux, FreeBSD, and so on). Version 1.0.0 was released in July 1996, and as of today, Squid is capable of running on over a dozen different Unix variants. It is also capable of being used as a client-side cache (allowing the client to cache web pages or other content), and as a reverse proxy. If it is being used as a reverse proxy, it is being used server side to cache pages from one or more web servers.

Proxy servers were quite commonplace in the days when dialup internet access was common. The reason for this is obvious. If you have at best a 56 Kbps internet connection, then it is faster to retrieve a local copy of a web page than it would be to acquire the remote copy of the page. As broadband internet connections have become more commonplace, proxy servers have become less commonplace. If you have a fast enough internet connection, using a proxy server might actually take longer than it would take to retrieve the page directly. The reason for this is obvious if you consider what happens when you request a web page through a proxy. First, you make a request to the proxy. Next, the proxy must check to see if there is a newer version of the web page available. If there is a newer version, it must retrieve the page, cache it, and send it to the client. If not, it will send a copy of the cached page.

If the page has been updated, then it is pretty obvious that the time required to retrieve the page is longer, since we end up eventually requesting the page from a remote web server, which we would have done if we didn't have a proxy, but now we have added another step to the process. But even if the page has not been updated, there is some overhead associated with checking to see if the page has been updated. Thus, in many cases, using a web proxy is slower than directly accessing websites.

However, there are some situations where using a web proxy can be advantageous. Let's assume that 25 users on your network simultaneously request a web page (imagine a classroom-type situation, or perhaps one in which users are simultaneously reading online documentation for a product). If there is no proxy, then 25 separate requests for the same web page are consuming your bandwidth. If, however, you have a web proxy and a cached local copy, the page can be sent to your network users at LAN speed instead of internet speed, and without consuming any of your internet bandwidth.

To begin Squid configuration, once it is installed, follow these steps:

1. Navigate to **Services** | **Squid Proxy Server**.
2. There are ten separate tabs on this page, but the default tab is **General**. From this tab, you should be able to get Squid up and running.
3. The **Enable Squid Proxy** checkbox controls whether the Squid proxy is active; checking it activates Squid.
4. The **Keep Settings/Data** checkbox, if checked, preserves settings and data across package reinstalls.
5. The **Proxy Interfaces** list box allows you to select to which interfaces the proxy server will bind.

6. The **Proxy Port** edit box allows you to specify on which port the proxy server will listen; the default is `3128`.
7. The **ICP Port** edit box allows you to specify the port on which the proxy server will send and receive ICP queries to and from neighbor caches.
8. By default, such queries are not allowed. The **Allow Users on Interface** checkbox, if checked, will allow users connected to interfaces selected in the **Proxy Interfaces** list box to use the proxy.
9. The **Resolve DNS IPv4 First** checkbox enables forcing DNS IPv4 lookup first:

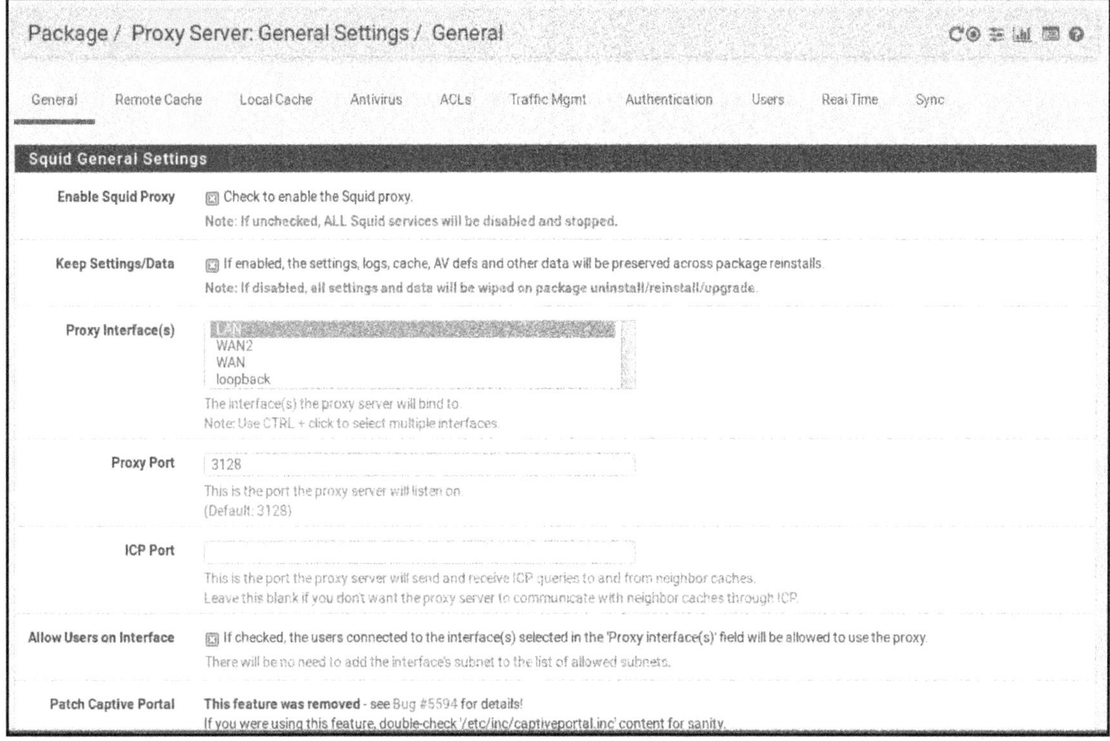

Configuring general settings in Squid

Starting with version 1.1.9, Squid supports using ICMP **round trip time** (**RTT**) measurements to select the best location to forward a cache miss.

Checking the **Disable ICMP** checkbox, however, disables the Squid ICMP pinger helper, forcing Squid to rely on ICP reply times in determining where to forward cache misses.

Finally, the **Use Alternate DNS Servers for the Proxy Server** edit box allows you to specify DNS servers other than the servers configured in the pfSense DNS forwarder/resolver.

If you check the **Transparent HTTP Proxy** checkbox, pfSense will forward all requests that have port `80` as their destination to the Squid proxy server without any additional configuration being necessary.

In the **Transparent Proxy Interface(s)** list box, you can choose the interfaces on which Squid will transparently intercept requests.

The **Bypass Proxy for Private Address Destination** checkbox, if checked, will cause Squid to not forward traffic to private address space (`10.x.x.x`, `172.16.x.x` to `172.31.x.x` and `192.168.x.x`) addresses.

The **Bypass Proxy for These Source Addresses** edit box allows you to specify IPs, networks, hostnames, or aliases for which the proxy server will not be invoked if they are the source; instead, these hosts will be able to pass directly through the firewall.

The **Bypass Proxy for These Destination IPs** edit box allows you to specify IPs, networks hostnames or aliases to which the proxy server will not be invoked if they are the destination.

The next section is **SSL Man In the Middle Filtering**. The **HTTPS/SSL Interception** checkbox, if checked, will enable SSL filtering.

If this option is not enabled, then port `443` traffic will not be filtered by Squid even if Squid is being run in transparent mode. The **SSL Intercept Interface** list box allows you to select the interfaces on which Squid will intercept SSL requests. The **SSL Proxy port** edit box allows you to specify the port on which the proxy will listen to intercept SSL. The **CA** drop-down box allows you to select a **Certificate Authority** (**CA**) to use when SSL interception is enabled. You should install the CA certificate as a trusted root CA on each computer on which you want to filter SSL to avoid an SSL error on each connection. The **SSL Certificate Daemon Children** edit box allows you to specify the number of SSL certificate daemon children to start. You may need to increase this if Squid is going to be used in busy environments. The **Remote Cert Checks** list box allows you to select which remote SSL certificate checks to perform on SSL traffic. Finally, the **Certificate Adapt** list box allows you to pass SSL certificate information on to users in order to allow the end user to make an informed decision on whether to trust a server certificate.

The **Enable Access Logging** checkbox, if checked, will enable the access log. This, of course, will use up even more disk space, so you should not enable this unless you have enough disk space. The **Log Store Directory** edit box allows you to specify where the logs will be stored. The **Rotate Logs** edit box allows you to choose how many days of log files will be kept. By default, rotation is disabled. The **Log Pages Denied By SquidGuard** checkbox, if checked, will make it possible for pages denied by Squid to be included in the logs.

The next section of the page is called **Headers Handling, Language and Other Customizations**. This section includes such options as setting the hostname and email address to display on error pages, and the ability to suppress the Squid version string in HTTP headers and HTML error pages (this can be useful if you don't want end users to know which Squid version is being used). By clicking the **Show Advanced** button, we can see a number of advanced options. The **Integrations** list box allows you to add Squid options added from packages such as `SquidGuard`. The **Custom ACLS (Before Auth)** list box allows you to put custom options that will be added to the configuration before Squid processes the authentication **access control list** (**ACL**) lines. Any options places in the **Custom ACLS (After Auth)** line will be executed after the ACL lines.

There are several other tabs with options. The **Remote Cache** tab allows you to specify remote Squid proxy servers from which web pages can be forwarded, which can help reduce network latency and incorporate redundancy into the network. Clicking on the **Add** button allows you to add configuration information about a remote server. Remote caches can be configured hierarchically. The three options for cache hierarchy are as follows:

- **Parent**: This is typically a more distant cache, such as your ISP's cache.
- **Sibling**: Closer caches are usually configured as siblings. You can have more than one sibling, and Squid will query them simultaneously.
- **Multicast**: You can cut down on network traffic by setting up a multicast address for a cache.

Note that the difference between a parent and a sibling is, to some extent, academic. When Squid queries more than one cache, it does not query each cache in sequence, but instead sends all ICP queries at the same time. Squid will get the page from the fastest-responding cache. The designation of a cache as a parent is significant because Squid will go to a parent cache when there is no response from a sibling cache; when there is no response from parent caches, by default Squid will attempt to go directly to the origin server.

Multicast can be used to increase the efficiency of cache requests. Unlike unicast (one-to-one communication) and broadcast (one-to-everyone on the subnet), multicast packets are one-to-many, and unlike broadcast packets, they can traverse network segments. This can be helpful in a scenario where multiple caches are being used. For example, if your cache hierarchy has four caches, to find out if a web page is cached, a host would normally have to query each of the four caches, which consumes bandwidth. If you configure a multicast address, however, the host can just send one packet to the multicast address. Once the packet reaches the local subnet, each cache can pick up the packet and reply. This cuts down considerably on traffic between networks.

There are also several options for determining which cache is selected:

- **Default**: The first peer to respond to an ICP query is used as the source.
- **Round-robin**: This is a simple load balancing method. Squid maintains a counter for each cache. The cache with the lowest counter is used (and its counter is incremented).
- **Weighted-round-robin**: Parent caches are used in round-robin fashion, with each cache having its own counter, but caches with lower RTTs are given greater weight.
- **CARP**: Not to be confused with Common Address Redundancy Protocol, this **CARP** refers to **Cache Array Routing Protocol**. This method entails taking the URL requested and feeding it into a hash function that generates large numbers. These numbers all fit in a certain range, and by dividing the range by however many caches we have, we can send the request to one of the caches based on this hash value.
- **Userhash**: Similar to CARP, but the hashing is done based on the client **proxy_auth** or **ident** username.
- **Sourcehash**: The hash function takes as input the client source IP.
- **Multicast-siblings**: If the peer is of type multicast, you can use this option.

Also of interest on this page is the **ICP Settings** section. In the **ICP Port** edit box, you can specify a port to connect to the upstream proxy with the ICP protocol. The default value is `7`, which disables ICP communication. In the **ICP Options** drop-down box, you can select an ICP mode for the cache being configured:

- **no-query**: Do not allow ICP queries from this cache to the remote cache
- **multicast-responder**: The peer being configured is a member of a multicast group

- **closest-only**: For **ICP_IP_MISS** replies (the cache did not have the page requested), we'll only forward **CLOSEST_PARENT_MISSes** (parent with lowest RTT) and never **FIRST_PARENT_MISSes** (fastest weighted RTT)
- **background-ping**: Only send ICP queries to this neighbor infrequently

The **Local Cache** tab, as the name implies, controls settings for the Squid cache on the local firewall. The **Cache Replacement Policy** drop-down box allows you to select from amongst several cache replacement policy options:

- **Least Recently Used** (**LRU**): This algorithm discards the least recently used items first.
- **Greedy Dual Size Frequency** (**Heap GDSF**): This algorithm keeps smaller popular objects in the cache at the expense of larger popular objects.
- **Least Frequently Used with Dynamic Aging** (**Heap LFUDA**): This algorithm keeps popular objects in the cache regardless of their size. Thus, a large popular object may keep smaller objects out of the cache.
- **Least Recently Used** (**Heap LRU**): Algorithm implemented with a heap.

There are also several options on this page for controlling the hard disk cache size, as well as the cache location and the threshold at which cache replacement occurs (the point at which the cache replacement policy is invoked to evict certain items from the cache). You can also select the hard disk cache system, and you can force a wiping of the cache on this page if necessary.

The **Antivirus** tab allows you to use Squid in conjunction with **Clam Antivirus** (**ClamAV**). Clam AV is a free and open source antivirus program licensed under the GNU GPL. The **Enable** checkbox, if checked, enables ClamAV. The **Client Forward Options** drop-down box allows you to choose what client information to forward to ClamAV. The **Enable Manual Configuration** drop-down box allows you to select manual configuration mode, which causes ClamAV to ignore any options set on this tab; instead, it uses the configuration settings from the configuration files (`squidclamav.conf`, `c-icap.conf`, `c-icap.magic`, `freshclam.conf`, and `clamd. conf`). These configuration files can be edited from this page by scrolling down and clicking on the **Show Advanced** button.

The **Redirect URL** edit box allows you to specify a URL to send users to when a virus is found. If no URL is specified here, the default Squid/pfSense web GUI error URL is used. Checking the **Google Safe Browsing** checkbox enables Google Safe Browsing. The Google Safe Browsing database includes information about harmful websites, such as websites that may be phishing sites or sources of malware. It should be noted that this option consumes a significant amount of RAM. The **Exclude Audio/Video Streams** checkbox, if checked, will disable antivirus scanning of streamed video and audio.

The **ClamAV Database Update** drop-down box allows you to select the database update interval. If you are using Google Safe Browsing, the interval should be set to one hour. You can also click on the **Update AV** button to update the database now. You can also schedule updates with the cron daemon. The **Regional ClamAV Database Update Mirror** drop-down box allows you to select a regional database mirror. Finally, the **Optional ClamAV Database Update Servers** edit box allows you to specify additional ClamAV databases (separated by semicolons).

The **ACLs** tab is where you can configure the **access control lists** (**ACLs**) for Squid. The **Allowed Subnets** list box is where you can enter subnets that are allowed to use the proxy. The interfaces specified on the **General** tab in the **Proxy Interfaces** list box do not have to have their subnets added. However, if you want to add subnets other than the subnets of the interfaces selected in **Proxy Interfaces**, you can add them here.

The **Unrestricted IPs** list box allows you to add unrestricted IP addresses and/or networks. These entries will not be subject to the access control directives specified on the **ACLs** tab. The **Banned Hosts Addresses** list box allows you to enter IP addresses and/or networks that will not be allowed to use the proxy. The **Whitelist** list box allows you to enter domains that will be accessible to users, while the **Blacklist** list box allows you to enter domains that will be blocked for proxy users. The **Block User Agents** edit box allows you to enter user agents that will be blocked for proxy users. This field is useful if you want to prevent users on your network from using certain types of software (for example, torrent clients). The **Block MIME Types (Reply Only)** list box allows you to enter MIME types that will be blocked for users that use the proxy. This is useful for blocking JavaScript, among other types.

The next section on the page is **Squid Allowed Ports**. The **ACL Safe Ports** edit box allows you to enter ports on which traffic will be allowed to pass, in addition to the default list of ports (the default ports are `21`, `70`, `80`, `210`, `280`, `443`, `488`, `563`, `591`, `631`, `777`, `901`, and `1025-65535`). The **ACL SSL Ports** edit box allows you to specify ports on which SSL connections will be allowed, in addition to the default list (`443` and `563`).

The **Traffic Mgmt** tab allows you to have some degree of control over your users' bandwidth consumption. The **Maximum Download Size** and **Maximum Upload Size** edit boxes allow you to set the maximum total download and upload sizes (in kilobytes) respectively. Of particular interest is the last section of the page: **Squid Transfer Quick Abort Settings**. By default, Squid continues downloading aborted requests which are almost done downloading. This may be undesirable in some cases (for example, slow links).

Users may repeatedly request and abort downloads, thus tying up file descriptors and bandwidth. The parameters in this section allow you to control under what circumstances a transfer continues or is aborted. Thus, we get the **Finish transfer if less than x KB remaining**, **Abort transfer if more than x KB remaining**, and **Finish transfer if more than x % finished** edit boxes.

By default, proxy users are not required to provide authentication, but if you want to require authentication, you can do so on the **Authentication** tab. The **Authentication Method** drop-down box allows you to select what form of authentication takes place. The default is **None**, but **Local** is supported (authentication through Squid), as well as **LDAP**, **RADIUS**, **Captive Portal** and **NT Domain**. You can also specify subnets that will not be asked for authentication to access the proxy in the **Subnets That Don't Need Authentication** list box.

If you selected **Local** as the **Authentication Method** on the **Authentication** tab, you will have to enter users via the **Users** tab. Click on the **Add** button to add a user. There are fields for **Username**, **Password**, and a **Description** field where you can enter a brief non-parsed description.

The **Real Time** tab allows you to view information about Squid as it is running. You can view the access logs here, the cache logs, SquidGuard logs, and ClamAV logs. You can also filter the logs using the options in the **Filtering** section. You can specify the number of lines that will be displayed, and you can also filter the results by typing a regular expression into the **String filter** edit box.

The **Sync** tab allows you to do an XMLRPC sync of the Squid proxy to another firewall. There are three options in the **Enable Sync** drop-down box:

- **Do not sync this package configuration**: This is the default; no sync is performed
- **Sync to configured system backup server**: Sync to the CARP backup firewall (or firewalls)
- **Sync to host(s) defined below**: Allows you to specify the hosts to which Squid will sync

The **Sync Timeout** drop-down allows you to choose the XMLRPC timeout (the default is `250` seconds). The **Replication Targets** subsection allows you to specify the IP address and/or hostname and port of hosts to which Squid will sync. You can also specify a **Replication Protocol** (either HTTP or HTTPS), as well as an **Admin Password**. Click on the **Add** button to add a host. You also need to check the **Enable** checkbox to enable replication.

Issues with Squid

Although Squid is an extremely popular and useful package, there are some issues you should consider. First, Squid ACLs take precedence over any rules defined on the interfaces to which Squid binds. For example, assume that we have a rule for LAN to block access to a certain website. We subsequently install Squid and configure it to bind to LAN without configuring any of the ACLs (including the blacklist). Access to the site is not blocked by Squid. Once Squid is enabled, access to the blocked website will be possible, even though there is a firewall rule blocking the site.

The solution, of course, is to navigate to **Services** | **Squid Proxy Server**, then click on the **ACL** tab, and add the website to the **Blacklist** list box. The **Blacklist** list box also accepts regular expressions, so if you want to specify a wildcard, you could do that as well. Since Squid makes it easier to block multiple websites, this should not be a problem. But if all you want to do is block a few websites, you might find that using firewall rules is the better solution, as it doesn't require the overhead of running a proxy server. You could even block multiple websites using aliases, and block them on multiple interfaces using floating rules.

Squid reverse proxy server

As mentioned earlier, Squid can also be used as a reverse proxy server. In this situation, Squid is caching content for one or more web servers, reducing the load on the servers. You can configure the reverse proxy server by navigating to **Services** | **Squid Reverse Proxy**. There are several tabs, but the default tab is **General**.

The first setting is the **Reverse Proxy Interfaces** list box, which allows you to select one or more interfaces to which the reverse proxy will bind. Since the reverse proxy will be serving content to remote users, you probably want to bind it to **WAN** (or possibly to multiple WAN-type interfaces). In the **User Defined Reverse Proxy IPs**, you can specify user-defined IPs to which Squid will bind. You also need to specify the external fully qualify domain name of the WAN IP address in the **External FQDN** edit box. You can use Squid as a reverse proxy for both HTTP traffic and HTTPS traffic, but you have to enable them separately; there are two separate checkboxes on the page: **Enable HTTP Reverse Proxy** and **Enable HTTPS Reverse Proxy**. You can also specify different HTTP and HTTPS ports than the defaults of `80` and `443`.

pfBlockerNG

pfBlockerNG, the next generation of pfBlocker, is a relatively new package that blocks countries and IP ranges. It was designed to combine the features of Countryblock and IPblocklist. pfBlocker is a good package to have if you are running an email server, as it allows you to quickly block the top countries from which spam originates. In addition, you do not even need to come up with your own block lists, as there are several free block lists available on the web.

Once you have installed pfBlockerNG, you need to run `geoipupdate` in order to update the GeoIP2 databases, which provide information about users, including country and approximate location. To do so, type in the following at the console or at **Diagnostics** | **Command Prompt**:

```
/usr/local/bin/geoipupdate.sh
```

To begin pfBlockerNG configuration, navigate to **Firewall** | **pfBlockerNG**. There are several tabs, but the default tab is the **general** tab. The first setting is the **Enable pfBlockerNG** checkbox, which, if checked, enables pfBlockerNG. The **Keep Settings** checkbox, if checked, will maintain pfBlockerNG's settings across a reinstall or upgrade (if this option is not checked, these settings will be erased). The **CRON settings** drop-down boxes allow you to select the interval at with the **MaxMind** interface is updated.

The **Global Logging** checkbox, if checked, enables the logging of firewall rules. You can check the **Disable Maxmind Updates** to disable the download of the monthly country database update. You can also set the maximum daily download failure threshold in the **Download Failure Threshold** drop-down box. Finally, you can set the number of lines in the log files in the **Logfile Size** drop-down box.

The **Inbound Firewall Rules** list box allows you to select the interfaces to which the inbound rules apply. You probably want to select **WAN** here. The adjacent drop-down box allows you to select what action to take when inbound rules are applied. You probably want to keep this set to **Block**. The **Outbound Firewall Rules** list box allows you to select one or more interfaces on which outbound traffic will be blocked. If you want to do this (in order to prevent the users on your network from connecting to IP addresses which are on the block lists), you should select **LAN** here and possibly also select additional internal interfaces. The corresponding drop-down box allows you to select what action to take when outbound rules are applied. The default value of **Reject** is probably what you want here; this will tell the users on your network what is happening when they try to connect to forbidden sites.

The **OpenVPN Interface** checkbox, if checked, will add auto-rules for OpenVPN. The **Floating Rules** checkbox enables you to ensure that auto-rules are generated in the **Floating Rules** tab. This is helpful if you want to ensure the auto-rules are in a single place. The **Rule Order** drop-down box allows you to select in what order the rules are placed; by default, pfBlocker rules take precedence over all other rules.

The **Update** tab allows you to configure some of the update settings for pfBlockerNG. The **Update Settings** section includes a **Status** subsection which informs you of the next time cron will update the pfBlocker database. There is also a section called **Force Options** if you wish to force an update. There are three options for forcing updates: **Update**, which just updates at the current time; **Cron**, which does an update, but does it as a cron job; and **Reload**, which just reloads the rules. If you choose **Reload**, you can choose to reload **All**, just the IP ranges (**IP**), or the blacklist(s) (**DNSBL**). As you update, any log activity will be reported in the **Log** section.

The **Country** tab allows you to quickly block any of the top countries from which spam originates. There are two top 20 spammer country lists: one for IPv4 and another for IPv6. You can select countries by pressing *Ctrl* (one country) or *Shift* (multiple countries) and clicking on countries. The **List Action** drop-down box allows you to select what happens to traffic from the selected countries. The options are: **Disabled**, **Deny**, **Permit**, **Match** and **Alias**. The **Deny**, **Permit** and **Match** options have three options each. You can deny/permit/match inbound connections, outbound connections, or both. You can choose **Alias** if you want to create an alias for traffic that matches this rule.

There are two additional sections on this page: **Advanced Inbound Firewall Rule Settings** and **Advanced Outbound Firewall Rule Settings**. These sections allow you to configure options similar to the options available for other firewall rules. For example, the **Custom Protocol** drop-down box will cause this rule to only match if the traffic matches the protocol set here. The **Custom DST Port** and **Custom Destination** fields require that you use aliases, not actual ports and IP addresses.

If you want to select specific countries, click on the appropriate continent tab in pfBlockerNG (**Africa**, **Asia**, **Europe**, **North America**, **Oceania** or **South America**) and select the countries in the list boxes at the top of the page. You can also whitelist a country by selecting on of the **Permit** options in the **List Action** drop-down box. The options on these pages are identical to the options on the main **Country** tab. The **Proxy and Satellite** tab allows you to match traffic to and from proxies and/or satellite providers.

You can also add your own IP lists by specifying a URL for a public block list that will then be automatically downloaded and then periodically update it. To enable this feature, click on the **DNSBL** tab. The main tab in this section will enable you to configure DNSBL list retrieval. Clicking on the **Enable DNSBL** checkbox enables DNS block lists. You can also enter a virtual IP in the **DNSBL Virtual IP** field. You can also enter a listening port and SSL listening port on this page. You can also select the interface you want DNSBL to listen on (the default is **LAN**, whichever interface is chosen, it should be a local interface). You can also check the **DNSBL Firewall Rule** checkbox to create a floating firewall rule, which will allow traffic from interfaces selected in the accompanying list box to access **DNSBL virtual IP**.

The **Alexa Whitelist** section allows you use Alexa's top 1 million sites list. To do so, check the **Enable Alexa** checkbox. You can also select a subset of this list to whitelist by selecting an option in the **number of AlexaTop Domains to Whitelist** drop-down box; the options range from 1,000 to all 1 million. In the **Alexa TLD Inclusion** list box, you can select **top-level domains** (**TLDs**) to whitelist (the defaults are `.com`, `.net`, `.org`, `.ca`, `.co`, and `.io`). In the **Custom Domain Suppression** section, you can enter URLs to whitelist.

The **DNSBL Feeds** tab is where you actually add and configure blacklists. You can do so by clicking on this tab and then clicking on the **Add** button. You need to enter **DNS GROUP Name** for each entry and you can also enter a **Description**. In the **DNSBL** subsection, you can select a **Format** (**Auto** or **rsync**) and a **State** (**ON**, **OFF**, **HOLD**, or **FLEX**). You must also specify **Source**, which can be either a URL or a local file. In the **Header/Label** field, you must enter a unique identifier. You can add more than one blacklist by clicking on the **Add** button and adding another entry.

There is a **List Action** drop-down box where you can select what action to take on the blacklisted items. The **Update Frequency** drop-down box allows you to select how often list files will be downloaded. In the **Weekly (Day of the Week)** drop-down box, you can select the day of the week to update, which is only required if you choose **Weekly** in **Update Frequency**. The **Enable Alexa Whitelist** checkbox, if checked, will result in pfBlocker whitelisting sites that were otherwise blocked if they appear in Alexa. You can also add a custom domain name block list in the **Custom Block List** section.

The **DNSBL EasyList** tab allows you to add one or more EasyList feeds to your pfBlocker NG setup. The EasyList feeds provide lists of ad servers and trackers that you can block at the firewall level. You can choose two different EasyList feeds:

- **EasyList w/o Elements**: EasyList without element hiding. The practice of element hiding hides sections of a page that previously contained advertising.
- **EasyPrivacy**: An optional filter list that removes all forms of tracking.

You can also select different categories to block, such as **EASYLIST Adservers**, **EASYLIST Adult Adservers**, and **EASYLIST trackers**. You can choose an update frequency for the list, and you can also filter this list through Alexa to enable certain sites that show up on Alexa's list of top sites.

The **IPv4** and **IPv6** tabs allow you to add lists of IP addresses or ranges of IP addresses to filter. You can do this by clicking on either the **IPv4** or **IPv6** tab and clicking on the **Add** button. Each entry must be given a name, which is specified in the **Alias Name** field. Your list can either be accessible via a URL or locally.

The **Reputation** tab allows you to enable pfBlocker to search for repeat offenders in each IP range. If there are enough offenders in a subnet, then the entire subnet will be blocked rather than just the individual IP addresses. For the purposes of this algorithm, subnets are always **/24** ranges. The **Enable Max** checkbox, if checked, enables the search for repeat offenders. The **[Max] Setting** drop-down box allows you to select the maximum number of repeat offenders which will be allowed in a single IP range. The default is `5`, but you can allow up to 50 repeat offenders in a subnet.

pMax and **dMax** allow you to perform further analysis on repeat offenders. pMax will look for repeat offenders in subnets but will not use the country exclusions, whereas dMax will look for repeat offenders, but will apply country exclusions. In the **Country Code Settings** section, you can ignore repeat offenders in select countries.

The **Alerts** tab enables you to view alerts, as well as control how many alerts are displayed. Under **Alert Settings**, you can control the number of **Deny**, **DNSBL**, **Permit**, and **Match** entries are shown (the defaults are `25`, `5`, `5`, and `5`). Under **Alert Filter**, you can filter the results based on such criteria as date, source and destination IP address, source and destination port, and protocol.

The **Logs** and **Sync** tabs are similar to the **Logs** and **Sync** tabs in Squid and SquidGuard. The **Logs** tab allows you to view the logs, and the **Sync** tab allows you to perform an XMLRPC sync with a CARP backup node or to a specified host.

Installation of the pfBlockerNG package results in the pfBlockerNG widget appearing on the pfSense dashboard. This widget provides you with a summary of pfBlockerNG activity. The table provides information about each alias, the number of sites blocked by the alias (**Count**), the number of packets blocked by the alias (**Packets**), and the last update time of the alias (**Updated**).

ntopng

`ntopng` is computer software for monitoring network traffic. It is designed to be the successor to ntop (**ntopng** = **ntop Next Generation**). There are versions of ntop for virtually every Unix platform, Windows and mac OS X. It can monitor network traffic, and does the following:

- It allows you to sort traffic by many criteria (for example, IP address, port, and protocol)
- It allows you to identify top talkers and listeners
- It provides flow reports
- It stores persistent traffic statistics
- It allows you to geolocate hosts and display reports based on host location

It can do all this and more with a simple web frontend and is not very resource intensive; its CPU/memory footprint is small. The **ntopng** package has been recently removed from the pfSense package list because it will not compile. According to the documentation for pfSense 2.3, however, **ntopng** will soon return to the package list.

To configure ntopng, navigate to **Diagnostics** | **ntopng Settings**. The **Enable ntopng** checkbox must be checked in order for ntopng to work. The **Keep Data/Settings** checkbox, if checked, will result in settings, graphs and traffic data being retained across package reinstalls and upgrades (if not checked, the settings will be wiped under these circumstances). You can enter an admin password on this page as well.

The **Interface** list box allows you to select the interfaces on which ntop will collect information. The **DNS Mode** drop-down box allows you to select how name resolution is handled. The default is **Decode DNS responses and resolve local numeric IPs only**, but you can choose to resolve all IPs, no IPs, and you can also choose not to decode DNS responses. You can also get data from GeoIP for location information about IP addresses; to update this data, click on the **Update GeoIP Data** button.

The **Local Networks** drop-down box determines how local networks are defined by ntopng. You can select **Consider all RFC1918 networks local**, so that all IPs within local addresses spaces will be considered local, **Consider selected interface networks local**, or **Consider only LAN interface local**. The **Historical Data Storage** checkbox, if checked, enables historical data storage, but this consumes a great deal of disk space. The **Delete (Historical) Data** button allows us to delete this data. Finally, checking the **Disable Alerts** checkbox disables all alerts generated by ntopng.

Once you have enabled and configured ntopng, you can click on the **Access ntopng** tab. Clicking on this tab simply redirects you to port `3000` of your pfSense firewall, which allows you to access the ntopng web GUI.

The **Active Flows** page displays information about current sessions. The information presented includes the application (if known), level four protocol (TCP or UDP), the client IP address, server IP address, and the duration of the connection. The **Breakdown** column graphically shows how much of the traffic for the session is on the client side and how much is on the server side. Finally, the **Bytes** column informs you how much data has been transferred during the session.

The **Top Flow Talkers** page displays both the local and remote IP addresses that generate the most traffic on your network. There is also a graph that displays which application layer protocols are used the most.

The **Local Hosts Matrix** field displays which local hosts connect to each other, and how much traffic is generated. Finally, the hosts page provides a breakdown of each local interface: its IP address, MAC address, and the total traffic sent and traffic received by the interface.

Nmap

Nmap, short for **network map**, is a program that is used to discover hosts and services on a computer network. Hence, it creates a map of the network. It is often used for network security audits, but it is also useful for routine administrative tasks. When you run Nmap, you receive a list of scanned targets as an output. The output depends upon which options are used, but you will always get a list of interesting ports, what services are running on those ports, and the state of the port (open, filtered, closed, or unfiltered). These states can be defined as follows:

- **Open**: If a port is listed as open, then an application is listening on this port; in other words, it is waiting for connections.
- **Filtered**: The port is blocked by a firewall. As a result, it could be open or closed, but Nmap cannot tell which is the case.
- **Closed**: No applications are listening on the port.
- **Unfiltered**: The port responds to Nmap's probes, but Nmap cannot tell if the port is open or closed.

To begin using Nmap, navigate to **Diagnostics** | **NMap**. Enter the IP address or hostname you want to scan in the **IP or Hostname** edit box. In the **Interface** drop-down box, select the source interface. The **Scan Method** drop-down box is where you select the manner in which the port scan is done. The options are as follows:

- **SYN**: As you probably know, establishing a TCP connection involves a three-way handshake which is initiated with a **SYN** packet being sent by the client. The server responds with an acknowledgment that the **SYN** packet was received (**SYN-ACK**), and the client responds with an acknowledgment to which the server need not respond. With this method, Nmap initially sends a **SYN** packet. If it receives a **SYN/ACK** response (or a **SYN** packet), then the port is marked as open. If Nmap receives an **RST** (reset) response, the port is marked as closed. If there is no response, the port is marked as filtered.
- **TCP connect()**: This method involves issuing a TCP `connect()` command through the Berkeley Sockets API (this is the API used by FreeBSD). This method is slower and more likely to be logged than a SYN scan.
- **Ping**: This method involves sending ping requests to scanned ports.
- **UDP**: With this method, Nmap sends a UDP packet to every scanned port. In some cases, a protocol-specific payload is also sent. This potentially increases the response rate in cases where a port is commonly associated with a specific protocol. The remote host will either respond with a UDP packet or not. If a response is received, the port will be marked as open. If there is no response, the port will be marked as **Open** | **Filtered**.
- If an ICMP port unreachable error is received, the port is marked as closed, but other ICMP unreachable errors result in the port as being marked as filtered. One problem with UDP scanning is that it tends to take much longer than TCP scanning; open UDP ports rarely respond (keep in mind UDP is a stateless protocol); therefore, if Nmap doesn't get a response after a timeout period, it will resend a UDP packet just to make sure the packet wasn't lost in transmission. If the port is closed or filtered and an ICMP error is returned, this reply should be returned relatively quickly, but some operating systems limit the number of ICMP replies within a time period. Still, it is good practice to include a UDP scan in your security audit.
- **ARP**: This is the preferred method for scanning local hosts. Sending an **Address Resolution Protocol**) request to a local host is, in most cases, faster and more reliable than doing an IP-based scan, so unless there are other reasons for not using ARP, you should use this on local networks.

There are also several checkboxes, which correspond to different Nmap command line options:

- `-P0`: Do not attempt to ping hosts before scanning. Sometimes, networks do not allow ICMP echo requests/responses through their firewall. If you are scanning such a network, you may want to skip this step even though it is part of the Nmap network discovery process.
- `-sV`: Attempt to identify service versions. With this option, if a TCP or UDP port is discovered, Nmap version detection will communicate with those ports, and try to determine what is running. It will try to determine the service protocol (for example, FTP, SSH, HTTP, and so on), the application name (for example, Apache), the version number, and sometimes other miscellaneous details.
- `-O`: Enable Operating System detection. This activates remote host identification via TCP/IP fingerprinting (it looks at the network stack and compares it with a database of known OS fingerprints to try and determine the OS of the host).

It should be noted that the options on the Nmap page represent only a fraction of the options available for Nmap. They may be enough for your purposes, but it may be beneficial to read the Nmap documentation and, if there is an Nmap option that cannot be invoked from this page, run Nmap from the command line, either by dropping to the shell from the console or via SSH, or by navigating to **Diagnostics** | **Command Prompt**.

HAProxy

HAProxy, as mentioned in `Chapter 8`, *Redundancy and High Availability*, is a pfSense package that implements load balancing and incorporates many features not available with pfSense's built-in load balancer. Once HAProxy is installed, HAProxy is added to the services menu; navigating there reveals that there are several tabs. The most significant of these are **Settings** (general settings), **Frontend** (allows you to configure one or more frontends), and **Backend** (allows you to configure one or more backends). There are also tabs for **Files** (allows you to add error files, which show custom error pages, and Lua scripts, which allow you to perform custom fetches and service implementations), **Stats and Stats FS** (both display the stats page, which can also be reached via **Status** | **HAProxy Stats**), and **Templates** (allows you to create templates for custom configurations).

Example – load balancing a web server

As a means of demonstrating some of the options available with HAProxy, we will show HAProxy in action by revisiting an example from `Chapter 8`, *Redundancy and High Availability*, in which we load balanced three Apache web servers.

Once we install HAProxy, we navigate to **Services** | **HAProxy** to begin configuration and click on the **Settings** tab. We will not check the Enable HAProxy checkbox right away; rather, we will do that last after all other configuration has been completed. There is a **Maximum connections** edit box which allows us to set the maximum number of per-process concurrent connections, along with some guidelines on how much memory connections will use. Unless your pfSense firewall has an unusually high amount of memory, it behooves you to limit the number of concurrent connections; in this case, we enter `5000`.

The next option is **Number of processes to start**, which defaults to 1 if left blank. The instructions recommend keeping this setting at the default value, which is what we will do. The **Reload behavior** checkbox, if checked, will force the old HAProxy process to stop when HAProxy is restarted, even if it is still serving old connections. In other words, old connections will be dropped when HAProxy is restarted, which is not what we want, so we will leave this option unchecked. We will also assume that in this case, we are not running a CARP failover group, so we will leave the **Carp monitor** drop-down box set to **Disabled**.

Scrolling down to **Stats tab, 'internal' stats port**, we set **Internal stats port** - this can be any unused port. Under Logging, we want to log HAProxy activity to the local pfSense systemlog, so we enter `/var/run/log` in the **Remote syslog host** edit box. We scroll past the **Global DNS resolvers for haproxy** section, but we want to add email notifications, so under **Global email notifications** we add a mail server. Under **Name**, we enter an appropriate name (example, `Local mail server`); under **Mailserver**, we enter the IP address of the local email server (assume that the email server, like the web servers, are part of the DMZ network, and that the IP address is `192.168.2.20`); for **Mailserverport**, we enter `25` - the default SMTP port. We also check the checkbox to the left of these edit boxes. **Mail level** allows us to define the maximum log level for which emails will be sent. Since we only want to receive emails if the situation is critical or worse, we set **Mail level** to **Critical**. **Mail myhostname** allows us to define the hostname to be used as the sender of the emails and **Mail from** allows us to define the email address which will be seen as the sender. For these two parameters, the actual value used is not important to the functioning of email notifications, but we should follow any conventions we have been using in configuring our network.

Finally, there is one last setting in this section whose value is important: **Mail to**, which allows us to set the email address to which notifications will be sent. In the **Tuning** section, we set **Max SSL Diffie-Hellman** size to **2048**. When we are done, we scroll to the bottom of the page and click on the **Save** button and then the **Apply Changes** button at the top of the page. There is also a **Show** button at the bottom of the page which, if clicked on, will show the current `/var/etc/haproxy/haproxy.cfg` configuration file, reflecting any changes that have been made.

We click on the **Backend** tab (it's easier to configure the frontend after the backend has already been configured) and click on the **Add** button to begin backend configuration. we enter an appropriate **Name** (example, `WEBSERVERS`), and click on the down arrow under Server list to begin adding the backend web servers. You might recall that the IP addresses for the servers were `192.168.2.11`, `192.168.2.12`, and `192.168.2.13`. We give the server a **Name** (example, `WEB1`); under Address we enter `192.168.2.11`, and under Port we enter `443`. We check the SSL checkbox, and for now we leave **Weight** unchanged.

Underneath the basic server configuration are a number of options related to SSL certificate verification. Essentially, if our servers use SSL, we have the option of verifying the client's SSL certificate against certificates that have been added with the **Cert. Manager**. In this case, we will assume that the web servers are configured to do SSL verification and not take advantage of this feature.

We repeat the server configuration process for each of the other servers, three in total, in each case setting the port to `443`, enabling SSL on each of them and leaving **Weight** unchanged. We scroll down to **Loadbalancing options**, click on the plus icon in the right portion of the column to expand this section, and choose **Least Connections** as the load balancing Option. Scrolling down, there are two sections that are worth noting. There is the **Health checking** section, which allows us to set a number of parameters controlling how HAProxy checks to see if a server is still up. A number of protocols are supported; HTTP is the default but LDAP, MySQL, SMTP and SSL are supported, to name a few. The **Stick table persistence** section allows you make sure separate requests from a single client go to the same backend. There are different criteria we can use to determine if a client is the same client. One is the SSL ID, the IP address (IPv4 or IPv6), or a cookie (standard cookie or RDP cookie). We will leave the defaults in these sections unchanged and click on the **Save** button and then the **Apply Changes** button.

We next click on the **Frontend** tab and click on the **Add** button to begin frontend configuration. We enter an appropriate **Name** (which can be the same name as the backend), an appropriate **Description** (example, Apache web server load balancing group) and leave the **Status** set to **Active**. For the **Listen address**, we want to use our **WAN** address, so we leave that at its default setting. Our web server is using HTTPS, so we change the **Port** to `80`, and also check the **SSL Offloading** checkbox. We also check the checkbox in the leftmost column of this row. Then we scroll down to the **Default backend, access control lists and actions** section and set **Default Backend** to the backend we configured in the previous step (**WEBSERVERS**). We then click on the **Save** button and click on the **Apply Changes** button.

HAProxy setup is complete, but we still need to create a rule to allow port `443` traffic on the **WAN** interface. We navigate to **Firewall | Rules**, and on the **WAN** tab we click on one of the Add buttons. Most of the settings can be kept at their defaults (**Action**, **Interface**, and **Protocol** are all by default at their correct settings), but we want to set **Destination Port Range** to `443` to allow HTTPS traffic on this port to pass through (port `443` is one of the presets in the drop-down box, although you can type it into the edit box as well). We enter a brief description (example, `Allow web server traffic`) and click on the **Save** button and then click on the **Apply Changes** button. After making sure the rule order is correct, we navigate back to **Services | HAProxy**, click on the **Settings** tab, and then check the **Enable HAProxy** checkbox. Then we scroll down, click on **Save**, and click on **Apply Changes**. To confirm that the load balancing pool is up and running, navigate to **Status | HAProxy Stats** and check.

Other packages

There are also a number of other packages that, while not likely to be utilized by most pfSense users, are nonetheless useful and deserve mention. For the most part, these packages are more likely to be useful in corporate-type deployments, so if you are installing pfSense in such an environment and the stock pfSense installation does not provide the functionality you require, you may want to review this section to see if any of the packages discussed meet your needs.

Snort

Snort is an open source network intrusion prevention system and intrusion detection system. Among its features, it can do real-time traffic analysis and packet logging. It can be run in three different modes:

- **Packet sniffing mode**: In this mode, Snort simply intercepts traffic on your network in a manner similar to how a program like Wireshark would.
- **Packet logging mode**: This mode is useful for network traffic debugging. Packets are logged to a disk.
- **Network intrusion prevention mode**: In this mode, Snort monitors network traffic, and analyzes it against a user-defined rule set. The program can perform a specific action based on the rule that has been matched.

Snort provides its own rules which you can use for intrusion detection. You can pay for a subscription or you can obtain the community rules for free. Even if you don't pay for a subscription, if you create an account on Snort.org, you can download the registered user rule packages.

Once you have installed Snort, you can begin configuration by navigating to **Services** | **Snort** and clicking on the **Global Settings** tab. Note that you can enable the download of the rules simply by checking a checkbox. The **Enable Snort VRT** checkbox, if checked, downloads the free registered user or paid subscriber rules, while checking the **Enable Snort GPLv2** checkbox enables downloading of the community rules (which, as mentioned, are free of charge).You can also enable the download of **Emerging Threats** (**ET**) rules. The **Enable ET Open** checkbox, if checked, enables downloading of the open source version of ET rules, while checking **Enable ET Pro** enables the downloading of ET Pro rules, which requires signing up for an ET Pro account.

If you are using Snort, you may want to use the Open AppID plugin. This plugin enables Snort to detect, monitor, and manage application usage. If so, you will have to download the Sourcefire Open AppID detectors, and checking the **Enable OpenAppID** checkbox makes this possible. Open AppID was introduced in February 2014, and there are already more than 1,500 applications that can be detected by this plugin.

The **Rules Update Settings** section allows you to control when rules are updated. In order to enable auto-updates, you must choose an option other than **NEVER** in the **Update Interval** drop-down box. You may also specify a start time for updates in the **Update Start Time** edit box. In this section, there is also an option to hide deprecated rules categories in the GUI and remove them from the configuration (the **Hide Deprecated Rules Categories** checkbox).

The **General Settings** section contains a few more options. The **Remove Blocked Hosts Interval** drop-down box allows you to select the amount of time hosts will be blocked. The **Remove Blocked Hosts Interval** checkbox, if checked, will clear all blocked hosts added by Snort when the package is removed. If you check the **Keep Snort Settings after Deinstall** checkbox, Snort settings will be retained after package removal. Finally, the **Startup/Shutdown Logging** checkbox, if checked, will output detailed messages to the system log when Snort is starting and stopping.

Once you have configured these options, you can click on the **Updates** tab and see what rules have been enabled in your configuration. There is also an **Update Your Rule Set** section which has two buttons. **Update Rules** automatically checks and applies any new posted updates for enabled rules packages. The **Force Update** button, if clicked, will zero out the MD5 hashes, thus forcing a download of the entire rules packages. You can also view the log file on this page by clicking on **View Log page**, or clear the log by clicking on **Clear Log**.

Snort is configurable on a per interface basis; you can configure interfaces by clicking on the **Snort Interfaces** tab. There, you can click on the **Add** tab to add a new interface. Once you choose an interface to inspect traffic on (in the **Interface** drop down), you can choose whether to automatically block hosts that generate a Snort alert (the **Block Offenders** checkbox). You can also choose the pattern matcher algorithm in the **Search Method** drop-down box. The default algorithm is AhoCorasick Binary NFA (**AC-BNFA**), but there are a number of other options, some of which require more resources than others.

The **Split ANY-ANY** checkbox, if checked, enables the splitting of an **ANY-ANY** port group. An *ANY-ANY* rule is a rule which will match any address and any port, for example:

```
alert tcp any any ->192.168.1.0/24 53
```

This will generate an alert when a host on any IP address and any port tries to connect to port `53` of any host on the `192.168.1.0` subnet. The default behavior of Snort is to add an *ANY-ANY* port rule to every non-ANY-ANY port group. This way, only one evaluation needs to be done per packet. But, suspending this behavior (not putting an *ANY-ANY* rule into every other port group) can significantly reduce the memory footprint, at a cost of requiring two group evaluations per packet.

The **Choose the Networks Snort Should Inspect and Whitelist** section allows you to choose **Home Net** and an **External Net** that will be whitelisted. You can also specify a suppression or filtering list in the **Alert Suppression and Filtering** drop-down box. Finally, you can specify additional parameters in the **Advanced Configuration PassThrough** list box.

The **Iface Categories** tab allows you to select the rulesets Snort will load at the startup for this interface. Any rulesets you have downloaded or created should be visible on this page. You can also enable automatic flowbit resolution on this tab (flowbits allow you to track the state of a flow during a TCP session; automatic flowbit resolution automatically converts old rules that do not use the `fileidentify.rules` category to the new format).

The **Iface Rules** tab allows you to enable and disable individual rules. You can choose from decoder rules, pre-processor rules, and sensitive data rules. You can also enable and disable any custom rules you have defined. The **Iface Variables** tab allows you to define the values of certain predefined variables used in rules.

The **Alerts** tab allows you to view alerts on a per-interface basis. The **Interface to Inspect** drop-down box allows you to select an interface, and the adjacent edit box allows you to determine how many lines appear. The **Auto-refresh view** checkbox will result in the page updating automatically as new alerts are generated. You can also download the alert log by clicking on the **Download** button and clear the log by clicking on the **Clear** button. The **Blocked** tab allows you to view hosts that have been blocked by Snort. You can choose the number of blocked hosts that appear on this page (the default is `500`), and there is a **Refresh** checkbox to auto-refresh the page's contents. You can also download the list of blocked hosts by clicking on the **Download** button.

The **Pass Lists** tab allows you to generate whitelists, which you can do by clicking on this tab and then clicking on the **Add** button. To make life easier, there are some sets of IP addresses that can be added to the list just by clicking on a checkbox: namely **firewall connected local networks**, **WAN gateways**, **WAN DNS servers**, **virtual IPs**, and **VPN addresses**. You can also add a configured alias to the list.

The **Suppress** tab allows you to define suppression lists in a similar manner; to do so, click on the tab and click on the **Add** button. After entering a name and description for the list, simply add the suppression rules into the appropriate list box. The rules must follow Snort's format for such rules.

The **SID (Signature ID) Mgmt** tab has a single option. The **Enable Automatic SID State Management** checkbox enables automatic management of rule state and content using criteria specified in configuration files. If you enable this option, Snort will generate a series of configuration files which will appear in the **SID Management Configuration Files** section. You can add, upload and download these configuration files from this section (the configuration files can be downloaded individually via the download icons in the table, or as a single gzip archive using the **Download** button). You can also add and delete configuration files within this section. You will need to specify the enable SID, disable SID, and modify SID files.

Most likely, none are selected by default, so you will have to create or generate separate files for each of these and specify them in the corresponding drop-down boxes. The **SID State Order** drop-down box determines which file is executed first: the disable SID file or the enable SID file. Check the **Rebuild** button to rebuild the rules from the selected configuration files.

The **Log Mgmt** tab allows you to control a number of log settings. The **Remove Snort Logs on Package Uninstall** checkbox, if checked, will remove the Snort log files on uninstall. The **Auto Log Management** checkbox allows you to enable automatic unattended management of the Snort logs using the parameters specified in the **Log Directory Size Limit** section and the **Log Size and Retention Limits** section. The **Log Directory Size Limit** edit box imposes a hard limit on the combined log directory size, while the **Log Size and Retention Limits** edit box allows you to control the size of individual logs.

The **Sync** tab is essentially identical to the **Sync** tab in such applications as Squid. It allows you to sync Snort settings via XMLRPC. The sync target can either be part of a CARP failover group or any arbitrarily defined node. Moreover, you can select more than one replication target by entering the information in the **Replication Targets** subsection, entering the relevant information, clicking on the **Add** button, and repeating the process.

Example – using Snort to block social media sites

In `Chapter 4`, *Using pfSense as a Firewall*, we covered several examples of using pfSense firewall rules to block certain websites. It quickly became apparent that blocking websites with this method is easy when the website uses a single IP address, but when the website uses multiple IP addresses, it was problematic. If the website uses a fixed set of IP addresses, it is easy enough to create an alias for them and to make sure the rule blocks all addresses covered by the alias. Some popular social media sites such as YouTube and Facebook, however, are constantly updating the pool of IP addresses they use, thus rendering this method difficult to utilize, because unless we constantly update our list of IP addresses, the rule becomes ineffective.

Snort, however, provides another way of trying to block these sites, and while it is not foolproof, it requires much less overhead than the process outlined in `Chapter 4`, *Using pfSense as a Firewall*. The process described below assumes the following:

- Snort has been installed using the Package Manager and has been enabled
- Snort has been enabled on the WAN interface

If those preconditions are not met and you want to try implementing these rules, make sure Snort is installed and enabled on the WAN interface. No additional configuration is necessary.

To begin, we navigate to **Services** | **Snort** and from the **Snort Interfaces** tab, we find the entry for WAN and click on the **Edit** icon for it. A second row of tabs will appear controlling different settings for the WAN interface; we click on the **WAN rules** tab. Make sure **Category Selection** is set to custom.rules and enter the following rules into the **Defined Custom Rules** text box:

```
alert tcp any any <> any any (msg: "YouTube detected";
pcre:"/youtube\.com|www\.youtube\.com/"; sid:4000001)
alert tcp any any <> any any (msg: "Facebook detected";
pcre:"/facebook\.com/"; sid:4000002)
```

Explaining what these rules do requires some exposition on Snort's rule syntax, so now is a good time to cover this subject:

- **alert**: This is the rule action. There are five default actions: **alert** (generate an alert and log the packet); **log** (log the packet); **pass** (ignore the packet); **activate** (alert and turn on another dynamic rule); **dynamic** (remain idle until turned on by an activate rule, then turn into a log rule). We can block IP addresses that generate an alert, so we choose alert.
- **tcp**: This is the protocol field, which can be either **tcp**, **udp**, or **icmp**. Web traffic is TCP, so we choose **tcp**.
- **any any**: These fields refer to the source of the traffic. The first field is the IP address, which is formed by a numeric portion and a CIDR. Thus, it can refer to an entire subnet. You can use the negation operator (`!`) to match any address not in the subnet. `any`, as you may have guessed, will match any IP address. The second field is the port, which can be `any` to match any port, or a port number. Two numbers separated by a colon (`:`) indicates a range of ports; for example, `5000:5010` denotes ports `5000` to `5010`. As with IP addresses, you can use the negation operator.
- **<>**: This is the direction operator. -> refers to traffic flowing from source to destination; <- refers to traffic flowing from destination to source; <> refers to traffic flowing in both directions. We want to match traffic flowing in both directions, so we choose <>.
- **msg**: This prints a message in alerts and packet logs. We are looking for YouTube traffic in the first rule and Facebook traffic in the second rule, as the `msg` field indicates.

- **pcre**: This is the field where we tell Snort what we want to match. **pcre** stands for Perl-Compatible Regular Expression; another popular option to use for this field is `content`, but `pcre` allows us a bit more flexibility in specifying the text we want to match. Note that the regular expression is contained within double quotes (`"`) and is also contained by forward slashes (`/`). For YouTube, we want to match both `youtube.com` and `www.youtube.com`, so we specify both and place an or operator (`|`) between the two. Note that we have to use the backslash character (`\`) as an escape sequence before each dot (`.`). Other options for this field include `nocase` (make the match case insensitive) and `offset` (skip a certain number of bytes before doing the comparison).
- **sid**: This is the unique identifier for the rule. Each `sid` must be unique, and we should use numbers over `4,000,000` to avoid conflicts with popular rule providers.

When we are done adding the rules, we click the **Save** button to save and force a reload of the rules. The rules we added only generate alerts, however, so to block these sites we must click on the **WAN Settings** tab scroll down to **Alert Settings**, and make sure that **Block Offenders** is enabled. When this option is enabled, Snort will block any host that generates an alert. When we are done, we scroll down and click on the **Save** button.

After adding these rules to Snort, both YouTube and Facebook should be blocked. To test this out, try to access both sites and click on the **Alerts** tab in Snort; the log should be filled with `YouTube detected` and `Facebook detected` messages. The IP addresses of the hosts that generated alerts should find their way onto the blocked hosts list; you can view this by clicking on the **Blocked** tab.

These rules have their shortcomings. For starters, we are looking for users trying to access certain hostnames (`www.youtube.com`, `facebook.com`, and `youtube.com`); if the user types the IP address into the browser, they could circumvent our attempt to block the traffic (that is, assuming that the IP address has not already been added to the blocked hosts list). It should be generally effective in blocking these sites, however, and provides a baseline for further experimentation with Snort rules.

FRRouting

As mentioned in `Chapter 10`, *Routing and Bridging*, **FRRouting** is a package that supports multiple dynamic routing protocols. Namely, it supports BGP, OSPF, and OSPF6. It is designed to take the place of Quagga OSPF and is incompatible with both Quagga and OpenOSPF. Installation of FRRouting will result in the automatic uninstalling of Quagga or OpenOSPF, if either of these packages are already installed.

Upon installation of FRRouting, four new items will appear in the **Services** menu: **FRR BGP**, **FRR Global/Zebra**, **FRR OSPF**, and **FRR OSPF6**. Each of these menu items takes you to a separate tab within the FRRouting configuration, so you also have the option of navigating between the configuration for each of these items by clicking on the corresponding tabs.

If you navigate to **Services | Global/Zebra**, you can review the global settings as well as the settings for the Zebra daemon, which supports multiple protocols. Observe that the **General Settings** section has a setting called **CARP Status IP**. If this option is set and the CARP status IP indicates that CARP is in backup mode, FRR will not be started, but if it is promoted to master, FRR will start. Thus FRR is compatible with CARP failover groups, although you still must install and configure FRR on each firewall within the group.

The **Route Handling** section allows you to route specified subnets differently. You can enable the **Do Not Accept** option, which will cause routing protocols controlled by FRR to reject traffic from the specified subnet. You can also enable **Null Route**, which will cause FRR to drop traffic destined for the specified subnet. There is also a **Static Route Target** option (you can select a gateway or interface), which allows you to enter traffic from a subnet into FRR/Zebra's static routing table for route redistribution.

There are also two tabs, one called **Access Lists** and another called **Prefix Lists**. The **Access Lists** tab allows you to define a list of networks that are either allowed or denied in specific contexts. The **Prefix Lists** tab allows you to do the same thing, only instead of networks, you are defining portions of networks that are either allowed or denied in specific contexts.

You can utilize these lists in the next tab, **Route Maps**. Much like firewall rules allow you to match traffic based on a set of criteria and take action, route maps allow you to match traffic based on selected criteria and either route the traffic a certain way or possibly deny the traffic. Like firewall rules, route maps are evaluated in a certain order, and the first route map to match the traffic is executed while subsequent route maps are ignored as far as the matched traffic is concerned. The order in which route maps are evaluated depends on the value in the **Sequence** field, with lower-numbered route maps being evaluated first.

As of this writing, FRR is still a relatively new package, so if you value stability above all else, you may opt for Quagga OSPF instead. Otherwise, FRR is the recommended choice if you need to deploy BGP or OSPF, and especially if you need to run multiple routing protocols.

Zabbix

Zabbix is an enterprise-level, open source (it's licensed under the GPL v. 2) monitoring software for both networks and applications. One Zabbix server can monitor hundreds of devices, and Zabbix can automatically discover servers and network devices. It is capable of monitoring services without installing any software on the monitored server, but you can also install agents on hosts that will collect data such as CPU load, memory, network, and disk utilization on behalf of the Zabbix server.

pfSense has packages for the Zabbix agent and Zabbix proxy, so you can install the agent or the proxy or both. The difference between the two is that while a Zabbix agent simply collects data from a local host and sends it to the Zabbix server, a Zabbix proxy can monitor remote hosts, collect performance and availability data, and offload the Zabbix server. Thus, it can perform many of the functions that the Zabbix server would otherwise have to do. In fact, it is somewhat easier to list the things a Zabbix proxy cannot do:

- A proxy cannot calculate triggers
- A proxy cannot process events
- A proxy cannot send alerts
- A proxy cannot execute remote commands

Most other functions that a Zabbix server can perform, such as Zabbix agent checks, built-in web monitoring, network discovery and low-level discovery (which is a way of automatically creating items, triggers, and graphs for devices as they are discovered) can be done by a Zabbix proxy. Also, if there's a firewall between the agents and the Zabbix server, having a single Zabbix proxy collect data from the agents makes configuration easier, as you only need to create one firewall rule to allow traffic between the Zabbix server and the proxy.

Zabbix agent and Zabbix proxy configuration are similar. Installing them adds items to the **Services** menu called **Zabbix Agent MajorNumber.MinorNumber** and **Zabbix Proxy MajorNumber.Minor Number**. As of this writing, the latest version of Zabbix is 3.4. In both configuration pages, there are fields where you can enter a list of Zabbix servers, as well as a list of Zabbix servers and ports for active checks. You can also set a **Listen IP** if you will be listening for a Zabbix server connection on a specific interface; the default is `0.0.0.0`, which will cause pfSense to listen on all interfaces. You can also set the **Listen Port**.

Both the agent and proxy configuration have a section called **TLS-RELATED Parameters**. These settings control how the agent should send data to the proxy or server: either **Unencrypted**, with TLS and a pre-shared key (**psk**) or with TLS and a certificate (**cert**). You can also control what connections the agent or proxy will accept, with the same options. There are also options to select a certificate authority (**TLS CA**), a certificate (**TLS Cert**), and a text box where you can enter a pre-shared key (**TLS PSK**).

The one significant difference between Zabbix agent and proxy configuration is that the proxy configuration page has a section called **SNMP Trap Monitoring** which enables you to start the SNMP trapper process on the proxy. You can also specify a temporary file to be used for passing SNMP trap data from the SNMP daemon to the proxy in the **SNMP Trapper File** field.

There are several versions of both the Zabbix agent and proxy available on the packages list, presumably so administrators can make a suitable trade-off between stability and functionality. Installing and configuring Zabbix may be overkill, especially if you are setting up a network for home or a small office/home office, but if you need to administer a large network with no local administrators, Zabbix provides an easy way of centralizing host monitoring.

Summary

In this chapter, we took a look at some of the more significant packages available for pfSense. More packages have been added over the past few years, and as a result, if the stock pfSense installation doesn't provide what you need, there's a good chance that a third-party package exists that does. Packages implementing proxy servers, network monitoring, and network intrusion detection/prevention are among the most popular ones, but in addition to that, there are packages for load balancing and routing, among others. This chapter covered what the author believes to be the most important packages, but be sure to look through the complete package list before giving up the search for the package you require.

In the final chapter, we will cover a topic that is essential to creating and maintaining a computer network but is often overlooked: troubleshooting.

Questions

Answer the following questions:

1. What two methods can be used to install pfSense packages?
2. What is the default port on which a Squid proxy will listen?
3. We have added a firewall rule to block access to a certain website from all local networks and we have confirmed that the rule works as intended. (a) After we install the Squid proxy server, what will be the outcome when we try to access this website? (b) After we enable the Squid proxy server, what will be the outcome when we try to access the website? For both (a) and (b), assume we have not done any additional configuration to Squid.
4. If we want to block a country from accessing our network, what package provides the easiest way of doing this?
5. Identify the different states of interesting ports in an Nmap probe.
6. If we want to add a load balancing group and also want email notifications if a server in the group goes down, which package should we install?
7. Identify the three modes in which Snort can be run.
8. Identify the three different protocols that can be specified in a Snort rule.
9. Identify any package that can be used for network monitoring (there are several).
10. (a) What is the difference between a Zabbix agent and a Zabbix proxy? (b) We want to enable SNMP trap monitoring. What Zabbix package should we install?

Further reading

Vacche, Andrea and Lee, Stefano. *Mastering Zabbix: Second Edition*. Birmingham/Mumbai: Packt Publishing, September 2015. Print. If you're interested in deploying Zabbix on your network, this book provides a comprehensive guide.

12
Diagnostics and Troubleshooting

If you are implementing or maintaining a network, it is almost certain that at some point something will go wrong. This could be a result of human error (for example, a misconfiguration issue), hardware failure, or a software problem. In such circumstances, your troubleshooting skills will be put to the test. The aim of this chapter is to help you develop your troubleshooting skills, by discussing both some common networking problems and the tools that can be used to diagnose them.

The following topics will be covered in this chapter:

- Troubleshooting basics
- pfSense troubleshooting tools

Technical requirements

To work through the examples in this chapter, you will need a working pfSense system either on a functioning network or in a virtual environment. For diagnostics, you will need at least one node on the network, running either Linux or Windows.

Troubleshooting basics

Implementing effective network troubleshooting involves a multi-step approach. These steps both provide a framework for troubleshooting and help reduce the amount of time spent resolving problems:

1. **Identify the problem**: This seems obvious, but we often assume that we know the exact scope of the problem, when we might be better served gathering information, identifying symptoms, and, when applicable, questioning users. If there is more than one problem, we should recognize it as such so we can approach each problem individually. Sometimes, the end users are good sources of information. For example, you can ask a user how the system behaves during normal operation and compare it to how the system currently behaves. Recreate the problem, if possible, and try to isolate the location of the problem.
2. **Formulate a theory of probable cause**: A single problem can have many causes, but if you have done your homework with information gathering and if you apply a modicum of common sense, you can eliminate many of these causes. Often, the most obvious solution is the correct one; looking at the easiest solution first is a reasonable approach. Keep in mind, however, that your initial theory may be incorrect and you may have to consider other theories.
3. **Test the theory**: Once you have established a theory of probable cause, you should attempt to confirm the theory. If the theory can be confirmed, then you can move on to the next step. If not, you need to formulate another theory.
4. **Establish a plan**: Once you think you have identified the cause, you need to establish a plan of action. This becomes more important when troubleshooting in enterprise-level environments. Implementing a solution may involve taking systems offline, and you have to determine when they will be taken offline and for how long. In many cases, your organization may have formal or informal procedures for taking the system offline. This often includes scheduling a time – often during non-working hours – when the work will be done. Nonetheless, once you have a plan in place, you should be able to implement a solution.
5. **Implement the solution**: Once the corrective change has been made to your network, you still need to test the solution. You can't assume that the solution has worked without testing it, and often you need to be mindful that early results may be deceiving, and you may need to test it again to make sure the solution has worked.

6. **Verify system functionality**: Sometimes a solution that fixes one problem creates another. This is why it is important to verify full system functionality before you decide the solution was successful. In fact, it might be best to assume that the changes you make will affect the network in one way or another and determine how it will affect it.
7. **Document the problem and solution**: Documenting the solution involves keeping a record of all the steps taken while solving the problem. Documenting both failures and successes can save you time in the future, and in large organizations, keeping a record of the person who implemented the solution can be helpful if someone in the organization has a question about it.

If the problem was initially reported by an end user, you might also consider providing feedback to the user. Such feedback might not only encourage users to report problems in the future, but you might be able to provide information as to how the problem could have been avoided in the first place.

One of the ways we can evaluate problems is to use the seven-layer OSI model and try to determine what layer or layers the problem is on:

- **Physical layer**: This covers such problems as damaged or dirty cabling, or terminations, high levels of signal attenuation, and insufficient cable bandwidth. It also covers such problems as wireless interference or access points malfunctioning.
- **Data link layer**: This covers such problems as MAC address misconfiguration and VLAN misconfiguration or sub-optimal VLAN performance. It also encompasses some protocol issues such as improper L2TP or OSPF configuration.
- **Network layer**: This covers such problems as damaged or defective networking devices, misconfigured devices, sub-optimal device configuration, authentication issues, and lack of sufficient network bandwidth.
- **Transport layer**: This covers issues with the TCP and UDP protocols.
- **Session/Presentation/Application layers**: This covers problems related to applications and application layer protocols (for example, FTP and SMTP).

Common networking problems

There are also some issues that come up so often in the networking world that we would be remiss if we did not take note of them. You can consider the following problems as obvious possible causes that, in many scenarios, should be considered before other, less obvious possible causes are considered.

Wrong subnet mask or gateway

This one is very simple: if the subnet mask specified on the host does not match the subnet mask for the network, then communicating with the network will not be possible. Finding the subnet mask is usually quite easy. In recent versions of Windows, such information can be obtained by navigating to **Settings** | **Network Connections**, right-clicking on the network adapter you are using, and selecting **Properties**. There should be a list box displaying the installed protocols; scroll down to **internet Protocol Version 6** or **Internet Protocol Version 4** depending on what version you are using, and click on the **Properties** button. This should show you what the subnet mask is.

In Linux, finding the subnet mask is just as easy. For example, in Ubuntu or Mint Linux, click on the networking icon in the tray on the right end of the taskbar (the icon should look like two interconnected cables if you have a wired connection or a series of arcs if you have a wireless connection). This should launch the **Network Connections** dialog box. Find your connection (for example, **Wired Connection 1**) and double-click on it. This will launch the **Editing** dialog box, where you can change settings for the connection. Click on either the **IPv4 Settings** or **IPv6 Settings** tab to find the subnet mask.

Correct configuration of the subnet mask should allow intra-network communications, but a missing or misconfigured gateway setting will prevent a host from communicating with other networks. You should confirm that the gateway is set correctly, and since the gateway is often specified in the same place as the subnet mask, this should not be difficult to do.

Wrong DNS configuration

The DNS provides us with a means of translating hostnames into IP addresses. If a DNS server is not specified at all, then the host will not be able to take advantage of DNS services. If the correct DNS server is not specified (for example, if the primary server is incorrect), then DNS resolution can take longer than necessary, thus giving the impression that internet access is slower than it actually is.

A good indicator that DNS configuration is incorrect is if you can ping a site if you specify the IP address, but the ping fails when you specify the hostname (and ping returns an *unknown hostname* or a similar error). If this happens, you should definitely check the DNS configuration, first on the host and then on the firewall.

Duplicate IP addresses

All IP addresses on a network must be unique. This includes network cards, routers and access points. If a network device is on the LAN, then its IP address must be unique on the LAN. If it is connected to the internet, then it must be unique on the internet. Problems with duplicate IP addresses can range from receiving error messages informing you of the existence of duplicate IP addresses to not being able to connect to the network from the device with duplicate address.

Obviously, the use of DHCP, in which assignment of IP addresses is managed by the DHCP server, and IPv6, which has a greater number of private addresses to assign, greatly cuts down on the possibility of duplicate IP addresses. Duplicate addresses are most likely to happen on IPv4 networks in which the IP addresses are statically assigned.

Network loops

As mentioned in `Chapter 10`, *Routing and Bridging*, there can only be a single path between two network devices. If there is more than one path, then the looping can generate a broadcast storm that brings your network to its knees. It is especially a concern if you have bridged one or more interfaces on your network. One way to prevent looping is to manually configure network ports to ensure there is only one path to each device. The more likely scenario, however, is that you utilize a protocol such as **Spanning Tree Protocol** (**STP**), or its successor, **Rapid Spanning Tree Protocol** (**RSTP**).

Another situation where looping can occur is when the information in the routing table is incorrect, either through a manual misconfiguration or a failure in automatic route detection. Such errors are often easy to detect, because as with physical loops, they will quickly bog down a network.

Routing issues

In `Chapter 10`, *Routing and Bridging*, we described how to set up a static route in pfSense. Static routes can easily cause problems on a network, since a change in network topology can render a static route incorrect. Therefore, if you make changes to your network and you have static routes, you should consider how the changes impact these static routes and make changes to them accordingly.

Port configuration

By default, pfSense will block all ports on the WAN side of the router. Therefore, if a remote user tries to connect to a port on a local host, the user will be blocked from doing so. In order to connect to a port on a local host, there must be a port forwarding rule forwarding the traffic to the host, and there must be a rule on the network to which the local host is connected permitting such traffic (in pfSense, NAT port forwarding has an option for auto-generating firewall rules that correspond to port forwarding rules, thus ensuring that both steps can be completed at the same time).

Black holes

Sometimes, network traffic is dropped without the source ever being informed that the traffic never reached its intended target. The error can only be detected by monitoring network traffic. Such a situation is referred to as a black hole.

One such scenario is when a host tries to connect to an IP address that was assigned to a host that is down or to an IP address that was never assigned to a host. Although TCP has mechanisms for communicating a failure to connect back to the original host, often the packets are just dropped. Moreover, if you are using a protocol such as UDP that is both connectionless and unreliable, then there are no means of communicating back to the original host that the IP address is dead.

Another common situation is with **Maximum Transmission Unit** (**MTU**) black holes. This happens when an MTU packet is larger than the maximum MTU size allowed on a network, and the **Don't Fragment** (**DF**) flag is set in the IP header. If this happens, any device whose MTU is smaller than the packet's size will drop the packet. The solution here is to make sure **Path MTU Discovery** (**PMTUD**) is running on all network devices. PMTUD solves this problem by sending back a **Fragmentation Needed** ICMP message back, thus causing the offending device to reduce its MTU size. Some network devices block ICMP messages for security reasons, however, and if this is the case on your network, you could end up with black hole connections: the TCP three-way handshake will be completed, but when data is transferred, the connection will hang because of the MTU size mismatch.

One possible solution is to use the RFC 4821 version of PMTUD. This version uses TCP or another protocol to probe the patch with progressively larger packets. Another solution is to change the **maximum segment size** (**MSS**) of all TCP connections lower than the Ethernet default of `1500`.

Physical issues

You should also be aware that there are many issues related to cabling that can cause problems, and are often overlooked as a potential cause. The most common form of network cabling used in homes and offices is **unshielded twisted pair** (**UTP**), with fiber optic cabling being the more expensive alternative. UTP cabling is susceptible to various forms of interference. One such form is crosstalk, when the signal from one cable bleeds into another cable. This often happens when two cables are run too close to each other. **Near end crosstalk** (**NEXT**) is when an outgoing data transmission leaks into an incoming transmission. **Far end crosstalk** (**FEXT**) is when a transmitting station at the other end of a transmission line leaks into the receiving line. One of the ways you can minimize crosstalk is to purchase high-quality UTP cable, in which the twisted pairs are twisted more tightly; the greater the number of twists, the less crosstalk.

EMI can also reduce signal strength. Computer monitors and fluorescent lighting both create an electromagnetic field and can cause problems with UTP network cabling. **Radio frequency interference** (**RFI**) from objects such as cell phones can also be an issue. The solution to this problem is to run network cabling away from such devices.

The signal in a UTP cable is susceptible to attenuation if the cable is too long. Keep in mind that the maximum length for Cat 5 and Cat 6 UTP cabling is 100 meters. If there are intermittent network problems and you notice that the cables are too long, this may be the problem. If you can't shorten the cable run, then installing a repeater will solve this problem.

One way to avoid all these problems is to install fiber optic cabling. Because fiber-based media uses light transmissions instead of electronic signals, the issues discussed in this section, such as crosstalk, EMI, and attenuation become nonissues. Fiber optic cabling is also a secure medium, as accessing the data signals requires physically tapping into the media, which is difficult to do.

Unfortunately, the high cost of fiber-opting cabling precludes a lot of organizations from implementing it in their networks. Moreover, fiber optic media is incompatible with most electronic equipment, requiring you to purchase fiber-compatible network equipment. Thus, while fiber optic cabling will continue to play a role in networking, particularly in serving as the media for the internet, WANs and **metropolitan area networks** (**MANs**), its impact on smaller networks will likely be limited for the foreseeable future.

It is generally a good idea to check cabling. If you suspect that Ethernet cabling is damaged, try swapping it with new cabling. Make sure that you are using the right type of cabling for the connection. Check to make sure that devices at both ends of the cable are on and that the ports are enabled and functioning. If you suspect that a device is not doing auto-negotiation properly, you may want to plug in another device and see if it works.

Wireless issues

If the issue is with a node that relies on a wireless adapter, then you will want to make sure that the wireless adapter is functioning. Make sure the wireless adapter is enabled; if the device is an iOS or an Android device, make sure it is not in airplane mode and that the WiFi adapter is on and is ready to connect. Check the settings for the wireless **service set identifier** (**SSID**) and verify that the device is configured to use the SSID that corresponds to the correct network. If the SSID to which you need to connect is not showing up in the list of available wireless networks on the client, check to make sure SSID broadcasts are enabled on the access point or router. You can also simply type in the SSID on the client; this should enable you to connect even if the SSID is hidden. Make sure the SSID is matched exactly, including the case of the letters.

You may want to make sure that the device is capable of connecting to the frequency band supported by the wireless access point or router. The following table lists the bands supported by different 802.11 wireless standards:

802.11 standard	**Band**
802.11a, 802.11g, 802.11n, 802.11ac	5 GHz
802.11b, 802.11n	2.4 GHz
802.11ad (WiGig)	60 GHz
802.11af (White-Fi, Super Wi-Fi)	54-790 GHz
802.11ah	Below 1 GHz
802.11aj	45 GHz
802.11ay (in development)	60 GHz

As you can see, the most common wireless standards currently in use (802.11b/g/n/ac) use either the 2.4 or 5 GHz band or both. To connect older 802.11a or 802.11b, enable Mixed Mode on your wireless access point or router so that the slower rates used by these standards are enabled. If the client supports multiple 802.11 modes but is trying to connect over a long distance, you may have to enabled Mixed Mode so the client can connect using one of the slower modes.

When verifying wireless functionality, check to see what IP subnet is assigned to the SSID, as well as the router that should be reachable via this subnet. Verify that the client is receiving an IP address that belongs to this subnet. Log in to the router and verify that the client is connecting to the router and that an IP address is being assigned to the client. In pfSense, the easiest way to confirm this is to check **Status** | **DHCP Leases** or **DHCPv6 Leases**.

Another matter to consider is whether the security parameters on the client and the access point/router match. There are several security algorithms for wireless networking. A detailed discussion of them is beyond the scope of this chapter, but they are worth mentioning:

- **Wired Equivalent Privacy** (**WEP**): Introduced as part of the original 802.11 standard in 1997, this algorithm had keys of either 40 or 104 bits. To connect via WEP, the client sends an authentication request to the access point, and the access point replies with a clear-text challenge. The client encrypts the challenge and sends it to the access point. The access point decrypts this and, if it matches the challenge, the client is authenticated. A major weakness of WEP is that the challenge is sent in the clear and it is thus possible to intercept the challenge and use this to derive the keystream used for authentication. It also used an encryption key that is manually entered on devices that support it and does not change. WEP is generally considered insecure and has been deprecated in favor of WPA/WPA2.
- **Wi-Fi Protected Access** (**WPA**): Introduced in 2003, this algorithm was designed to address the main weaknesses of WPA, and employs the **Temporal Key Integrity Protocol** (**TKIP**), which dynamically generates a new 128-bit encryption key for each packet. There are two versions: WPA-Personal, which supports 128-bit encryption keys and 256-bit shared keys, and WPA-Enterprise, which requires authentication via a RADIUS server.

- **WPA2**: Introduced in 2004, this algorithm added support for **CCMP** (**Counter Mode Cipher Block Chaining Message Authentication Code Protocol**), an AES-based encryption protocol. As with WPA, WPA2 has WPA2-Personal and WPA2-Enterprise versions.
- **WPA3**: Announced in January 2018, this algorithm will support 192-bit encryption keys and per-user encryption.

If your access point/router uses WPA-Personal or WPA2-Personal, make sure the encryption method is set to WPA-PSK or WPA2-PSK and enter the same passphrase on both devices. If you must support both WPA and WPA2, make sure the access point/router supports both TKIP and AES encryption and that both are enabled. If you are using WPA-Enterprise or WPA2-Enterprise, it is a bit more complicated as you must set up the client to use RADIUS authentication; the next section covers RADIUS configuration issues.

RADIUS issues

If you use WPA-Enterprise or WPA2-Enterprise on your network, clients must be authenticated via a RADIUS server, and even if you don't use those wireless standards, RADIUS provides an effective way of providing centralized authentication. Troubleshooting RADIUS issues involves both ensuring that the access point/router can connect to the RADIUS server, and that the client can log in to the RADIUS server.

Verify that the RADIUS server has a secret configured and that it is set up to accept connections from the access point/router, which should be configured to connect to RADIUS with a matching secret. Also, verify connectivity between the access point/router and the RADIUS server. There are different ways of doing this but using the ping utility is the easiest way.

You may find that the RADIUS server is up and running and connected to the network, but the client's log in attempts are rejected. If so, make sure the client is using the **Extensible Authentication Protocol** (**EAP**) to log in and that it matches the type the RADIUS server requires. Some of the common options include:

- EAP Transport Layer Security (EAP-TLS): This was defined in RFC 5216, and was the original wireless LAN EAP authentication protocol.
- Protected Extensible Authentication Protocol (PEAP): Encapsulates an EAP session within an encrypted TLS tunnel.
- EAP Tunneled Transport Layer Security (EAP-TTLS): With this protocol, authentication takes place within an encrypted tunnel. Supported in Windows 8 and subsequent versions of Windows.

- EAP Flexible Authentication via Secure Tunneling (EAP-FAST): Another variant of EAP which creates an encrypted tunnel, this version of the protocol uses a **Protected Access Credential** (**PAC**) to establish a tunnel in which client credentials are checked.

If your RADIUS server uses EAP-TTLS or EAP-FAST, you will need to install an 802.1X supplicant program on the client. Also make sure that other EAP-specific settings match on both the RADIUS server and the client. If you are still having issues, you may want to refer to your RADIUS server's documentation for further guidance. A LAN analyzer or a packet sniffer such as Wireshark can be of use in debugging protocol issues.

pfSense troubleshooting tools

pfSense provides a great deal of information and data related to the functioning of your network, and this information and data can be extremely helpful when troubleshooting network issues. One of the first places you'll probably want to start looking is in the logs, so we'll begin with them.

System logs

To access the system logs, navigate to **Status** | **System Logs**. There are several tabs in this section, but the default tab is **System**. Note that different subcategories (for example, **Firewall** and **DHCP**) have their own tabs where you can view log entries related to such activity, which simultaneously makes it easier to find log activity for a specific subcategory and also reduces clutter on the **System** tab. The **System** tab is itself divided into several subcategories: **General**, **Gateways**, **Routing**, **DNS Resolver**, and **Wireless**.

pfSense logs are stored in such a way as to not overflow the available disk space. The logs have a binary circular log file format; these log files are a fixed size and they store a maximum of 50 entries. If the limit is reached, older log entries are overwritten by newer ones. If you want to retain these logs, you can copy them to another server with syslog.

The **General** tab includes entries for several different services, including pfBlocker, VPN tunnels, and Dynamic DNS. The default log order is chronological, although you can show the log entries in reverse order by clicking on the **Settings** tab and checking the **Forward/Reverse Display** checkbox. Note that there is an **Advanced Log Filter** section at the top of the page (this section can be expanded by clicking on the plus icon on the right of the section heading).

This section allows you to filter the log entries by several criteria: by time, process, **process ID** (**PID**), the quantity of entries displayed (the default is **50**), and the message contained in the log entry. Each of these fields except for **Quantity** can contain a regular expression as well. To filter the logs, click on the **Apply Filter** button.

You can control many log settings by clicking on the **Settings** tab. We already mentioned the **Forward/Reverse Display** checkbox, which allows you to show the log entries in reverse order. The **GUI Log Entries** edit box allows you to control the number of log entries displayed in the GUI (but not the number of entries in the actual log files). The next option, the **Log file size (Bytes)** edit box, allows you to change the size of each log file. By default, each log file is approximately 500 KB. Since there are about 20 log files, the disk space used by log files by default is about 10 MB. If you want to retain more than 50 entries per log file, you can increase this number. Be aware, however, that increasing this value increases every log file size, so make sure you have enough disk space available. For example, if you specify 1,048,576 here (1 MB), the total amount of disk space used will be 20 MB, and each log will contain 100 entries.

The next subsection is **Log firewall default blocks**. The **Log packets matched from the default block rules in the ruleset** checkbox, if checked, will log packets that are blocked by the implicit default block rule. By default, all internetwork traffic is blocked, and unless traffic is explicitly allowed elsewhere, if this option is set, this blocked traffic will be logged. If the log packets matched from the default pass rules put in the ruleset are checked, pfSense will log packets that are allowed by the implicit default pass rule. Since you generally don't want to log traffic that is allowed to pass, by default this option is not checked. The **Log packets blocked by 'Block Bogon Networks' rules** and the **Log packets blocked by 'Block Private Networks' rules** checkboxes, if checked, log packets blocked by those rules.

If the **Web Server Log** checkbox is checked, errors from the web server process for the pfSense GUI or the captive portal will appear in the main system log. The **Raw Logs** checkbox, if checked, will show the logs without being interpreted by the log parser. The raw log file, though more difficult to read, can be helpful in troubleshooting as it provides detailed information that is left out in the parsed log output.

The next option is the **Where to show rule descriptions** drop-down box. This option allows you to show a description of the applied rule in the firewall log. The options are as follows:

- **Don't load descriptions**: This is the default option
- **Display as column**: The applied firewall rule will appear as an additional column
- **Display as second row**: The applied firewall rule will appear below the corresponding log entry

The **Local Logging** checkbox, if checked, will disable writing log files to the local disk. If you click the **Reset Log Files** button will clear all local log files and reinitialize them as empty logs. This will also restart the DHCP daemon. If you have made any changes to settings on this page, you should click on the **Save** button before clearing the log files.

The next section is the **Remote Logging Options** section. Checking the **Enable Remote Logging** checkbox allows you to send log messages to a remote syslog server. If you check this option, a number of other options will appear. The **Source Address** drop-down box allows you to choose to which IP address the syslog daemon will bind. The choices include each interface on your pfSense system (which normally would include at least the WAN and LAN interfaces) and localhost. If one of these options is selected, then remote syslog servers must all be of that IP type (either **IPv4** or **IPv6**). In order to mix IPv4 and IPv6 syslog servers, select **Default (any)** to bind to all interfaces. Also, if an IP address cannot be located on the chosen interface, the daemon will bind to all addresses.

The **IP Protocol** drop-down box allows you to select the IP type of the address specified in the **Source Address** drop-down box. However, if an IP address of the type selected here is not found, the other type will be tried. The **Remote log servers** edit boxes allow you to specify the IP addresses and ports of up to three syslog servers. Finally, the **Remote Syslog Contents** checkboxes allow you to select what events are sent to the syslog server(s). Keep in mind that you must configure the syslog daemon on the remote server to accept syslog messages from pfSense. When you are done making changes, click on the **Save** button.

Dashboard

You can also gather a great deal of information from the pfSense dashboard, which you can access by navigating to **Status** | **Dashboard** (the dashboard is also the first page you see when you log in to the web GUI). The dashboard contains a great deal of information about your pfSense system, such as the uptime, CPU usage, memory usage, the version being run, and whether an upgrade is available. The dashboard was redesigned for version 2.3 (and, with the release of version 2.4, now supports multiple languages); you can choose the number of columns in the display under **General Setup**. If you resize the width of your web browser, the dashboard will resize to a single column, thus ensuring that you do not have to scroll left and right. There is also an **Interfaces** widget which displays the interfaces, their speed, and their IP addresses. You can add widgets to the page by clicking on the plus sign on the right side of the title bar. There are widgets for gateways, traffic graphs, CARP status, load balancer status, and many packages have their own widgets. The dashboard updates every few seconds, so you don't have to hit the **Reload** button.

Interfaces

You can view information about the status of interfaces by navigating to **Status | Interfaces**. Information about all interfaces is available here, including the following:

- The device name of the interface (for example, `fxp0`, `em1`, and so on)
- Interface status (**Up** or **Down**)
- The MAC address of the interface
- IP address, subnet mask, and gateway (for WAN-type interfaces)
- The number of packets that have passed (in and out), that have been blocked (in and out)
- The number of errors and collisions

If an interface has been configured to receive its IP address via DHCP (this is likely true for all WAN-type interfaces on your system), you can renew the DHCP lease via this page.

Services

Most system and package services display their status on the **Services** page, which can be viewed by navigating to **Status | Services**. On this page, you will find a table which lists the name of the service (**Service**), a brief description (**Description**), and whether the service is running or stopped (**Status**). There is also an **Actions** column. By clicking on the appropriate icon for a service, you can either start a stopped service or restart/stop a running service. Normally, it is not necessary to control services in such a way, but you may need to do so in a troubleshooting scenario.

There are three additional icons that appear in some, but not all entries in the **Services** table:

- **Related settings**: This is the icon that looks like three sliders. This links to the settings page for the service.
- **Related status**: This icon looks like a bar graph. Many of the services listed have their own page on the **Status** menu, and if they do, it is linked to here.
- **Related log entries**: This icon looks like a logbook page. If the service has its own tab in **Status | Logs**, it will be linked to here.

Monitoring

By navigating to **System** | **Monitoring**, you can view another useful set of data relating to the real time operation of your pfSense system. There are two sections on this page: a graph (**Interactive Graph**) and a summary of the information in the graph (**Data Summary**). There are several pieces of information available on this page, and they relate to the percentage of CPU usage attributable to different processes:

- **User util.**: User-related processes
- **Nice util.**: Nice (low-priority) processes
- **System util.**: Non-nice system processes
- **Interrupt**: System interrupts

There is also a column representing the grand total of processes. Each entry includes the minimum, maximum, and average percentage of CPU usage for each category.

Traffic graphs

You can view traffic graphs for each interface by navigating to **Status** | **Traffic Graph**. You can select the interface for which a graph is generated in the **Interface** drop-down box. Information displayed in the table adjacent to the graph is sorted in descending order based on either bandwidth in or bandwidth out, depending on what is selected in the **Sort by** drop-down box. The **Filter** drop-down box allows you to display either only local traffic or only remote traffic in the table (the default selection is **All**). The **Display** drop-down box allows you to select what is displayed in the **Host Name or IP** column: the IP address, the hostname, a description, or the **fully qualified domain name** (**FQDN**).

Firewall states

Sometimes when troubleshooting, it is helpful to view information about the firewall states. These states can be viewed several different ways from within the pfSense web GUI and the console.

States

One way to view the states table is to navigate to **Diagnostics** | **States**. This table provides information about each state table entry, including the interface, protocol, the direction of the traffic, the socket status, and the number of packets and bytes exchanged. By using the options in the **State Filter** section, you can filter the state table entries by interface or by a regular expression. By clicking on the **Reset States** tab, you can also clear the state table, if necessary.

States summary

If you just need an overview of state information rather than information about each individual entry, you can navigate to **Diagnostics** | **States Summary**. Here, you will find sections in which states are organized by source IP, by destination IP, the total per IP, and by IP pair. This page is useful for seeing if an IP address has an unusual number of states.

pfTop

pfTop is available in both the web GUI (by navigating to **Diagnostics** | **pfTop**), and at the console (it is 9 on the console menu). pfTop provides a live view of the state table and the total amount of bandwidth utilized by each state. If you are using pfTop from the console, type `q` to quit; this will return you to the console menu.

Most of the column headings in pfTop are self-explanatory. For example, the default view provides the following column headings: **PR**, **D**, **SRC**, **DEST**, **STATE**, **AGE**, **EXP**, **PKTS**, and **BYTES**.

PR stands for protocol; **D** stands for direction (in or out); **SRC** and **DEST** stand for source and destination, respectively; **AGE** indicates how long it has been since the entry was created; **EXP** indicates when the entry expires; **PKTS** indicates the number of packets that have been handled by the rule; and **BYTES** indicates the number of bytes.

STATE indicates the state of the connection in the format **client:server**. Since the states will not fit into an 80-column table, pfTop uses integers, such as 1:0. The numbers signify the following:

Number	**State**
0	`TCP_CLOSED`
1	`TCP_LISTEN`
2	`TCP_SYN_SENT`
3	`TCP_SYN_RECEIVED`
4	`TCP_ESTABLISHED`
5	`TCP_CLOSE_WAIT`
6	`TCP_FIN_WAIT_1`
7	`TCP_CLOSING`
8	`TCP_LAST_ACK`
9	`TCP_FIN_WAIT_2`
10	`TCP_TIME_WAIT`

Thus, an entry of **1:0** indicates that the state on the client side is `TCP_LISTEN`, and the state on the server side is `TCP_CLOSED`.

One of the advantages of using pfSense within the web GUI is that it is very easy to change the output to suit your needs. The **View** drop-down menu allows you to choose how pfTop displays its output. There are several options, including:

- **label**: The **LABEL** column represents the rule that is being invoked, and how many packets, bytes, and states are accounted for by the rule
- **long**: Displays the protocol, source, destination, gateway, state, and age of each entry
- **queue**: If the traffic shaper is configured, it will display results organized by queue
- **rules**: This option will display each rule being invoked in the rightmost column, and the number of states associated with each rule

There is also a **Sort by** drop-down box, which allows you to sort output in descending order by several categories (for example, **Bytes**, **Age**, **Destination Address**, **Source Address**, and others). The **Maximum # of States** drop-down box allows you to control the number of states that appear on the page.

If you run pfTop from the console, it will be running in interactive mode, which means that pfTop will read commands from the terminal and act upon them accordingly; characters will be processed as soon as they are typed, and the display will be updated immediately after the characters are processed.

Refer to the pfTop man page for a full listing of commands available in interactive mode, as well as pfTop command-line options.

tcpdump

Often the most effective way of troubleshooting a networking problem is through packet capturing, also known as packet sniffing. One way of capturing packets is to use the command-line tool **tcpdump**, which is part of the default pfSense installation. tcpdump is a command-line utility used to capture and analyze packets; details can either be displayed on the screen or saved to a file. It uses the **libpcap** library for packet capturing.

The results of packet capture will differ depending on which interface's traffic you capture. As a result, you should give some consideration as to which interface's traffic you choose to capture, and in some cases, you may want to capture traffic from several interfaces at the same time. In order to use **tcpdump**, you will have to use the underlying device names of the interfaces. If you don't remember what they are, you can navigate to **Interfaces** | **(assign)** within the web GUI. The console menu also lists each interface and has a separate column for the device name. Another way of retrieving a list of interface names is to issue to following command from the console shell:

```
tcpdump -D
```

Then, to run `tcpdump` on a single interface, type the following:

```
tcpdump -iinterface_name
```

Here, `interface_name` is the device name (for example, `fxp0`, `em1`, and so on). Alternatively, you can run `tcpdump` without any command-line options to capture packets from all interfaces.

If you run tcpdump, you may notice that the hostname of the source and destination is displayed. By default, `tcpdump` does a DNS lookup on IP addresses. As a result, `tcpdump` can generate a considerable amount of DNS traffic; however, you can prevent this. By default, `tcpdump` runs continuously until you press *Ctrl* + *C*, but you can limit the number of packets captured with the `-c` option, for example:

```
tcpdump -c 10
```

This will cause tcpdump to capture `10` packets and then stop running. The default maximum capture size for each packet is 64 K, but in many cases, you may only want to see what's in the header. You can use the `-s` parameter to limit the amount of each packet captured, for example:

```
tcpdump -s 96
```

This will only capture the first `96` bytes of each packet.

tcpdump allows you to save packet capture files in `pcap` format for later analysis.

This is useful, especially if you want to load the files onto another computer running Wireshark or some other graphical network protocol analyzer. To save the output to a file, use the `-w` option, like this:

```
tcpdump -w filename
```

Be aware that when you are using this option, the frames will not be displayed on the screen, as they otherwise would be. Also, be aware that the file will be saved in pcap (packet capture), rather than ASCII, format.

By default, `tcpdump` puts your network interface into promiscuous mode so that shows every frame on the wire, not just frames being sent to its MAC address. In modern networks, this should not be much of a problem, as most networks employ switches, and the interface generally will only receive traffic it should receive. If you have hubs on your network, however, running `tcpdump` in promiscuous mode can result in you capturing a great deal of traffic that may not be of interest to you. By using the `-p` option, which runs `tcpdump` in non-promiscuous mode, you can improve the signal-to-noise ratio and focus on traffic destined for the interface on which you are capturing packets.

You can control the verbosity of tcpdump's output with the `-v` flag. This flag only controls the output on the screen and not the contents of `tcpdump` output saved to a file (assuming that output is being saved). In addition to `-v`, you may also choose `-vv` or `-vvv`, which provides additional verbosity for screen output. If you invoked the `-w` option to write to a file along with one of the verbosity options, then `tcpdump` will report the number of packets captured at 10-second intervals.

The `-e` option causes `tcpdump` to display the MAC addresses of the source and destination of the packet as well as 802.1Q VLAN tag information.

You may notice that `tcpdump` displays packet sequence numbers. You may also notice that when displaying multiple packets from the same source/destination, the first packet in a series of packets has large sequence numbers, but all subsequent packets have smaller numbers. This is because `tcpdump` switches to relative sequence numbers in order to save display space. To see only actual sequence numbers, use the `-S` flag.

If you want a simple frontend for tcpdump, you can use the tcpdump page in the web GUI instead. To do so, navigate to **Diagnostics** | **Packet Capture**. Once there, use the **Interface** drop-down box to select the interface whose packets will be captured (note that there does not seem to be an option to capture all interfaces on this page). Checking the **Promiscuous** checkbox enables promiscuous mode. The **Address Family** drop-down box allows you to select IPv4 packets, IPv6 packets, or both. The **Protocol** drop-down box has several options: you can capture any packets (**Any**), or the following: **ICMP**, **Exclude ICMP**, **ICMPv6**, **Exclude ICMPv6**, **TCP**, **Exclude TCP**, **UDP**, **Exclude UDP**, **ARP**, **Exclude ARP**, **CARP**, **Exclude CARP**, **pfsync**, **Exclude pfsync**, **ESP**, and **Exclude ESP**.

The **Host Address** edit box allows you to specify a source or destination IP address or subnet (in CIDR notation). Tcpdump will look for the address specified in either field. You can negate the IP address by preceding the value with **!**, in which case tcpdump will match everything except the IP address. Multiple IP addresses or CIDR subnets may be specified here; comma separated values (`,`) perform a Boolean AND, while separating addresses with a pipe (`|`) performs a Boolean OR. If this field is left blank, then all packets on the specified interface that meet the other criteria specified will be captured, regardless of the source or destination IP address.

If you specify a port in the **Port** edit box, tcpdump will look for the port in either field. If you leave this field blank, tcpdump will not filter by port. The **Packet Length** edit box lets you specify the number of bytes of each packet that will be captured. The default value is `0`, which will cause the entire frame to be captured. The **Count** edit box allows you to specify the number of packets `tcpdump` will grab. The default value is `100`; specifying 0 will result in `tcpdump` continuously capturing packets.

The **Level of detail** drop-down box controls the amount of detail that will be displayed after you hit **Stop** when packets have been captured. The options are **Normal**, **Medium**, **High**, and **Full**. This option does not affect the level of detail in the packet capture file if you choose to download it when the packet capture completes.

The **Reverse DNS Lookup** checkbox, if checked, will result in tcpdump performing a reverse DNS lookup on all IP addresses. As noted when discussing the command-line options for tcpdump, doing a reverse DNS lookup generates considerable DNS traffic and also creates delays, and therefore is not generally recommended. When you are done selecting options on this page, click on the **Start** button.

Once you click on **Start**, you should see a **Packet capture is running** message across the bottom of the page, and the **Start** button should become a **Stop** button. Once you click on the **Stop** button, a **Packets Captured** listbox will appear at the bottom of the page with information about the packets captured. You can change the level of detail by changing the value in the **Level of Detail** edit box and clicking on **View Capture** to update the display. Finally, you can save the packet capture by clicking on the **Download Capture** button; this will save the capture as a **.cap** file which can be opened by many network protocol analyzers such as Wireshark.

tcpflow

tcpflow, like tcpdump, allows you to view the text contents of network packets in real time. Whereas `tcpdump` is more suited to capturing packets as well as protocol information, `tcpflow` is better suited for viewing the actual data flow between two hosts. One significant difference between tcpflow and `tcpdump` is that while `tcpdump` displays output to the console by default, `tcpflow` writes the output to a file by default. In order to display tcpflow's output on the console, you can use the `-c` option.

Much of the syntax of `tcpflow` is similar to that of `tcpdump`, for example:

```
tcpflow -i fxp0 -c host 172.16.1.2 and port 80
```

This would capture packets on the `fxp0` interface with either a source or destination of `172.16.1.2` port `80`. Here are some of the options available for `tcpflow`:

Option	Description	tcpdump equivalent
`-bmax_bytes`	Capture no more than `max_bytes` per flow	`-c`
`-c`	Console print	NA (default)
`-ddebug_level`	Debug level	
`-iiface`	Capture packets from interface `iface`	`-i`
`-p`	Do not put the interface in promiscuous mode	`-p`
`-r file`	Read packets from file, when file was created using tcpdump's `-w` option	`-r`
`-s`	Convert all non-printable characters to the . character before displaying or saving output	NA
`-v`	Verbose operation (equivalent to `-d` 10)	`-v`

Unlike `tcpdump, tcpflow` is not part of the default pfSense installation.

ping, traceroute and netstat

ping, **traceroute**, and **netstat** are old command-line utilities used to test the reachability of hosts, provide routing information, and give information about network connections. They often are the first tools used by network technicians when testing networks. They can prove invaluable when troubleshooting networks. Both **ping** and **traceroute** are accessible from pfSense's web GUI, although they are more commonly used from the console.

ping

The purpose of ping is to measure the **round-trip time** (**RTT**) for messages sent from a source host to a destination host that are then echoed back to the source. It uses **internet Control Message Protocol** (**ICMP**), sending ICMP Echo Request packets to the destination host and waiting for an ICMP Echo Reply.

The first item reported is the size of the packet received. The default size is 56 bytes, but an ICMP `ECHO_REQUEST` packet contains an additional 8 bytes of an ICMP header followed by an arbitrary amount of data. Thus, the size reported is 64 bytes. Next is the destination IP address. By default, ping displays the IP address to which the hostname resolves rather than the hostname.

The `icmp_seq` field reveals the ordering of the ICMP packets. ping reports on each packet as it is received, and the packets are not necessarily received in the same order as they are sent, although when the networks are functioning properly, they usually are. TTL stands for **time to live**. The **TTL** field is reduced by one by every router en route to its destination. If the **TTL** field reaches zero before the packet arrives, then an ICMP error is sent back (**ICMP Time Exceeded**). As you may have guessed, the default start value used by ping in Linux is 64. Finally, the last field is the RTT of each packet, which is a good measure of the latency of a connection.

Once the results for each packet are reported, ping reports aggregate statistics for the ping session. The number of packets transmitted and received is reported, as well as the percentage of packet loss. On the final line, we see the minimum RTT, the average RTT, the maximum RTT, and the standard deviation.

One caveat that should be made concerning ping is that many firewalls block ICMP traffic, rendering the ping utility useless with hosts behind restrictive firewalls. In fact, pfSense blocks such traffic by default, so if you want to ping your hosts from the other side of the firewall, you will have to explicitly allow such traffic. Even so, you may have occasion to ping a network you don't control that blocks ICMP traffic. In such cases, you may be better off utilizing a utility that relies on TCP or UDP for sending packets, since such protocols are much less likely to be blocked by most firewalls. One such utility is tcpping, and it has a similar syntax to `ping`. If you are pinging to local hosts, you can use arping, which uses the **Address Resolution Protocol** (**ARP**) request method to resolve IP addresses.

To install tcpping, you must first install `tcptraceroute` and then install **tcpping**, which is a script that utilizes `tcptraceroute`. You can install `tcptraceroute` from the repositories. If you are using Debian/Ubuntu/Mint Linux, type the following at the console:

```
sudo apt-get install tcptraceroute
```

For CentOS/Red Hat Enterprise Level, the command is:

```
sudo yum install tcptraceroute
```

Then you have to install tcpping, which can be done with the `wget` command:

```
cd /usr/bin
```

```
sudo wget http://www.vdberg.org/~richard/tcpping
```

You'll also want to set permissions for `tcpping`, which you can do with `chmod`:

```
sudo chmod 755 tcpping
```

To see the command line options for `tcpping`, type the following at the console:

```
tcpping --help
```

This caveat aside, the ping utility is useful in a number of different troubleshooting scenarios:

- Ping can help us determine if there is network connectivity between two hosts.
- Ping can help us determine if there is an unacceptable rate of packet loss. We may have connectivity between two hosts, but if the packet loss rate is consistently high, network performance will undoubtedly suffer.
- Ping is a good tool for measuring latency between two hosts.

As an example of the last of these scenarios, you might consider pinging a well-known host (for example, `google.com`) and measuring the latency in a number of different scenarios: for example, on a broadband connection, on a DSL connection, on a mobile connection, through a VPN, and so on.

You may have noticed that when we invoked the `ping` command under Linux, we used one flag: the `-c` flag, which limits the number of packets sent. Without the `-c` flag, `ping` would have sent packets continuously until we pressed *Ctrl* + *C* at the console. This is just one of many flags and options available for ping. The following table covers some of the more commonly used ping options:

Option	Description	Windows equivalent
`-c count`	Stop after receiving count `ECHO_RESPONSE` packets	`-n count`
`-D`	Set the `DF` bit	`-f`
`-f`	Flood ping; output packets as fast as they come back (use with caution)	NA
`-i wait`	Wait seconds before sending each packet	NA
`-mttl`	Set the ttl for each packet.	`-I ttl`
`-S source_addr`	Use `source_addr` as the source address in outgoing packets; useful for forcing the IP address to be something other than the IP address on which the `ping` packet is sent out on (only works if the IP address is one of the host's IP addresses)	`-S source_addr`
`-s packetsize`	Specify the number of data bytes to be sent (the default is `56`)	`-lpacketsize`
`-t timeout`	Specify a timeout, in seconds, before ping exits regardless of how many packets have been received	NA
`-v`	Verbose output; ICMP packets other than `ECHO_RESPONSE` packets are also displayed	NA

Be aware that this is not an exhaustive list of ping options; consult the ping man page for a complete listing of them.

If you are running ping from the Windows command prompt, the output is similar, with some exceptions:

- By default, ping sends four packets instead of sending packets. To send packets continuously, use the `-t` option. To send an arbitrary number of packets, use the `-n` count option.
- The default packet size is 32 bytes.
- The summary does not show the standard deviation.

Other than that, the behavior of ping under Windows is similar to its behavior under Linux, although it seems to have fewer command-line options. The preceding table lists some of the Windows ping flag equivalents.

You can also invoke ping from within the pfSense web GUI. To do so, navigate to **Diagnostics** | **Ping**. In the **Hostname** edit box, specify the hostname or IP address to ping. You can specify the protocol in the **IP Protocol** drop-down box (**IPv4** or **IPv6**). In the **Source Address** drop-down box, you can set a source address for the ping. Finally, in the **Maximum number of pings** edit box, you can set the maximum number of pings (the default is `3`). When you are done configuring the ping settings, click on the **Ping** button.

traceroute

traceroute (or **tracert**, as it is known under Windows) is a network diagnostic tool for IP networks. Its purpose is twofold: to display the path of packets, as well as the transit delays along each step (known as a hop). The RTT of each hop is recorded, and the sum of the mean times in each hop is a measure of the total time to establish the connection. By default, **traceroute** outputs the results of each hop, as well as the final results. **traceroute** sends three packets, and it proceeds unless all three are lost more than twice. In this case, the connection is considered lost and the route/path cannot be evaluated.

traceroute is available at the Windows command prompt (as **tracert**), but it is not part of most default Linux installations. Instead, it is available from the repositories, both as a standalone package (**traceroute**) and as part of the inetutils utilities (**inetutils-traceroute**). The output of **traceroute** is relatively simple. The first column displays the hop count. The final column displays the IP address and hostname (if available) of the host/router. The middle three columns display the RTT of each of the three packets sent.

The only required parameter is the hostname or IP address of the destination host. There are, however, many other options available, as shown in the following table:

Option	Description
`-e`	Firewall evasion mode; uses fixed destination ports for UDP, UDP-lite, TCP, and SCTP probes
`-ffirst_ttl`	Set the TTL for the first outgoing packet
`-F`	Set the DF bit
`-d`	Enable socket-level debugging
`-I`	Use ICMP ECHO instead of UDP datagrams
`-M first_ttl`	Set the TTL value used in outgoing probe packets
`-P proto`	Set the protocol (`proto`) used in outgoing probe packets; the currently supported values are UDP, UDP-Lite, TCP, SCTP, GRE, and ICMP
`-ssrc_addr`	Use `src_addr` as the IP address in outgoing probe packets to force the source address to something other than the IP address of the interface the probe packet is sent on (only works if the IP address is the address of one of the interfaces on the host)
`-S`	Print a summary of how many probes were not answered at each hop
`-v`	Verbose output (all received ICMP packets shown)
`-w`	Set the time to wait for a response to a probe (default is `5` seconds)

I omitted the **Windows Equivalent** column on this table, since few of the options available for **traceroute** under Linux exist for the Windows version. If you need to use another protocol, you can use the `-P` option; there is also a utility called **tcptraceroute** (available for Linux), which sends TCP probe packets.

You can also invoke **traceroute** from the web GUI. To do so, navigate to **Diagnostics** | **Traceroute**. Type in the hostname or IP address in the **Hostname** edit box. You can select the protocol (**IPv4** or **IPv6**) in the **IP Protocol** drop-down box. You can select the source address for the trace in the **Source Address** drop-down box. In the **Maximum number of hops** drop-down box, you can set the maximum number of network hops to trace (the maximum number is 20; the default is `18`). You can enable DNS lookup by checking the **Reverse Address Lookup** checkbox. Finally, you can change the protocol used by **traceroute** from UDP to ICMP by checking the **Use ICMP** checkbox. When you are done configuring settings, click on the **Traceroute** button.

netstat

netstat is a network utility that displays a variety of statistics for network connections on a system. It displays incoming and outgoing connections, routing tables, and a number of other network statistics. Under Linux, it is considered deprecated, and you are advised to use `dss` instead (part of the `iproute2` package), although netstat may still work, depending on which distribution you are using.

netstat, without any command-line arguments, will display a list of active sockets for each network protocol. If you invoke netstat under Linux, it will also display a list of active Unix domain sockets. There are several columns of output. **Proto** stands for protocol, with a 6 in the column denoting use of IPv6. **Recv-Q** tells you how many packets have not yet been copied from the socket buffer by the application. **Send-Q** tells you how many packets have been sent, but for which an **ACK** packet has not yet been received. **Local Address** indicates the IP address/hostname and port of the local end of the connection, while **Foreign Address** indicates the IP address/hostname and port of the remote end of the connection. Finally, **State** indicates the state of the socket. This column may be left blank, since there are no states in **RAW** and usually no states used in UDP.

For active Unix domain sockets, there are several columns not present under active internet connections. **RefCnt** stands for reference count, which is the number of attached processes connected via this socket. The **Flags** column contains a number of flags that are used on both connected and unconnected sockets, such as **SO_ACCEPTON** (displayed as **ACC**), **SO_WAITDATA** (**W**) and **SO_NOSPACE** (**N**). The **Type** column indicates the type of socket access. **DGRAM** indicates that the socket is in datagram (connectionless) mode, while **STREAM** indicates that the socket is a stream (connection) socket. **RAW** indicates a raw socket. The **State** column will contain one of several different states: **FREE** indicates that the socket is not allocated; **LISTENING** indicates that the socket is listening for a connection request. **CONNECTING** indicates the socket is about to establish a connection, while **CONNECTED** indicates the socket is already connected. Finally, **DISCONNECTING** indicates the socket is disconnecting. The **I-Node** and the **Path** columns show the `inode` and path of the file object representing the process attached to the socket.

As with **ping** and **traceroute**, there are many command-line options; here are some of the more useful ones:

Option	Description	Windows equivalent
`-faddress_family`	Limit the display to a specific `address_family` (for example, inet, inet6, unix)	NA

`-p protocol`	Limit the display to a specific protocol (tcp, udp, icmp, and so on)	`-p protocol`
`-r`	Display the content of routing tables	`-r`
`-rs`	Display routing statistics	NA
`-n`	Do not resolve addresses and ports; instead show addresses and ports as numbers	`-n`
`-W`	Avoid truncating addresses even if this causes some fields to overflow	NA

Troubleshooting scenarios

Having covered troubleshooting techniques and tools, we now have a chance to put them into use by considering a real-world example. Keep in mind that some problems have multiple potential causes, and you may have to gather some information before making a conjecture as to the root cause.

VLAN configuration problem

First, let's consider an issue that I encountered when configuring a switch discussed in `Chapter 3`, *VLANs*. I installed a TP-Link TL-SG108E switch on my network, and had planned to set up two VLANs using this switch. I had given some consideration as to how the VLANs would be configured, and I settled on the following:

- Each VLAN would be assigned three ports (the TL-SG108E is an eight-port switch; thus, six ports would be assigned to VLANs, leaving two ports to act as trunk ports)
- One VLAN (DEVELOPERS) would be assigned the network `192.168.10.x`; the other VLAN would be assigned the VLAN `192.168.20.x`
- The DEVELOPERS VLAN would be assigned a VLAN ID of `10`; the ENGINEERING VLAN would be assigned a VLAN of `20` (thus, the VLAN IDs would match the third octet of the network)

Since I wanted to set up 802.1q VLANs, I started the TP-Link Easy Smart Configuration Utility and selected VLAN from the sidebar menu, and then selected the 802.1q menu. I set up **1** as the default VLAN, and tagged ports `3` to `5` with a VLAN ID of `10` and tagged ports `6` to `8` with a VLAN ID of `20`. After clicking on the **Apply** button, I continued configuration in pfSense. After creating the two VLANs, I set up interfaces for each of them, and enabled the DHCP server on both interfaces. The switch was connected to the parent interface of the VLANs.

If everything worked as expected, connecting a computer to one of the VLAN ports should have resulted in outgoing traffic from the port being tagged with a VLAN ID. pfSense should have then assigned a DHCP lease for the VLAN whose VLAN ID matches the ID of the packets. Unfortunately, DHCP assignment never took place, and the computer connected to the VLAN port could not access the network.

Referring back to our troubleshooting procedure, I had identified the problem - the VLANs were not functioning as they should - but I would have to gather more information before formulating a theory as to the probable cause. Being more familiar with configuring pfSense than with configuring the TL-SG108E, I decided to check the DHCP and VLAN settings in pfSense to eliminate those as likely causes of the problem. Finding nothing wrong with either the DHCP or VLAN settings in the pfSense web GUI, I began to focus on the switch's settings.

When I launched the Easy Smart Configuration Utility again, I discovered that there was a separate page for PVID configuration. **PVID** (**Port VLAN ID**) is the default VLAN ID of the port. I set ports **3-5** to have a default VLAN ID of **10** and ports `6` to `8` to have a default VLAN ID of `20`, leaving ports `1` and `2` having a default VLAN ID of `1`. After clicking on the **Apply** button, I disabled and re-enabled the Ethernet connection on the computer being used to test the VLANs. Still, there was no DHCP assignment and no network connectivity.

I checked the configuration settings again and could not find anything obviously wrong, but I noticed that the **Port Based VLAN** option only allows you to set the VLAN ID between 1 and 8. I considered the possibility that the allowed VLAN IDs were `1` to `8`. Thus, I had a theory of probable cause and could move on to testing the theory.

Establishing a plan was not difficult; I was testing the theory on my test network, which is as far removed from an enterprise level environment as possible. Thus, I could try out setting the VLAN IDs to lower values without much concern for its effect on the network. I set the DEVELOPERS VLAN ID to `2` and the ENGINEERING VLAN to `3`. I made the same changes to the PVID, setting the PVID for the DEVELOPERS ports to `2` and the ENGINEERING ports to `3`.

When I disabled and re-enabled the connection on the computer connected to the switch, the computer was assigned a DHCP lease and I was able to access other networks. Thus, setting the VLAN IDs to lower numbers seemed to solve the problem, but I still was unsure whether setting up PVIDs was necessary or not. Therefore, I set the PVIDs back to `1` for all the ports and tested connectivity again. This time, the same problem recurred (no DHCP assignment or network connectivity).

Thus, it seemed that in order for 802.1q VLAN tagging to work with this switch, both PVIDs had to be configured and VLAN IDs had to be set to a number between 1 and 8. Once I confirmed that setting the VLAN IDs to higher numbers did not work, I set them back to `2` for DEVELOPERS and `3` for ENGINEERING , thus implementing the solution. Finally, I verified system functionality, confirming that the solution I had implemented had not created other problems, and I documented the results.

What conclusions can we draw from the approach I employed here? I probably should have spent more time gathering information; because I was configuring this switch for the first time, I assumed that it was a switch configuration issue, an assumption that turned out to be correct. Nonetheless, the tried and true method of formulating a theory of probable cause, testing the theory, and then repeating the process until a solution is found served me well. Also, it's important to remember that finding the solution isn't the end of the process; you still have to implement the solution, verify system functionality, and document the results.

Summary

In this chapter, we covered some troubleshooting fundamentals, including some basic steps you can employ in any troubleshooting scenario. We also covered some common networking problems and some troubleshooting tools you can use. Some of these tools, such as pfTop, are exclusive to pfSense/BSD, but many others, such as ping, traceroute, and netstat, can be found on multiple platforms, including Linux and Windows. Finally, we put these fundamentals into practice by considering a real-world VLAN configuration issue.

Needless to say, this chapter barely scratches the surface of network troubleshooting, and if you want to learn more about it, there are copious amounts of material available, both in book form and online. Of course, there is no substitute for practical experience, and there is a great deal you can learn from building and maintaining networks. Acquiring troubleshooting skills is something that will aid you not just in mastering pfSense, but in understanding networking in general.

Questions

Answer the following questions:

1. What is the final step in troubleshooting a networking problem?
2. A site can be reached by pinging the IP address but pinging the hostname fails. What is a likely cause of this?
3. Name a wireless standard that uses the 2.4 GHz range (there are two).
4. Which wireless encryption standard sends challenges in the clear and is generally considered insecure now?
5. Identify a method of determining whether an interface is up or down from within the pfSense web GUI.
6. What tool can be used to monitor the pfSense state table, and can be used from within the web GUI or the command line?
7. What tool can be used to ping a site that blocks ICMP traffic but allows TCP traffic?
8. What are the two main purposes of traceroute?

Assessments

Chapter 1 – Revisiting pfSense Basics

1. Demilitarized zone (DMZ).
2. CPU: 500 MHz or greater; RAM: 512 MB; disk space: 1 GB.
3. 1 KB.
4. Checksums ensure the integrity of a download; running a checksum on a binary guarantees that the download has completed and that the binaries have not been tampered with by a third party.
5. (a) ZFS. (b) UFS (DOS is also an acceptable answer).
6. At the console/shell and in the web GUI.
7. The following are all valid answers: Static; DHCP; PPTP; PPPoE; PPP; L2TP.
8. (a) Enabled. (b) Disabled. (c) The reason Block Private Networks is blocked on the WAN interface is that private addresses by definition are nonroutable and therefore should never pass through the WAN interface. On the LAN interface and other local interfaces, however, we generally want private addresses to work.
9. Via **Setup Wizard and System | General Setup**.
10. The following are all valid answers: Hostname, Domain, DNS Servers, Timezone, NTP Server, WAN Interface, LAN Interface, Password.

Chapter 2 – Advanced pfSense Configuration

1. (a) Transport Control Protocol (TCP). (b) 67 and 68. (c) User Datagram Protocol (UDP). (d) 67 and 68.
2. M flag: 0; O flag: 1; L flag: 1; A flag: 1.
3. DNS Resolver (the default) and DNS Forwarder.
4. (a) UDP. (b) 53.

5. It can be updated much more rapidly than traditional DNS, making it suitable for scenarios in which the IP address associated with a domain name will change rapidly.
6. User Manager, Voucher, and RADIUS.
7. <input name="auth_voucher" type="text">.
8. Global Positioning System (GPS) or Pulse Per Second (PPS).
9. The structure into which management data is hierarchically organized in an SNMP-managed network.
10. 161.

Chapter 3 – VLANs

1. 802.1Q.
2. 1, 4094.
3. Switch spoofing, double tagging.
4. 7.
5. It increases the number of possible VLANs (16,752,649 with a single level of nesting, with even more VLANs possible if there are multiple levels of nesting).
6. Increased throughput, redundancy.
7. None (we have to create rules to allow access from VLANs to other networks ourselves).
8. Trunk ports and VLAN ports.
9. PVID.
10. Static, Dynamic Trunking Protocol (DTP), VLAN Trunking Protocol (VTP).

Chapter 4 – Using pfSense as a Firewall

1. The principle of least privilege.
2. **Block** will drop traffic silently, while **Reject** will send back a packet (RST for TCP or ICMP Port Unreachable for UDP).
3. We will be able to connect to Recode; the block rule will have no effect because it was placed after the "Allow LAN to any" rule.

4. We will not be able to connect to Recode; the block rule will match the traffic to Recode before the "Allow LAN to any" rule.
5. (a) We will not be able to connect to Recode; the new "default allow" rule will be invoked after the block rule. (b) We will be able to connect to Recode; the new "default allow" rule will be invoked before the block rule. (c) The default "Allow LAN to any" rules have no effect on traffic flow anymore because they are never reached; the floating "default allow" rule is invoked first.
6. **IP**, **Network**, **Port**, **URL**.
7. (a) Navigate to **Firewall** | **Aliases**, click on the IP tab, click on **Add**, and enter each IP address manually; (b) navigate to **Diagnostics** | **DNS Lookup**, perform a DNS lookup, and create an alias from it; (c) navigate to **Firewall** | **Aliases**, click on the **Import** button, do a bulk import.
8. **IP Alias**.

Chapter 5 – Network Address Translation

1. Classless networks (CIDR), private networks (RFC 1918 networks), and IPv6. Any two would be acceptable.
2. No; we do not need to alter the Outbound NAT settings because outbound NAT rules were generated for each of the non-WAN interfaces.
3. Two rules (one for IPsec and the other for all other traffic).
4. 1:1 NAT.
5. The port forwarding traffic will be blocked by the firewall.
6. We normally don't care what the source of the incoming traffic is.
7. (a) 7000; (b) 3389.
8. (a) Multihoming and route aggregation are both valid answers. (b) DHCPv6.

Chapter 6 – Traffic Shaping

1. To ensure that network traffic conforms to certain predefined constraints.
2. (a) Priority queuing (PRIQ), class-based queuing (CBQ), and Hierarchical Fair-Service Curve (HFSC). (b) Class-based queuing. (c) Hierarchical Fair-Service Curve.
3. No; we can only implement it with third-party packages such as Snort.

4. (a) The Multiple Lan/Wan configuration wizard; (b) the Dedicated Links wizard.
5. Explicit Congestion Notification.
6. The Floating Rules tab.
7. None; we have to manually enable each interface.
8. By navigating to **Status** | **Queues** and looking under the **Length** column.

Chapter 7 – Virtual Private Networks

1. Peer-to-peer and client-server.
2. (a) IPsec, L2TP, and OpenVPN. (b) L2TP.
3. Authentication Headers (AH), Encapsulating Security Protocol (ESP), and Security Association (SA).
4. (a) The connection will fail because when the **Key Exchange version** is set to **Auto** and pfSense is the initiator, it will use IKEv2 (since the other firewall is using IKEv1, there will be a mismatch). (b) The connection will succeed because pfSense as the initiator will again use IKEv2, and the protocols will match.
5. (a) 500; (b) 1194.
6. Challenge-Handshake Authentication Protocol (CHAP), MS-CHAPv2, and Password Authentication Protocol (PAP).
7. Elliptic-curve Diffie-Hellman (ECDH).
8. Lightweight Directory Access Protocol (LDAP) and Remote Authentication Dial-In User Protocol (RADIUS).

Chapter 8 – Redundancy and High Availability

1. Any three of these: random, round robin, weighed round robin, least connection, least traffic, least latency, IP hash, URL hash, SDN adaptive.
2. Client-side load balancing: easy to implement and effective. Server-side load balancing: better able to guarantee load balancing; transparent to client; more secure; we can provide a message to client when all servers are down.
3. **Load balancing** and **Failover**.

4. The most likely cause is that I forgot to update the alias for the server pool to include the new server. Since the firewall rule to allow traffic to pass to the server pool uses this alias, it allows traffic to pass to every server except the new one.
5. (a) Yes; (b) no; (c) yes; (d) no.
6. No; we do not have to create a virtual IP for the PFSYNC interface because use it to pass synchronization data between firewalls; we don't want any redundancy on this interface.
7. The firewall rule will get overwritten when data is synchronized with the master firewall.
8. Because, if the Advertising frequency is the same on two or more backup firewalls, if the master goes down, two or more backup firewalls will try to become master at the same time.
9. Use HAProxy and select Least Connections as the load balancing for Balance when configuring the backend.
10. Navigate to **Status** | **CARP (failover)** and click on the **Enter Persistent CARP Maintenance Mode** button.

Chapter 9 – Multiple WANs

1. Service-Level Agreement (SLA).
2. Routing in which routing decisions are dictated by administrative policy.
3. (a) Load balancing. (b) Failover.
4. Traffic between local interfaces will be routed through the original WAN interface and will never reach the gateway group; pfSense's default behavior is to route external traffic to the primary **WAN** interface.
5. You are configuring an OPT_WAN interface and the OPT_WAN's DNS server is not the same as the Monitor IP. We do not have to configure a static route for the primary WAN interface because external traffic is routed to it by default, and we do not have to configure a static route if the OPT_WAN's DNS server is the same as the Monitor IP because pfSense will add a static route for the Monitor IP.
6. One for each **OPT_WAN** interface (and one for each **1:1 NAT** mapping, if we have any).
7. Use Sticky Connections.

8. Acceptable answers: The load balancing gateway group isn't working properly; the web page is cached and therefore isn't refreshing when we reload it; the connections are weighted such that the secondary connection handles very little traffic; Use Sticky Connections or some other persistent connection option is enabled; other users are on the network and generating a share of the connections going to the nonprimary connections.

Chapter 10 – Routing and Bridging

1. Routing involves moving traffic between networks (internetwork traffic), whereas bridging involves connecting segments on the same network (intranetwork traffic).
2. (a) Distance vector protocols. (b) Link-state protocols.
3. Enable **Static route filtering** in **System** | **Advanced** (**Firewall and NAT** tab) or create firewall rules to deal with the static routes.
4. (a) routed. (b) Quagga OSPF or FRR (FRRouting). (c) FRR.
5. Adding one or more gateways.
6. Spanning Tree Protocol (STP) and Rapid Spanning Tree Protocol (RSTP).
7. Looping.
8. The routing table found at **Diagnostics** | **Routes**.

Chapter 11 – Extending pfSense with Packages

1. The web GUI and the command line.
2. 3128.
3. (a) Access to the website will still be blocked because the installation of Squid does not enable Squid by default. (b) Access to the website will be possible because Squid takes precedence over firewall rules, and we have not added the site to Squid's blacklist.

4. pfBlockerNG.
5. HAProxy.
6. Packet sniffing mode, packet logging mode, and network intrusion prevention mode.
7. Ntopng, nmap, Zabbix, and Suricata would all be acceptable answers.
8. A Zabbix agent collects information from the local host and passes it on to the Zabbix server, whereas a Zabbix proxy collects information from hosts and is capable of offloading the Zabbix server so that the workload can be distributed.

Chapter 12 – Diagnostics and Troubleshooting

1. Documenting the problem and solution.
2. A DNS failure.
3. 802.11b and 802.11n.
4. Wireless Encryption Privacy (WEP).
5. **Status** | **Interfaces**, or use the Dashboard.
6. pfTop.
7. tcpping.
8. (1) To show the path of packets and (2) to display the transit delays along each step.

Another Book You May Enjoy

If you enjoyed this book, you may be interested in another book by Packt:

pfSense 2 Cookbook
Matt Williamson

ISBN: 978-1-84951-486-6

- Determine your deployment scenario, hardware/throughput/interface requirements, form-factor, and which platform version of pfSense is right for you
- Secure remote access using the SSH and/or HTTPS protocols
- Add, assign, and configure network interfaces
- Configure essential networking services (such as DHCP, DNS, Dynamic DNS)
- Create aliases, firewall rules, NAT port-forward rules, and rule schedules
- Enable external Remote Desktop Access to an internal machine, following a complete example of the core pfSense functionality
- Configure the PPTP, IPSec, L2TP, and/or OpenVPN services
- Create virtual IPs, a virtual LAN, 1:1 and outbound NAT rules, gateways, static routes, and bridged interfaces
- Configure traffic-shaping and Quality of Service (QoS)

- Create multiple WAN interfaces in load-balanced or failover configurations
- Configure firewall redundancy with a CARP firewall failover
- Configure external logging with syslog
- Use a variety of built-in networking tools such as Ping and traceroute
- Configuration backup/restoration and automatic configuration-file backup
- Update the pfSense firmware
- Monitor and view all sorts of system and feature statuses/logs using RRD graphs and status monitoring tools

Leave a review - let other readers know what you think

Please share your thoughts on this book with others by leaving a review on the site that you bought it from. If you purchased the book from Amazon, please leave us an honest review on this book's Amazon page. This is vital so that other potential readers can see and use your unbiased opinion to make purchasing decisions, we can understand what our customers think about our products, and our authors can see your feedback on the title that they have worked with Packt to create. It will only take a few minutes of your time, but is valuable to other potential customers, our authors, and Packt. Thank you!

Index

D

E

F

G

H

I

K

L

M

N

O

P

Q

R

S

T

CPSIA information can be obtained
at www.ICGtesting.com
Printed in the USA
BVHW05s1211210518
516872BV00022BA/982/P